SOCIOLOGY

A BRIEF INTRODUCTION

Sociology Around the World

The countries that are identified on this map are cited in the book, either in the context of research studies or in relevant statistical data. Refer to the subject index for specific page references.

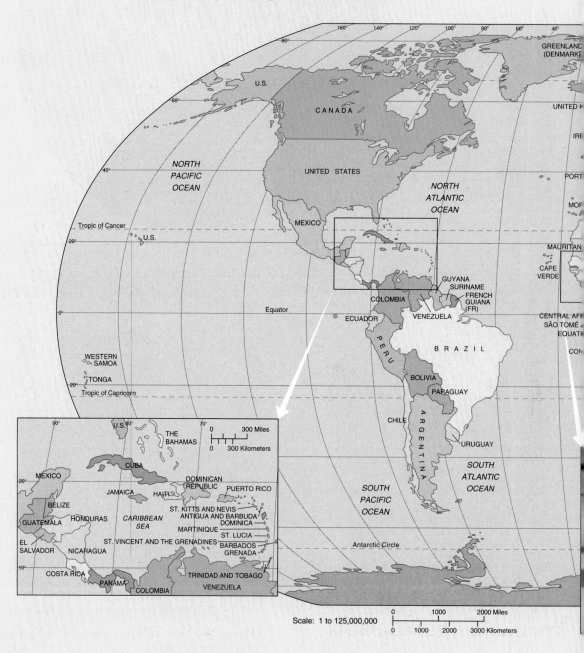

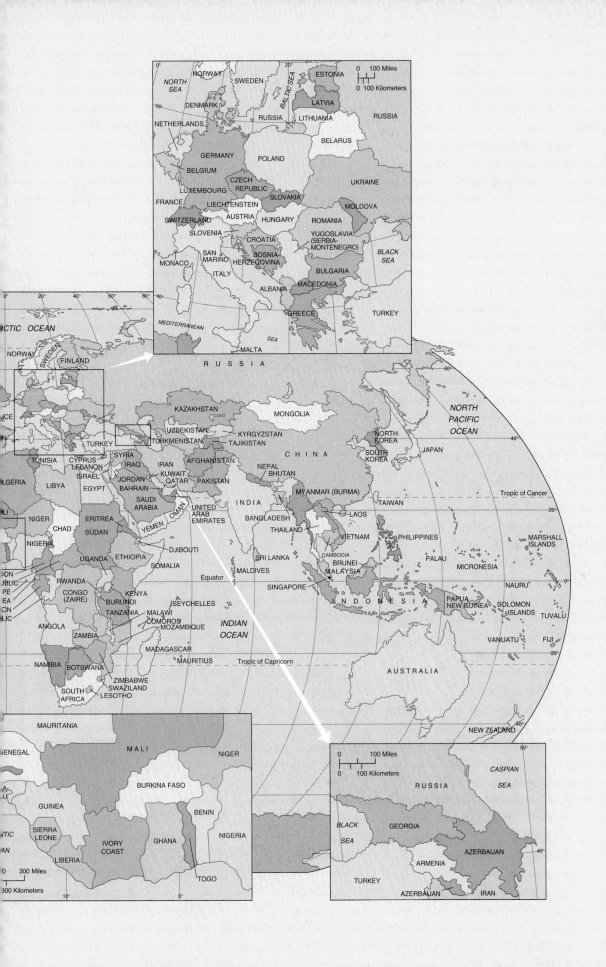

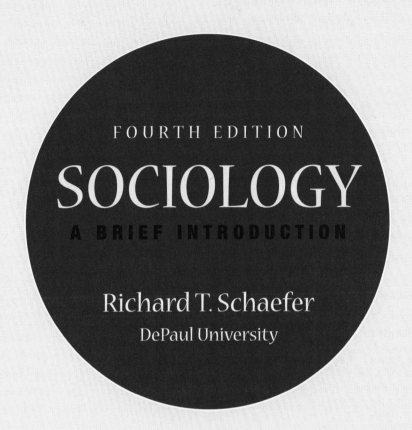

FOURTH EDITION

SOCIOLOGY

A BRIEF INTRODUCTION

Richard T. Schaefer

DePaul University

McGraw Hill

Boston   Burr Ridge, IL   Dubuque, IA   Madison, WI   New York   San Francisco   St. Louis
Bangkok   Bogotá   Caracas   Kuala Lumpur   Lisbon   London   Madrid   Mexico City
Milan   Montreal   New Delhi   Santiago   Seoul   Singapore   Sydney   Taipei   Toronto

McGraw-Hill Higher Education

A Division of The **McGraw-Hill** *Companies*

SOCIOLOGY: A BRIEF INTRODUCTION

Published by McGraw-Hill, an imprint of The McGraw-Hill
Companies, Inc., 1221 Avenue of the Americas, New York, NY 10020.

This book is printed on acid-free paper.

3 4 5 6 7 8 9 0 VNH/VNH 0 9 8 7 6 5 4 3 2

ISBN 0-07-242641-1 (student edition)
ISBN 0-07-243554-2 (annotated instructor's edition)

Editorial director: *Phillip A. Butcher*
Sponsoring editor: *Sally Constable*
Developmental editor: *Rhona Robbin*
Editorial assistant: *Alyson DeMonte*
Marketing manager: *Daniel M. Loch*
Project manager: *Kimberly D. Hooker*
Senior production supervisor: *Lori Koetters*
Photo research coordinator: *David Tietz*
Photo researcher: *Elyse Rieder*
Supplement coordinator: *Nate Perry*
Media technology producer: *Laurel Miller*
Cover design: *Laurie J. Entringer*
Interior design: *Laurie J. Entringer*
Cover images: *Stephanie Carter, Christopher
Baldwin, José Ortega, Noma
© The Stock Illustration Source*
Compositor: *GTS Graphics, Inc.*
Typeface: *10/12 Minion*
Printer: *Von Hoffmann Press, Inc.*

Library of Congress Cataloging-in-Publication Data

Library of Congress Card Number: 2001086136

INTERNATIONAL EDITION ISBN 0-07-112077-7

www.mhhe.com

Dedication

*To my mother-in-law,
Violet Erlandson, and to the
memory of my father-in-law,
Stanley B. Erlandson.
R.T.S.*

About the Author

RICHARD T. SCHAEFER:
Professor, DePaul University;
B.A. Northwestern University
M.A., Ph.D. University of Chicago

Growing up in Chicago at a time when neighborhoods were going through transitions in ethnic and racial composition, Richard T. Schaefer found himself increasingly intrigued by what was happening, how people were reacting, and how these changes were affecting neighborhoods and people's jobs. His interest in social issues caused him to gravitate to sociology courses at Northwestern University, where he eventually received a B.A. in sociology.

"Originally as an undergraduate I thought I would go on to law school and become a lawyer. But after taking a few sociology courses, I found myself wanting to learn more about what sociologists studied, and fascinated by the kinds of questions they raised." This fascination led him to obtain his M.A. and Ph.D. in sociology from the University of Chicago. Dr. Schaefer's continuing interest in race relations led him to write his master's thesis on the membership of the Ku Klux Klan and his doctoral thesis on racial prejudice and race relations in Great Britain.

Dr. Schaefer went on to become a professor of sociology. He has taught introductory sociology for 31 years to students in colleges, adult education programs, nursing programs, and even a maximum-security prison. Dr. Schaefer's love of teaching is apparent in his interaction with his students. "I find myself constantly learning from the students who are in my classes and from reading what they write. Their insights into the material we read or current events that we discuss often become part of future course material and sometimes even find their way into my writing."

Dr. Schaefer is author of the seventh edition of *Sociology* (McGraw-Hill, 2001). Dr. Schaefer is also the author of *Racial and Ethnic Groups,* now in its ninth edition (Prentice Hall, 2002), and *Race and Ethnicity in the United States,* second edition (Prentice Hall, 2001). His articles and book reviews have appeared in many journals, including *American Journal of Sociology; Phylon: A Review of Race and Culture; Contemporary Sociology; Sociology and Social Research; Sociological Quarterly;* and *Teaching Sociology.* He served as president of the Midwest Sociological Society in 1994–1995.

Dr. Schaefer's advice to students is to "look at the material and make connections to your own life and experiences. Sociology will make you a more attentive observer of how people in groups interact and function. It will also make you more aware of people's different needs and interests—and perhaps more ready to work for the common good, while still recognizing people's individuality."

Contents in Brief

Contents

1 UNDERSTANDING SOCIOLOGY   2

2 SOCIOLOGICAL RESEARCH   26

10 STRATIFICATION BY GENDER AND AGE 256

11 THE FAMILY AND INTIMATE RELATIONSHIPS 288

12 RELIGION AND EDUCATION 318

13 GOVERNMENT AND THE ECONOMY 350

14 POPULATION AND HEALTH 378

List of Boxes

 Sociology in the Global Community

 Research in Action

Eye
on the Media

Taking
Sociology
to Work

Social Policy Sections

List of Maps

Preface

"What has sociology got to do with me or with my life?" Any student might well ask this question before signing up for a sociology course. Here are some things for that student to consider: Are you influenced by what you see on television? Do you use the Internet? Do you know someone with a tattoo? Did you neglect to vote in the last election? Are you familiar with binge drinking on campus? Do you use alternative medicine? These are just a few of the everyday life situations described in this book that sociology can shed light on, revealing patterns and meanings.

Sociology also looks at large social issues. It seeks to unravel the factors behind the transfer of thousands of jobs from the United States to the developing countries of the Third World. It assesses the ways in which the availability of computer technology and the Internet may increase or reduce inequality. Sociology investigates the social forces that promote prejudice, the persistence of slavery today, the issues surrounding bilingual education, the social networks established by women, the process of growing old in different cultures, and the factors that lead someone to join a social movement and work for social change. These issues, along with many others, are of great interest to me, but it is the sociological explanations for them that I find especially compelling. The introductory sociology class provides the ideal laboratory in which to confront our society and our global neighbors.

After more than 30 years of teaching sociology to students in colleges, adult education programs, nursing programs, an overseas program based in London, and even a maximum-security prison, I am firmly convinced that the discipline can play a valuable role in teaching critical thinking skills. Sociology can help students to better understand the workings of their own lives as well as of their society and other cultures. The distinctive emphasis on social policy found in this text shows students how to use the sociological imagination in examining such public policy issues as sexual harassment, the AIDS crisis, welfare reform, the death penalty, and privacy and censorship in an electronic age.

My hope is that, through their reading of this book, students will begin to think like sociologists and will be able to use sociological theories and concepts in evaluating human interactions and institutions. From the introduction of the concept of sociological imagination in Chapter 1—which draws on a study that a colleague and I conducted of the food bank system of the United States—this text stresses the distinctive way in which sociologists examine and question even the most familiar patterns of social behavior.

The first seven editions of *Sociology* have been well received; it is currently used in more than 500 colleges and universities. But some instructors have sought a more concise overview of the discipline that would permit them to assign additional material or projects. This brief introduction to sociology was developed to meet that demand.

Sociology: A Brief Introduction, Fourth Edition, includes all the distinctive features that have been popular with instructors and students who use the more comprehensive volume, including these three especially important focal points:

- **Comprehensive and balanced coverage of theoretical perspectives throughout the text.** Chapter 1 introduces, defines, and contrasts the functionalist, conflict, and interactionist perspectives. It explores their distinctive views of such topics as television (Chapter 1), social institutions (Chapter 5), deviance (Chapter 7), the family (Chapter 11), education (Chapter 12), and health and illness (Chapter 14).
- **Strong coverage of issues pertaining to gender, age, race, ethnicity, and class in all chapters.** Examples of such coverage include social policy sections on bilingualism (Chapter 3), rethinking welfare (Chapter 8), immigration policy (Chapter 9), and sexual harassment (Chapter 6); boxes on women's social networks (Chapter 5), urban poverty and joblessness (Chapter 8), prejudice against Arab Americans and Muslim Americans (Chapter 9), domestic violence (Chapter 11), squatter settlements and gated communities (Chapter 15); and sections on the social construction of race (Chapter 9) and the contingency or temporary workforce (Chapter 13).
- **Use of cross-cultural material throughout the text.** A major part of Chapter 8 treats the topic of stratification from a global perspective. This chapter introduces world systems analysis, dependency theory, and modernization theory and examines multinational corporations and the global economy. Every chapter presents global material and makes use of cross-cultural examples. Among the topics examined are

The global "McDonaldization of society" (Chapter 3)

Neglect of children in Eastern European orphanages (Chapter 4)

The status of women around the world (Chapter 10)

Issues of aging around the world (Chapter 10)

Transmission of cultural values (Chapter 12)

Population policy in China (Chapter 14)

Homelessness worldwide (Chapter 15)

A sociological interpretation of the Soviet collapse (Chapter 16)

The global disconnect in technology (Chapter 16)

As in the longer text, I take great care to introduce the basic concepts and research methods of sociology and to reinforce this material in all chapters. The most recent data are included, making this book even more current than the seventh edition of *Sociology.*

Content

Sociology: A Brief Introduction is divided into 16 chapters that study human behavior concisely from the perspective of sociologists. The opening chapter ("Understanding Sociology") presents a brief history of the discipline and introduces the basic theories and perspectives used in sociology. Chapter 2 ("Sociological Research") describes the major research methods.

The next five chapters focus on key sociological concepts. Chapter 3 ("Culture") illustrates how sociologists study the behavior we have learned and share. Chapter 4 ("Socialization") reveals how humans are most distinctively social animals who learn the attitudes and behavior viewed as appropriate in their particular cultures. We examine social interaction and social structure in Chapter 5 and the workings of groups and organizations in Chapter 6. Chapter 7 ("Deviance and Social Control") reviews how we conform to and deviate from established norms.

The next three chapters consider the social hierarchies present in societies. Chapter 8 ("Stratification in the United States and Worldwide") introduces us to the presence of social inequality, while Chapter 9 ("Racial and Ethnic Inequality") and Chapter 10 ("Stratification by Gender and Age") analyze specific types of inequality.

The following chapters examine the major social institutions of human society. Marriage, kinship, and divorce are some of the topics examined in Chapter 11 ("The Family and Intimate Relationships"). Other social institutions are considered in Chapter 12 ("Religion and Education") and Chapter 13 ("Government and the Economy").

The final chapters of the text introduce major themes in our changing world. Chapter 14 ("Population and Health") helps us understand the impact of these issues on our society and around the world. In Chapter 15 we examine the importance of communities and the environment in our lives. Chapter 16 ("Social Movements, Social Change, and Technology") presents sociological analysis of the process of change and has a special focus on technology and the future.

Special Features

Poster Art

Each chapter opens with a reproduction of a poster or piece of graphic art that illustrates a key theme or concept of the chapter. Accompanying captions help readers to grasp the relevance of the artwork to the chapter.

Chapter Opener

The chapter openers convey the excitement and relevance of sociological inquiry by means of lively excerpts from writings of sociologists and others who explore sociological topics. These openers are designed to expose students to vivid writing on a broad range of topics and to stimulate their sociological imagination. For example, Chapter 3 begins with Horace Miner's classic take on Nacirema culture. Chapter 5 opens with a description of Zimbardo's mock prison study. Cornel West's musings on being a single father introduce Chapter 11. Later, in Chapter 15, Kai Erikson reflects on the value of sociology in understanding the connection between the population and the environment.

Chapter Overview

The opening excerpt is followed by a chapter overview that links the excerpt to key themes of the chapter and describes the content of the chapter in narrative form.

Key Terms

I have given careful attention to presenting understandable and accurate definitions of each key term. These terms are highlighted in bold italics when they are introduced. A list of key terms and definitions in each chapter—with page references—follows the end of the chapter. In addition, the glossary at the end of the book includes the definitions of the textbook's key terms and the page references for each term.

Research in Action

These sections, which appear in almost every chapter, present sociological findings on topics such as binge drinking, school-related violence, and gated communities.

Sociology in the Global Community

These sections, which appear in almost every chapter, provide a global perspective on topics such as disability as a master status, domestic violence, and population policy in China.

Eye on the Media

New to this edition, these sections illustrate how the media affect, and are affected by, social trends and events. Topics featured in these sections include the social construction of rock music as a social problem, coalition building in *Survivor,* the lack of diversity on network television, and political activism on the Internet.

Taking Sociology to Work

These sections profile individuals who majored in sociology and use its principles in their work. While these people work in a variety of occupations and professions, they all share a conviction that their background in sociology has been valuable in their careers.

Illustrations

The photographs, cartoons, figures, and tables are closely linked to the themes of the chapters. The maps, titled "Mapping Life Nationwide" and "Mapping Life Worldwide," show the prevalence of social trends. A world map highlighting those countries used as examples in the text appears in the front matter to this book.

Social Policy Sections

The social policy sections that close all but one of the chapters play a critical role in helping students to think like sociologists. They apply sociological principles and theories to important social and political issues being debated by policymakers and the general public. These include bilingual education (Chapter 3), the death penalty (Chapter 7), reproductive technology (Chapter 11), religion in the schools (Chapter 12), and financing health care (Chapter 14). All the policy sections now present a global perspective.

Cross-Reference Icons

When the text discussion refers to a concept introduced earlier in the book, an icon in the margin points the reader to the exact page.

Chapter Summaries

Each chapter includes a brief numbered summary to aid students in reviewing the important themes.

Critical Thinking Questions

After the summary, each chapter includes critical thinking questions that will help students analyze the social world in which they participate. Critical thinking is an essential element in the sociological imagination.

Additional Readings

An annotated list of books concludes each chapter; these works have been selected as additional readings because of their sociological soundness and their accessibility for introductory students.

Internet Connection Exercises

Three exercises in each chapter take students online to analyze social issues relevant to chapter topics. Throughout the text an icon signals where more information and/or updates are available on the book's website.

Endpapers

The front endpaper features a description of what the world would look like if it were a village of a thousand people. The back endpaper summarizes the applications used in the book to illustrate sociology's major theoretical approaches.

What's New in the Fourth Edition?

The most important changes in this edition include the following (refer as well to the chapter-by-chapter list of changes on pp. xxiii–xxv and to the *Visual Preview* on pp. xxix–xxxvi):

Content

- Inviting new openers drawing on the vivid writings of sociologists and others writing on sociological topics

- "Eye on the Media" boxes that illustrate how the media affect and are affected by social events.

Pedagogy

- Discussion questions at the end of boxes and social policy sections
- Cross-reference icons
- More examples relevant to students' lives
- More cross-cultural examples, including a global focus in the social policy boxes
- More direct and engaging writing style

Map and Illustration Program

- Expanded map program: Two kinds of maps, "Mapping Life Nationwide" and "Mapping Life Worldwide," are featured throughout the text
- Use of poster art at the beginning of each chapter to illustrate key sociological concepts
- "Sticker" captions within figures draw attention to major points in the graphs

This edition has been thoroughly updated. It includes the most recent data and research findings, many of which were published in the last three years. Recent data from the Census Bureau, Bureau of Labor Statistics, Current Population Reports, the Population Reference Bureau, the World Bank, the United Nations Development Programme, and the Centers for Disease Control have been incorporated.

A more complete, chapter-by-chapter listing of the most significant new material in this edition follows.

● What's New in Each Chapter

CHAPTER 1 Understanding Sociology

- Opening excerpt from tattoo study by Katherine Irwin
- Section on "What Is Sociological Theory?"
- Eye on the Media box: Looking at Television from Three Perspectives
- Section on "Sociology and the Social Sciences"
- Expanded discussion of Durkheim, including anomie

CHAPTER 2 Sociological Research

- Opening excerpt from *Streetwise* by Elijah Anderson
- Global box on a study of China's "send-down" policy

- Gun control case study (with figure) to illustrate scientific method
- Discussion of causal logic and correlation (with figure)
- Discussion of reliability and validity of research results
- Updated discussion of using Internet for surveys
- Section on qualitative and quantitative research and ethnography
- Field experiment measuring effects of police action in domestic assault cases
- Discussion of effects of race and gender in conducting research
- Research box on framing survey questions about interracial friendships (with figure)
- Social policy section on studying human sexuality (with figure)

CHAPTER 3 Culture

- Opening excerpt from *Nacirema* by Horace Miner
- Media box on rock music as a social problem
- Illustration of pickpocket argot (subculture section)
- Example of culture shock on Navajo reservation
- Examples of national defenses against cultural invasion
- Updated discussion of bilingualism section, incorporating new test results

CHAPTER 4 Socialization

- Opening excerpt from *Peer Power* by Patricia A. Adler and Peter Adler
- Box on raising Amish children
- Coverage of peer harassment
- Taking Sociology to Work box
- Additional cross-cultural examples of socialization
- More examples of television's benign socializing influence
- Discussion of influence of technology on socialization in family life
- Section on teenagers in the workforce (with figure)

CHAPTER 5 Social Interaction and Social Structure

- Discussion of online groups and emerging electronic social networks, including "texting"
- Discussion of gender/occupational role conflict

- Discussion of how taking medication for HIV affects social interaction
- Discussion of networking among women leaving welfare rolls
- Discussion of gendered and racist environments in social institutions

CHAPTER 6 Groups and Organizations

- Opening excerpt from *The McDonaldization of Society* by George Ritzer
- Discussion of teenage in-group/out-group conflicts, including Columbine High School tragedy
- Expanded discussion of coalitions (including transracial community organizations and the anti-tobacco coalition)
- Eye on the Media box on coalition building in the TV show *Survivor*
- Introduction of Weber's ideal type as key term in bureaucracy discussion
- Discussion of alienation in workplace
- Example of domestic workers in California in discussion of bureaucratization in small-group settings
- Expanded discussion of impact of telecommuting on workplace

CHAPTER 7 Deviance and Social Control

- Opening excerpt from *Victimless Crime? Prostitution, Drugs, Homosexuality, Abortion* by Robert F. Meir and Gilbert Geis
- Research box on binge drinking in college, with figure
- Section on social stigma
- Global box on social control campaigns in Singapore
- Section on deviance and technology, with figure on digital piracy
- Discussion of racial profiling
- Discussion of social constructionist perspective
- Discussion of transnational organized crime

CHAPTER 8 Stratification in the United States and Worldwide

- Opening excerpt from *Nike Culture* by Robert Goldman and Stephen Papson
- Discussion of student anti-sweatshop movement
- Comparison of CEOs' salaries around the world
- Discussion of monetary value of women's unpaid labor

- Discussion of multidimensional measures of social class
- Discussion of the "digital divide" between haves and have-nots
- Global box on inequality in Japan

CHAPTER 9 Racial and Ethnic Inequality

- Opening excerpt from article "Of Race and Risk" by Patricia J. Williams
- Media box on diversity issues in network TV
- Illustration of changing race and ethnicity in United States from 1500 to 2100
- Map showing concentrations of racial and ethnic populations in the United States
- Expanded discussion of mixed racial ancestry
- Discussion of the advantages of "White privilege"
- Illustration of immigration patterns in the United States, 1820s–1990s

CHAPTER 10 Stratification by Gender and Age

- Opening excerpt from *The Beauty Myth* by Naomi Wolf
- Comparison of women's labor force participation around the world
- Discussion and table on gender norm "transgressions"
- Map showing states with restrictions on public funding of abortions
- Table summarizing theories of aging
- Discussion of elder gay concerns

CHAPTER 11 The Family and Intimate Relationships

- Opening excerpt from *The War Against Parents* by Sylvia Ann Hewlett and Cornel West
- Focus on "intimate relationships" as well as "family"
- Discussion of dating and love relationships on campus
- Section on interactionist view of family
- Discussion of relationships formed via the Internet
- Discussion of arranged marriages at home and abroad
- Updated discussion of divorce rates, with new figure on marriage and divorce trends
- Discussion of official recognition of same-sex partnership in other countries
- Discussion of preselection of a baby's sex

CHAPTER 12 Religion and Education

- Opening excerpt from *For This Land* by Vine Deloria Jr.
- Discussion of impact of Internet on religion
- Expanded discussion of liberation theology
- Discussion of Muslim ritual, the *hajj*
- Discussion of impact of taking courses on the Internet
- Section on home schooling
- Section on adult education, with figure
- Social policy section on religion in the schools

CHAPTER 13 Government and the Economy

- Opening excerpt from *Diversity in the Power Elite* by Richard L. Zweigenhaft and G. William Domhoff
- Discussion of how female politicians receive different media coverage from male politicians
- Discussion of interest groups representing Internet-based companies
- Media box on political activism on the Internet
- Section on changing face of the workforce, reflecting increase of women and minorities (with figure)
- Section on social dynamics of e-commerce

CHAPTER 14 Population and Health

- Opening excerpt from *The Scalpel and the Silver Bear* by Dr. Lori Arviso Alvord
- Global box on China's population policy
- Discussion of racism in medical treatment
- Discussion of federal initiative to achieve 100 percent access and zero health disparities, with map of availability of physicians by state
- Section on role of government in health care
- Discussion of neglect of women in medical research

CHAPTER 15 Communities and the Environment

- Opening excerpt from *A New Species of Trouble* by Kai Erikson
- Case study of technology in Blacksburg, Virginia (electronic village)
- Overview of major influences on cities in the past and predictions about future changes
- Discussion of "green" effect of recycling programs and Internet purchases
- Discussion of gentrification and its impact on homelessness

CHAPTER 16 Social Movements, Social Change, and Technology

- Opening excerpt from *The Nudist on the Night Shift* by Po Bronson
- Media box on virtual social movements on the Internet
- Expanded discussion of differences of utilization of Internet by race
- Updated discussion of technology and Internet use by gender
- Discussion of opposition to genetically modified food
- New section on gender and social movements
- Discussion of McDonaldization of biotechnology

Support for Instructors

PRINT RESOURCES

Annotated Instructor's Edition

An annotated instructor's edition (AIE) of the text, prepared by Mark Kassop of Bergen Community College in New Jersey, offers page-by-page annotations to assist instructors in using textbook material. These include several categories: Let's Discuss (ideas for classroom discussion); Student Alerts (which anticipate common student misconceptions); Policy Pointers (which show tie-ins between important concepts and social policy applications); Theory (examples of the application of the functionalist, conflict, interactionist, and labeling perspectives); Methods (examples of the use of surveys, observation, experiments, and existing sources); Global View (examples of cross-cultural material); Race/ Ethnicity (material on racial and ethnic minorities in the United States); Gender (material on women, men, and gender issues); and Contemporary Culture (examples of popular culture).

Instructor's Resource Manual

This manual, prepared by Richard T. Schaefer and Mark Kassop, provides sociology instructors with detailed key points, additional lecture ideas (among them alternative social policy issues), class discussion topics, essay questions, topics for student research (along with suggested research materials for each topic), and suggested additional readings (unlike those in the text itself, these are meant for instructors rather than students). Media materials are suggested for each chapter, including videotapes and films.

Test Bank

The test bank that accompanies the text features short-answer questions, multiple-choice questions and essay questions for each chapter; they will be useful in testing students on basic sociological concepts, application of theoretical perspectives, and recall of important factual information. Correct answers and page references are provided for all multiple-choice questions.

In addition to the printed format, the test bank is available on disk and on CD-ROM for computerized test construction.

Primis Customized Readers

An array of first-rate readings is available to adopters in a customized electronic database. Some are classic articles from the sociological literature; others are provocative pieces written especially for McGraw-Hill by leading sociologists.

Internet Guide

A guide to sociology surfing on the Internet assists students in using the many dimensions and services of the World Wide Web.

McGraw-Hill/Dushkin

Any of the Dushkin publications can be packaged with this text at a discount: Annual Editions, Taking Sides, Sources, Global Studies. For more information, please visit the website at **http://www.dushkin.com.**

DIGITAL RESOURCES

PageOut: The Course Website Development Center

 PageOut was designed for the professor just beginning to explore web options. In less than an hour, even the novice computer user can create a course website with a template provided by McGraw-Hill (no programming knowledge required). PageOut lets you offer your students instant access to your syllabus, lecture notes, and original material. Students can even check their grades online. And, you can pull any of the McGraw-Hill content from the Schaefer website and Online Learning Center into your website. PageOut also provides a discussion board where you and your students can exchange questions and post announcements, as well as an area for students to build personal web pages.

To find out more about PageOut: The Course Website Development Center, ask your McGraw-Hill representative for details, or fill out the form at **www.mhhe.com/pageout.**

Interactive e-Source with Making the Grade CD-ROM

 This remarkable CD-ROM intertwines the complete text with media resources and offers students a nonlinear approach to learning. With Interactive e-Source, students can instantly explore various topics and concepts with an assortment of video clips (including footage of this text's author in Singapore), website links, and interactive maps and graphs. Along the way, students can refer to an audio tutor for a helping hand with difficult topics. Students can also highlight the text and customize the content with electronic notes that can be shared with other e-Source users. And, students can test themselves with interactive study questions and other learning aids.

Online Learning Center Website

 Instructors (and students) are invited to visit the book's Online Learning Center, the text-specific website, at **www.mhhe.com/schaefer4.** Here you and your students will find an extensive variety of resources and activities, including quizzes, key terms, chapter overviews, learning objectives, PowerPoint slides, and more. It's also possible to link directly to Internet sites from the Online Learning Center. And, you can use any of the material from the Online Learning Center in a course website that you create using PageOut. An icon appears in the boxes, policy sections, and Internet Connection exercises throughout the text, reminding students and instructors to visit the Online Learning Center home page for current material and activities relating to these popular sections.

PowerWeb

 Offered free with the text, PowerWeb is a turnkey solution for adding the Internet to a course. PowerWeb is a password-protected website developed by McGraw-Hill/Dushkin, which offers instructors (and students):

- Course-specific materials
- Refereed course-specific web links and articles
- Student study tools—quizzing, review forms, time management tools, web research
- Interactive exercises

- Weekly updates with assessment
- Informative and timely world news
- Access to Northern Light Research Engine (received multiple Editor's Choice awards for superior capabilities from *PC Magazine*)
- Material on how to conduct web research
- Message board for instructors
- Daily news feed of topic-specific news

For further information, visit the PowerWeb website at **http://mhhe/NewMedia/dushkin/index.html#powerweb**.

PowerPoint Slides

Adopters of *Sociology* can also receive a set of 140 color PowerPoint slides, developed by Richard T. Schaefer. These slides include figures, tables, and maps drawn from academic and governmental sources, a few of which reproduce material from the textbook. Instructors are welcome to generate overhead transparencies from the slides if they wish to do so.

Instructor's Resource CD

This CD-ROM includes the contents of the instructor's resource manual, test banks, PowerPoint slides, and more for instructors' convenience in customizing multimedia lectures.

SocCity

SocCity is a veritable melting pot of sociology cybersources, information, and Internet activities for students and instructors alike. Just click on any of the four buttons on the left side of your screen and get started (**www.mhhe.com/socscience/sociology**).

Primis Online

Professors can customize this book by selecting the chapters they want to use in their course. Through McGraw-Hill's Primis Online, professors have the ability to adapt this title by chapter, change its order, or add readings from our vast database of content. Primis Online offers professors the choice between custom printed textbooks or electronic eBooks. To learn more, contact your McGraw-Hill sales representative or visit our website at **www.mhhe.com/primis/online**.

VIDEO RESOURCES

McGraw-Hill offers adopters a variety of videotapes that are suitable for classroom use in conjunction with the textbook.

 Support for Students

Interactive e-Source with Making the Grade CD-ROM

This remarkable CD-ROM intertwines the complete text with media resources and offers students a nonlinear approach to learning. With Interactive e-Source, students can instantly explore various topics and concepts with an assortment of video clips (including footage of this text's author in Singapore), website links, and interactive maps and graphs. Along the way, students can refer to an audio tutor for a helping hand with difficult topics. Students can also highlight the text and customize the content with electronic notes that can be shared with other e-Source users. And, students can test themselves with interactive study questions and other learning aids.

Online Learning Center Website

 Students (and instructors) are invited to visit the book's Online Learning Center, the text-specific website, at **www.mhhe.com/schaefer4**. Here you will find an extensive variety of resources and activities, including quizzes, key terms, chapter overviews, learning objectives, PowerPoint slides, and more. It's also possible to link directly to Internet sites from the Online Learning Center. An icon appears in the boxes, policy sections, and Internet Connection exercises throughout the text, reminding students and instructors to visit the Online Learning Center home page for current material and activities relating to these popular sections.

PowerWeb

 Offered free with the text, PowerWeb is a password-protected website developed by McGraw-Hill/Dushkin, giving students:

- Web links and articles
- Study tools—quizzing, review forms, time management tools, web research
- Interactive exercises
- Weekly updates with assessment
- Informative and timely world news
- Access to Northern Light Research Engine (received multiple Editor's Choice awards for superior capabilities from *PC Magazine*)

- Material on how to conduct web research
- Daily news feed of topic-specific news

Student's Guide

The student's guide includes standard features such as detailed key points, definitions of key terms, multiple-choice questions, fill-in questions, and true–false questions. Some chapters include a "Name that Sociologist" section. Perhaps the most distinctive feature is the social policy exercise, which is closely tied to the social policy section in the text. All study guide questions are keyed to specific pages in the textbook, and page references are provided for key points and definitions of key terms.

Acknowledgments

Virginia Joyner collaborated with me on the fourth edition, bringing fresh insight into presenting the sociological imagination. Robert P. Lamm had been part of several previous brief and comprehensive editions of *Sociology*, and his contributions are still apparent.

I deeply appreciate the contributions to this book made by my editors. Rhona Robbin, a senior development editor at McGraw-Hill, has continually and successfully challenged me to make each edition better than its predecessor.

I have received strong support and encouragement from Phillip Butcher, editorial director, and Sally Constable, sponsoring editor. Additional guidance and support were provided by Alyson DeMonte, editorial assistant; Kimberly Hooker, project manager; Laurie Entringer, designer; Elyse Rieder, photo editor; and Diane Kraut, permissions editor. I would also like to express appreciation to Melissa Haeffner and Todd Fuist for their research assistance.

I would also like to acknowledge the contributions of the following individuals: Mark Kassop of Bergen Community College in New Jersey for his work on the instructor's resource manual, as well as the annotations that appear in the annotated instructor's edition; Kenrick Thompson of Arkansas State University for preparing the test items for the Interactive e-Source CD-ROM that is packaged with each copy of the text; and John Tenuto of the College of Lake County in Illinois for developing the Internet exercises in the text and for his contributions to the annotated instructor's edition.

Academic Reviewers

I would like to express my thanks to the following people who have reviewed all or various portions of the manuscript:

Sally Caldwell
Southwest Texas State University

Mirelle Cohen
Green River Community College

Kelly A. Dagan
Kent State University

Lee F. Hamilton
New Mexico State University

Jeanne Humble
Lexington Community College

Janet Hund
Long Beach City College

William L. Smith
Georgia Southern University

Tracy Faye Tolbert
California State University, Long Beach

James E. Trela
University of Maryland, Baltimore County

Jacquelyn Troup
Cerritos College

As is evident from these acknowledgments, the preparation of a textbook is truly a team effort. The most valuable member of this effort continues to be my wife, Sandy. She provides the support so necessary in my creative and scholarly activities.

I have had the good fortune to be able to introduce students to sociology for many years. These students have been enormously helpful in spurring on my own sociological imagination. In ways I can fully appreciate but cannot fully acknowledge, their questions in class and queries in the hallway have found their way into this textbook.

Richard T. Schaefer
schaeferrt@aol.com

As a full-service publisher of quality educational products, McGraw-Hill does much more than just sell textbooks to your students. We create and publish an extensive array of print, video, and digital supplements to support instruction on your campus. Orders of new (versus used) textbooks help us to defray the cost of developing such supplements, which is substantial. Please consult your local McGraw-Hill representative to learn about the availability of the supplements that accompany Sociology. If you are not sure who your representative is, you can find him or her by using the Rep Locator at www.mhhe.com.

A Visual Preview of the Fourth Edition

The fourth edition of *Sociology: A Brief Introduction* continues its tradition of teaching students how to think critically about society and their own lives from a wide range of classical and contemporary sociological perspectives.

New Intriguing Chapter Openers

Chapter openers convey the excitement and relevance of sociological inquiry by means of lively excerpts from writings of sociologists and others who explore sociological topics.

New Provocative Chapter-Opening Art

Each chapter opens with a reproduction of a poster or piece of graphic art that illustrates a key theme or concept of the chapter. Accompanying captions help readers grasp the relevance of the artwork to the chapter.

Helpful Chapter Overviews

Chapter overviews provide a bridge between the chapter-opening excerpt and the content of the chapter.

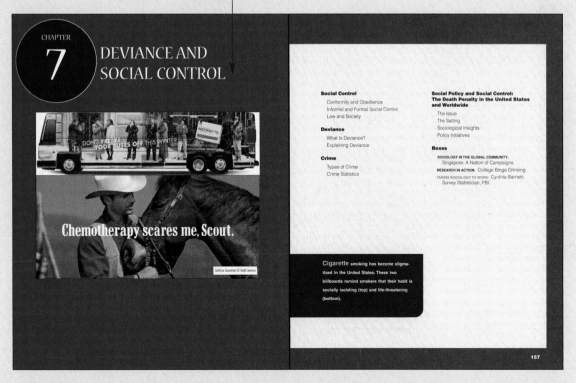

Timely "Sociology in the Global Community" Boxes

These boxes provide a global perspective on topics such as disability as a master status, domestic violence, and squatter settlements.

Sociology in the Global Community 7-2 Singapore: A Nation of Campaigns

www.mhhe.com/schaefer4

"Males with Long Hair Will Be Attended to Last!" "Throwing Litter from Apartments Can Kill!" "No Spitting!" These are some of the posters sponsored by the Singapore government in its effort to enforce social norms in this small nation of some four million people living in a totally urbanized area in southeast Asia.

While Singapore is governed by a democratically elected parliament, one party has dominated the government since its independence in 1965. And it has not hesitated to use its authority to launch a number of campaigns to shape the social behavior of its citizens. In most cases these campaigns are directed against "disagreeable" behavior—littering, spitting, chewing gum, failing to flush public toilets, teenage smoking, and the like. Courtesy is a major concern, with elaborate "Courtesy Month" celebrations scheduled to both entertain and educate the populace.

Some campaigns take on serious issues and are backed by legislation. For example, in the 1970s the government asked its citizens to "Please Stop at Two" in family planning; tax and schooling benefits rewarded those who complied. However, this campaign was so successful that in the 1980s the government began a "Have Three or More If You Can Afford to" campaign. In this case it provided school benefits for larger families. In another attempt at social control, the government has launched a "Speak Mandarin" campaign to encourage the multiethnic, multilingual population to accept Mandarin as the dialect of choice.

Courtesy is a major concern, with elaborate "Courtesy Month" celebrations scheduled to both entertain and educate the populace.

For the most part, Singaporeans cheerfully accept their government's admonitions and encouragement. They see the results of being clean and courteous: Singapore is a better place to live. Corporations also go along with the government and even help to sponsor some of the campaigns. As one corporate sponsor noted: "If (people) see Singapore as a clean country, they will view companies here as clean." Political scientist Michael Haas refers to this compliance as "the Singapore puzzle": citizens of Singapore accept strict social control dictates in exchange for continuing prosperity and technological leadership in the world.

Let's Discuss

1. How would you react to an administration-sponsored campaign at your college against drinking? What would be some positive aspects of such a campaign? What would be some negative aspects?
2. Why do you think these social control campaigns work in Singapore? If there was a strong two-party system there, do you think the campaigns would be as prevalent and as effective? Why or why not?

Sources: Dorai 1998; Haas 1999; Haub and Cornelius 2000; Instituto del Tercer Mundo 1999.

had installed or made plans to install such surveillance cameras, and the use of public surveillance had spread to the United States. Supporters of surveillance believe that it will make the public feel more secure. Moreover, it can be cheaper to install and maintain cameras than to put more police officers on street patrol. For critics, however, the use of surveillance cameras brings to mind the grim, futuristic world presented by Britain's own George Orwell (1949) in his famous novel *1984*. In the world of *1984*, an all-seeing "Big Brother" represented an authoritarian government that watched people's every move and took immediate action against anyone who questioned the oppressive regime (Halbfinger 1998; Uttley 1993).

Law and Society

Some norms are so important to a society they are formalized into laws controlling people's behavior. ***Law*** may be defined as governmental social control (Black 1995). Some laws, such as the prohibition against murder, are directed at all members of society. Others, such as fishing and hunting regulations, primarily affect particular categories of people. Still others govern the behavior of social institutions (corporate law and laws regarding the taxing of nonprofit enterprises).

p. 61

Sociologists have become increasingly interested in the creation of laws as a social process. Laws are created in response to perceived needs for formal social control. Sociologists have sought to explain how and why such perceptions arise. In their view, law is not merely a static body of rules handed down from generation to generation. Rather, it reflects continually changing standards of what is right and wrong, of how violations are to be determined, and of what sanctions are to be applied (Schur 1968).

Sociologists representing varying theoretical perspectives agree that the legal order reflects underlying social values. Therefore, the creation of criminal law can be

164

Stimulating "Research in Action" Boxes

These boxes present sociological findings on topics such as binge drinking, why young people don't vote, and women's social networks.

New Thought-Provoking "Eye on the Media" Boxes

These boxes illustrate how the media affect—and are affected by—social trends and events. Topics featured in these boxes include rock music as a social problem, the lack of diversity on network television, and political activism on the Internet.

Research in Action 12-2 Violence in the Schools

www.mhhe.com/schaefer4

Littleton, Colorado; Jonesboro, Arkansas; West Paducah, Kentucky; Pearl, Mississippi; Edinboro, Pennsylvania; Springfield, Oregon—these are now more than just the names of small and medium-size cities. They resonate with the sound of gunshots, of kids killing kids on school grounds. As a result, people no longer perceive schools as safe havens. But how accurate is that impression?

Studies of school violence put the recent spate of school killings in perspective:

- A child has less than one in a million chance of being killed at school.
- The number of people shot and killed in school in the 1997–1998 school year was 40 (including adults), about average over the last six years.
- According to the Center for Disease Control, 99 percent of violent deaths of school-aged children in 1992–1994 occurred *outside* school grounds.
- Fewer students are now being found with guns in school.
- Data from the National School Safety Center at Pepperdine University suggest there has been a 27 percent decline in school-associated violent deaths from 1992 through the 1997–1998 school year.
- Twenty-three times more children are killed in gun *accidents* than in school killings.

Schools, then, are safer than neighborhoods, but people still are unnerved by the perception of an alarming rise in schoolyard violence that has been generated by heavy media coverage of the recent incidents. Some conflict theorists object to the huge outcry about recent violence in schools. After all, they note, violence in and around inner-city schools has a long history. It seems that only when middle-class White children are the victims does school violence become a plank on the national policy agenda. When violence hits the middle class, the problem is viewed not as an extension of delinquency, but as a structural issue in need of legislative remedies, such as gun control.

Meanwhile, feminists observe that virtually all the offenders are male and, in some instances, such as in the case of Jonesboro, the victims are disproportionately female. The precipitating factor for violence is often a broken-off dating relationship—yet another example of violence of men against women (or, in this case, boys against girls).

A child has less than one in a million chance of being killed at school.

Increasingly, efforts to prevent school violence are focusing on the ways in which the socialization of young people in the United States contributes to violence. For example, the *Journal of the American Medical Association* published a study of Second Step, a violence prevention curriculum for elementary school students that teaches social skills related to anger management, impulse control, and empathy. The study evaluated the impact of the program on urban and suburban elementary school students and found that it appeared to lead to a moderate decrease in physically aggressive behavior and an increase in neutral and prosocial behavior in school. However, one can never undertake such efforts early enough. The "peaceful play" program in Illinois shows *preschoolers* how to resolve their disputes in a nonviolent fashion. Other approaches to preventing violence include stiffer regulations of gun sales and gun ownership, longer school days, and afterschool programs (to keep young people occupied during unsupervised hours).

Some people believe that a key ingredient to prevention of violence, in or out of school, is greater parental supervision and responsibility for their children. In her book *A Tribe Apart*, Patricia Hersch (1998) documents the lives of eight teens growing up in a Virginia suburb over a three-year period. Her conclusion: Children need meaningful adult relationships in their lives. Former Secretary of Education Richard Riley cites studies showing that youths who feel connected to their parents and schools are less likely to engage in high-risk behavior.

Let's Discuss

1. Has a shooting or other violent episode ever occurred at your school? If so, how did students react? Do you feel safer at school than at home, as experts say you are?
2. What steps have administrators at your school taken to prevent violence? Have they been effective, or should other steps be taken?

Sources: Bowles 1999; Chaddock 1998; Department of Education 1999; Donohue, Schiraldi, and Ziedenberg 1998; D. Grossman et al. 1997; Hersch 1998; National Center for Education Statistics 1998; S. Schaefer 1996.

pressure in all three of these areas. First, the amount of formal schooling required for teaching remains high, and now the public has begun to call for new competency examinations for teachers. Second, the statistics cited above demonstrate that teachers' salaries are significantly lower than those of many professionals and skilled workers. Finally, as we have seen, the overall prestige of the teaching profession has declined in the last decade. Many teachers have become disappointed and frustrated and have left the educational world for other careers in other professions.

340

Eye on the Media 6-1 Surviving *Survivor*—A Sociological View

www.mhhe.com/schaefer4

Richard, Kelly, Rudy, and Susan all want to get ahead of other members of their group. So they agree to form a coalition aimed at keeping the other members from advancing or from receiving precious resources. Sometimes the coalition breaks down, but in the end they prevail. Along the way they give out disinformation, deny their collusion, and even appear to be friendly to those they scheme against.

Sound like office politics? It well could be, but you probably recognize the four coalition members as the final four castaways in the first *Survivor*, the hit TV show in the summer of 2000. This four-person coalition, calling itself the "Tagi Alliance," turned on fellow members of the Tagi tribe, voting them off the island one by one at tribal councils, and eventually banded against the remaining contestants in the merged tribe the last 6 weeks of the 12-episode contest. Coalitions like theirs occur in all organizations from schools to corporate board rooms.

The *Survivor* castaways knew that after the 39 days of filming, they would have nothing to do with one another beyond publicity appearances.

But what would sociologists have to say about the *Survivor* coalition? They would be quick to point out that this coalition does not truly represent everyday coalition-building. Coalitions can be temporary, but usually the members have to weigh the long-term social consequences of what they do against others. The *Survivor* castaways knew that after the 39 days of filming, they would have nothing to do with one another beyond publicity appearances. While the stakes were high ($1 million to the final survivor) and emotions were high, there were virtually no long-term social implications. For example, Susan expressed her strong dislike of Kelly in an emotional speech at the final tribal council, but what did it matter? They were not coworkers or classmates or family members.

The "Tagi Alliance": Kelly, Rudy, Susan, and Richard (left to right).

Many observers have billed this type of show as "reality TV" and use the term to describe such offshoots as *Big Brother* and *Chains of Love*. Sociologists, however, would note there is nothing real about taking 16 middle-class (or better) individuals from the United States and placing them on the island of Pulau Tiga to compete for a million dollar windfall. That island is a part of Malaysia, a nation representative of much of the world's people who would welcome just one of the *Survivor* castaways' pre-island paychecks. Malaysia has a per capita gross national product of $3,670 a year, compared to $29,240 in the United States. Now that is reality!

Let's Discuss

1. Put yourself in the place of one of the TV show's castaways. Would you have joined a coalition? What would have been the advantages and disadvantages of such an action?
2. Did you watch the 2000 *Survivor* show? If so, why do you think the ringleader of the coalition won the contest? Would you have voted for him against Kelly to be the winner? Why or why not?

Source: For GNP data, Haub and Cornelius 2000.

within a three-person group. If two roommates in an apartment are perpetually sniping at each other, the third roommate may attempt to remain on good terms with each and arrange compromise solutions to problems. Finally, a member of a triad can choose to employ a *divide-and-rule* strategy. This is the case, for example, with a coach who hopes to gain greater control over two assistants by making them rivals (Nixon 1979).

Coalitions

As groups grow to the size of triads or larger, we can expect coalitions to develop. A ***coalition*** is a temporary or permanent alliance geared toward a common goal. Coalitions can be broad-based or narrow, and can take on many different objectives. Sociologist William Julius Wilson (1999b) has described community-based organizations in Texas that include Whites and Latinos,

139

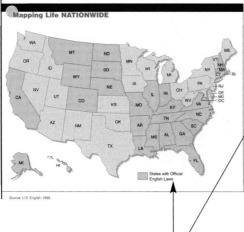

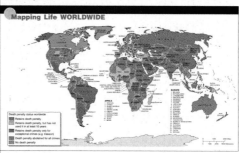

Expanded Map Program

Two kinds of maps—"Mapping Life Nationwide" and "Mapping Life Worldwide"—are featured throughout the text. A map of the world at the beginning of the book shows readers the countries referenced in the text.

Effective Tables

Easy-to-read tables present the latest findings and summarize important concepts.

Distinctive Social Policy Sections

These discussions provide a sociological perspective on contemporary social issues such as welfare reform, immigration, and affirmative action. These sections provide a global view of the issues and are organized around a consistent heading structure to make the material more accessible.

Motivational "Taking Sociology to Work" Boxes

"Taking Sociology to Work" boxes profile individuals who majored in sociology and use its principles in their work.

A Wealth of Media Resources

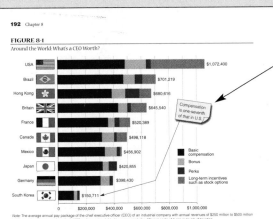

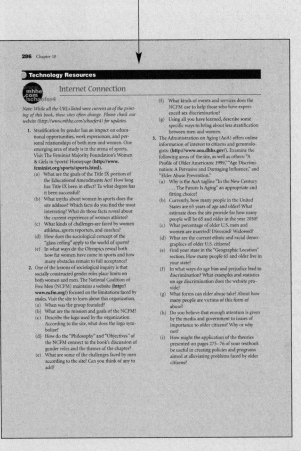

New Innovative "Sticker" Captions

Captions within figures draw attention to major points in the graphs.

New Helpful Cross-Reference System

Key concepts that have been introduced at an earlier point in the text are highlighted with an icon that includes a page number for review purposes.

Internet Connection Exercises

Two or three exercises at the end of each chapter take students online to analyze social issues relevant to chapter content. Web icons featured throughout the book signal that related information and exercises can be found on the book's website.

New Interactive e-Source with Making the Grade CD-ROM

An expanded version of the text is available on CD-ROM. With this CD, you can instantly explore various topics and concepts with an assortment of video clips (including footage of this text's author in Singapore), and website links. You can also highlight text material electronically and test yourself with interactive quizzes and other learning tools.

Online Learning Center

The Online Learning Center is a text-specific website (www.mhhe.com/schaefer4) that offers students and professors a variety of resources and activities. Material from this website can be used in creating the PageOut website.

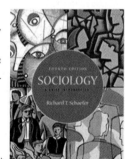

Online Learning Center

Student Center
Instructor Center
Information Center

Preferences
Feedback
Help Center

Sociology: A Brief Introduction, 4/e

Richard T. Schaefer

"I am firmly convinced that sociology can play a valuable role in teaching critical thinking skills. *Sociology: A Brief Introduction* can help students to better understand the workings of their own lives as well as of their society and other cultures." —Richard T. Schaefer

The fourth edition of *Sociology: A Brief Introduction*, like its predecessors, reflects Rick Schaefer's mission to bring readers a concise, up-to-date text that teaches students how to think critically about society and their own lives from a wide range of classical and contemporary perspectives. Combining balanced coverage of theory with current research findings, distinctive social policy sections, examples and issues of interest to students, and abundant learning aids and exercises, *Sociology: A Brief Introduction* is a text that will help students to develop a sociological imagination and perspective.

To support and extend the content of the fourth edition of *Sociology: A Brief Introduction*, the text-specific Online Learning Center offers students and professors a variety of resources and activities, including updates to the text's boxes and Internet Connection exercises, quizzes, annotated web links, PowerPoint slides, and more. And, instructors can use any of the material from the Online Learning Center in a course website created using PageOut, a template-driven website development program offered by McGraw-Hill.

SocCity Website

SocCity is a veritable melting pot of sociology cybersources, information, and Internet activities for students and instructors (www.mhhe.com/socscience/sociology). Just click on any of the four buttons on the left side of your screen to get started.

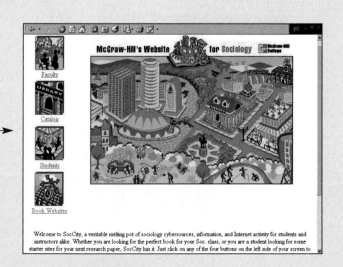

Welcome to SocCity, a veritable melting pot of sociology cybersources, information, and Internet activity for students and instructors alike. Whether you are looking for the perfect book for your Soc. class, or you are a student looking for some starter sites for your next research paper, SocCity has it. Just click on any of the four buttons on the left side of your screen to

PageOut: The Course Website Development Center

Designed for the instructor just beginning to explore web options. PageOut allows even the novice computer user to create a course website with a template provided by McGraw-Hill.

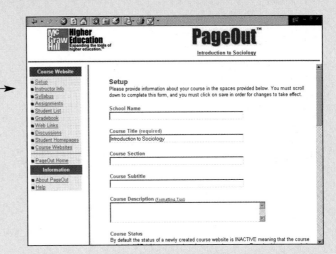

New PowerWeb

Offered free with the text, Power Web is a turnkey solution for adding the Internet to a course. A password-protected website developed by McGraw-Hill/Dushkin, PowerWeb offers instructors and students course-specific materials, Web links and articles, student study tools, and more.

SOCIOLOGY

A BRIEF INTRODUCTION

UNDERSTANDING SOCIOLOGY

Sociology places us in the context of groups, cultures, and societies. People interact in all three of these settings in the Olympic games. This poster promotes the bid of Osaka, Japan, for the 2008 Summer Olympics.

I first walked into the Blue Mosque in the spring of 1996, when I came to accompany a friend getting her first tattoo. Before entering the clean, comfortable, and friendly shop, I had never thought about getting permanent body art myself. In fact, I had specifically promised my family that I would never become tattooed. After watching my friend go through the experience, I changed my mind and began wondering what forms of body modification I could sport myself. The shop's congenial atmosphere made it easy to return several times while choosing my own piercings and eventually my own tattoo. During my visits, I formed friendships with all the artists, and started dating and eventually married the shop's owner, Lefty. Our home became a stopping ground for tattooists traveling through town and a social center for the shop. . . .

My tattoo recreational life became a research interest after Lefty and I took a vacation to California. Renting a car and roaming the California coastline, we visited a score of tattoo shops, talked about the meaning of tattoos in society, and noted the many changes taking place in the tattoo industry. At the end of one of these conversations, Lefty mentioned that someone should do a study chronicling these changes. As a graduate student in Sociology looking for a dissertation topic, I quickly stepped up to the research task and Lefty willingly assumed the responsibility of key informant. . . .

As a tattooist's wife and a shop regular, I gained a unique view of this social world. Over the two-year participant observation study, I visited the shop between one hundred to two hundred times and was present during thousands of conversations between the tattoo artists at home and at social occasions. . . .

While at home and during social functions, I focused on the social world of professional tattooists while listening to daily conversations regarding their interactions with clients, their hopes, their frustrations, and their goals. The first time tattooees at the Blue Mosque were a unique set made up equally of men and women, ranging in age (18–60) more than heavily tattooed clients of the shop, and were more likely to be middle or upper middle class. My observations reflect the largely conventional, middle class experience of getting a first tattoo. *(Irwin 1999a)* ■

What makes tattooing an appropriate subject for study in sociology? Uniting all sociological studies is their focus on *patterns* of human behavior. Katherine Irwin's tattoo research, for example, tracked the dramatic change in what it meant to get a tattoo in the 1990s, as opposed to earlier periods, when tattooing was primarily associated with fringe groups like biker gangs, punk rockers, and skinheads. First-time tattoo clients of the 1990s, Irwin found, increasingly fit the image of avant-garde or hip individuals, seeking to make a statement about their identities but not to cut themselves off from mainstream society. By continuing to interact with that society, whether as students, or employees, or just members of conventional families, they were in fact making tattooing appear less unconventional. The tattoo has gradually become a badge of trendy social status, instead of a symbol of outcast status (Irwin 1998, 1999b, 2000).

Sociologists are not concerned with what one individual does or does not do, but with what people do as members of a group or interacting with one another, and what that means for the individuals and for society as a whole. Tattooing is, in fact, a subject that sociologists can study in any number of ways. They might examine its history (going back as far as 30,000 years) or its use in different groups and cultures. One study, for example, specifically looks at how the tattoos of prison gang members communicate their status, rank, and personal accomplishments. Another focuses is on the emergence of Christian tattoo parlors, which offer images of Christ or banners that blaze "Born Again" (E. Gale 1999; Mascia-Lees and Sharpe 1992; Phelan and Hunt 1998).

As a field of study, then, sociology is extremely broad in scope. You will see throughout this book the range of topics sociologists investigate—from suicide to TV viewing habits, from Amish society to global economic patterns, from peer pressure to pickpocketing techniques. Sociology looks at how others influence our behavior as well as how major social institutions like the government, religion, and the economy affect us.

This chapter will explore the nature of sociology as a field of inquiry and an exercise of the "sociological imagination." We'll look at the discipline as a science and consider its relationship to other social sciences. We will evaluate the contributions of three pioneering thinkers—Émile Durkheim, Max Weber, and Karl Marx—to the development of sociology. Next we will discuss a number of important theoretical perspectives used by sociologists. Finally, we will consider the ways sociology helps us to develop our sociological imagination. ■

What Is Sociology?

Sociology is the systematic study of social behavior and human groups. It focuses primarily on the influence of social relationships on people's attitudes and behavior and on how societies are established and change. This textbook deals with such varied topics as families, the workplace, street gangs, business firms, political parties, genetic engineering, schools, religions, and labor unions. It is concerned with love, poverty, conformity, discrimination, illness, technology, and community.

The Sociological Imagination

In attempting to understand social behavior, sociologists rely on an unusual type of creative thinking. C. Wright Mills (1959) described such thinking as the *sociological imagination*—an awareness of the relationship between an individual and the wider society. This awareness allows all of us (not just sociologists) to comprehend the links between our immediate, personal social settings and the remote, impersonal social world that surrounds us and helps to shape us.

A key element in the sociological imagination is the ability to view one's own society as an outsider would, rather than only from the perspective of personal experiences and cultural biases. Consider something as simple as the practice of eating while walking. In the United States we think nothing of seeing people consuming ice cream cones or sodas or candy bars as they walk along. Sociologists would see this as a pattern of acceptable behavior because others regard it as acceptable. Yet sociologists need to go beyond one culture to place the practice in perspective. This "normal" behavior is quite unacceptable elsewhere. For example, in Japan people do not eat while walking. Streetside sellers and vending machines dispense food everywhere, but the Japanese will stop to eat or drink whatever they buy before they continue on their way. In their eyes, to engage in another activity while eating shows disrespect for the food preparation, even if the food comes out of a vending machine.

The sociological imagination allows us to go beyond

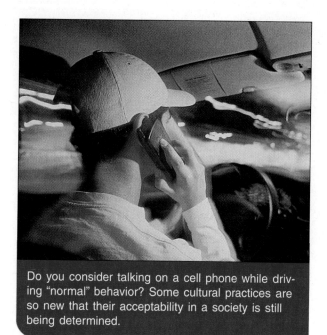

Do you consider talking on a cell phone while driving "normal" behavior? Some cultural practices are so new that their acceptability in a society is still being determined.

personal experiences and observations to understand broader public issues. Unemployment, for example, is unquestionably a personal hardship for a man or woman without a job. However, C. Wright Mills pointed out that when unemployment is a social problem shared by millions of people, it is appropriate to question the way that a society is structured or organized. Similarly, Mills advocated using the sociological imagination to view divorce not simply as the personal problem of a particular man or woman, but rather as a societal problem, since it is the outcome of many marriages. And he was writing this in the 1950s, when the divorce rate was but a fraction of what it is today (I. Horowitz 1983).

Sociological imagination can bring new understanding to daily life around us. Since 1992, sociologists David Miller and Richard Schaefer (this textbook's author) have studied the food bank system of the United States, which distributes food to hungry individuals and families. On the face of it, food banks seem above reproach. After all, as Miller and Schaefer learned in their research, more than one out of four children in the United States are hungry. One-third of the nation's homeless people report eating one meal per day or less. What could be wrong with charities redistributing to pantries and shelters food that just a decade ago was destined for landfills? In 1997, for example, Second Harvest, a food distribution organization, distributed one billion pounds of food from hundreds of individual and corporate donors to more than 50,000 food pantries, soup kitchens, and social service agencies.

Many observers would uncritically applaud the distribution of tons of food to the needy. But let's look

deeper. While supportive of and personally involved in such efforts, Miller and Schaefer (1993) have drawn on the sociological imagination to offer a more probing view of these activities. They note that powerful forces in our society—such as the federal government, major food retailers, and other large corporations—have joined in charitable food distribution arrangements. Perhaps as a result, the focus of such relief programs is too restricted. The homeless are to be fed, not housed; the unemployed are to be given meals, not jobs. Relief efforts assist hungry individuals and families without challenging the existing social order (for example, by demanding a redistribution of wealth). Of course, without these limited successes in distributing food, starving people might assault patrons of restaurants, loot grocery stores, or literally die of starvation on the steps of city halls and across from the White House. Such critical thinking is typical of sociologists, as they draw on the sociological imagination to study a social issue—in this case, hunger in the United States (Second Harvest 1997; Vladimiroff 1998).

Sociology and the Social Sciences

Is sociology a science? The term *science* refers to the body of knowledge obtained by methods based on systematic observation. Just like other scientific disciplines, sociology engages in organized, systematic study of phenomena (in this case, human behavior) in order to enhance understanding. All scientists, whether studying mushrooms or murderers, attempt to collect precise information through methods of study that are as objective as possible. They rely on careful recording of observations and accumulation of data.

Of course, there is a great difference between sociology and physics, between psychology and astronomy. For this reason, the sciences are commonly divided into natural and social sciences. *Natural science* is the study of the physical features of nature and the ways in which they interact and change. Astronomy, biology, chemistry, geology, and physics are all natural sciences. *Social science* is the study of various aspects of human society. The social sciences include sociology, anthropology, economics, history, psychology, and political science.

These academic disciplines have a common focus on the social behavior of people, yet each has a particular orientation. Anthropologists usually study past cultures and preindustrial societies that continue today, as well as the origins of men and women; this knowledge is used to examine contemporary societies, including even industrial societies. Economists explore the ways in which people produce and exchange goods and services, along with money and other resources. Historians are concerned with the peoples and events of the past and their significance for us today. Political scientists study international relations, the workings of government, and the exercise of power and authority. Psychologists investigate personality and individual behavior. So what does sociology focus on? It emphasizes the influence that society has on people's attitudes and behavior and the ways in which people shape society. Humans are social animals; therefore, sociologists scientifically examine our social relationships with people.

Let's consider how the different social sciences might approach the hotly debated issue of handgun control. Many people today, concerned about the misuse of firearms in the United States, are calling for restrictions on the purchase and use of handguns. Political scientists would look at the impact of political action groups, such as the National Rifle Association (NRA), on lawmakers. Historians would examine how guns were used over time in our country and elsewhere. Anthropologists would focus on the use of weapons in a variety of cultures as means of protection as well as symbols of power. Psychologists would look at individual cases and assess the impact handguns have on their owners as well as on individual victims of gunfire. Economists would be interested in how firearm manufacture and sales affect communities. Sociologists would gather data to inform policymakers. For example, they would examine data from different states to evaluate the effect of gun restrictions on the incidence of firearm accidents or violent crimes involving firearms. They might also look at the kind of data shown in Table 1-1, which gives an idea of who owns handguns in the United States. They would ask: What explanations can be offered for the significant gender, racial, age, and geographic differences in gun ownership? How would these differences affect the formulation of social policy by city, state, and federal governments? Sociologists might also look at data that show how the United States compares to other nations in handgun ownership and use.

Sociologists put their imagination to work in a variety of areas—including aging, criminal justice, the family, human ecology, and religion. Throughout this textbook, the sociological imagination will be used to examine the United States (and other societies) from the viewpoint of respectful but questioning outsiders.

Sociology and Common Sense

Sociology focuses on the study of human behavior. Yet we all have experience with human behavior and at least some knowledge of it. All of us might well have theories about why people get tattoos, for example, or why people become homeless. Our theories and opinions typically come from "common sense"—that is, from our experiences and conversations, from what we read, from what we see on television, and so forth.

Table 1-1	Gun Ownership in the United States
Sex	
Men	47%
Women	27
Race	
Whites	40%
Non-Whites	19
Age	
18–29	28%
30–49	37
50–64	46
65+	36
Region	
South	46%
Midwest	39
East	29
West	33

Note: Based on a national survey February 1999.
Source: Gallup Poll in M. Gillespie 1999.

In our daily lives, we rely on common sense to get us through many unfamiliar situations. However, this commonsense knowledge, while sometimes accurate, is not always reliable, because it rests on commonly held beliefs rather than on systematic analysis of facts. It was once considered "common sense" to accept that the earth was flat—a view rightly questioned by Pythagoras and Aristotle. Incorrect commonsense notions are not just a part of the distant past; they remain with us today.

In the United States, "common sense" tells us that an "epidemic" of teen pregnancies accounts for most unwed births today, creating a drag on the welfare system. "Common sense" tells us that people panic when faced with natural disasters, such as floods and earthquakes, or even in the wake of tragedies such as the 1995 Oklahoma City bombing. However, these particular "commonsense" notions—like the notion that the earth is flat—are untrue; neither of them is supported by sociological research. The proportion of unwed mothers in their teens is declining; in fact, women who are *not* in their teens account for most of the unwed mothers, and they make up an estimated 93 percent of women on welfare (Luker 1996, 1999). Disasters do not generally produce panic. In the aftermath of disasters and even explosions, greater social organization and structure emerge to deal with a community's problems. In the United States, for example, an emergency "operations group" often coordinates public services and

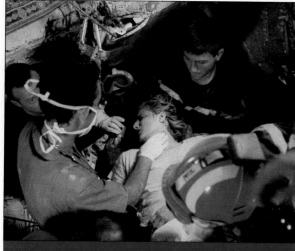

Do disasters produce panic or an organized, structured response? Common sense might tell us the former, but, in fact, disasters bring out a great deal of structure and organization to deal with their aftermath. A French rescue team is pulling this young woman from the rubble caused by a devastating earthquake in Turkey in 1999. Even Greece, Turkey's traditional "enemy," sent relief workers to aid in this disaster. The favor was returned when an earthquake struck Athens later that year.

even certain services normally performed by the private sector, such as food distribution. Decision making becomes more centralized in times of disaster.

Like other social scientists, sociologists do not accept something as a fact because "everyone knows it." Instead, each piece of information must be tested and recorded, then analyzed in relationship to other data. Sociology relies on scientific studies in order to describe and understand a social environment. At times, the findings of sociologists may seem like common sense because they deal with facets of everyday life. The difference is that such findings have been *tested* by researchers. Common sense now tells us that the earth is round. But this particular commonsense notion is based on centuries of scientific work upholding the breakthrough made by Pythagoras and Aristotle.

What Is Sociological Theory?

Why do people commit suicide? One traditional commonsense answer is that people inherit the desire to kill themselves. Another view is that sunspots drive people to take their own lives. These explanations may not seem especially convincing to contemporary researchers, but they represent beliefs widely held as recently as 1900.

Sociologists are not particularly interested in why any one individual commits suicide; they are more concerned with the social forces that systematically cause some people to take their own lives. In order to undertake this research, sociologists develop a theory that offers a general explanation of suicidal behavior.

We can think of theories as attempts to explain events, forces, materials, ideas, or behavior in a comprehensive manner. Within sociology, a **theory** is a set of statements that seeks to explain problems, actions, or behavior. An effective theory may have both explanatory and predictive power. That is, it can help us to see the relationships among seemingly isolated phenomena as well as to understand how one type of change in an environment leads to others.

Émile Durkheim (1951, original edition 1897) looked into suicide data in great detail and developed a highly original theory about the relationship between suicide and social factors. He was primarily concerned not with the personalities of individual suicide victims, but rather with suicide *rates* and how they varied from country to country. As a result, when he looked at the number of reported suicides in France, England, and Denmark in 1869, he also examined the populations of these nations to determine their rates of suicide. He found that whereas England had only 67 reported suicides per million inhabitants, France had 135 per million and Denmark had 277 per million. The question then became: "Why did Denmark have a comparatively high rate of reported suicides?"

Durkheim went much deeper into his investigation of suicide rates, and the result was his landmark work *Suicide,* published in 1897. Durkheim refused to automatically accept unproven explanations regarding suicide, including the beliefs that cosmic forces or inherited tendencies caused such deaths. Instead, he focused on such problems as the cohesiveness or lack of cohesiveness of religious, social, and occupational groups.

Durkheim's research suggested that suicide, while a solitary act, is related to group life. Protestants had much higher suicide rates than Catholics did; the unmarried had much higher rates than married people did; soldiers were more likely to take their lives than civilians were. In addition, it appeared that there were higher rates of suicide in times of peace than in times of war and revolution, and in times of economic instability and recession rather than in times of prosperity. Durkheim concluded that the suicide rates of a society reflected the extent to which people were or were not integrated into the group life of the society.

Émile Durkheim, like many other social scientists, developed a theory to explain how individual behavior can be understood within a social context. He pointed out the influence of groups and societal forces on what had always been viewed as a highly personal act. Clearly, Durkheim offered a more *scientific* explanation for the causes of suicide than that of sunspots or inherited tendencies. His theory has predictive power, since it suggests that suicide rates will rise or fall in conjunction with certain social and economic changes.

Of course, a theory—even the best of theories—is not a final statement about human behavior. Durkheim's theory of suicide is no exception; sociologists continue to examine factors that contribute to differences in suicide rates around the world and to a particular society's rate of suicide. For example, although the overall rate of suicide in New Zealand is only marginally higher than in the United States, the suicide rate among young people is 41 percent higher in New Zealand. Sociologists and psychiatrists from that country suggest that their remote, sparsely populated society maintains exaggerated standards of masculinity that are especially difficult for young males. Gay adolescents who fail to conform to their peers' preference for sports are particularly vulnerable to suicide (Shenon 1995; for a critique of Durkheim's work, see Douglas 1967).

The Development of Sociology

People have always been curious about sociological matters—such as how we get along, what we do, and whom we select as our leaders. Philosophers and religious authorities of ancient and medieval societies made countless observations about human behavior. They did not test or verify these observations scientifically; nevertheless, these observations often became the foundation for moral codes. Several of the early social philosophers predicted that a systematic study of human behavior would one day emerge. Beginning in the nineteenth century, European theorists made pioneering contributions to the development of a science of human behavior.

Early Thinkers: Comte, Martineau, and Spencer

The nineteenth century was an unsettling time in France. The French monarchy had been deposed earlier in the revolution of 1789, and Napoleon had subsequently suffered defeat in his effort to conquer Europe. Amidst this chaos, philosophers considered how society might be improved. Auguste Comte (1798–1857), credited with being the most influential of these philosophers of the early 1800s, believed that a theoretical science of society and systematic investigation of behavior were needed to improve society. He coined the term *sociology* to apply to the science of human behavior.

Writing in the 1800s, Comte feared that the excesses of the French Revolution had permanently impaired France's stability. Yet he hoped that the study of social behavior in a systematic way would eventually lead to more rational human interactions. In Comte's hierarchy of sciences, sociology was at the top. He called it the "queen" and its practitioners "scientist-priests." This French theorist did not simply give sociology its name; he also presented a rather ambitious challenge to the fledgling discipline.

Scholars were able to learn of Comte's works largely through translations by the English sociologist Harriet Martineau (1802–1876). But Martineau was a pathbreaker in her own right as a sociologist. She offered insightful observations of the customs and social practices of both her native Britain and the United States. Martineau's book *Society in America* (1962, original edition 1837) examines religion, politics, child rearing, and immigration in the young nation. Martineau gives special attention to social class distinctions and to such factors as gender and race.

Martineau's writings emphasized the impact that the economy, law, trade, and population could have on the social problems of contemporary society. She spoke out in favor of the rights of women, the emancipation of slaves, and religious tolerance. In Martineau's (1896) view, intellectuals and scholars should not simply offer

Harriet Martineau, an early pioneer of sociology, studied social behavior both in her native England and in the United States.

observations of social conditions; they should act upon their convictions in a manner that will benefit society. In line with this view, Martineau conducted research on the nature of female employment and pointed to the need for further investigation of this important issue (Lengermann and Niebrugge-Brantley 1998).

Another important contributor to the discipline of sociology was Herbert Spencer (1820–1903). A relatively prosperous Victorian Englishman, Spencer (unlike Martineau) did not feel compelled to correct or improve society; instead, he merely hoped to understand it better. Drawing on Charles Darwin's study *On the Origin of Species,* Spencer applied the concept of evolution of the species to societies in order to explain how they change, or evolve, over time. Similarly, he adapted Darwin's evolutionary view of the "survival of the fittest" by arguing that it is "natural" that some people are rich while others are poor.

Spencer's approach to societal change was extremely popular in his own lifetime. Unlike Comte, Spencer suggested that societies are bound to change eventually; therefore, one need not be highly critical of present social arrangements or work actively for social change. This position appealed to many influential people in England and the United States who had a vested interest in the status quo and were suspicious of social thinkers who endorsed change.

Émile Durkheim

Émile Durkheim made many pioneering contributions to sociology, including his important theoretical work on suicide. The son of a rabbi, Durkheim (1858–1917) was educated in both France and Germany. He established an impressive academic reputation and was appointed as one of the first professors of sociology in France. Above all, Durkheim will be remembered for his insistence that behavior must be understood within a larger social context, not just in individualistic terms.

As one example of this emphasis, Durkheim (1947, original edition 1912) developed a fundamental thesis to help understand all forms of society through intensive study of the Arunta, an Australian tribe. He focused on the functions that religion performed for the Arunta and underscored the role that group life plays in defining that which we consider religious. Durkheim concluded that, like other forms of group behavior, religion reinforces a group's solidarity.

Another of Durkheim's main interests was the consequences of work in modern societies. In his view, the growing division of labor found in industrial societies as workers became much more specialized in their tasks led to what he called *anomie*. **Anomie** refers to the loss of direction that a society feels when social control of individual behavior has become ineffective. The state of anomie occurs when people have lost their sense of purpose or direction, often during a time of profound social change. In a period of anomie, people are so confused and unable to cope with the new social environment that they may resort to taking their own lives.

Durkheim was concerned about the dangers that alienation, loneliness, and isolation might pose for modern industrial societies. He shared Comte's belief that sociology should provide direction for social change. As a result, he advocated the creation of new social groups—between the individual's family and the state—which would ideally provide a sense of belonging for members of huge, impersonal societies. Unions would be an example of such a group.

Like many other sociologists, Durkheim did not limit his interests to one aspect of social behavior. Later in this book, we will consider his thinking on crime and punishment, religion, and the workplace. Few sociologists have had such a dramatic impact on so many different areas within the discipline.

Max Weber

Another important early theorist was Max Weber (pronounced "VAY-ber"). Born in Germany in 1864, Weber took his early academic training in legal and economic history, but he gradually developed an interest in sociology. Eventually, he became a professor at various German universities. Weber taught his students that they should employ **Verstehen,** the German word for "understanding" or "insight," in their intellectual work. He pointed out that we cannot analyze much of our social behavior by the kinds of objective criteria we use to measure weight or temperature. To fully comprehend behavior, we must learn the subjective meanings people attach to their actions—how they themselves view and explain their behavior.

For example, suppose that a sociologist was studying the social ranking of individuals in a fraternity. Weber would expect the researcher to employ *Verstehen* to determine the significance of the fraternity's social hierarchy for its members. The researcher might examine the effects of athleticism or grades or social skills or seniority on standing within the fraternity. He or she would seek to learn how the fraternity members relate to other members of higher or lower status. While investigating these questions, the researcher would take into account people's emotions, thoughts, beliefs, and attitudes (L. Coser 1977).

We also owe credit to Weber for a key conceptual tool: the ideal type. An *ideal type* is a construct, a made-up model that serves as a measuring rod against which actual cases can be evaluated. In his own works, Weber identified various characteristics of bureaucracy as an ideal type (discussed in detail in Chapter 6). In presenting this model of bureaucracy, Weber was not describing any particular business, nor was he using the term *ideal* in a way that suggested a positive evaluation. Instead, his purpose was to provide a useful standard for measuring just how bureaucratic an actual organization is (Gerth and Mills 1958). Later in this textbook, we use the concept of ideal type to study the family, religion, authority, and economic systems and to analyze bureaucracy.

Although their professional careers coincided, Émile Durkheim and Max Weber never met and probably were unaware of each other's existence, let alone ideas. This was certainly not true of the work of Karl Marx. Durkheim's thinking about the impact of the division of labor in industrial societies was related to Marx's writings, while Weber's concern for a value-free, objective sociology was a direct response to Marx's deeply held convictions. Thus, it is not surprising that Karl Marx is viewed as a major figure in the development of sociology as well as several other social sciences (see Figure 1-1).

Karl Marx

Karl Marx (1818–1883) shared with Durkheim and Weber a dual interest in abstract philosophical issues and the concrete reality of everyday life. Unlike the others, Marx was so critical of existing institutions that a conventional academic career was impossible, and although he was born and educated in Germany, he spent most of his life in exile.

Marx's personal life was a difficult struggle. When a paper that he had written was suppressed, he fled his native land for France. In Paris, he met Friedrich Engels (1820–1895), with whom he formed a lifelong friendship. They lived at a time when European and North American economic life was increasingly being dominated by the factory rather than the farm.

In 1847, Marx and Engels attended secret meetings in London of an illegal coalition of labor unions, known as the Communist League. The following year, they prepared a platform called *The Communist Manifesto*, in which they argued that the masses of people who have no resources other than their labor (whom they referred to as the *proletariat*) should unite to fight for the overthrow of capitalist societies. In the words of Marx and Engels:

> The history of all hitherto existing society is the history of class struggles. . . . The proletarians have nothing to lose but their chains. They have a world to win. WORKING MEN OF ALL COUNTRIES UNITE! (Feuer 1959:7, 41).

After completing *The Communist Manifesto*, Marx returned to Germany, only to be expelled. He then moved to England, where he continued to write books and

FIGURE 1-1

Early Social Thinkers

	Émile Durkheim 1858–1917	**Max Weber** 1864–1920	**Karl Marx** 1818–1883
Academic training	Philosophy	Law, economics, history, philosophy	Philosophy, law
Key works	1893—*The Division of Labor in Society* 1897—*Suicide: A Study in Sociology* 1912—*Elementary Forms of Religious Life*	1904–1905—*The Protestant Ethic and the Spirit of Capitalism* 1922—*Wirtschaft und Gesellschaft*	1848—*The Communist Manifesto* 1867—*Das Kapital*

essays. Marx lived there in extreme poverty. He pawned most of his possessions, and several of his children died of malnutrition and disease. Marx clearly was an outsider in British society, a fact that may well have affected his view of Western cultures.

In Marx's analysis, society was fundamentally divided between classes that clash in pursuit of their own class interests. When he examined the industrial societies of his time, such as Germany, England, and the United States, he saw the factory as the center of conflict between the exploiters (the owners of the means of production) and the exploited (the workers). Marx viewed these relationships in systematic terms; that is, he believed that an entire system of economic, social, and political relationships maintained the power and dominance of the owners over the workers. Consequently, Marx and Engels argued that the working class needed to overthrow the existing class system. Marx's influence on contemporary thinking has been dramatic. Marx's writings inspired those who were later to lead communist revolutions in Russia, China, Cuba, Vietnam, and elsewhere.

Even apart from the political revolutions that his work fostered, Marx's influence on contemporary thinking has been dramatic. Marx emphasized the *group* identifications and associations that influence an individual's place in society. This area of study is the major focus of contemporary sociology. Throughout this textbook, we will consider how membership in a particular gender classification, age group, racial group, or economic class affects a person's attitudes and behavior. In an important sense, we can trace this way of understanding society back to the pioneering work of Karl Marx.

Modern Developments

Sociology today builds on the firm foundation developed by Émile Durkheim, Max Weber, and Karl Marx. However, the discipline of sociology has certainly not remained stagnant over the last century. While Europeans have continued to make contributions to the discipline, sociologists from throughout the world and especially the United States have advanced sociological theory and research. Their new insights have helped them to better understand the workings of society.

Charles Horton Cooley (1864–1929) was typical of the sociologists who came to prominence in the early 1900s. Cooley was born in Ann Arbor, Michigan, and received his graduate training in economics but later became a sociology professor at the University of Michigan. Like other early sociologists, he had become interested in this "new" discipline while pursuing a related area of study.

Cooley shared the desire of Durkheim, Weber, and Marx to learn more about society. But to do so effectively, Cooley preferred to use the sociological perspective to look first at smaller units—intimate, face-to-face groups such as families, gangs, and friendship networks. He saw these groups as the seedbeds of society in the sense that they shape people's ideals, beliefs, values, and social nature. Cooley's work increased our understanding of groups of relatively small size.

In the early 1900s, many leading sociologists in the United States saw themselves as social reformers dedicated to systematically studying and then improving a corrupt society. They were genuinely concerned about the lives of immigrants in the nation's growing cities, whether these immigrants came from Europe or from the rural American south. Early female sociologists, in particular, often took active roles in poor urban areas as leaders of community centers known as *settlement houses*. For example, Jane Addams (1860–1935), an active member of the American Sociological Society, cofounded the famous Chicago settlement, Hull House.

Addams and other pioneering female sociologists commonly combined intellectual inquiry, social service work, and political activism—all with the goal of assisting the underprivileged and creating a more egalitarian society. For example, working with the Black journalist and educator Ida B. Wells, Addams successfully prevented the implementation of a racial segregation policy in the Chicago public schools. Addams' efforts to establish a juvenile court system and a women's trade union also reflect the practical focus of her work (Addams 1910, 1930; Deegan 1991; Lengermann and Niebrugge-Brantley 1998).

A postage stamp honored social reformer Jane Addams, an early pioneer both in sociology and in the settlement house movement.

By the middle of the twentieth century, however, the focus of the discipline had shifted. Sociologists for the most part restricted themselves to theorizing and gathering information; the aim of transforming society was left to social workers and others. This shift away from social reform was accompanied by a growing commitment to scientific methods of research and to value-free interpretation of data. Not all sociologists were happy with this emphasis. A new organization, the Society for the Study of Social Problems, was created in 1950 to deal more directly with social inequality and other social problems.

Sociologist Robert Merton (1968) made an important contribution to the discipline by successfully combining theory and research. Born in 1910 of Slavic immigrant parents in Philadelphia, Merton subsequently won a scholarship to Temple University. He continued his studies at Harvard, where he acquired his lifelong interest in sociology. Merton's teaching career has been based at Columbia University.

Merton produced a theory that is one of the most frequently cited explanations of deviant behavior. He noted different ways in which people attempt to achieve success in life. In his view, some may not share the socially agreed-upon goal of accumulating material goods or the accepted means of achieving this goal. For example, in Merton's classification scheme, "innovators" are people who accept the goal of pursuing material wealth but use illegal means to do so, including robbery, burglary, and extortion. Merton bases his explanation of crime on individual behavior—influenced by society's approved goals and means—yet it has wider applications. It helps to account for the high crime rates among the nation's poor, who may see no hope of advancing themselves through traditional roads to success. Chapter 7 discusses Merton's theory in greater detail.

Merton also emphasized that sociology should strive to bring together the "macro-level" and "micro-level" approaches to the study of society. *Macrosociology* concentrates on large-scale phenomena or entire civilizations. Thus, Émile Durkheim's cross-cultural study of suicide is an example of macro-level research. More recently, macrosociologists have examined international crime rates (see Chapter 7), the stereotype of Asian Americans as a "model minority" (see Chapter 9), and the population patterns of Islamic countries (see Chapter 14). By contrast, *microsociology* stresses study of small groups and often uses experimental study in laboratories. Sociological research on the microlevel has included studies of how divorced men and women, for example, disengage from significant social roles (see Chapter 5); of how conformity can influence the expression of prejudiced attitudes (see Chapter 7); and of how a teacher's expectations can affect a student's academic performance (see Chapter 12).

Contemporary sociology reflects the diverse contributions of earlier theorists. As sociologists approach such topics as divorce, drug addiction, and religious cults, they can draw on the theoretical insights of the discipline's pioneers. A careful reader can hear Comte, Durkheim, Weber, Marx, Cooley, Addams, and many others speaking through the pages of current research. Sociology has also broadened beyond the intellectual confines of North America and Europe. Contributions to the discipline now come from sociologists studying and researching human behavior in other parts of the world. In describing the work of today's sociologists, it is helpful to examine a number of influential theoretical approaches (also known as *perspectives*).

Major Theoretical Perspectives

Sociologists view society in different ways. Some see the world basically as a stable and ongoing entity. They are impressed with the endurance of the family, organized religion, and other social institutions. Some sociologists see society as composed of many groups in conflict, competing for scarce resources. To other sociologists, the most fascinating aspects of the social world are the everyday, routine interactions among individuals that we sometimes take for granted. These three views, the ones most widely used by sociologists, are the functionalist, conflict, and interactionist perspectives. They will provide an introductory look at the discipline.

Functionalist Perspective

Think of society as a living organism in which each part of the organism contributes to its survival. This view is the *functionalist perspective,* which emphasizes the way that parts of a society are structured to maintain its stability.

Talcott Parsons (1902–1979), a Harvard University sociologist, was a key figure in the development of functionalist theory. Parsons had been greatly influenced by the work of Émile Durkheim, Max Weber, and other European sociologists. For over four decades, Parsons dominated sociology in the United States with his advocacy of functionalism. He saw any society as a vast network of connected parts, each of which helps to maintain the system as a whole. The functionalist approach holds that if an aspect of social life does not contribute to a society's stability or survival—if it does not serve some identifiably useful function or promote value consensus among members of a society—it will not be passed on from one generation to the next.

Let's examine prostitution as an example of the functionalist perspective. Why is it that a practice so widely condemned continues to display such persistence and vitality? Functionalists suggest that prostitution satisfies needs of patrons that may not be readily met through more socially acceptable forms such as courtship or marriage. The "buyer" receives sex without any responsibility for procreation or sentimental attachment; at the same time, the "seller" makes a living through this exchange.

Such an examination leads us to conclude that prostitution does perform certain functions that society seems to need. However, this is not to suggest that prostitution is a desirable or legitimate form of social behavior. Functionalists do not make such judgments. Rather, advocates of the functionalist perspective hope to explain how an aspect of society that is so frequently attacked can nevertheless manage to survive (K. Davis 1937).

Manifest and Latent Functions

Your college catalog typically states various functions of the institution. It may inform you, for example, that the university intends to "offer each student a broad education in classical and contemporary thought, in the humanities, in the sciences, and in the arts." However, it would be quite a surprise to find a catalog that declared, "This university was founded in 1895 to keep people between the ages of 18 and 22 out of the job market, thus reducing unemployment." No college catalog will declare that this is the purpose of the university. Yet societal institutions serve many functions, some of them quite subtle. The university, in fact, *does* delay people's entry into the job market.

Robert Merton (1968) made an important distinction between manifest and latent functions. *Manifest functions* of institutions are open, stated, conscious functions. They involve the intended, recognized consequences of an aspect of society, such as the university's role in certifying academic competence and excellence. By contrast, *latent functions* are unconscious or unintended functions and may reflect hidden purposes of an institution. One latent function of universities is to hold down unemployment. Another is to serve as a meeting ground for people seeking marital partners.

Dysfunctions

Functionalists acknowledge that not all parts of a society contribute to its stability all the time. A *dysfunction* refers to an element or a process of society that may actually disrupt a social system or lead to a decrease in stability.

We consider many dysfunctional behavior patterns, such as homicide, as undesirable. Yet we should not automatically interpret dysfunctions as negative. The evaluation of a dysfunction depends on one's own values or, as the saying goes, on "where you sit." For example, the official view in prisons in the United States is that inmates' gangs should be eradicated because they are dysfunc-

Military chaplains fill a function in society by providing inspiration and solace to those serving their country. This Navy chaplain is leading a field prayer service for the soldiers stationed in Kosovo in 1999 as part of the NATO-led peacekeeping military force.

tional to smooth operations. Yet some guards have actually come to view the presence of prison gangs as functional for their jobs. The danger posed by gangs creates a "threat to security," requiring increased surveillance and more overtime work for guards (Hunt et al. 1993:400).

Conflict Perspective

In contrast to functionalists' emphasis on stability and consensus, conflict sociologists see the social world in continual struggle. The *conflict perspective* assumes that social behavior is best understood in terms of conflict or tension between competing groups. Such conflict need not be violent; it can take the form of labor negotiations, party politics, competition between religious groups for members, or disputes over the federal budget.

Throughout most of the 1900s, the functionalist perspective had the upper hand in sociology in the United States. However, the conflict approach has become increasingly persuasive since the late 1960s. The widespread social unrest resulting from battles over civil rights, bitter divisions over the war in Vietnam, the rise of the feminist and gay liberation movements, the Watergate scandal, urban riots, and confrontations at abortion clinics offered support for the conflict approach—the view that our social world is characterized by continual struggle between competing groups. Currently, the discipline of sociology accepts conflict theory as one valid way to gain insight into a society.

The Marxist View

As we saw earlier, Karl Marx viewed struggle between social classes as inevitable, given the exploitation of workers under capitalism. Expanding on Marx's work, sociologists and other social scientists have come to see conflict not merely as a class phenomenon but as a part of everyday life in all societies. Thus, in studying any culture, organization, or social group, sociologists want to know who benefits, who suffers, and who dominates at the expense of others. They are concerned with the conflicts between women and men, parents and children, cities and suburbs, and Whites and Blacks, to name only a few. Conflict theorists are interested in how society's institutions—including the family, government, religion, education, and the media—may help to maintain the privileges of some groups and keep others in a subservient position. Their emphasis on social change and redistribution of resources makes conflict theorists more "radical" and "activist" than functionalists (Dahrendorf 1958).

A Racial View: W. E. B. Du Bois

One important contribution of conflict theory is that it has encouraged sociologists to view society through the eyes of those segments of the population that rarely influence decision making. Early Black sociologists such as W. E. B. Du Bois (1868–1963) conducted research that they hoped would assist the struggle for a racially egalitarian society. Du Bois believed that knowledge was essential in combating prejudice and achieving tolerance and justice. Sociology, Du Bois contended, had to draw on scientific principles to study social problems such as those experienced by Blacks in the United States. In addition, Du Bois made a major contribution to sociology through his in-depth studies of urban life—both White and Black.

Du Bois had little patience for theorists such as Herbert Spencer who seemed content with the status quo. He advocated basic research on the lives of Blacks that would separate opinion from fact. In this way he documented their relatively low status in Philadelphia and Atlanta. Du Bois believed that the granting of full political rights to Blacks was essential to their social and economic progress in the United States. Many of his ideas challenging the status quo did not find a receptive audience within either the government or the academic world. As a result, Du Bois became increasingly involved with organizations whose members questioned the established social order, and he helped to found the National Association for the Advancement of Colored People, better known as the NAACP (Green and Driver 1978).

The addition of diverse views within sociology in recent years has led to some helpful research, especially for African Americans. For many years, African Americans were understandably wary of participating in medical research studies, because those studies had been used for such purposes as justifying slavery or determining the impact of untreated syphilis. Now, however, African American sociologists and other social scientists are working to involve Blacks in useful ethnic medical research in such areas as diabetes and sickle cell anemia, two disorders that strike Black populations especially hard (St. John 1997).

The ideas of W. E. B. Du Bois challenged the status quo in both academic and political circles. The first Black person to receive a doctorate from Harvard University, he later helped organize the National Association for the Advancement of Colored People (NAACP).

The Feminist View

Feminist theory builds in important ways on the conflict perspective, but it is also sensitive to the need for social integration advocated by functionalists. Like other conflict theorists, feminist scholars see gender differences as a reflection of the subjugation of one group (women) by another group (men). Drawing on the work of Marx and Engels, contemporary feminist theorists often view women's subordination as inherent in capitalist societies. Some radical feminist theorists, however, view the oppression of women as inevitable in *all* male-dominated societies, including those labeled as *capitalist, socialist,* and *communist* (Tuchman 1992).

As is true of the work of African American sociologists,

feminist scholarship in sociology has broadened our understanding of social behavior by taking it beyond the White male point of view. For example, a family's social standing is no longer defined solely by the husband's position and income. Feminist scholars have not only challenged stereotyping of women; they have argued for a gender-balanced study of society in which women's experiences and contributions are as visible as those of men (Brewer 1989; P. England 1999; Komarovsky 1991).

The feminist perspective has given sociologists new views of familiar social behavior. For example, past research on crime rarely considered women, and when it did, the studies tended to focus on "traditional" crimes by women like shoplifting. Such a view tended to ignore the role that women play in all types of crime as well as the disproportionate role that they play as *victims* of crime. Research conducted by Meda Chesney-Lind and Noelie Rodriguez (1993) showed that nearly all women in prison had suffered physical and/or sexual abuse when they were young; half had been raped. Contributions by both feminist and minority scholars have enriched all the sociological perspectives.

Interactionist Perspective

Workers interacting on the job, encounters in public places like bus stops and parks, behavior in small groups—these are all aspects of microsociology that catch the attention of interactionists. Whereas functionalist and conflict theorists both analyze large-scale society-wide patterns of behavior, the **interactionist perspective** generalizes about everyday forms of social interaction in order to understand society as a whole. In the 1990s, for example, the workings of juries became a subject of public scrutiny. High-profile trials ended in verdicts that left some people shaking their heads. Long before jury members were being interviewed on their front lawns following trials, interactionists tried to better understand behavior in the small-group setting of a jury deliberation room.

Interactionism is a sociological framework for viewing human beings as living in a world of meaningful objects. These "objects" may include material things, actions, other people, relationships, and even symbols.

While functionalist and conflict approaches were initiated in Europe, interactionism developed first in the United States. George Herbert Mead (1863–1931) is widely regarded as the founder of the interactionist perspective. Mead taught at the University of Chicago from 1893 until his death. His sociological analysis, like that of Charles Horton Cooley, often focused on human interactions within one-to-one situations and small groups. Mead was interested in observing the most minute forms of communication—smiles, frowns, nodding of one's head—and in understanding how such individual behavior was influenced by the larger context of a group or society. Despite his innovative views, Mead only occasionally wrote articles, and never a book. He was an extremely popular teacher, and most of his insights have come to us through edited volumes of lectures that his students published after his death.

The interactionist perspective is sometimes referred to as the *symbolic interactionist perspective,* because interactionists see symbols as an especially important part of human communication. Members of a society share the social meanings of symbols. In the United States, for example, a salute symbolizes respect, while a clenched fist signifies defiance. However, another culture might use different gestures to convey a feeling of respect or defiance.

Consider the different ways various societies portray suicide without the use of words. People in the United States point a finger at the head (shooting); urban Japanese bring a fist against the stomach (stabbing); and the South Fore of Papua, New Guinea, clench a hand at the throat (hanging). These types of symbolic interaction are classified as forms of **nonverbal communication,** which can include many other gestures, facial expressions, and postures.

Since Mead's teachings have become well known, sociologists have expressed greater interest in the interactionist perspective. Many have moved away from what may have been an excessive preoccupation with the large-scale (macro) level of social behavior and have redirected their attention toward behavior that occurs in small groups (microlevel).

Erving Goffman (1922–1982) popularized a particular type of interactionist method known as the **dramaturgical approach.** The dramaturgist compares everyday life to the setting of the theater and stage. Just as actors project certain images, all of us seek to present particular features of our personalities while we hide other qualities. Thus, in a class, we may feel the need to project a serious image; at a party, we want to look relaxed and friendly.

The Sociological Approach

Which perspective should a sociologist use in studying human behavior? Functionalist? Conflict? Interactionist?

Sociology makes use of all three perspectives (see Table 1-2), since each offers unique insights into the same issue. Think about how Katherine Irwin went about studying the tattoo culture in the United States today (described in the chapter opening). She focused on the tattoo's use as a symbol of hip social status (functionalist perspective), and she examined the tensions between a

Table 1-2 **Comparing Major Theoretical Perspectives**

	Functionalist	Conflict	Interactionist
View of society	Stable, well integrated	Characterized by tension and struggle between groups	Active in influencing and affecting everyday social interaction
Level of analysis emphasized	Macro	Macro	Micro analysis as a way of understanding the larger macro phenomena
Key concepts	Manifest functions Latent functions Dysfunction	Inequality Capitalism Stratification	Symbols Nonverbal communication Face-to-face
View of the individual	People are socialized to perform societal functions	People are shaped by power, coercion, and authority	People manipulate symbols and create their social worlds through interaction
View of the social order	Maintained through cooperation and consensus	Maintained through force and coercion	Maintained by shared understanding of everyday behavior
View of social change	Predictable, reinforcing	Change takes place all the time and may have positive consequences	Reflected in people's social positions and their communications with others
Example	Public punishments reinforce the social order	Laws reinforce the positions of those in power	People respect laws or disobey them based on their own past experience
Proponents	Émile Durkheim Talcott Parsons Robert Merton	Karl Marx W. E. B. Du Bois C. Wright Mills	George Herbert Mead Charles Horton Cooley Erving Goffman

parent and a child who decides to get tattooed, and the disapproval an employer might show toward a tattooed employee (conflict perspective). Research into the actual process of getting tattooed, including the negotiations between the tattoo artist and the tattooee, made use of the interactionist perspective. As another example, Box 1-1 shows how television might look from the functionalist, conflict, and interactionist points of view.

No one approach to a particular issue is "correct." This textbook assumes that we can gain the broadest understanding of our society by drawing on all three perspectives in the study of human behavior and institutions. These perspectives overlap as their interests coincide but can diverge according to the dictates of each approach and of the issue being studied. A sociologist's theoretical orientation influences his or her approach to a research problem in important ways.

Developing the Sociological Imagination

In this book, we will be illustrating the sociological imagination in several different ways—by showing theory in practice and research in action; by speaking across race, gender, class, and national boundaries; and by highlighting social policy throughout the world.

Theory in Practice

We will illustrate how the three sociological perspectives—functionalist, conflict, and interactionist—are helpful in understanding today's issues, whether it be capital punishment or financing health care. Sociologists do not necessarily declare "here I am using functionalism," but their research and approaches do tend to draw on one

Eye on the Media

1-1 Looking at Television from Three Perspectives

Television to most of us is that box sitting on the shelf or table that diverts us, occasionally entertains us, and sometimes puts us to sleep. But sociologists would look much deeper at the medium. Here is what they would find using the three sociological perspectives.

FUNCTIONALIST VIEW

In examining any aspect of society, including television, functionalists emphasize the contribution it makes to overall social stability. Functionalists regard television as a powerful force in communicating the common values of our society and in promoting an overall feeling of unity and social solidarity:

- Television vividly presents important national and international news. On a local level, television communicates vital information on everything from storm warnings and school closings to locations of emergency shelters.
- Television programs transmit valuable learning skills (*Sesame Street*) and factual information (the National Geographic series on PBS).
- Television "brings together" members of a community or even a nation by broadcasting important events and ceremonies (inaugurations, press conferences, parades, and state funerals) and through coverage of disasters such as the 1986 *Challenger* explosion and the 1995 bombing in Oklahoma City.
- Television contributes to economic stability and prosperity by promoting and advertising services and (through shopping channels) serving as a direct marketplace for products.

CONFLICT VIEW

Conflict theorists argue that the social order is based on coercion and ex-

ploitation. They emphasize that television reflects and even exacerbates many of the divisions of our society and world, including those based on gender, race, ethnicity, and social class:

- Television is a form of big business in which profits are more important than the quality of the product (programming).
- Television's decision makers are overwhelmingly White, male, and prosperous; by contrast, television programs tend to ignore the lives and ambitions of subordinate groups, among them working-class people, African Americans, Hispan-

> **On a local level, television communicates vital information on everything from storm warnings and school closings to locations of emergency shelters.**

ics, gays and lesbians, people with disabilities, and older people.
- Television distorts the political process, as candidates with the most money (often backed by powerful lobbying groups) buy exposure to voters and saturate the air with attack commercials.
- By exporting *Beverly Hills 90210*, *Baywatch*, and other programs around the world, U.S. television undermines the distinctive traditions and art forms of other societies and encourages their cultural and economic dependence on the United States.

INTERACTIONIST VIEW

In studying the social order, interactionists are especially interested in shared understandings of everyday be-

havior. Consequently, interactionists examine television on the microlevel by focusing on how day-to-day social behavior is shaped by television:

- Television literally serves as a babysitter or a "playmate" for many children for long periods of their lives.
- Friendship networks can emerge from shared viewing habits or from recollections of a cherished series from the past. Family members and friends often gather for parties centered on the broadcasting of popular events such as the Super Bowl or the Academy Awards or even series like *Survivor*.
- The frequent appearance of violence in news and entertainment programming creates feelings of fear and may actually make interpersonal relations more aggressive.
- The power of television encourages political leaders and even entertainment figures to carefully manipulate symbols (through public appearances) and attempt to convey self-serving definitions of social reality.

Despite their differences, functionalists, conflict theorists, and interactionists would agree that there is much more to television than simply "entertainment." They would also agree that television and other popular forms of culture are worthy subjects for serious study by sociologists.

Let's Discuss

1. What functions does television serve? What might be some "dysfunctions"?
2. If you were a television network executive, which perspective would influence your choice of programs? Why?

1-2 Women in Public Places Worldwide

By definition, a public place, such as a sidewalk or a park, is open to all persons. Even some private establishments, such as restaurants, are intended to belong to people as a whole. Yet sociologists and other social scientists have found that societies define access to these places differently for women and men.

In many Middle Eastern societies, women are prohibited from public places and are restricted to certain places in the house. In such societies, the coffeehouse and the market are considered male domains. Some other societies, such as Malagasy, strictly limit the presence of women in "public places" yet allow women to conduct the haggling that is a part of shopping in open-air markets. In some West African societies, women actually control the marketplace. In various eastern European countries and Turkey, women appear to be free to move about in public places, but the coffeehouse remains the exclusive preserve of males. Similarly in Taiwan today, wine houses are the exclusive domains of businessmen; even female managers are unwelcome. Contrast this with coffeehouses and taverns in North America, where women and men mingle freely and even engage each other in conversation as total strangers.

While casual observers may view both private and public space in the United States as gender-neutral, private all-male clubs do persist, and even in public spaces women experience some inequality. Erving Goffman, an interactionist, conducted classic studies of public spaces, which he found to be innocuous settings for routine interactions, such as "helping" encounters when a person is lost and asks for directions. But sociologist Carol Brooks Gardner

> Women are well aware that a casual helping encounter with a man in a public place can too easily lead to undesired sexual queries or advances.

has offered a feminist critique of Goffman's work: "Rarely does Goffman emphasize the habitual disproportionate fear that women can come to feel in public toward men, much less the routine trepidation that ethnic and racial minorities and the disabled can experience" (1989:45). Women are well aware that a casual helping encounter with a man in a public place can too easily lead to undesired sexual queries or advances. Whereas Goffman suggests that

street remarks about women occur rarely—and that they generally hold no unpleasant or threatening implications—Gardner (1989:49) counters that "for young women especially, . . . appearing in public places carries with it the constant possibility of evaluation, compliments that are not really so complimentary after all, and harsh or vulgar insults if the woman is found wanting." She adds that these remarks are sometimes accompanied by tweaks, pinches, or even blows, unmasking the latent hostility of many male-to-female street remarks.

According to Gardner, many women have a well-founded fear of the sexual harassment, assault, and rape that can occur in public places. She concludes that "public places are arenas for the enactment of inequality in everyday life for women and for many others" (1989:56).

Let's Discuss

1. How would a coffeehouse in Turkey differ from one in Seattle, Washington? What might account for these differences?

2. Do you know a woman who has encountered sexual harassment in a public place? How did she react? How has her social behavior been changed by the experience?

Sources: Cheng and Liao 1994; Gardner 1989, 1990, 1995; Goffman 1963b, 1971; Rosman and Rubel 1994; D. Spain 1992.

or more theoretical frameworks, as will become clear in the pages to follow.

Research in Action

Sociologists actively investigate a variety of issues and social behavior. We have already seen that such research might involve the meaning of tattoos and decision making in the jury box. Often the research has direct applications to improving people's lives, as in the case of increas-

ing the participation of African Americans in diabetes testing. Throughout the rest of the book, the research performed by sociologists and other social scientists will shed light on group behavior of all types.

Speaking across Race, Gender, Class, and National Boundaries

Sociologists include both men and women, people from a variety of socioeconomic backgrounds (some privileged and many not), and individuals from a wealth of ethnic, national, and religious origins. In their work, sociologists seek to draw conclusions that speak to all people—not just the affluent or powerful. This is not always easy. Insights into how a corporation can increase its profits tend to attract more attention and financial support than do, say, the merits of a needle exchange program for low-income, inner-city residents. Yet sociology today, more than ever, seeks to better understand the experiences of *all* people. In Box 1-2, we take a look at how a woman's role in public places is defined differently from that of a man in different parts of the world.

Social Policy throughout the World

One important way we can use the sociological imagination is to enhance our understanding of current social issues throughout the world. Beginning with Chapter 2, which focuses on research, each chapter will conclude with a discussion of a contemporary social policy issue. In some cases, we will examine a specific issue facing national governments. For example, government funding of child care centers will be discussed in Chapter 4, Socialization; sexual harassment in Chapter 6, Groups and Organizations; and the search for shelters in Chapter 15, Communities and the Environment. These social policy sections will demonstrate how fundamental sociological concepts can enhance our critical thinking skills and help us to better understand current public policy debates taking place around the world.

In addition, sociology has been used to evaluate the success of programs or the impact of changes brought about by policymakers and political activists. Chapter 8, Stratification in the United States and Worldwide, includes a discussion of research on the effectiveness of welfare reform experiments. Chapter 14, Population and Health, considers the issue of financing health care in the United States and other nations, partly by drawing on studies showing that some people may be vulnerable to a lower quality of medical care than others. These discussions underscore the many practical applications of sociological theory and research.

Sociologists expect the next quarter of a century to be perhaps the most exciting and critical period in the history of the discipline. This is because of a growing recognition—both in the United States and around the world—that current social problems *must* be addressed before their magnitude overwhelms human societies. We can expect sociologists to play an increasing role in the government sector by researching and developing public policy alternatives. It seems only natural for this textbook to focus on the connection between the work of sociologists and the difficult questions confronting the policymakers and people of the United States.

● Chapter Resources

Summary

Sociology is the systematic study of social behavior and human groups. In this chapter, we examine the nature of sociological theory, the founders of the discipline, theoretical perspectives of contemporary sociology, and ways to exercise the "sociological imagination."

1. An important element in the *sociological imagination*—which is an awareness of the relationship between an individual and the wider society—is the ability to view our own society as an outsider might, rather than from the perspective of our limited experiences and cultural biases.

2. Knowledge that relies on "common sense" is not always reliable. Sociologists must test and analyze each piece of information that they use.

3. In contrast to other *social sciences,* sociology emphasizes the influence that groups can have on people's behavior and attitudes and the ways in which people shape society.

4. Sociologists employ *theories* to examine the relationships between observations or data that may seem completely unrelated.

5. Nineteenth-century thinkers who contributed sociological insights included Auguste Comte, a French philosopher; Harriet Martineau, an English sociologist; and Herbert Spencer, an English scholar.

6. Other important figures in the development of sociology were Émile Durkheim, who pioneered work on suicide; Max Weber, who taught the need for "insight" in intellectual work; and Karl Marx, who emphasized the importance of the economy and of conflict in society.

7. In the twentieth century, the discipline of sociology is indebted to the U.S. sociologists Charles Horton Cooley and Robert Merton.

8. *Macrosociology* concentrates on large-scale phenomena or entire civilizations, whereas *microsociology* stresses study of small groups.
9. The *functionalist perspective* of sociology emphasizes the way that parts of a society are structured to maintain its stability. Social change should be slow and evolutionary.
10. The *conflict perspective* assumes that social behavior is best understood in terms of conflict or tension between competing groups. Social change, spurred by conflict and competition, should be swift and revolutionary.

11. The *interactionist perspective* is primarily concerned with fundamental or everyday forms of interaction, including symbols and other types of nonverbal communication. Social change is ongoing, as individuals get shaped by society and in turn shape it.
12. Sociologists make use of all three perspectives, since each offers unique insights into the same issue.
13. This textbook makes use of the sociological imagination by showing theory in practice and research in action; by speaking across race, gender, class, and national boundaries; and by highlighting social policy around the world.

Critical Thinking Questions

1. What aspects of the social and work environment in a fast-food restaurant would be of particular interest to a sociologist because of his or her "sociological imagination"?
2. What are the manifest and latent functions of a health club?

3. How might the interactionist perspective be applied to a place where you have been employed or to an organization you joined?

Key Terms

Anomie   The loss of direction felt in a society when social control of individual behavior has become ineffective. (page 10)

Conflict perspective   A sociological approach that assumes that social behavior is best understood in terms of conflict or tension between competing groups. (14)

Dramaturgical approach   A view of social interaction that examines people as if they were theatrical performers. (16)

Dysfunction   An element or a process of society that may disrupt a social system or lead to a decrease in stability. (14)

Functionalist perspective   A sociological approach that emphasizes the way that parts of a society are structured to maintain its stability. (13)

Ideal type   A construct or model that serves as a measuring rod against which actual cases can be evaluated. (10)

Interactionist perspective   A sociological approach that generalizes about fundamental or everyday forms of social interaction. (16)

Latent functions   Unconscious or unintended functions; hidden purposes. (14)

Macrosociology   Sociological investigation that concentrates on large-scale phenomena or entire civilizations. (13)

Manifest functions   Open, stated, and conscious functions. (14)

Microsociology   Sociological investigation that stresses study of small groups and often uses laboratory experimental studies. (13)

Natural science   The study of the physical features of nature and the ways in which they interact and change. (6)

Nonverbal communication   The sending of messages through the use of posture, facial expressions, and gestures. (16)

Science   The body of knowledge obtained by methods based upon systematic observation. (6)

Social science   The study of various aspects of human society. (6)

Sociological imagination   An awareness of the relationship between an individual and the wider society. (5)

Sociology   The systematic study of social behavior and human groups. (5)

Theory   In sociology, a set of statements that seeks to explain problems, actions, or behavior. (8)

Verstehen   The German word for "understanding" or "insight"; used to stress the need for sociologists to take into account people's emotions, thoughts, beliefs, and attitudes. (10)

Additional Readings

Du Bois, W. E. B. 1996. *The Philadelphia Negro: A Social Study.* With a new introduction by Elijah Anderson. Philadelphia: Temple University Press. The reissuing of this classic work, which first appeared in 1899, documents the timelessness of Du Bois' observations a century ago.

Glassner, Barry. 1999. *The Culture of Fear.* New York: Basic Books. Glassner looks at how people's fears of crime, drug use, and other social problems are growing, even though the social reality often does not match the public perceptions.

Levin, Jack. 1999. *Sociological Snapshots 3: Seeing Social Structure and Change in Everyday Life.* Thousand Oaks, CA: Pine Forge Press. The sociological imagination is employed to look at everything from elevator culture and television soap operas to religious cults and the death penalty.

McDonald, Lynn. 1994. *Women Founders of the Social Sciences.* Ottawa, Can.: Carlton University Press. The author examines the important but often overlooked contributions of such pioneers as Mary Wollstonecraft, Harriet Martineau, Beatrice Webb, Jane Addams, and many more.

● Technology Resources

Internet Connection

Note: While all the URLs listed were current as of the printing of this book, these sites often change. Please check our website (http://www.mhhe.com/schaefer4) for updates.

1. Sociologists use three main theoretical perspectives when analyzing the social world, including events both historical and current. Log onto Yahoo! (**http://www.yahoo.com**) and choose one of the breaking stories from the "In the News" section. Follow the links given, reading articles and viewing pictures from online newspapers and networks on your chosen story. Next, apply functionalist, conflict, and interactionist perspectives to the story (Table 1-2 in your text will be especially helpful).

   (a) How would Karl Marx and conflict thinkers view such an event? Is there tension and struggle between groups? Which groups?

   (b) How would Émile Durkheim and functionalist thinkers examine the story? Can you apply concepts such as manifest functions, latent functions, and dysfunctions?

   (c) What would be the perspective of George Herbert Mead and other interactionists? What symbols are being used to describe the story by the media? Can you apply dramaturgy to the events? Are players in the story trying to project a certain image using symbols?

   (d) Which perspective did you find to be the most interesting? Is one perspective better suited than the others to analyze the story? Why or why not?

2. Sociology has as its subject matter a vast array of topics—from the Amish to *Verstehen,* and everything social in between. Linda Lambert and The University of Texas at San Antonio offer a series of Internet links that allow visitors to learn about more than 25 areas of Sociological Concentrations (**http://csbs.utsa.edu/social&policy/soc/masters/topics.html**). Log on to the site and investigate three different areas and the associated links that interest you. For each area, answer the following questions:

   (a) What is the name of the area of concentration? Why did you choose this area over the others offered on the site?

   (b) What kinds of issues are explored by sociologists in this particular field? Why is it important for researchers to focus on such issues?

   (c) What fact or statistic from the links did you find the most interesting or surprising? Why?

   (d) Are any governmental agencies or community organizations also conducting research in this area?

   (e) In what ways is this specific area similar to your other two choices? In what ways is it different?

   (f) What connections, if any, do you see between sociology and other academic disciplines/majors?

   (g) Which areas of concentration would you be most interested in pursuing? Why?

3. Sociologists in the twenty-first century owe a debt of intellectual gratitude to early thinkers and pioneers such as Émile Durkheim, Karl Marx, and Max Weber. To learn about many of the thinkers listed in Chapter 1, visit SocioRealm (**http://www.geocities.com/CollegePark/Quad/5889/index.htm**), a site constructed by Jessica Champlin. Choose two of the theorists offered and visit the links associated with them; read some of their original works and biographies. For each theorist, answer the following:

   (a) When did the thinker live? What important historical events were occurring during this time? Did any of these historical events shape his or her sociological imagination and views on society?

   (b) After reading some of the original works, how would you summarize this person's perspectives? Which of the three main sociological perspectives—functionalism, conflict, or interactionism—would you say this thinker is most associated with? Why?

   (c) What facts did you find most interesting about this person in his or her life story or sociological contributions?

   (d) How do the ideas of this thinker compare and contrast with your other selection? Which of the two thinkers' ideas did you like the most? Why?

Interactive e-Source with Making the Grade

An expanded version of text is available on CD-ROM. With this CD, you can instantly explore various topics and concepts with an assortment of video clips (including footage of this text's author in Singapore), and website links. You can also highlight text material electronically and test yourself with interactive quizzes and other learning tools.

Online Learning Center   www.mhhe.com/schaefer4

Visit the *Online Learning Center*, this textbook's specific website, at **www.mhhe. com/schaefer4.** There you will find a variety of resources and activities for each chapter that will assist you in learning and mastering the material in the book. These include quizzes, key terms, chapter overviews, learning objectives, PowerPoint slides, and more. You can also link directly to Internet sites from the Online Learning Center, including those found in the Internet Connection sections at the end of each chapter.

PowerWeb

Using the password found on the gold and black card that was shrinkwrapped with your book, visit *PowerWeb*, a website that provides a wealth of resources including quizzes, links to related websites, interactive exercises, time management tips, articles, and a guide to doing research on the web. You will also find daily news on relevant topics.

SocCity

Explore SocCity, a veritable melting pot of sociology cybersources, information, and Internet activity for students and instructors alike. Whether you are looking for the perfect book for your Sociology class, or you are a student looking for some starter sites for your next research paper, SocCity has it.

Appendix   CAREERS IN SOCIOLOGY

An undergraduate degree in sociology doesn't just serve as excellent preparation for future graduate work in sociology. It also provides a strong liberal arts background for entry-level positions in business, social services, foundations, community organizations, not-for-profit groups, law enforcement, and governmental jobs. Many fields—among them marketing, public relations, and broadcasting—now require investigative skills and an understanding of diverse groups found in today's multiethnic and multinational environment. Moreover, a sociology degree requires accomplishment in oral and written communication, interpersonal skills, problem solving, and critical thinking—all job-related skills that may give sociology graduates an advantage over those who pursue more technical degrees (Benner and Hitchcock 1986; Billson and Huber 1993).

Consequently, while few occupations specifically require an undergraduate degree in sociology, such academic training can be an important asset in entering a wide range of occupations (American Sociological Association 1993, 1999). Just to bring this home, a number of chapters highlight a real-life professional who describes how the study of sociology has helped in his or her career. Look for the "Taking Sociology to Work" boxes.

The accompanying figure summarizes sources of employment for those with BA or BS degrees in sociology. It shows that the areas of human services, the not-for-profit sector, business, and government offer major career opportunities for sociology graduates. Undergraduates who know where their career interests lie are well advised to enroll in sociology courses and specialties best suited for those interests. For example, students hoping to become health planners would take a class in medical sociology; students seeking employment as social science research assistants would focus on courses in statistics and methods. Internships, such as placements at city planning agencies and survey research organizations, afford another way for sociology students to prepare for careers. Studies show that students who choose an internship placement have less trouble finding jobs, obtain better jobs, and enjoy greater job satisfaction than students without internship placements (Salem and Grabarek 1986).

Many college students view social work as the field

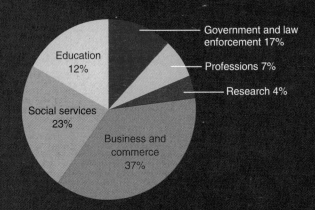

Source: Schaefer 1998b.

most closely associated with sociology. Traditionally, social workers received their undergraduate training in sociology and allied fields such as psychology and counseling. After some practical experience, social workers would generally seek a master's degree in social work (MSW) to be considered for supervisory or administrative positions. Today, however, some students choose (where it is available) to pursue an undergraduate degree in social work (BSW). This degree prepares graduates for direct service positions such as caseworker or group worker.

Many students continue their sociological training beyond the bachelor's degree. More than 215 universities in the United States have graduate programs in sociology that offer PhD and/or master's degrees. These programs differ greatly in their areas of specialization, course requirements, costs, and research and teaching opportunities available to graduate students (American Sociological Association 2001).

Higher education is an important source of employment for sociologists with graduate degrees. About 75 percent of recent PhD recipients in sociology sought employment in colleges and universities. These sociologists teach not only majors committed to the discipline but also students hoping to become doctors, nurses, lawyers, police officers, and so forth.

For sociology graduates interested in academic careers, the road to a PhD degree (or doctorate) can be long and difficult. This degree symbolizes competence in original research; each candidate must prepare a book-length study known as a *dissertation*. Typically, a doctoral

Classroom Tip The ASA offers such brochures as "Majoring in Sociology: A Guide for Students," "The Sociology Major as Preparation for Careers in Business and Organizations," and "Careers in Sociology."

for Racial and Ethic Minority Group in the U.S.A

merican Indians: The first American

e making of Black Americans in V   ca

- slavery

The challenge of black leadership

rican American=

education

employment & incom

Sociology students put in many years and a great deal of work on the way to a PhD. Fortunately, the job market for instructors is looking much better than in years past as the size of the college student population steadily grows.

student in sociology will engage in four to seven years of intensive work, including the time required to complete the dissertation. Yet even this effort is no guarantee of a job as a sociology professor.

The good news is that over the next 10 years, the demand for instructors is expected to increase because of high rates of retirement among faculty from the baby-boom generation, as well as the anticipated slow but steady growth in the college student population in the

United States. Nonetheless, anyone who launches an academic career must be prepared for considerable uncertainty and competition in the college job market (American Sociological Association 1999; B. Huber 1985).

Of course, not all people working as sociologists teach or hold doctoral degrees. Take government, for example. The Census Bureau relies on people with sociological training to interpret data for other government agencies and the general public. Virtually every agency depends on survey research—a field in which sociology students can specialize—in order to assess everything from community needs to the morale of the agency's own workers. In addition, people with sociological training can put their academic knowledge to effective use in probation and parole, health sciences, community development, and recreational services. Some people working in government or private industry have a master's degree (MA or MS) in sociology; others have a bachelor's degree (a BA or BS).

Currently, about 22 percent of the members of the American Sociological Association use their sociological skills outside the academic world, whether in social service agencies or in marketing positions for business firms. A renewed interest in applied sociology has led to the hiring of an increasing number of sociologists with graduate degrees by businesses, industry, hospitals, and nonprofit organizations. Indeed, studies show that many sociology graduates are making career changes from social service areas to business and commerce. As an undergraduate major, sociology is excellent preparation for employment in many parts of the business world (Billson 1994).

Whether you take a few courses in sociology or actually complete a degree, you will benefit from the critical thinking skills developed in this discipline. Sociologists emphasize the value of being able to analyze, interpret, and function within a variety of working situations; this is an asset in virtually any career. Moreover, given the rapid technological change evident in the last decade and the expanding global economy, all of us will need to adapt to substantial social change, even in our own careers. Sociology provides a rich conceptual framework that can serve as a foundation for flexible career development and can assist us in taking advantage of new employment opportunities (American Sociological Association 1999, 1995).

How America Knows What America Needs

This Is Your Future. Don't Leave It Blank.

U.S. Department of Commerce
Economics and Statistics Administration
U.S. CENSUS BUREAU

USCENSUSBUREAU

United States
Census
2000

gests that 40 percent of all gun owners use them for recreational purposes, 20 percent in the line of work, and 40 percent for self-protection (J. Wright 1995). Roth and Koper, in effect, had to sort out the different functions of firearms and specifically measure the impact of one piece of legislation on the dysfunctional use of assault weapons. Other researchers might define the issue of gun control from a different perspective. For example, one might use the conflict approach to see how powerful interests work to prevent changes in gun licensing procedures. Interactionists might look at behavior patterns in gun clubs or interaction among gun enthusiasts.

Reviewing the Literature

By conducting a *review of the literature*—the relevant scholarly studies and information—researchers refine the problem under study, clarify possible techniques to be used in collecting data, and eliminate or reduce avoidable mistakes. Government control of firearms is relatively recent, but there is no lack of relevant research. For example, the researchers found material in the respected *Journal of the American Medical Association* that considered the impact of an earlier ban on the import of several models of assault rifles. That study found that while sales surged and prices increased prior to imposition of the ban, criminal use declined, suggesting that high prices and hoarding made the guns less accessible to criminal users. Other research material concluded that certain types of crime such as burglary in the home or small business may be reduced if law-abiding citizens are armed. Roth and Koper were interested in seeing which findings would be replicated (American Medical Association Council on Scientific Affairs 1992; Cook and Leitzel 1996; J. Lott 1998).

Formulating the Hypothesis

After reviewing earlier research and drawing on the contributions of sociological theorists, the researchers then *formulate the hypothesis*. A **hypothesis** is a speculative statement about the relationship between two or more factors known as *variables*. Income, religion, occupation, and gender can all serve as variables in a study. We can define a **variable** as a measurable trait or characteristic that is subject to change under different conditions.

Researchers who formulate a hypothesis generally must suggest how one aspect of human behavior influences or affects another. The variable hypothesized to cause or influence another is called the **independent variable**. The second variable is termed the **dependent variable** because its action "depends" on the influence of the independent variable.

Roth and Koper hypothesized that banning certain assault weapons would make them less available and thus would reduce the number of crimes involving such weapons. The independent variable is the enactment of the federal legislation. The researchers would look closely at any data prior to and following the legislation. The dependent variables influenced by the independent variable are the availability of weapons and incidence of crime. These variables proved to be complicated because the researchers had to differentiate between weapons covered by the ban and similar weapons not affected by the ban. Furthermore, measuring crime is limited to *reported* crime; the researchers acknowledged they could not measure incidents that were unreported to law enforcement agencies. Roth and Koper recognized that the announcement of an impending ban on assault weapons would increase demand for them and drive up the price. Therefore, they hypothesized that speculators, rather than potential criminals, would be most likely to buy the weapons prior to the ban.

Identifying independent and dependent variables—in this case, passing a law and measuring the outcome—is a critical step in clarifying cause-and-effect relationships in society. As shown in Figure 2-2, **causal logic** involves the relationship between a condition or variable and a particular consequence, with one event leading to the

FIGURE 2-2

Causal Logic

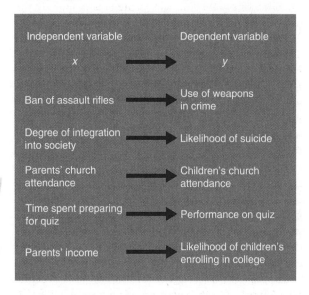

In *causal logic* an independent variable (often designated by the symbol *x*) influences a dependent variable (generally designated as *y*); thus, *x* leads to *y*. For example, parents who attend church regularly (*x*) are more likely to have children who are churchgoers (*y*). Notice that the first two pairs of variables are taken from studies already described in this textbook.

Whether it is the census or any other type of research, sampling methods have a direct impact on the accuracy of the results.

other. Under causal logic, the degree of integration into society may be directly related to or produce a greater likelihood of suicide. Similarly, the time students spend reviewing material for a quiz may be directly related to or produce a greater likelihood of getting a high score on the quiz.

p.8

A *correlation* exists when a change in one variable coincides with a change in the other. Correlations are an indication that causality *may* be present; they do not necessarily indicate causation. For example, data indicate that working mothers are more likely to have delinquent children than are mothers who do not work outside the home. This correlation is actually caused by a third variable: family income. Lower-class households are more likely to have a full-time working mother; at the same time, reported rates of delinquency are higher in this class than in other economic levels. Consequently, while having a mother who works outside the home is correlated with delinquency, it does not *cause* delinquency. Sociologists seek to identify the *causal* link between variables; this causal link is generally advanced by researchers in their hypotheses.

Collecting and Analyzing Data

How do you test a hypothesis to determine if it is supported or refuted? You need to collect information, using one of the research designs described later in the chapter. The research design guides the researcher in collecting and analyzing data.

Selecting the Sample

In most studies, social scientists must carefully select what is known as a *sample*. A **representative sample** is a selection from a larger population that is statistically typical of that population. There are many kinds of samples, but the one social scientists most frequently use is the random sample. In a **random sample,** every member of an entire population being studied has the same chance of being selected. Thus, if researchers want to examine the opinions of people listed in a city directory (a book that, unlike the telephone directory, lists all households), they might call every 10th or 50th or 100th name listed. This would constitute a random sample. The advantage of using specialized sampling techniques is that sociologists do not need to question everyone in a population.

It is all too easy to confuse the careful scientific techniques used in representative sampling with the many *nonscientific* polls that receive much more media attention. For example, television viewers and radio listeners are encouraged to e-mail their views on today's headlines or on political contests. Obviously the results of such polls reflect nothing more than the views of those who happened to see the television program (or hear the radio broadcast) and took the time, perhaps at some cost, to register their opinions. These data do not necessarily reflect (and indeed may distort) the views of the broader population. Not everyone has access to a television or radio or has the time to watch or listen to a program or has the means and/or inclination to send e-mail. Similar problems are raised by "mail-back" questionnaires found in many magazines and by "mall intercepts" where shoppers are asked about some issue. Even when these techniques include answers from tens of thousands of people, their accuracy will be far less than that of a carefully selected representative sample of 1,500 respondents (S. Roberts 1974).

Sampling has become a hot issue in census taking. Every 10 years the U.S. government seeks to count every

Sociology in the Global Community

2-1 "Sent-down" in China

Imagine arriving at school and learning that the entire college was being closed and that, in fact, the government was closing *all* universities. Furthermore, since there was no school for you to attend, you were now being taken to the countryside to work on farms so the country could increase agricultural production.

This is basically what happened to students in China from 1967 to 1978, a period historians refer to as the Cultural Revolution, when China was trying to rid itself of outside influences. During this time, 17 million young urban people—about a third of the youth entering the labor force—were the victims of the government's "send-down" policy. They were forced to live and work in rural areas rather than attend school or work at government jobs they may have held.

Sociologists Xueguang Zhou and Liren Hou of Duke University were interested in what impact these state policies had on the people's lives. To learn more, the researchers decided to interview those who were "sent-down" as well as comparable people who were not sent to rural areas. They did their representative sampling in several stages: first selecting cities from different geographical areas, then systematically selecting blocks within those cities, and finally randomly selecting

> **17 million young urban people were the victims of the government's "send-down" policy.**

and interviewing adults within the blocks. They accumulated a sample of 2,793 people, of whom 855 had been sent-down.

Zhou and Hou found that those who stayed in rural areas more than six years were likely to marry later, have fewer children, and hold poorer jobs than those who spent less time or those who stayed in urban areas. While these differences may be expected, some findings were surprising. For example, those who were sent-down for only a few years were more likely to graduate from college than those young people who were never sent-down. The researchers argue that many of the youths who left "early" from rural areas were well-connected politically and therefore probably came from more prosperous backgrounds. Also, these young people may have resolved to quickly overcome the adverse effects of the state policy.

Let's Discuss

1. How did the researchers make sure their sample was representative? Do you think selecting names from a phone book would produce the same results? How would you go about selecting a sample population?

2. Describe the independent and dependent variables in this study. (Refer to page 31 if you need to.)

Source: Zhou and Hou 1999.

---

resident; the results determine everything from political representation to allocation of federal aid to the states. The effort to count every household has always been difficult and inevitably results in some inaccuracies. For example, the number of households "missed" in the 1990 census amounted to some 4 to 5 million people. As federal dollars grow in importance, the "undercount," as it is called, has taken on greater significance. That is why the Bureau of the Census proposed using sampling in the 2000 census as a means to estimate data for those households that fail to respond to initial efforts to collect data. But sampling has political consequences. The undercounted people most likely to be added to the population count by the use of "sampling" are minorities and poor people, who traditionally support Democrats. In 1999 the Supreme Court ruled that sampling may not be used to determine congressional apportionment, but is acceptable in other census surveys used to determine allocations for government programs (J. Greenburg 1999).

Sampling is a complex aspect of research design. In Box 2-1, we consider the approach some researchers took when trying to create an appropriate sample of people in the world's most populous nation—China. We'll also see how they made use of data from the sample.

Ensuring Validity and Reliability

The scientific method requires that research results be both valid and reliable. *Validity* refers to the degree to which a measure or scale truly reflects the phenomenon under study. A valid measure of the ban on assault rifles depended on gathering accurate data. Firearms vary in numerous specific ways. Fortunately for the researchers the legislation clarified in exacting detail just what the ban covered. But this meant Roth and Koper had to become knowledgeable about such matters as where the ammunition magazine was placed, whether the barrel was threaded, and the weight of firearms loaded as opposed to unloaded. All these factors and more determined whether the data collected were relevant to their study or not.

Reliability refers to the extent to which a measure

provides consistent results. Reliability was less of a concern with Roth and Koper since the process for reporting gun sales, clearance checks for permits, and reporting of crime incidents were already well-established prior to the beginning of their social research. However, they looked closely at data collection from different states to see if they could detect any potential reliability problems.

Developing the Conclusion

Scientific studies, including those conducted by sociologists, do not aim to answer all the questions that can be raised about a particular subject. Therefore, the conclusion of a research study represents both an end and a beginning. It terminates a specific phase of the investigation, but it should also generate ideas for future study. Both Roth and Koper see a need to continue the research to gauge the lasting impact of the assault rifle ban.

Supporting Hypotheses

Sociological studies do not always generate data that support the original hypothesis. In many instances, a hypothesis is refuted, and researchers must reformulate their conclusions. Unexpected results may also lead sociologists to reexamine their methodology and make changes in the research design.

Roth and Koper's research applied an understanding of social behavior to the impact of social policies. In the short term it appears that fewer of the banned weapons were used in crimes (see Figure 2-3). When the ban went into effect the number of assault weapon traces placed by law enforcement agencies decreased dramatically. This seems to confirm the findings of the earlier research published in the *Journal of the American Medical Association.* Following the ban there did not appear to be a reduction in multiple-gunshot victims, so characteristic of rapid-fire assault rifles. However, other evidence suggests that the 1994 ban may have contributed to a reduction in the *overall* gun murder rate of about 11 percent and to fewer murders of police officers by criminals armed with assault weapons.

Controlling for Other Factors

A *control variable* is a factor held constant to test the relative impact of the independent variable. For example, if researchers wanted to know how adults in the United States feel about restrictions on smoking in public places, they would probably attempt to use a respondent's smoking behavior as a control variable. That is, how do smokers versus nonsmokers feel about smoking in public places? Consequently, the researchers would compile separate statistics on how smokers and nonsmokers feel about antismoking regulations.

In Summary: The Scientific Method

Let us briefly summarize the process of the scientific method through a review of the example. Roth and Koper *defined a problem* (the question of what effect the assault weapon ban had on crime). They *reviewed the literature* (other studies of firearms control) and *formulated a hypothesis* (the ban of certain assault weapons would make them less available and thus would reduce crimes involving such weapons). They *collected and analyzed the data,* making sure the data were valid and reliable. Finally, they *developed the conclusion:* in the short term, at least, it appears that fewer banned weapons were used in crime than before the ban went into effect.

Major Research Designs

An important aspect of sociological research is deciding how to collect the data. A *research design* is a detailed plan or method for obtaining data scientifically. Selection of a research design is a critical step for sociologists and requires creativity and ingenuity. This choice will directly influence both the cost of the project and the amount of time needed to collect the results of the research. Research designs that sociologists regularly use to generate data include surveys, observation, experiments, and existing sources.

Surveys

Almost all of us have responded to surveys of one kind or another. We may have been asked what kind of detergent we use, which presidential candidate we intend to vote for,

FIGURE 2-3

Impact of Assault Rifle Ban

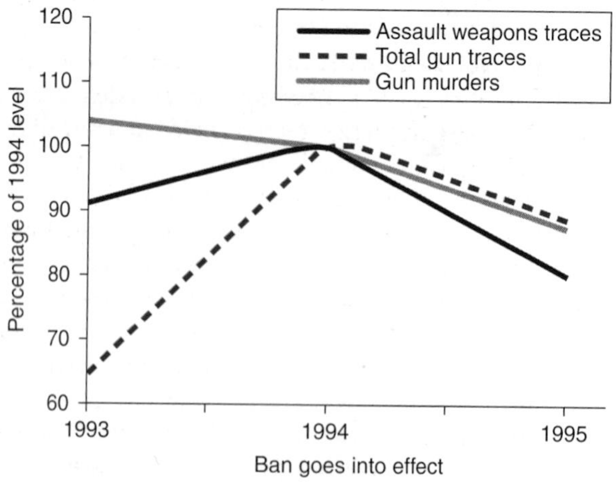

Source: Roth and Koper 1999a:6.

Research in Action

2-2 Framing Survey Questions about Interracial Friendships

Do White people really have Black friends, and vice versa? Many surveys have attempted to gauge the amount of White-Black interaction. But unless the questions are phrased carefully, it is possible to overestimate just how much "racial togetherness" is taking place.

Sociologist Tom Smith, who heads up the respected General Social Survey,

> Unless the questions are phrased carefully, it is possible to overestimate just how much "racial togetherness" is taking place.

noticed that a high proportion of Whites and African Americans indicate they have friends of the other race. But is this, in fact, true? When Smith and his fellow researchers analyzed data from the 1998 General Social Survey they found that response rates varied according to how the question was phrased.

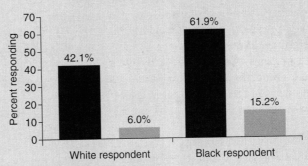

■ Percent who say they have a close friend who is black or white

■ Percent who name a close friend who is of a different race

White respondent: 42.1%, 6.0%
Black respondent: 61.9%, 15.2%

Source: Smith 2001.

For example, when asked to give the names of friends they feel close to, only 6 percent of Whites listed a close friend of a different race or ethnicity. Yet when asked whether any of their friends that they feel close to was Black, 42.1 percent of Whites said "yes" to having a close Black friend. The accompanying figure shows the results for both White and Black respondents.

Let's Discuss

1. Why do you think people responded so differently to these two questions? How would you frame a question to get an accurate picture of interracial friendships?
2. Do you have close friends of another race? If asked to list your close friends, would you list someone from a different race?

Source: Smith 2001.

or what our favorite television program is. A *survey* is a study, generally in the form of an interview or questionnaire, that provides sociologists with information concerning how people think and act. Among the United States' best-known surveys of opinion are the Gallup poll and the Harris poll. As anyone who watches the news during presidential campaigns knows, these polls have become a staple of political life.

When you think of surveys, you may recall seeing many "person on the street" interviews on local television news shows. While such interviews can be highly entertaining, they are not necessarily an accurate indication of public opinion. First, they reflect the opinions of only those people who happen to be at a certain location. Such a sample can be biased in favor of commuters, middle-class shoppers, or factory workers, depending on which

street or area the newspeople select. Second, television interviews tend to attract outgoing people who are willing to appear on the air, while they frighten away others who may feel intimidated by a camera. As we've seen, a survey must be based on precise, representative sampling if it is to genuinely reflect a broad range of the population.

In preparing to conduct a survey, sociologists must not only develop representative samples; they must exercise great care in the wording of questions. An effective survey question must be simple and clear enough for people to understand it. It must also be specific enough so that there are no problems in interpreting the results. Even questions that are less structured ("What do you think of programming on educational television?") must be carefully phrased to solicit the type of information desired. Box 2-2 illustrates the different results that different phrasing of a question can produce. Surveys can be indispensable sources of information, but only if the sampling is done properly and the questions are worded accurately.

There are two main forms of surveys: the *interview* and the *questionnaire.* Each of these has its own advantages. An interviewer can obtain a high response rate because people find it more difficult to turn down a personal request for an interview than to throw away a written questionnaire. In addition, a skillful interviewer can go beyond written questions and "probe" for a subject's underlying feelings and reasons. On the other hand, questionnaires have the advantage of being cheaper, especially when large samples are used.

Studies have shown that characteristics of the interviewer have an impact on survey data. For example, women interviewers tend to receive more feminist responses from female subjects than do male researchers, and African American interviewers tend to receive more detailed responses about race-related issues from Black subjects than do White interviewers. The possible impact of gender and race only indicates again how much care social research requires (D. Davis 1997; L. Huddy et al. 1997).

This African city in the Ivory Coast provides a rich setting for observation research. An ethnographer would take note of the interaction of Western and African cultures in the everyday street life.

Observation

Investigators who collect information through direct participation and/or observation of a group, tribe, or community under study are engaged in *observation.* This method allows sociologists to examine certain behaviors and communities that could not be investigated through other research techniques.

Observation research is the most common form of *qualitative research,* which relies on what is seen in field or naturalistic settings more than on statistical data. Generally, such studies focus on small groups or communities rather than large groups or whole nations. An increasingly popular form of qualitative research in sociology today is ethnography. *Ethnography* refers to efforts to describe an entire social setting through extended, systematic observation. Elijah Anderson's study, described at the beginning of this chapter, involved not just understanding behavior of pedestrians but also understanding all facets of life in two urban neighborhoods. Anthropologists rely heavily on ethnography. Much as an anthropologist seeks to understand the people of some Polynesian island, the sociologist

as an ethnographer seeks to understand and present to us an entire way of life in some setting.

Quantitative research collects and reports data primarily in numerical form. Most of the survey research discussed so far in this book has been this type of research. While quantitative research can make use of larger samples than qualitative research, it can't look at a topic in as great depth. Neither type of research is necessarily better; indeed usually we are best informed when we rely on studies using a variety of research designs that look at both qualitative and quantitative aspects of the same subject.

In some cases, the sociologist actually "joins" a group for a period of time to get an accurate sense of how it operates. This is called *participant observation.* In the tattoo study described in Chapter 1 as well as p. 4 in Anderson's study of "eye work," the researcher was a participant observer.

During the late 1930s, in a classic example of participant-observation research, William F. Whyte moved into a low-income Italian neighborhood in Boston. For nearly four years, he was a member of the social circle of "corner boys" that he describes in *Street Corner Society.* Whyte revealed his identity to these men and joined in their conversations, bowling, and other leisure-time activities. His goal was to gain greater insight into the community that these men had established. As Whyte (1981:303) listened to Doc, the leader of the group, he "learned the answers to questions I would not even have had the sense to ask if I had been getting my information solely on an interviewing basis." Whyte's work was especially valuable, since, at the time, the academic world had little direct knowledge of the poor and tended to rely for information on the records of social service agencies, hospitals, and courts (Adler and Johnson 1992).

The initial challenge that Whyte faced—and that every participant observer encounters—was to gain acceptance into an unfamiliar group. It is no simple matter for a college-trained sociologist to win the trust of a religious cult, a youth gang, a poor Appalachian community, or a circle of skid row residents. It requires a great deal of patience and an accepting, nonthreatening type of person.

Observation research poses other complex challenges for the investigator. Sociologists must be able to fully understand what they are observing. In a sense, then, researchers such as William F. Whyte or Elijah Anderson must learn to see the world as the group sees it in order to fully comprehend the events taking place around them.

This raises a delicate issue. If the research is to be successful, the observer cannot allow the close associations or even friendships that inevitably develop to influence the subjects' behavior or the conclusions of the study. Anson Shupe and David Bromley (1980), two sociologists who have used participant observation, have likened this challenge to that of "walking a tightrope." Even while working hard to gain acceptance from the group being studied, the participant observer *must* maintain some degree of detachment.

Managers may rely on observation research to improve working conditions or productivity. For example, when Norway's shipping industry was faced with severe cutbacks, a team of researchers worked aboard a merchant ship as part of an effort to improve the social organization and efficiency of Norway's fleet. Similarly, when faced with growing competition in the photocopying industry, Xerox Corporation employed a research team to propose cost-cutting measures to managers and union leaders. In each case, the methodology of participant observation proved useful in solving practical problems (W. Whyte 1989).

Experiments

When sociologists want to study a possible cause-and-effect relationship, they may conduct experiments. An *experiment* is an artificially created situation that allows the researcher to manipulate variables.

In the classic method of conducting an experiment, two groups of people are selected and matched for similar characteristics such as age or education. The researchers then assign the subjects to one of two groups—the experimental or the control group. The *experimental group* is exposed to an independent variable; the *control group* is not. Thus, if scientists were testing a new type of antibiotic drug, they would administer that drug to an experimental group but not to a control group.

Sociologists don't often rely on this classic form of experiment because it generally involves manipulating human behavior in an inappropriate manner, especially in a laboratory setting. However, sociologists do try to recreate experimental conditions in the field. For example, they may compare children's performance in two schools that use different curricula. Another area of investigation that has led to several experimental studies in the field is an examination of police action in domestic assault cases. Emergency calls to a household where domestic violence is occurring account for a significant part of a police officer's work. Sociologists Anthony Pate and Edwin Hamilton (1992) studied cases in Dade County (Miami) Florida in which officers did or did not arrest the violent suspect and then looked at the effect of the arrest or nonarrest on future incidents of assault in the household. In other words, they compared cases where no arrest was made (the control group) with incidents where the suspect was arrested (experimental group). They found that an arrest did have a deterrent effect if the suspect was employed. Pate and Hamilton

Does arresting someone for domestic assault deter future incidents of violence? An experiment in Miami, Florida, studied this question by making use of control and experimental groups.

How do people respond to being observed? Evidently these employees at the Hawthorne plant enjoyed the attention paid them when researchers observed them at work. No matter what variables were changed, the workers increased their productivity every time, including when the level of lighting was *reduced*.

Use of Existing Sources

Sociologists do not necessarily have to collect new data in order to conduct research and test hypotheses. The term *secondary analysis* refers to a variety of research techniques that make use of publicly accessible information and data. In the case study of the effect of the ban on certain assault rifles, the researchers made use of existing data. Generally, in conducting secondary analysis, researchers utilize data in ways unintended by the initial collectors of information. For example, census data are compiled for specific uses by the federal government but are valuable for marketing specialists in locating everything from bicycle stores to nursing homes.

Sociologists consider secondary analysis to be *nonreactive*, since it does not influence people's behavior. As an example, Émile Durkheim's statistical analysis of suicide neither increased nor decreased human self-destruction. Subjects of an experiment or observation research are often aware that they are being watched—an awareness that can influence their behavior—but this is not the case with secondary analysis. Researchers, then, can avoid the Hawthorne effect by using secondary analysis.

There is one inherent problem, however: the researcher who relies on data collected by someone else may not find exactly what is needed. Social scientists studying family violence can use statistics from police and social service agencies on *reported* cases of spouse abuse and child abuse. Yet such government bodies have no precise data on *all* cases of abuse.

Many social scientists find it useful to study cultural, economic, and political documents, including newspapers, periodicals, radio and television tapes, the Internet, scripts, diaries, songs, folklore, and legal papers, to name some examples (see Table 2-1). In examining these sources, researchers employ a technique known as *content analysis,* which is the systematic coding and objective recording of data, guided by some rationale.

Using content analysis, Erving Goffman conducted a pioneering exploration of how advertisements in 1979 portrayed women as inferior to men. Women typically were shown being subordinate to or dependent on others or being instructed by men. They used caressing and touching gestures more than men. Even when presented in leadership-type roles, women were likely to be shown in seductive poses or gazing out into space. Similarly, researchers today

concluded that while an arrest may be a sobering experience for any individual, the impact of being taken to a police station is greater if a person is employed and is forced to explain what is happening in his or her personal life to a boss.

In some experiments, as in observation research, the presence of a social scientist or other observer may affect the behavior of people being studied. The recognition of this phenomenon grew out of an experiment conducted during the 1920s and 1930s at the Hawthorne plant of the Western Electric Company. A group of researchers set out to determine how to improve the productivity of workers at the plant. The investigators manipulated such variables as the lighting and working hours to see what impact changes in them had on productivity. To their surprise, they found that *every* step they took seemed to increase productivity. Even measures that seemed likely to have the opposite effect, such as reducing the amount of lighting in the plant, led to higher productivity.

Why did the plant's employees work harder even under less favorable conditions? Their behavior apparently was influenced by the greater attention being paid to them in the course of the research and by the novelty of being subjects in an experiment. Since that time, sociologists have used the term *Hawthorne effect* to refer to subjects of research who deviate from their typical behavior because they realize that they are under observation (S. Jones 1992; Lang 1992; Pelton 1994).

Table 2-1	Existing Sources Used in Sociological Research

Most Frequently Used Sources

Census data

Crime statistics

Birth, death, marriage, and divorce statistics

Other Sources

Newspapers and periodicals

Personal journals, diaries, e-mail, and letters

Records and archival material of religious organizations, corporations, and other organizations

Transcripts of radio programs

Videotapes of motion pictures and television programs

Webpages

Song lyrics

Scientific records (such as patent applications)

Speeches of public figures (such as politicians)

Votes cast in elections or by elected officials on specific legislative proposals

Attendance records for public events

Videotapes of social protests and rallies

Literature, including folklore

from the distant past. For example, sociologist Karen Barkey (1991) examined village court records from the seventeenth-century Ottoman Empire (centered in modern-day Turkey) to assess the extent of peasant rebellions against the empire and, more specifically, its tax policies. Barkey could hardly have relied on surveys, observations, or experiments to study the Ottoman Empire; like other scholars studying earlier civilizations, she turned to secondary analysis.

Ethics of Research

A biochemist cannot inject a serum into a human being unless the serum has been thoroughly tested and the subject agrees to the shot. To do otherwise would be both unethical and illegal. Sociologists must also abide by certain specific standards in conducting research—a *code of ethics.* The professional society of the discipline, the American Sociological Association (ASA), first published the *Code of Ethics* in 1971 (most recently revised in 1997), which put forth the following basic principles:

1. Maintain objectivity and integrity in research.
2. Respect the subject's right to privacy and dignity.
3. Protect subjects from personal harm.
4. Preserve confidentiality.
5. Seek informed consent when data are collected from research participants or when behavior occurs in a private context.
6. Acknowledge research collaboration and assistance.
7. Disclose all sources of financial support (American Sociological Association 1997).

Content analysis of recent films finds this unstated message: smoking is cool. In this still from *Fight Club*, Brad Pitt is shown enjoying his cigarette. If the movie industry is made aware of the extent of smoking in films and the message that sends to young viewers, perhaps it will try to alter the message.

are analyzing films to look at the increase in smoking in motion pictures, despite increased public health concerns. This type of content analysis can have clear social policy implications if it draws the attention of the motion picture industry to the message it may be delivering (especially to young people) that smoking is acceptable, even desirable. For example, a 1999 content analysis found that tobacco use appeared in 89 percent of the 200 most popular movie rentals (Goffman 1979; Kang 1997; and Roberts et al. 1999).

These examples underscore the value of using existing sources in studying contemporary material. Researchers have learned, in addition, that such analysis can be essential in helping us to understand social behavior

On the surface, the basic principles of the ASA's *Code of Ethics* probably seem clear-cut. How could they lead to any disagreement or controversy? However, many delicate ethical questions cannot be resolved simply by reading the seven points above. For example, should a sociologist engaged in participant-observation research *always* protect the confidentiality of subjects? What if the subjects are members of a religious cult allegedly engaged in unethical and possibly illegal activities? What if the sociologist is interviewing political activists and is questioned by a grand jury about his or her research?

Most sociological research uses *people* as sources of information—as respondents to survey questions, subjects of observation, or participants in experiments. In all cases, sociologists need to be certain that they are not invading the privacy of their subjects. Generally, this is handled by assuring those involved of anonymity and by guaranteeing that personal information disclosed will remain confidential. However, a study by William Zellner raised important questions about the extent to which sociologists can threaten people's right to privacy.

Accident or Suicide?

An ethical issue—with the right to know posed against the right to privacy—became apparent in research on automobile accidents in which fatalities occur. Sociologist William Zellner (1978) wanted to learn if fatal car crashes are sometimes suicides that have been disguised as accidents in order to protect family and friends (and perhaps to collect otherwise unredeemable insurance benefits). These acts of "autocide" are by nature covert.

In his efforts to assess the frequency of such suicides, Zellner sought to interview the friends, coworkers, and family members of the deceased. He hoped to obtain information that would allow him to ascertain whether the deaths were accidental or purposeful. Zellner told the people approached for interviews that his goal was to contribute to a reduction of future accidents by learning about the emotional characteristics of accident victims. He made no mention of his suspicions of autocide, out of fear that potential respondents would refuse to meet with him.

Zellner eventually concluded that at least 12 percent of all fatal single-occupant crashes are suicides. This information could be valuable for society, particularly since some of the probable suicides actually killed or critically injured innocent bystanders in the process of taking their own lives. Yet the ethical questions still must be faced. Was Zellner's research unethical because he misrepresented the motives of his study and failed to obtain his subjects' informed consent? Or was his deception justified by the social value of his findings?

Are some people who die in single-occupant car crashes actually suicides? One sociological study of possible "autocides" concluded that at least 12 percent of such accident victims have in fact committed suicide. But the study also raised some ethical questions concerning the right to know and the right to privacy.

The answers to these questions are not immediately apparent. Zellner appeared to have admirable motives and took great care in protecting confidentiality. He did not reveal names of suspected suicides to insurance companies, though Zellner did recommend that the insurance industry drop double indemnity (payment of twice the person's life insurance benefits in the event of accidental death) in the future.

Zellner's study raised an additional ethical issue: the possibility of harm to those who were interviewed. Subjects were asked if the deceased had "talked about suicide" and if they had spoken of how "bad or useless" they were. Could these questions have led people to guess the true intentions of the researcher? Perhaps, but according to Zellner, none of the informants voiced such suspicions.

More seriously, might the study have caused the bereaved to *suspect* suicide—when before the survey they had accepted the deaths as accidental? Again, there is no evidence to suggest this, but we cannot be sure.

Given our uncertainty about this last question, was the research justified? Was Zellner taking too big a risk in asking the friends and families if the deceased victims had spoken of suicide before their death? Does the right to know outweigh the right to privacy in this type of situation? And who has the right to make such a judgment? In practice, as in Zellner's study, it is the *researcher,* not the subjects of inquiry, who makes the critical ethical decisions. Therefore, sociologists and other investigators bear the responsibility for establishing clear and sensitive boundaries for ethical scientific investigation.

Preserving Confidentiality

Like journalists, sociologists occasionally find themselves subject to questions from law enforcement authorities because of knowledge they have gained in conducting research. This uncomfortable situation raises profound ethical questions.

In May 1993, Rik Scarce, a doctoral candidate in sociology at Washington State University, was jailed for contempt of court. Scarce had declined to tell a federal grand jury what he knew—or even whether he knew anything—about a 1991 raid on a university research laboratory by animal rights activists. At the time, Scarce was conducting research for a book about environmental protestors and knew at least one suspect in the break-in. Curiously, although chastised by a federal judge, Scarce won respect from fellow prison inmates who regarded him as a man who "wouldn't snitch" (Monaghan 1993:A8).

The American Sociological Association supported Scarce's position when he appealed his sentence. Ultimately, Scarce maintained his silence, the judge ruled that nothing would be gained by further incarceration, and Scarce was released after serving 159 days in jail. In January 1994, the U.S. Supreme Court announced without comment that it had declined to hear Scarce's case on appeal. The Court's failure to consider his case led Scarce (1994, 1995) to argue that federal legislation is needed to clarify the rights of scholars and members of the press to preserve the confidentiality of research subjects.

Neutrality and Politics in Research

The ethical considerations of sociologists lie not only in the methods they use but also in the way they interpret results. Max Weber (1949, original edition 1904) recognized that personal values would influence the questions that sociologists select for research. In his view, that was per-

fectly acceptable, but under no conditions could a researcher allow his or her personal feelings to influence the *interpretation* of data. In Weber's phrase, sociologists must practice **value neutrality** in their research.

As part of this neutrality, investigators have an ethical obligation to accept research findings even when the data run counter to their own personal views, to theoretically based explanations, or to widely accepted beliefs. For example, Émile Durkheim challenged popular conceptions when he reported that social (rather than supernatural) forces were an important factor in suicide.

p. 8

Some sociologists believe that it is impossible for scholars to prevent their personal values from influencing their work. If that is true, then Weber's insistence on value-free sociology may lead the public to accept sociological conclusions without exploring the biases of the researchers. Furthermore, drawing on the conflict perspective, Alvin Gouldner (1970), among others, has suggested that sociologists may use objectivity as a sacred justification for remaining uncritical of existing institutions and centers of power. These arguments are attacks not so much on Weber himself as on how his goals have been incorrectly interpreted. As we have seen, Weber was quite clear that sociologists may bring values to their subject matter. In his view, however, they must not confuse their own values with the social reality under study (Bendix 1968).

Let's consider what might happen when researchers bring their own biases to the investigation. A person investigating the impact of intercollegiate sports on alumni contributions, for example, may focus only on the highly visible revenue-generating sports of football and basketball and neglect the so-called "minor sports" such as tennis or soccer that are more likely to involve women athletes. Despite the early work of W. E. B. Du Bois and Jane Addams, sociologists still need to be reminded that the discipline often fails to adequately consider *all* people's social behavior.

In her book *The Death of White Sociology* (1973) Joyce Ladner called attention to the tendency of mainstream sociology to treat the lives of African Americans as a social problem. More recently, feminist sociologist Shulamit Reinharz (1992) has argued that sociological research should not only be inclusive but also be open to bringing about social change and drawing on relevant research by nonsociologists. Both Reinharz and Ladner maintain that research should always analyze whether women's unequal social status has affected the study in any way. For example, one might broaden the study of firearms control to consider how the implications of gun control differ for women than for men. Do women need concealed handguns for safety, or are they more likely to be victimized by criminals wielding these weapons? The issue of value neutrality does not mean you can't have opinions, but it does mean you must work to overcome any biases, however unintentional, that you may bring to the research.

Peter Rossi (1987:73) admits that "in my professional work as a sociologist, my liberal inclinations have led me to undertake applied social research in the hope that . . . my research might contribute to the general liberal aim of social reform. . . ." Yet, in line with Weber's view of value neutrality, Rossi's commitment to rigorous research methods and objective interpretation of data has sometimes led him to controversial findings not necessarily supportive of his own liberal values. For example, when Rossi and a team of researchers carefully attempted to measure the extent of homelessness in Chicago in the mid-1980s, they arrived at estimates of the city's homeless population far below those offered (with little firm documentation) by the Chicago Coalition for the Homeless. Coalition members bitterly attacked Rossi for hampering social reform efforts by minimizing the extent of homelessness. Having been involved in similar controversies before, Rossi (1987:79) concludes that "in the short term, good social research will often be greeted as a betrayal of one or another side to a particular controversy." But he insists that such applied research is exciting to do and can make important long-term contributions to our understanding of social problems.

A homeless woman living in Chicago. Sociologist Peter Rossi came under attack by the Chicago Coalition for the Homeless for finding in a carefully researched study that the city's homeless population was far below the Coalition's estimate. The Coalition accused Rossi of hampering their efforts at social reform.

Technology and Sociological Research

Advances in technology have affected all aspects of life, and sociological research is no exception. The increased speed and capacity of computers have enabled sociologists to handle much larger sets of data. In the recent past, only people with large grants or major institutional support could easily work with census data. Now anyone with a desktop computer and modem can access information to learn more about social behavior. Moreover, data from foreign countries concerning crime statistics and health care are just as available as information from our own country.

Researchers usually rely on computers to deal with quantitative data—that is, numerical measures—but electronic technology is also assisting us with qualitative data, such as information obtained in observation research. Numerous software programs such as *Ethnograph* and *NUD*IST* allow the researcher not only to record his or her observations, like a word processing program, but also to identify common behavioral patterns or similar concerns expressed in interviews. For example, after observing students in a college cafeteria over several weeks and putting your observations into the computer, you could then group all your observations related to certain variables, such as "sorority" or "study group."

The Internet affords an excellent opportunity to communicate with fellow researchers as well as to locate useful information on social issues posted on websites. It would be impossible to calculate all the sociological postings on Internet mailing lists or World Wide Web sites. Of course, you need to apply the same critical scrutiny to Internet material that you would use on any printed resource.

How useful is the Internet for conducting survey research? That's unclear as yet. It is relatively easy to send out or post on an electronic bulletin board a questionnaire and solicit responses. It is an inexpensive way to reach large numbers of potential respondents and get a quick return of responses. However, there are some obvious dilemmas. How do you protect a respondent's anonymity? Second, how do you define the potential audience? Even if you know to whom you sent

KILJOONG KIM:
Associate Statistician, Nielsen Media Research

www.mhhe.com/schaefer4

Much of what we see on television is influenced by what Nielsen Media Research learns about our viewing habits. Kiljoong Kim uses his statistical skills to help select the samples and to analyze the data that come from the monitoring devices placed on the TVs of the sample population. The media networks use this information to decide what programming appeals to what kinds of audiences.

Kim says that one of the things he examines in television ratings is how they differ across racial groups. As he notes, "the top 25 shows for Whites are drastically different from the top 25 shows for African Americans." But Kim is intrigued by how results of the 2000 census may change things, since people who used to inaccurately classify themselves as Black or White are now given options to designate themselves as biracial or multi-racial for the first time in history. "That's one of the reasons sociology is getting more interesting. Things are constantly changing, including the composition of this society by race. It certainly has an impact on my professional career."

Kim's undergraduate training at the University of Wisconsin was in quantitative analysis. "I had to learn about computers and demography (like census data). Being a sociology major was very helpful for what I do now." After a year of doing educational research Kim realized that a lot of people in the same field had advanced degrees. He went on to get his master's degree in sociology at DePaul University, where he is currently teaching classes in statistics and quantitative research in sociology.

Kim's advice for students: Broaden your horizons. Don't feel pressured to declare a major right away, but try out different courses and see what you like. That's how he discovered sociology. Kim sees the value of studying math along with sociology, which is not surprising, given the type of work that he does.

Let's Discuss

1. Why would the study of both sociology and statistics be useful for a career like Kim's?
2. Using your sociological imagination, describe what sorts of information a sociologist might find useful from the analysis of TV ratings.

---

the questionnaire, the respondents may forward it on to others.

While web-based surveys are still in their early stages, the initial results are promising. For example, InterSurvey has created a pool of Internet respondents, initially selected by telephone to be a diverse and representative sample. Using similar methods to locate 50,000 adult respondents in 33 nations, the National Geographic Society conducted an online survey that focused on migration and regional culture. Social scientists are closely monitoring these new approaches to gauge how they might revolutionize one type of research design (W. Bainbridge 1999; R. Morin 2000).

Computers have tremendously extended the range and capability of sociological research, from allowing large amounts of data to be stored and analyzed to facilitating communication with other researchers via websites, newsgroups, and e-mail.

Studying Human Sexuality

The Issue

Here's a scene from *Veronica's Closet,* the NBC sitcom:

> Veronica and her ex-husband, Bryce, share joint custody of their dog, Buddy. Veronica knocks on the door of Bryce's apartment to exchange the dog, and is surprised when a young woman named Pepper answers. Pepper tells Veronica that Bryce has just recently hired her. Veronica asks sarcastically, "By the hour or for the whole night?" Pepper ignores the slur and responds energetically that she is Bryce's new assistant. Veronica then relents, "When I first saw you, I just thought—she's sleeping with my ex-husband." Pepper, in a young, bubbly voice, replies excitedly "Oh, I am!" (Kunkel et al. 1999:21)

You can find similar scenes from dozens of TV shows today. Human sexuality is a topic of drama and comedy as well as life. Certainly, it is an important aspect of human behavior. As we will see, however, it is a difficult topic to research because of all the preconceptions, myths, and beliefs we bring to the topic of sexuality. Yet, in this age of devastating sexually transmitted diseases, there is no time more important to increase our scientific understanding of human sexuality.

The Setting

We have few reliable national data on patterns of sexual behavior in the United States. Until recently, the only comprehensive study of sexual behavior was the famous two-volume Kinsey Report prepared in the 1940s (Kinsey et al. 1948, 1953). While the Kinsey Report is still widely quoted, the volunteers interviewed for the report were not representative of the nation's adult population. Since then, social scientific studies of sexual behavior have typically been rather limited in scope but still useful. For example, every two years the general public is interviewed as a part of the federally funded General Social Survey. In Figure 2-4, we see how attitudes about premarital sexual behavior have changed since the early 1970s.

In part, we have few reliable data on patterns of sexual behavior because it is difficult for researchers to obtain accurate information about this sensitive subject. Moreover, until AIDS emerged in the 1980s, there was little scientific demand for data on sexual behavior, ex-

cept for specific areas such as contraception. Finally, even though the AIDS crisis has reached dramatic proportions (as will be discussed in the social policy section of Chapter 5), government funding for studies of sexual behavior is controversial. Because the General Social Survey described above concerns *attitudes* rather than *behavior* of human sexuality, its funding has not been in jeopardy.

Sociological Insights

The controversy surrounding research on human sexual behavior raises the issue of value neutrality. And this becomes especially delicate when one considers the relationship of sociology to the government. The federal gov-

Research into sexual behavior in the United States is complicated by the sensitivity of the subject and the reluctance of government agencies to provide funding. Sociologists had to raise private funds to finance the National Health and Social Life Survey (NHSLS), a nationwide study of the sexual practices of adults.

Operational definition An explanation of an abstract concept that is specific enough to allow a researcher to measure the concept. (30)

Qualitative research Research that relies on what is seen in field or naturalistic settings more than on statistical data. (36)

Quantitative research Research that collects and reports data primarily in numerical form. (36)

Questionnaire A research instrument employed to obtain desired information from a respondent. (36)

Random sample A sample for which every member of the entire population has the same chance of being selected. (32)

Reliability The extent to which a measure provides consistent results. (33)

Representative sample A selection from a larger population that is statistically typical of that population. (32)

Research design A detailed plan or method for obtaining data scientifically. (34)

Scientific method A systematic, organized series of steps that ensures maximum objectivity and consistency in researching a problem. (29)

Secondary analysis A variety of research techniques that make use of publicly accessible information and data. (38)

Survey A study, generally in the form of interviews or questionnaires, that provides sociologists and other researchers with information concerning how people think and act. (35)

Validity The degree to which a scale or measure truly reflects the phenomenon under study. (33)

Value neutrality Objectivity of sociologists in the interpretation of data. (41)

Variable A measurable trait or characteristic that is subject to change under different conditions. (31)

Additional Readings

American Sociological Association. 1997. *Style Guide,* 2d ed. Washington, DC: ASA. This concise handbook (39 pages) provides guidance in writing clearly as well as citation format, including referencing electronic sources such as the Internet.

Denzin, Norman K., and Yvonna S. Lincoln (eds.). 2000. *Handbook of Qualitative Research,* 2d ed. Thousand Oaks, CA: Sage. The 40 articles in this anthology cover newer techniques used in conducting observation and biographical research, as well as ethical issues facing researchers.

Ericksen, Julia A. 1999. *Kiss and Tell: Surveying Sex in the Twentieth Century.* Cambridge, MA: Harvard University Press. Evaluates the methodology of the hundreds of surveys of human sexuality conducted by sociologists and other social scientists.

Internet Connection

Note: While all the URLs listed were current as of the printing of this book, these sites often change. Please check our website (http://www.mhhe.com/schaefer4) for updates.

1. Erving Goffman used content analysis in 1979 to examine the portrayal of men and women in magazines. Try your hand at a bit of content analysis by taking Goffman's research into cyberspace! Although this particular study will not be scientific, it will give you an introduction to this kind of research. First, review the material on researching existing sources in your textbook. Second, direct your web browser to the list of magazines featured (**http://dir.yahoo.com/Arts/Design_Arts/Fashion_and_Beauty/News_and_Media/Magazines/**). Next, choose two popular magazines directed toward women and two popular magazines for men. Link to those four magazine sites and answer the following questions for each:

   (a) What are the predominant colors and layouts of each site and of this month's magazine?

   (b) How are the models on the cover of the site portrayed? Specifically, describe the colors and styles of clothing, the body shapes and sizes, and facial expressions of the models.

   (c) Does the magazine feature women, men, or both on this month's cover or on the website's homepage itself?

   (d) What kind of topics and articles are found in the magazine? If you can look at back issues online, do there seem to be trends in terms of the topics or articles?

   (e) What differences and similarities did you find between those magazine websites directed to a male audience and those to female readers?

   (f) What conclusions could you draw from your examination? What kinds of methodological problems or challenges might a researcher face if she or he wanted to conduct a scientific update of Goffman's classic study?

2. Social scientists conduct their research under a code of ethics geared toward their discipline. Your book summarizes some of the important elements of the code for sociologists. Using your computer, examine the code of ethics for each of the following disciplines: sociology (The American Sociological Association—**http://www.asanet.org/members/ecoderev.html**), psychology (The American Psychological Association—**http://www.apa.org/ethics/**), and anthropology (The American Anthropological Association—**http://www.aaanet.org/committees/ethics/ethcode.htm**).

   (a) How does each code define and describe the issue of confidentiality?

   (b) In your opinion, what are some of the core values or most important ethical guidelines listed in each of the three codes? Why did you choose them?

   (c) What responsibilities to animal and human subjects does each code detail for researchers?

   (d) What responsibilities does each code list for those teaching sociology, psychology, and anthropology?

   (e) What does each code have to say—if anything—about neutrality and politics in research?

   (f) How do the three codes compare overall? Which code do you feel is the most complete and best suited to assisting researchers as they try to make ethical decisions? Why?

(g) What additions or changes, if any, would you make to the guidelines or issues of the socio-logical code?

3. One of the most important uses of the scientific method in social science research is to gather and interpret crime statistics. To learn more about how statistics are collected, visit Organized Crime: A Crime Statistics Site offered by Regina Schekall (**http://www.crime.org/**). Here you will find an online tutorial and crime statistics links. Explore the site and answer the following questions:

(a) What are the steps and processes by which researchers and law enforcement agencies obtain and gather crime statistics?

(b) What is the UCR? Which crime categories are used in the UCR?

(c) How are victim reports and surveys used to gain a better picture of crime in the United States?

(d) What are some of the problems and challenges in both gathering and interpreting crime data?

(e) Link to UCR data online through the site and check the most recent crime rates and statistics for murder-homicide. What statistic or fact surprised you the most and why?

(f) This site also allows visitors to link to various college and university campus police and safety sites. Try to find your own college or a college near you and link to their data. What kind of crimes are occurring on campus? If rates are reported over time, has there been a change over the last few semesters? What might account for the changes in crime rates, both on the college campus and in society in general?

Interactive e-Source with Making the Grade

Online Learning Center   www.mhhe.com/schaefer4

PowerWeb

SocCity

CHAPTER

3

CULTURE

Additional Readings

Kraybill, Donald B., and Steven M. Nott. 1995. *Amish Enterprises: From Plows to Profits.* Baltimore: Johns Hopkins University Press. An examination of how the Amish have adapted to capitalism in the United States while maintaining their distinctive values and subculture.

Lakoff, Robin Talmach. 2000. *Language War.* Berkeley: University of California Press. A linguist considers how language shapes a culture and the discussions within a society. Uses case studies of contemporary issues, such as the O. J. Simpson murder trial, the Ebonics controversy, and the Clinton sex scandal.

Weinstein, Deena. 2000. *Heavy Metal: The Music and Its Culture.* Cambridge, MA: Da Capo. A sociologist examines the subculture associated with "heavy metal" music and efforts to curtail this subculture.

Zellner, William M. 1995. *Countercultures: A Sociological Analysis.* New York: St. Martin's. An overview of six countercultures found in the United States: the Unification Church, the Church of Scientology, satanists, skinheads, survivalists, and the Ku Klux Klan.

Technology Resources

Internet Connection

Note: While all the URLs listed were current as of the printing of this book, these sites often change. Please check our website (http://www.mhhe.com/schaefer4) for updates.

1. Nonverbal communication is an important element in all cultures. Through gestures and body language, we can express ideas and feelings. As with all elements of culture though, specific forms of nonverbal communication differ among different groups. Visit **http://dir.yahoo.com/Arts/ Performing_Arts/Dance/Folk_and_Traditional/** to sample the meanings and forms of dances in differing groups. Choose three of the groups listed on the homepage. Then link to websites dedicated to their folk or traditional forms of dance. For each, answer the following questions:
   (a) Does the name of the dance itself hold any special meaning?
   (b) What purposes/functions does the dance serve for members of the group?
   (c) What is the history or origin of the dance?
   (d) Is the dance still performed today? Is it performed at a specific time of year or under certain conditions?
   (e) What symbolism and gestures do the dancers use? What ideas and feelings do they try to express?
   (f) What similarities and differences among the three groups and dances do you see?
   (g) Why would it be good for a social scientist studying dance forms in different cultures to keep in mind the concepts of cultural relativism, ethnocentrism, and culture shock?

2. Your text offers a contrast of subcultures and countercultures. In general, both groups are segments of society that share distinctive features, such as argots, beliefs, and particular dress codes. However, a counterculture conspicuously and deliberately opposes certain aspects of the larger culture in a way that a subculture does not. To see this difference in action, compare the Amish described through the links found at **http://dir.yahoo.com/ Society_and_Culture/Religion_and_ Spirituality/Faiths_and_Practices/Christianity/ Denominations_and_Sects/Amish** to street gangs described through the links found at **http://dir. yahoo.com/Society_and_Culture/Cultures_and_ Groups/Gangs/.** For each of the two groups, explore the following:
   (a) Identify the argot of the group. Describe some specific examples of special forms of verbal, written, and gestural communication. How are those gestures and words used to communicate? What kinds of messages are sent through the argot? In what ways can a subculture or counterculture make use of an argot to build solidarity among its members, while at the same time keeping outsiders at a distance?
   (b) What special clothing or dress codes are used? What symbols and messages do members communicate through clothing? What purpose does specialized dress serve for the group?
   (c) What are some of the special practices or beliefs of the group? Do these beliefs or practices put the group at odds with the larger culture? How so?

(d) What purpose or meaning can being a member of the group have for those who belong?

(e) Draw some comparisons and contrasts between the two groups. What do the Amish and street gangs have in common? In what ways are they different? Why would the Amish be labeled a subculture, but street gangs a counterculture? Do you agree with these labels? Why or why not?

3. The Web of Culture (**http://webofculture. com/refs/gestures.html/**) offers information on gestures and nonverbal communication around the world. Imagine that you are traveling different parts of the world on an important business venture. On the website, select two foreign regions or nations and read all about their forms of nonverbal communication. For each of your two choices, answer the following:

(a) What overall themes did you find after reading the information? How can gestures reflect the general values and beliefs of a people?

(b) Which gesture or norm about gestures surprised you the most? Why?

(c) What similarities did you find in the gestures of the places you selected and your own culture?

(d) If listed, identify one gesture that is considered rude or impolite in a society you chose. Why do you think that the gesture might be considered as such?

(e) Which gestures do you feel would be most important for a business person to remember as she or he travels through this area of the world? Why did you choose those gestures over others?

Interactive e-Source with Making the Grade

 Online Learning Center   www.mhhe.com/schaefer4

PowerWeb

SocCity

CHAPTER
4

SOCIALIZATION

3. The concepts of *Gemeinschaft* and *Gesellschaft* are crucial to the study of social life, especially when taking a historical viewpoint. As many nations continue to modernize, the *Gemeinschaft* way of life becomes less and less a part of daily experience. One subculture in the United States that still embraces the features of *Gemeinschaft* is the Amish. Maryalice Yakutchik chronicles her time among the Amish in words and pictures on Discovery Online's Amish Online website (**http://www.discovery.com/ area/exploration/amish/amish1.html**). Read her work and reflect on the ways of the Amish.

(a) Using Table 5-2 in your text, which of the features of *Gemeinschaft* communities can be applied to the Amish? Are there any features of *Gesellschaft* that could apply as well?

(b) Where does the Amish way of life fit best in Gerhard Lenski's sociocultural evolution model: hunting/gathering, horticultural, agrarian, industrial, or postindustrial? Why?

(c) What kinds of challenges do the Amish face as they try to maintain their way of life in the face of modernization, technology, tourism, and development?

(d) What part of Amish life interested or surprised you the most? Why?

(e) What are some of the benefits of adopting Amish perspectives? What are some of the drawbacks?

(f) Has the website and chapter changed the way you viewed the Amish? If you have seen the Amish portrayed in movies or television programs, how accurate were those portrayals in light of what you have now learned?

Interactive e-Source with Making the Grade

Online Learning Center   www.mhhe.com/schaefer4

PowerWeb

SocCity

GROUPS AND ORGANIZATIONS

the second annual
insect collector's
convention

december 23 & 24
at the los angeles
county arboretum
(818) 762-3762
for information

it—no big deal" attitude toward the behavior. Many find that taking five drinks in a row is fairly typical. As one student at Boston University noted, "Anyone that goes to a party does that or worse. If you talk to anyone college age, it's normal." Some colleges and universities are taking steps to make binge drinking a bit less "normal" by means of *social control*—banning kegs, closing fraternities and sororities, encouraging liquor retailers not to sell in high volume to students, and expelling students after three alcohol-related infractions.

Let's Discuss

1. Why do you think most college students regard binge drinking as a normal rather than a deviant behavior?
2. Which method of social control do you think would be most effective in stopping binge drinking on your campus?

FIGURE 7-1

College Binge Drinking

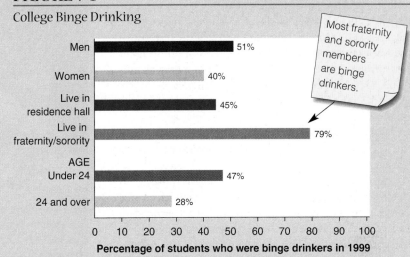

Most fraternity and sorority members are binge drinkers.

Percentage of students who were binge drinkers in 1999

Note: Based on a national survey of more than 14,000 college students in 1999. Binge drinking is defined as one drinking session of at least five drinks for men or four drinks for women during the two weeks prior to the self-administered questionnaire.

Source: Wechsler et al. 2000:203.

ducted an experiment at Smith College and found that statements people overhear others make influence their own expressions of opinion on the issue of racism.

A student confederate of the researchers approached 72 White students as each was walking across the campus to get responses for an opinion poll she said she was conducting for a class. At the same time, a second White student—actually another confederate working with the researchers—was stopped and asked to participate in the survey. Both students were then asked how Smith College should respond to anonymous racist notes actually sent to four African American students in 1989. The confederate always answered first. In some cases, she condemned the notes; in others, she justified them.

Blanchard and his colleagues (1991:102–103) conclude that "hearing at least one other person express strongly antiracist opinions produced dramatically more strongly antiracist public reactions to racism than hearing others express equivocal opinions or opinions more accepting of racism." A second experiment demonstrated that when the confederate expressed sentiments justifying racism, subjects were much *less* likely to express antiracist opinions than were those who heard no one else offer opinions. In these experiments, social control (through the process of conformity) influenced people's attitudes, or at least the expression of those attitudes. In the next section, we will see that social control (through the process of obedience) can alter people's behavior.

Obedience to Authority

If ordered to do so, would you comply with an experimenter's instruction to give people increasingly painful electric shocks? Most people would say no; yet, the research of social psychologist Stanley Milgram (1963,

1975) suggests that most of us *will* obey such orders. In Milgram's words (1975:xi), "Behavior that is unthinkable in an individual . . . acting on his own may be executed without hesitation when carried out under orders."

Milgram placed advertisements in New Haven, Connecticut, newspapers to recruit subjects for what was announced as a learning experiment at Yale University. Participants included postal clerks, engineers, high school teachers, and laborers. They were told that the purpose of the research was to investigate the effects of punishment on learning. The experimenter, dressed in a gray technician's coat, explained that in each testing, one subject would be randomly selected as the "learner" while another would function as the "teacher." However, this lottery was rigged so that the "real" subject would always be the teacher while an associate of Milgram's served as the learner.

At this point, the learner's hand was strapped to an electric apparatus. The teacher was taken to an electronic "shock generator" with 30 lever switches. Each switch was labeled with graduated voltage designations from 15 to 450 volts. Before beginning the experiment, subjects were given sample shocks of 45 volts to convince them of the authenticity of the experiment.

The experimenter instructed the teacher to apply shocks of increasing voltage each time the learner gave an incorrect answer on a memory test. Teachers were told that "although the shocks can be extremely painful, they cause no permanent tissue damage." In reality, the learner did not receive any shocks.

The learner deliberately gave incorrect answers and acted out a prearranged script. For example, at 150 volts, the learner would cry out, "Experimenter, get me out of here! I won't be in the experiment any more!" At 270 volts, the learner would scream in agony. When the shock reached 350 volts, the learner would fall silent. If the teacher wanted to stop the experiment, the experimenter would insist that the teacher continue, using such statements as "The experiment requires that you continue" and "You have no other choice; you *must* go on" (Milgram 1975:19–23).

The results of this unusual experiment stunned and dismayed Milgram and other social scientists. A sample of psychiatrists had predicted that virtually all subjects would refuse to shock innocent victims. In their view, only a "pathological fringe" of less than 2 percent would continue administering shocks up to the maximum level. Yet almost *two-thirds* of participants fell into the category of "obedient subjects."

Why did these subjects obey? Why were they willing to inflict seemingly painful shocks on innocent victims who had never done them any harm? There is no evidence that these subjects were unusually sadistic; few seemed to

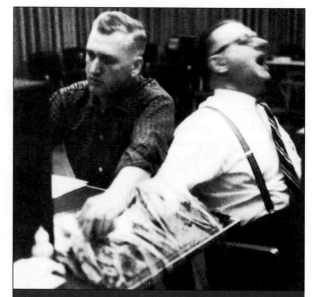

In one of Stanley Milgram's experiments, a supposed "victim" received an electric shock when his hand rested on a shock plate. At the 150-volt level, the "victim" would demand to be released, and would refuse to place his hand on the shock plate. The experimenter would then order the actual subject to force the "victim's" hand onto the plate, as shown in the photo. Though 40 percent of the true subjects stopped complying with Milgram at this point, 30 percent did force the "victim's" hand onto the shock plate, despite his pretended agony.

enjoy administering the shocks. Instead, in Milgram's view, the key to obedience was the experimenter's social role as a "scientist" and "seeker of knowledge."

Milgram pointed out that in the modern industrial world, we are accustomed to submitting to impersonal authority figures whose status is indicated by a title (professor, lieutenant, doctor) or by a uniform (the technician's coat). The authority is viewed as larger and more important than the individual; consequently, the obedient individual shifts responsibility for his or her behavior to the authority figure. Milgram's subjects frequently stated, "If it were up to me, I would not have administered shocks." They saw themselves as merely doing their duty (Milgram 1975).

From an interactionist perspective, one important aspect of Milgram's findings is the fact that subjects in follow-up studies were less likely to inflict the supposed shocks as they were moved physically closer to their victims. Moreover, interactionists emphasize the effect of *incrementally* administering additional dosages of 15 volts. In effect, the experimenter negotiated with the teacher and convinced the teacher to continue inflicting higher levels

Interactive e-Source with Making the Grade

 www.mhhe.com/schaefer4

 PowerWeb

SocCity

STRATIFICATION IN THE UNITED STATES AND WORLDWIDE

ASIEN-WOCHEN
JAM JAM
BEI McDONALD'S

much respect working as street cleaners? Functionalists say no, which is partly why they believe that a stratified society is universal.

In the view of Kingsley Davis and Wilbert Moore (1945), society must distribute its members among a variety of social positions. It must not only make sure that these positions are filled but also see that they are staffed by people with the appropriate talents and abilities. Rewards, including money and prestige, are based on the importance of a position and the relative scarcity of qualified personnel. Yet this assessment often devalues work performed by certain segments of society, such as women's work as homemakers or occupations traditionally filled by women or low-status work in fast-food outlets.

Davis and Moore argue that stratification is universal and that social inequality is necessary so that people will be motivated to fill functionally important positions. But, critics say, unequal rewards are not the only means of encouraging people to fill critical positions and occupations. Personal pleasure, intrinsic satisfaction, and value orientations also motivate people to enter particular careers. Functionalists agree but note that society must use some type of reward to motivate people to enter unpleasant or dangerous jobs and jobs that require a long training period. This response does not justify stratification systems in which status is largely inherited, such as slave or caste societies. Similarly, it is difficult to explain the high salaries our society offers to professional athletes or entertainers on the basis of how critical these jobs are to the survival of society (R. Collins 1975; Kerbo 2000; Tumin 1953, 1985).

Even if stratification is inevitable, the functionalist explanation for differential rewards does not explain the wide disparity between the rich and the poor. Critics of the functionalist approach point out that the richest 10 percent of households account for 20 percent of the nation's income in Sweden, 25 percent in France, and 30 percent in the United States. In their view, the level of income inequality found in contemporary industrial societies cannot be defended—even though these societies have a legitimate need to fill certain key occupations (World Bank 2000a:238–239).

Conflict View

The writings of Karl Marx are at the heart of conflict theory. Marx viewed history as a continuous struggle between the oppressors and the oppressed that would ultimately culminate in an egalitarian, classless society. In terms of stratification, he argued that the dominant class under capitalism—the bourgeoisie—manipulated the economic and political systems in order to maintain control over the exploited proletariat. Marx did not believe that stratification was inevitable, but he

did see inequality and oppression as inherent in capitalism (E. Wright et al. 1982).

Like Marx, contemporary conflict theorists believe that human beings are prone to conflict over such scarce resources as wealth, status, and power. However, where Marx focused primarily on class conflict, more recent theorists have extended this analysis to include conflicts based on gender, race, age, and other dimensions. British sociologist Ralf Dahrendorf is one of the most influential contributors to the conflict approach.

Dahrendorf (1959) modified Marx's analysis of capitalist society to apply to *modern* capitalist societies. For Dahrendorf, social classes are groups of people who share common interests resulting from their authority relationships. In identifying the most powerful groups in society, he includes not only the bourgeoisie—the owners of the means of production—but also the managers of industry, legislators, the judiciary, heads of the government bureaucracy, and others. In that respect, Dahrendorf has merged Marx's emphasis on class conflict with Weber's recognition that power is an important element of stratification (Cuff et al. 1990).

Conflict theorists, including Dahrendorf, contend that the powerful of today, like the bourgeoisie of Marx's time, want society to run smoothly so that they can enjoy their privileged positions. Because the status quo suits those with wealth, status, and power, they have a clear interest in preventing, minimizing, or controlling societal conflict.

One way for the powerful to maintain the status quo is to define and disseminate the society's dominant ideology. The term **dominant ideology** describes a set of cultural beliefs and practices that helps to maintain powerful social, economic, and political interests. For Karl Marx, the dominant ideology in a capitalist society serves the interests of the ruling class. From a conflict perspective, the social significance of the dominant ideology is that a society's most powerful groups and institutions not only control wealth and property, but, even more important, they control the means of producing beliefs about reality through religion, education, and the media (Abercrombie et al. 1980, 1990; Robertson 1988).

The powerful, such as leaders of government, also use limited social reforms to buy off the oppressed and reduce the danger of challenges to their dominance. For example, minimum wage laws and unemployment compensation unquestionably give some valuable assistance to needy men and women. Yet these reforms also serve to pacify those who might otherwise rebel. Of course, in the view of conflict theorists, such maneuvers can never entirely eliminate conflict, since workers will continue to demand equality, and the powerful will not give up their control of society.

Conflict theorists see stratification as a major source of societal tension and conflict. They do not agree with Davis and Moore that stratification is functional for a society or that it serves as a source of stability. Rather, conflict sociologists argue that stratification will inevitably lead to instability and to social change (R. Collins 1975; L. Coser 1977).

Lenski's Viewpoint

Let's return to the question posed earlier—"Is stratification universal?"—and consider the sociological response. Some form of differentiation is found in every culture, from the most primitive to the most advanced industrial societies of our time. Sociologist Gerhard Lenski, in his sociocultural evolution approach, described how economic systems change as their level of technology becomes more complex, beginning with hunting and gathering and culminating eventually with industrial society. In subsistence-based, hunting-and-gathering societies, people focus on survival. While some inequality and differentiation are evident, a stratification system based on social class does not emerge because there is no real wealth to be claimed.

p. 120

As a society advances in technology, it becomes capable of producing a considerable surplus of goods. The emergence of surplus resources greatly expands the possibilities for inequality in status, influence, and power and allows a well-defined rigid social class system to develop. In order to minimize strikes, slowdowns, and industrial sabotage, the elites may share a portion of the economic surplus with the lower classes, but not enough to reduce their power and privilege.

As Lenski argued, the allocation of surplus goods and services controlled by those with wealth, status, and power reinforces the social inequality that accompanies stratification systems. While this reward system may once have served the overall purposes of society, as functionalists contend, the same cannot be said for the large disparities separating the haves from the have-nots in current societies. In contemporary industrial society, the degree of social and economic inequality far exceeds the need to provide for goods and services (Lenski 1966; Nolan and Lenski 1999).

Stratification by Social Class

Measuring Social Class

We continually assess how wealthy people are by looking at the cars they drive, the houses they live in, the clothes they wear, and so on. Yet it is not so easy to locate an individual within our social hierarchies as it would be in slavery or caste systems of stratification. To determine someone's class position, sociologists generally rely on the objective method.

The **objective method** of measuring social class views class largely as a statistical category. Researchers assign individuals to social classes on the basis of criteria such as occupation, education, income, and residence. The key to the objective method is that the *researcher*, rather than the person being classified, identifies an individual's class position.

The first step in using this method is to decide what indicators or causal factors will be measured objectively, whether wealth, income, education, or occupation. The prestige ranking of occupations has proved to be a useful indicator of a person's class position. For one thing, it is much easier to determine accurately than income or wealth. The term **prestige** refers to the respect and admiration that an occupation holds in a society. "My daughter, the physicist" connotes something very different from "my daughter, the waitress." Prestige is independent of the particular individual who occupies a job, a characteristic that distinguishes it from esteem. **Esteem** refers to the reputation that a specific person has earned within an occupation. Therefore, one can say that the position of president of the United States has high prestige, even though it has been occupied by people with varying degrees of esteem. A hairdresser may have the esteem of his clients, but he lacks the prestige of a corporation president.

Table 8-1 ranks the prestige of a number of well-known occupations. In a series of national surveys, sociologists assigned prestige rankings to about 500 occupations, ranging from physician to newspaper vendor. The highest possible prestige score was 100, and the lowest was 0. Physician, lawyer, dentist, and college professor were the most highly regarded occupations. Sociologists have used such data to assign prestige rankings to virtually all jobs and have found a stability in rankings from 1925 to 1991. Similar studies in other countries have also developed useful prestige rankings of occupations (Hodge and Rossi 1964; Lin and Xie 1988; Treiman 1977).

Studies of social class tend to neglect the occupations and incomes of *women* as determinants of social rank. In an exhaustive study of 589 occupations, sociologists Mary Powers and Joan Holmberg (1978) examined the impact of women's participation in the paid labor force on occupational status. Since women tend to dominate the relatively low-paying occupations, such as bookkeepers and child care workers, their participation in the workforce leads to a general upgrading of the status of most male-dominated occupations. More recent research conducted in both the United States and Europe has assessed the occupations of husbands *and* wives in determining the class positions of families (Sørensen 1994). With more than half of all married women now working outside the home (see Chapter 10), this approach seems long overdue, but it also raises some questions. For example, how is class or status to be judged in dual-career families—by the occu-

Table 8-1 Prestige Rankings of Occupations

Occupation	Score	Occupation	Score
Physician	86	Secretary	46
Lawyer	75	Insurance agent	45
Dentist	74	Bank teller	43
College professor	74	Nurse's aide	42
Architect	73	Farmer	40
Clergy	69	Correctional officer	40
Pharmacist	68	Receptionist	39
Registered nurse	66	Barber	36
High school teacher	66	Child care worker	35
Accountant	65	Hotel clerk	32
Airline pilot	60	Bus driver	32
Police officer and detective	60	Truck driver	30
Prekindergarten teacher	55	Salesworker (shoes)	28
Librarian	54	Garbage collector	28
Firefighter	53	Waiter and waitress	28
Social worker	52	Bartender	25
Electrician	51	Farm worker	23
Funeral director	49	Janitor	22
Mail carrier	47	Newspaper vendor	19

Sources: J. Davis and Smith 1999:1,242–1,246; Nakao and Treas 1990, 1994; NORC 1994.

pation regarded as having greater prestige, the average, or some other combination of the two occupations?

Sociologists—and, in particular, feminist sociologists in Great Britain—are drawing on new approaches in assessing women's social class standing. One approach is to focus on the individual (rather than the family or household) as the basis of categorizing a woman's class position. Thus, a woman would be classified based on her own occupational status rather than that of her spouse (O'Donnell 1992).

Another feminist effort to measure the contribution of women to the economy reflects a more clearly political agenda. International Women Count Network, a global grassroots feminist organization, has sought to give a monetary value to women's unpaid work. Besides pro-

viding symbolic recognition of women's role in labor, this value would also be used to calculate pension programs and benefits that are based on wages received. In 1995 the United Nations placed an $11 trillion price tag on unpaid labor by women, largely in child care, housework, and agriculture. Whatever the figure today, the continued undercounting of many workers' contribution to a family and to an entire economy makes virtually all measures of stratification in need of reform (United Nations Development Programme 1995; Wages for Housework Campaign 1999).

Another complication in measuring social class is that advances in statistical methods and computer technology have multiplied the factors used to define class under the objective method. No longer are sociologists limited to annual income and education in evaluating a person's class position. Today, studies use as criteria the value of homes, sources of income, assets, years in present occupations, neighborhoods, and considerations regarding dual careers. Adding these variables will not necessarily paint a different picture of class differentiation in the United States, but it does allow sociologists to measure class in a more complex and multidimensional way.

Whatever the technique used to measure class, the sociologist is interested in real and often dramatic differences in power, privilege, and opportunity in a society. The study of stratification is a study of inequality. Nowhere is this more evident than in the distribution of wealth and income.

Consequences of Social Class

Wealth and Income

By all measures, income in the United States is distributed unevenly. Nobel prizewinning economist Paul Samuelson has described the situation in the following words: "If we made an income pyramid out of a child's blocks, with each layer portraying $500 of income, the peak would be far higher than Mount Everest, but most people would be within a few feet of the ground" (Samuelson and Nordhaus 1998:344).

Recent data support Samuelson's analogy. As Figure 8-2 shows, in 1999 the richest fifth of the population (or 20 percent of the nation)—earning $79,375 or more—accounted for 49 percent of total after-tax income. By contrast, the bottom fifth—earning $17,196 or less—accounted for only 4 percent of after-tax income.

There has been modest redistribution of income in the United States over the past 70 years. From 1929 through 1970, the government's economic and tax policies shifted income somewhat to the poor. However, in the last three decades—and especially during the 1980s—federal budgetary policies favored the affluent. Moreover, while the salaries of highly skilled workers and professionals have continued to rise, the wages of less skilled workers have *decreased* when controlled for inflation. As a result, the Census Bureau reports that regardless

FIGURE 8-2

Comparison of Distribution of Income and Wealth in the United States

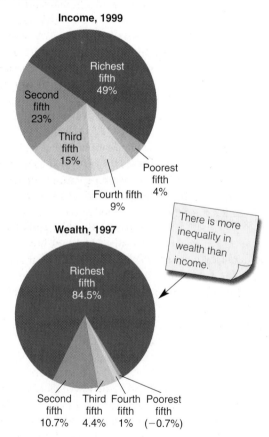

Note: Data on wealth do not add to 100 percent due to rounding.

Sources: Income data (household) are from Bureau of the Census 2000d: B6. Data on wealth are from Wolff 1999.

of the measure used, income inequality rose substantially between 1967 and the early 1990s, although it has remained unchanged since then (Bureau of the Census 2000d:xiii; Jones and Weinberg 2000).

Survey data show that only 38 percent of people in the United States believe that government should take steps to reduce the income disparity between the rich and the poor. By contrast, 80 percent of people in Italy, 66 percent in Germany, and 65 percent in Great Britain support governmental efforts to reduce income inequality. It is not surprising, then, that many European countries provide more extensive "safety nets" to assist and protect the disadvantaged. By contrast, the strong cultural value placed on individualism in the United States leads to greater possibilities for both economic success and failure (Lipset 1996).

Wealth in the United States is much more unevenly distributed than income. As Figure 8-2 shows, in 1997 the richest fifth of the population held 85 percent of the nation's wealth. Government data indicate that more than one out of every 100 households had assets over $2.4 million, while one-fifth of all households were in debt and therefore had a negative net worth. Researchers have also found a dramatic disparity in wealth between African Americans and Whites. This disparity is evident even when educational backgrounds are held constant: the households of college-educated Whites have about three times as much wealth as the households of college-educated Blacks (Hurst et al. 1996; Kennickell et al. 2000; Oliver and Shapiro 1995).

Poverty

Approximately one out of every nine people in this country lives below the poverty line established by the federal government. In 1999, 32.3 million people were living in poverty. The economic boom of the 1990s passed these people by. A 2000 Bureau of the Census report showed that one in five households had trouble meeting basic needs—everything from paying the utility bills to buying dinner. In this section, we'll consider just how we define "poverty" and who is included in that category (K. Bauman 1999; Dalaker and Proctor 2000:1).

Studying Poverty   The efforts of sociologists and other social scientists to better understand poverty are complicated by the difficulty of defining it. This problem is evident even in government programs that conceive of poverty in either absolute or relative terms. *Absolute poverty* refers to a minimum level of subsistence that no family should be expected to live below. This standard theoretically remains unchanged from year to year. Policies concerning minimum wages, housing standards, or school lunch programs for the poor imply a need to bring citizens up to some predetermined level of exis-

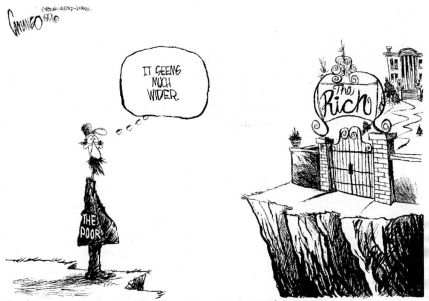

FOR EVERY GENERATION, THERE'S A GAP.

Other observers dispute this view. They argue that the poverty line may actually overestimate the number of low-income people because it fails to consider noncash benefits (such as Medicare, Medicaid, food stamps, public housing, and health care and other fringe benefits provided by some employers). In response, the Bureau of the Census has considered several different definitions of poverty; they showed at most a 1.4 percent lower rate. That is, if the official poverty threshold places 13 percent of the population in the category of the poor, the poverty estimate including *all* these noncash benefits would account for about 11.6 percent of the population (K. Short et al. 1999; Uchitelle 1999).

tence. For example, in 1997 the federal minimum wage rate was raised to $5.15 an hour. Even so, when one takes inflation into account, this standard was actually *lower* than what workers were guaranteed at any time from 1956 through 1982 (Bureau of the Census 1999a:497).

By contrast, **relative poverty** is a floating standard of deprivation by which people at the bottom of a society, whatever their lifestyles, are judged to be disadvantaged *in comparison with the nation as a whole*. Most of our country's current social programs view poverty in relative terms. Therefore, even if the poor of the 1990s are better off in absolute terms than the poor of the 1930s or 1960s, they are still seen as deserving special assistance from government.

One commonly used measure of relative poverty is the federal government's *poverty line*, a money income figure adjusted annually to reflect the consumption requirements of families based on their size and composition. The poverty line serves as an official definition of which people are poor. In 1999, for example, any family of four with a combined income of $17,029 or less fell below the poverty line. This definition determines which individuals and families will be eligible for certain government benefits (Dalaker and Proctor 2000:1).

In the 1990s, there was growing debate over the validity of the poverty line as a measure of poverty and a standard for allocating government benefits. Some critics charge that the poverty line is too low; they note that the federal government continues to use 20-year-old nutritional standards in assessing people's level of poverty. If the poverty line is too low, then government data will underestimate the extent of poverty in the United States, and many deserving poor citizens will fail to receive benefits.

Who Are the Poor?   Not only does the category of the poor defy any simple definition, it counters common stereotypes about "poor people." For example, many people in the United States believe that the vast majority of the poor are able to work but will not. Yet many poor adults *do* work outside the home, although only a portion (12 percent of all low-income adults) work full-time throughout the year. About 60 percent of poor adults do not work, primarily because they are ill or disabled, are maintaining a home, or are retired (Dalaker and Proctor 2000:18).

A sizable number of the poor live in urban slums, but a majority live outside these poverty areas. Poverty is no stranger in rural areas, ranging from Appalachia to hard-hit farming regions to Native American reservations. Included among the poor of the United States are elderly people, children living in single-parent families with their mothers, and over 10,000 men in military service who cannot adequately support their large families. Table 8-2 provides additional statistical information regarding these low-income people in the United States. (The situation of the most destitute poor in the United States and worldwide, the homeless, will be examined in the social policy section of Chapter 15.)

Since World War II, an increasing proportion of the poor people of the United States have been women— many of whom are divorced or never-married mothers. Currently, almost two out of every three adults classified as poor by the federal government are women. In 1959, female householders accounted for 26 percent of the nation's poor; by 1998, that figure had risen to 57 percent (see Table 8-2). This alarming trend, known as the

Table 8-2 Who Are the Poor in the United States?

Group	Percentage of the Population of the United States	Percentage of the Poor of the United States
Under 18 years old	26%	38%
18 to 64 years old	61	52
65 years and older	13	10
Whites (non-Hispanic)	83	46
Blacks	12	26
Hispanics	11	23
Asians and Pacific Islanders	4	4
Married couples and families with male householders	82	47
Families with female householders	18	53

Notes: Data are for 1999, as reported by the Bureau of the Census in 2000.

Source: Dalaker and Proctor 2000:vi.

feminization of poverty, is evident not just in the United States but around the world.

About half of all women in the United States living in poverty are "in transition," coping with an economic crisis caused by the departure, disability, or death of a husband. The other half tend to be economically dependent either on the welfare system or on friends and relatives living nearby. A major factor in the feminization of poverty has been the increase in families with women as single heads of the household (see Chapter 11). In 1999, 11.8 percent of all people in the United States lived in poverty, compared to 27.8 percent of households headed by single mothers. Conflict theorists and other observers trace the higher rates of poverty among women to three distinct factors: the difficulty in finding affordable child care, sexual harassment, and sex discrimination in the labor market (see Chapter 10) (Dalaker and Proctor 2000:vi).

p. 97
p. 148

During the last 20 years, female-headed families have become an increasing proportion of Canada's low-income population. This trend is also noticeable throughout Europe, in developing countries, and even in three widely differing nations whose legislation on behalf of women is the most advanced in the world: Israel, Sweden, and Russia. In these countries, national health care programs, housing subsidies, and other forms of government assistance cushion the impact of poverty somewhat, yet the feminization of poverty still advances (Abowitz 1986; Stanley 1995; Statistics Sweden 1999).

In 1995, 45 percent of poor people in the United States were living in central cities. These highly visible urban residents are the focus of most governmental efforts to alleviate poverty. Yet, according to many observers, the plight of the urban poor is growing worse, owing to the devastating interplay of inadequate education and limited employment prospects. Traditional employment opportunities in the industrial sector are largely closed to the unskilled poor. Past and present discrimination heightens these problems for low-income urban residents who are Black and Hispanic (Baugher and Lamison-White 1996:vii).

Sociologist William Julius Wilson (1980, 1987, 1989, 1996) and other social scientists have used the term **underclass** to describe the long-term poor who lack training and skills. While estimates vary depending on the definition, in 1990 the underclass comprised more than 3 million adults in the United States, not including the elderly. In central cities, about 49 percent of the underclass are African American, 29 percent are Hispanic, 17 percent are White, and 5 percent are "other" (O'Hare and Curry-White 1992).

Conflict theorists, among others, have expressed alarm at the portion of the nation's population living on this lower rung of the stratification hierarchy and at society's reluctance to address the lack of economic opportunities for these people. Often, portraits of the underclass seem to "blame the victims" for their own plight while ignoring other factors that push people into poverty. In Box 8-1 we consider Wilson's latest research into the persistence of urban poverty.

Poverty, of course, is not a new phenomenon. Yet the concept of the underclass describes a chilling development: individuals and families, whether employed or unemployed, who are beyond the reach of any safety net provided by existing social programs. Moreover, membership in the underclass is not an intermittent condition

Woodlawn, an urban neighborhood on Chicago's South Side, used to boast more than 800 commercial and industrial establishments. Today, some 50 years later, there are about 100 left, mostly barber shops, thrift stores, and small catering businesses. One Woodlawn resident described the changes on returning after an absence of many years: "I was just really appalled. . . . those resources are just gone, completely. . . . And . . . housing, everybody has moved, there are vacant lots everywhere" (Wilson 1996:5). Another South Side resident noted, "Jobs were plentiful in the past. You could walk out of the house and get a job. . . . Now, you can't find anything. . . . The majority they want to work but they can't find work" (p. 36). When opportunities cease to exist, discouragement sets in. An unmarried welfare mother of three put it this way: "Sometimes you can try and then you say 'I'm tired of trying' " (p. 77).

It has been more than 30 years since President Lyndon Johnson launched a series of federal programs known as the "war on poverty." Yet poverty is still with us as we move past the year 2000, and efforts continue to identify its causes and solutions. Sociologist and past president of the American Sociology Association William Julius Wilson has undertaken a major study of poverty using surveys, interviews, and existing census data from 1987 to the present. His Urban Poverty and Family Life Study (UPFLS) has investigated Chicago neighborhoods with poverty rates of at least 20 percent.

Wilson and his colleagues have noted that the jobless increasingly dominate low-income neighborhoods. As time passes, there are fewer and fewer middle-class households. The absence of full-time workers is especially noticeable in African American poor neighborhoods. As a local community becomes more jobless, it is less able to support neighborhood services such as a pharmacy or

hardware store or even a movie theater. As a result, these poverty neighborhoods become increasingly marginal to the economic, social, and cultural life of the city. Wilson sees this as a movement away from what the historian Albert Spear (1967) termed an *institutional ghetto* (where viable social institutions did exist) to the *jobless ghetto* of today.

What drives the persistence of poverty in urban areas? According to Wilson, it is primarily the exodus of decent-paying jobs, especially in the manufacturing sector. In the last several decades, almost all improvements in productivity have been associated with improved technology and skilled workers. Manufacturers no longer rely so much on assembly-line workers, who often enjoyed not only employment but also labor union fringe benefits and some protection from layoffs. A generation ago, the typical ghetto resi-

> **When opportunities cease to exist, discouragement sets in.**

dent might have worked as a machine operator or assembler, but today's resident, if even successful in finding wage labor, is working as a waiter or janitor. Not only have good-paying jobs disappeared from the urban center, but the new jobs that are available tend to be professional, managerial, and technical positions requiring years of postsecondary education.

For women, especially Black women, the situation is even worse. Wilson found that African American women were significantly isolated from people who were working, had some college education, or were married. This makes it even more difficult for people to move beyond the poverty areas into the larger economy and the better employment opportunities

William Julius Wilson, a sociologist at Harvard University, specializes in the study of urban poverty.

found there. Thus, in Wilson's view, it is the economy and the social structure that supports it, not the poor, that need reforming.

Reflecting on inner-city joblessness, Wilson proposes some initiatives, such as national performance standards in education in order to upgrade the minimum level of schooling that the youth in poverty areas receive. His research also shows the clear need for expansion of child care and other family support mechanisms. In addition, he calls for developing metropolitan solutions to bridge the central cities and suburbs. Wilson admits that these approaches are not likely to meet with political acceptance or be easily adopted, but they do underscore the idea that there is no simple solution to reducing poverty in urban areas if viable employment opportunities disappear.

Let's Discuss

1. Has a community you lived in or near seen jobs disappear? What changes took place in the neighborhood as a result?
2. What causes joblessness in urban areas? What can be done to counter it?

Source: Wilson 1996, 1999a.

Poverty hits women particularly hard throughout the world, a situation known as the "feminization of poverty." Shown here are women and children in India.

of society actually *benefit* from the existence of the poor. Gans has identified a number of social, economic, and political functions that the poor perform for society, among them the following:

- The presence of poor people means that society's dirty work—physically dirty or dangerous, dead-end and underpaid, undignified and menial jobs—will be performed at low cost.
- Poverty creates jobs for occupations and professions that "service" the poor. It creates both legal employment (public health experts, welfare caseworkers) and illegal jobs (drug dealers, numbers "runners").
- The identification and punishment of the poor as deviants uphold the legitimacy of conventional social norms p. 167 and "mainstream values" regarding hard work, thrift, and honesty.
- Within a relatively hierarchical society, the existence of poor people guarantees the higher status of the more affluent. As psychologist William Ryan (1976) has noted, affluent people may justify inequality (and gain a measure of satisfaction) by "blaming the victims" of poverty for their disadvantaged condition.
- Because of the lack of political power, the poor often absorb the costs of social change. Under the policy of deinstitutionalization, mental patients released from long-term hospitals have been "dumped" primarily into low-income communities and neighborhoods. Similarly, halfway houses for rehabilitated drug abusers are often rejected by more affluent communities and end up in poorer neighborhoods.

In Gans's view, then, poverty and the poor actually satisfy positive functions for many nonpoor groups in the United States.

Stratification and Life Chances

Max Weber saw class as closely related to people's *life chances*—that is, their opportunities to provide themselves with material goods, positive living conditions, and favorable life experiences (Gerth and Mills 1958). Life chances are reflected in such measures as housing, educa-

but a long-term attribute. The underclass is understandably alienated from the larger society and engages sporadically in illegal behavior. These illegal acts do little to encourage society to address the long-term problems of the underclass.

Analyses of the poor reveal that they are not a static social class. The overall composition of the poor changes continually, with some individuals and families moving above the poverty level after a year or two while others slip below it. Still, there are hundreds of thousands of people who remain in poverty for many years at a time. African Americans are more likely than Whites to be "persistently poor." Over a 20-year period, 12 percent of Whites lived below the poverty line for 5 or more consecutive years, and 5 percent of Whites lived below the poverty line for 7 or more consecutive years. In this same 20-year period, African Americans were twice as likely as Whites to experience long poverty spells. Two studies in 1998 documented that Hispanics are also displaying chronic or long-term periods of poverty. Both Hispanics and Blacks are less likely than Whites to leave the welfare rolls as a result of welfare reform discussed in the policy section of this chapter (J. DeParle 1998; Gottschalk et al. 1994; M. Naifeh 1998).

Explaining Poverty   Why is it that pervasive poverty continues within a nation of such vast wealth? Sociologist Herbert Gans (1995) has applied functionalist analysis to the existence of poverty and argues that various segments

This 1973 poster encouraged consumers to boycott grapes in support of the predominantly Mexican United Farm Workers Union, on strike to protest treatment of migrant farm workers in California. The godlike Aztec figure, shown with the "blood" of grapes dripping through his fingers, suggests the anger striking fieldworkers must have felt over their low pay and substandard living conditions.

Several years ago, at a moment when I was particularly tired of the unstable lifestyle that academic careers sometimes require, I surprised myself and bought a real house. Because the house was in a state other than the one where I was living at the time, I obtained my mortgage by telephone. I am a prudent little squirrel when it comes to things financial, always tucking away stores of nuts for the winter, and so I meet the criteria of a quite good credit risk. My loan was approved almost immediately.

I should repeat that to this point my entire transaction had been conducted by telephone. I should also note that I speak a Received Standard English, regionally marked as Northeastern perhaps, but not easily identifiable as black. With my credit history, my job as a law professor and, no doubt, with my accent, I am not only middle class but apparently match the cultural stereotype of a good white person. It is thus, perhaps, that the loan officer of the bank, whom I had never met, had checked off the box on the fair housing form indicating that I was white.

Race shouldn't matter, I suppose, but it seemed to in this case, so I took a deep breath, crossed out "white" and sent the contract back. That will teach them to presume too much, I thought. A done deal, I assumed. But suddenly the transaction came to a screeching halt. The bank wanted more money, more points, a higher rate of interest. Suddenly I found myself facing great resistance and much more debt. To make a long story short, I threatened to sue under the act in question [the Fair Housing Act], the bank quickly backed down and I procured the loan on the original terms.

What was interesting about all this was that the reason the bank gave for its newfound recalcitrance was not race, heaven forbid. . . . The reason they gave was that property values in that neighborhood were suddenly falling. They wanted more money to buffer themselves against the snappy winds of projected misfortune.

Initially, I was surprised, confused. The house was in a neighborhood that was extremely stable. I am an extremely careful shopper; I had uncovered absolutely nothing to indicate that prices were falling. It took my realtor to make me see the light. "Don't you get it," he sighed. "This is what always happens." And even though I suppose it was a little thick of me, I really hadn't gotten it: For of course, I was the reason the prices were in peril.

The bank's response was driven by demographic data that show that any time black people move into a neighborhood, whites are overwhelmingly likely to move out. In droves. In panic. In concert. Pulling every imaginable resource with them. From school funding to garbage collection to social workers who don't want to work in black neighborhoods. . . .

"I'll bet you'll keep your mouth shut the next time they plug you into the computer as white," laughed a friend when he heard my story. *(Williams 1997)* ∎

Some people believe that racial discrimination is a thing of the past in the United States—that it ended decades ago with the passage of civil rights legislation. But the experience of Patricia J. Williams, a professor of law at Columbia University, is a vivid reminder that race continues to shape the lives of even professional African Americans. Indeed, millions of African Americans, Asian Americans, Hispanic Americans, and many other racial and ethnic minorities have experienced the often bitter contrast between the "American dream" and the grim realities of poverty, prejudice, and discrimination. According to a recent national study, discrimination in mortgage lending actually *increased* between 1995 and 1999 (Turner and Skidmore 1999). Like class, the social definitions of race and ethnicity still affect people's place and status in a stratification system, not only in this country but throughout the world. High incomes and hard-earned professional credentials do not always override racial and ethnic stereotypes or protect those who fit them from the sting of racism.

This chapter focuses primarily on the meaning of race and ethnicity. We begin by identifying the basic characteristics of a minority group and distinguishing between racial and ethnic groups. The next section of the chapter will examine the dynamics of prejudice and discrimination. After considering the functionalist, conflict, and interactionist perspectives on race and ethnicity, we'll take a look at patterns of intergroup relations, particularly in the United States. Finally, the social policy section will explore issues related to immigration worldwide. ∎

Minority, Racial, and Ethnic Groups

Sociologists frequently distinguish between racial and ethnic groups. The term *racial group* is used to describe a group that is set apart from others because of obvious physical differences. Whites, African Americans, and Asian Americans are all considered racial groups in the United States. While race does turn on physical differences, it is the culture of a particular society that constructs and attaches social significance to these differences, as we will see later. Unlike racial groups, an *ethnic group* is set apart from others primarily because of its national origin or distinctive cultural patterns. In the United States, Puerto Ricans, Jews, and Polish Americans are all categorized as ethnic groups.

Minority Groups

A numerical minority is any group that makes up less than half of some larger population. The population of the United States includes thousands of numerical minorities, including television actors, green-eyed people, tax lawyers, and descendants of the Pilgrims who arrived on the *Mayflower*. However, these numerical minorities are not considered to be minorities in the sociological sense; in fact, the number of people in a group does not necessarily determine its status as a social minority (or dominant group). When sociologists define a minority group, they are primarily concerned with the economic and political power, or powerlessness, of that group. A *minority group* is a subordinate group whose members have significantly less control or power over their own lives than the members of a dominant or majority group have over theirs.

Sociologists have identified five basic properties of a minority group—unequal treatment, physical or cultural traits, ascribed status, solidarity, and in-group marriage (Wagley and Harris 1958):

1. Members of a minority group experience unequal treatment as compared to members of a dominant group. For example, the management of an apartment complex may refuse to rent to African Americans, Hispanics, or Jews. Social inequality may be created or maintained by prejudice, discrimination, segregation, or even extermination.

2. Members of a minority group share physical or cultural characteristics that distinguish them from the dominant group. Each society arbitrarily decides which characteristics are most important in defining the groups.

3. Membership in a minority (or dominant) group is not voluntary; people are born into the group. Thus, race and ethnicity are considered *ascribed* statuses. pp. 109–110 ◀

4. Minority group members have a strong sense of group solidarity. William Graham Sumner, writing in 1906, noted that people make distinctions between members of their own group (the *in-group*) and everyone else (the *out-group*). p. 136 ◀ When a group is the object of long-term prejudice and discrimination, the feeling of "us versus them" can and often does become extremely intense.

5. Members of a minority generally marry others from the same group. A member of a dominant group is often unwilling to marry into a supposedly inferior minority. In addition, the minority group's sense of solidarity encourages marriages within the group and discourages marriages to outsiders.

Race

The term *racial group* refers to those minorities (and the corresponding dominant groups) set apart from others by obvious physical differences. But what is an "obvious" physical difference? Each society determines which differences are important while ignoring other characteristics that could serve as a basis for social differentiation. In the United States, we see differences in both skin color and hair color. Yet people learn informally that differences in skin color have a dramatic social and political meaning, while differences in hair color do not.

When observing skin color, people in the United States tend to lump others rather casually into such categories as "Black," "White," and "Asian." More subtle differences in skin color often go unnoticed. However, this is not the case in other societies. Many nations of Central America and South America have color gradients distinguishing people on a continuum from light to dark skin color. Brazil has approximately 40 color groupings, while in other countries people may be described as "Mestizo Hondurans," "Mulatto Colombians," or "African Panamanians." What we see as "obvious" differences, then, are subject to each society's social definitions.

The largest racial minorities in the United States are African Americans (or Blacks), Native Americans (or American Indians), and Asian Americans (Japanese Americans, Chinese Americans, and other Asian peoples). Figure 9-1 provides information about the population of racial and ethnic groups in the United States over the past five centuries.

Biological Significance of Race

Viewed from a biological perspective, the term *race* would refer to a genetically iso-

lated group with distinctive gene frequencies. But it is impossible to scientifically define or identify such a group. Contrary to popular belief, there are no "pure races." Nor are there physical traits—whether skin color or baldness—that can be used to describe one group to the exclusion of all others. If scientists examine a smear of human blood under a microscope, they cannot tell whether it came from a Chinese or a Navajo, a Hawaiian or an African American. There is, in fact, more genetic variation *within* races than across them.

FIGURE 9-1

Racial and Ethnic Groups in the United States, 1500–2100 (Projected)

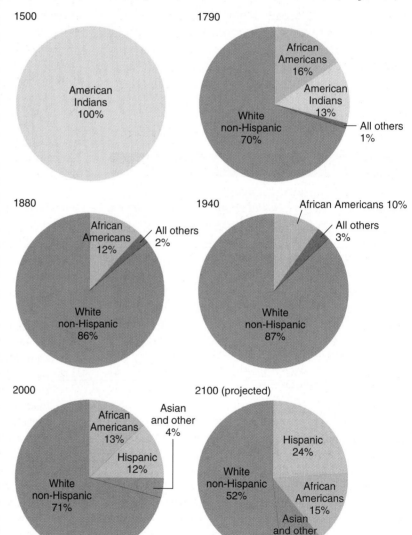

Sources: Author's estimate; Bureau of the Census 1975, 2000c; Thornton 1987.

The racial and ethnic composition of what is today the United States has been undergoing change not just for the last 50 years, but for the last 500. Five centuries ago the land was populated only by indigenous Native Americans.

Migration, exploration, and invasion have led to inter-mingling of races. Scientific investigations indicate that the percentage of North American Blacks with White ancestry ranges from 20 percent to as much as 75 percent. Recent DNA findings suggest that some Blacks today can even claim Thomas Jefferson as their ancestor. Such statistics undermine a fundamental assumption of life in the United States: that we can accurately categorize individuals as "Black" or "White" (Herskovits 1930; D. Roberts 1975).

Some people would like to find biological explanations to help social scientists understand why certain peoples of the world have come to dominate others (see the discussion of sociobiology in Chapter 4). Given the absence of pure racial groups, there can be no satisfactory biological answers for such social and political questions.

p. 84

Social Construction of Race

In the southern part of the United States, it was known as the "one-drop rule." If a person had even a single drop of "Black blood," that person was defined and viewed as Black, even if he or she *appeared* to be White. Clearly, race had social significance in the South, enough so that White legislators established official standards about who was "Black" and "White."

The one-drop rule was a vivid example of the *social construction of race*—the process by which people come to define a group as a race based in part on physical characteristics, but also on historical, cultural, and economic factors. It is an ongoing process subject to some debate, especially in a diverse society like the United States, where each year increasing numbers of children are born to parents of different racial backgrounds. Census Bureau estimates indicate that about 7 percent of the U.S. population could claim multiple racial ancestry in 1999; by the year 2030 that percentage of the population is expected to climb to 21 percent. Among Asian Americans the percentage of people claiming mixed ancestry is expected to reach 36 percent; among Native Americans, 89 percent; among Whites, 21 percent; among Blacks, 14 percent; and among Hispanics, 45 percent (Edmonston and Passel 1999).

Still, mixed racial ancestry is an identity that is not clearly defined in a society that literally thinks in "black" and "white" terms. Facing this social reality, the U.S. Census Bureau considered adding a "biracial" category to Census 2000. But trial studies showed that people were confused by this "new" term, and relatively few chose it. As a compromise, the Census 2000 for the first time allowed people to check off as many racial categories as they wish, so that one could, for example, check off "White," "American Indian," *and* "African American." Sociologists and others are eagerly awaiting the results of this oppor-tunity for people to individually express their blended racial identity.

A dominant or majority group has the power not only to define itself legally but to define a society's values. Sociologist William I. Thomas (1923), an early critic of theories of racial and gender differences, saw that the "definition of the situation" could mold the personality of the individual. To put it another way, Thomas, writing from the interactionist perspective, observed that people respond not only to the objective features of a situation or person but also to the *meaning* that situation or person has for them. Thus, we can create false images or stereotypes that become real in their consequences. *Stereotypes* are unreliable generalizations about all members of a group that do not recognize individual differences within the group.

In the last 30 years, critics have pointed out the power of the mass media to perpetuate false racial and ethnic stereotypes. Television is a prime example: Almost all the leading dramatic roles are cast as Whites, even in urban-based programs like *Friends.* Blacks tend to be featured mainly in crime-based dramas. (See Box 9-2 on pp. 240–241 for further discussion of the distorted picture of United States society presented on prime-time television programs.)

Self-Fulfilling Prophecy

In certain situations, we may respond to stereotypes in such a way that false definitions end up being accurate. In this phenomenon, called the *self-fulfilling prophecy,* a person or group that is described as having particular characteristics begins to display those very traits. When teachers and counselors tell a bright child from a working-class family that he would make a good carpenter or mechanic, for instance, they may discourage him from thinking of college or a profession. Seeing himself through their eyes as a tradesperson, he may well grow up to become a blue-collar worker. In assessing the impact of self-fulfilling prophecies, we can apply labeling theory, which emphasizes how a person comes to be labeled as deviant and even to accept a self-image of deviance.

p. 172

Self-fulfilling prophecies can be especially devastating for minority groups (see Figure 9-2). The dominant group in a society believes that subordinate group members lack the ability to perform in important and lucrative positions. So it denies them the training needed to become scientists, executives, or physicians, effectively locking the subordinate group into society's inferior jobs. The false definition has become real: in terms of employment, the minority has become inferior because it was originally defined as inferior and was prevented from achieving equality.

Because of this vicious circle, talented people from

FIGURE 9-2

The Self-Fulfilling Prophecy

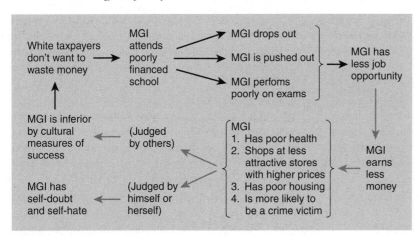

This figure shows the self-validating effects of definitions made by the dominant group. A minority group individual (MGI) attends a poorly financed school and is left unequipped to perform jobs that offer high status and high pay. He or she then gets a low-paying job and must settle for a lifestyle far short of society's standards. Since the person shares these standards, he or she may begin to feel self-doubt and self-hatred. Recent research, however, called this last phase of the cycle into question.

Note: MGI stands for "minority group individual." Arrows represent direction of negative cumulative effect.
Source: Schaefer 2000b.

minority groups may come to see the worlds of entertainment and professional sports as their only hope for achieving wealth and fame. It is no accident that successive waves of Irish, Jewish, Italian, Black, and Hispanic performers and athletes have made their mark on our society. Unfortunately, these very successes may convince the dominant group that its original stereotypes are valid—that these are the *only* areas of society in which minorities can excel. Furthermore, athletics and the arts are well-known in our society as highly competitive arenas. For every Gloria Estefan, Sammy Sosa, or Oprah Winfrey who "makes it," many, many more will end up disappointed (Allport 1979; Merton 1968).

Sociologist Harry Edwards (1984:9–13) agrees that the self-fulfilling prophecy of "innate Black athletic superiority" can have damaging consequences. Edwards points out that although this perception of athletic prowess may channel many African Americans into sports, only about 2,500 of them, at best, currently make a living in professional sports. In his view, Blacks should no longer put football playbooks ahead of textbooks, and the Black community should abandon its "blind belief in sport as an extraordinary route to social and economic salvation" (see also Gates 1991).

African Americans and other minorities do not always passively accept harmful stereotypes and self-fulfilling prophecies. In the 1960s and 1970s, many subordinate minorities in the United States rejected traditional definitions and replaced them with feelings of pride, power, and strength. "Black is beautiful" and "Red power" movements among Blacks and Native Americans were efforts to take control of their own lives and self-images. However, although a minority can make a determined effort to redefine a situation and resist stereotypes, the definition that remains most important is the one used by a society's powerful groups. In this sense, the historic White, Anglo-Saxon, Protestant norms of the United States still shape the definitions and stereotypes of racial and ethnic minorities.

Ethnicity

An ethnic group, unlike a racial group, is set apart from others because of its national origin or distinctive cultural patterns. Among the ethnic groups in the United States are peoples with a Spanish-speaking background, referred to collectively as *Hispanics* or *Latinos,* such as Puerto Ricans, Mexican Americans, Cuban Americans, and other Latin Americans. Other ethnic groups in this country include Jewish, Irish, Italian, and Norwegian Americans. While these groupings are convenient, they serve to obscure differences *within* these ethnic categories (as in the case of Hispanics) as well as to overlook the mixed ancestry of so many ethnic people in the United States.

The distinction between racial and ethnic minorities is not always clear-cut. Some members of racial minorities, such as Asian Americans, may have significant cultural differences from other groups. At the same time, certain ethnic minorities, such as Hispanics, may have obvious physical differences that set them apart from other residents of the United States.

Despite categorization problems, sociologists continue to feel that the distinction between racial groups and ethnic groups is socially significant. That is because in most societies, including the United States, physical differences tend to be more visible than ethnic differences.

West Indians show pride in their heritage at the annual West Indian Day parade in New York City. Many racial and ethnic minorities hold parades and celebrations to preserve and display their unique culture.

of prejudice. Prejudice tends to perpetuate false definitions of individuals and groups.

Sometimes prejudice results from *ethnocentrism*—the tendency to assume that one's culture and way of life represent the norm or are superior to all others. Ethnocentric people judge other cultures by the standards of their own group, which leads quite easily to prejudice against cultures viewed as inferior. p. 69

One important and widespread form of prejudice is *racism,* the belief that one race is supreme and all others are innately inferior. When racism prevails in a society, members of subordinate groups generally experience prejudice, discrimination, and exploitation. In 1990, as concern mounted about racist attacks in the United States, Congress passed the Hate Crimes Statistics Act. This law directs the Department of Justice to gather data on crimes motivated by the victim's race, religion, ethnicity, or sexual orientation.

In 1998 a total of 9,235 hate crimes were reported to authorities. Some 58 percent of these crimes against persons involved racial bias, while 16 percent reflected bias based on sexual orientation; 16 percent, religious bias; and 10 percent, ethnic bias. As Figure 9-3 shows, laws against such crimes vary from state to state (Department of Justice 1999a:58–59).

A particularly horrifying hate crime made the front pages in 1998: In Jasper, Texas, three White men with possible ties to race-hate groups tied up a Black man, beat him with chains, and then dragged him behind their truck until his body was dismembered. Numerous groups in the United States have been victims of hate crimes as well as generalized prejudice. In Box 9-1, we examine prejudice against Arab Americans and Muslims living in the United States.

The activity of organized hate groups appears to be increasing, both in reality and in virtual reality. While only a few hundred such groups may exist, there were at least 2,000 websites advocating racial hatred on the Internet in 1999. Particularly troubling were sites disguised as video games for young people, or as "educational sites" about crusaders against prejudice, like Martin Luther King, Jr. The technology of the Internet has allowed race-hate groups to expand far beyond their traditional southern base to reach millions (J. Sandberg 1999).

Partly as a result of this fact, stratification along racial lines is more resistant to change than stratification along ethnic lines. Members of an ethnic minority sometimes can become, over time, indistinguishable from the majority—although this process may take generations and may never include all members of the group. By contrast, members of a racial minority find it much more difficult to blend in with the larger society and to gain acceptance from the majority.

Prejudice and Discrimination

In recent years, college campuses across the United States have been the scene of bias-related incidents. Student-run newspapers and radio stations have ridiculed racial and ethnic minorities; threatening literature has been stuffed under the doors of minority students; graffiti endorsing the views of White supremacist organizations such as the Ku Klux Klan have been scrawled on university walls. In some cases, there have even been violent clashes between groups of White and Black students (Bunzel 1992; Schaefer 2000b).

Prejudice is a negative attitude toward an entire category of people, often an ethnic or racial minority. If you resent your roommate because he or she is sloppy, you are not necessarily guilty of prejudice. However, if you immediately stereotype your roommate on the basis of such characteristics as race, ethnicity, or religion, that is a form

FIGURE 9-3

Hate Crime Laws in the United States

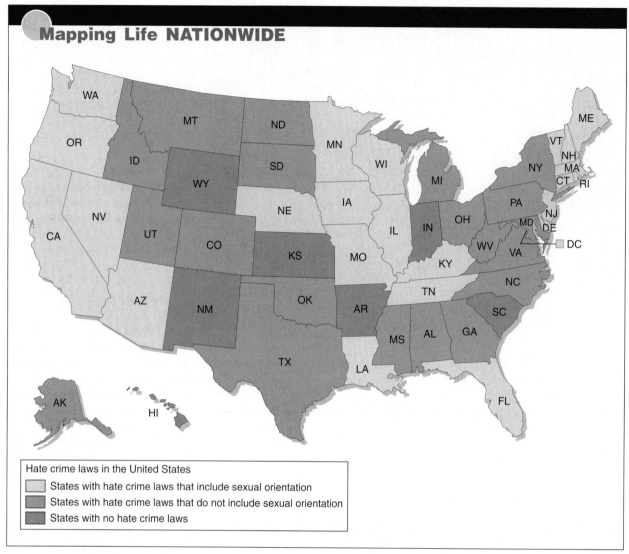

Source: Human Rights Campaign 2000.

Discriminatory Behavior

John and Glenn are alike in almost every way—about the same age, they are both Big Ten college graduates with good jobs. But they find they have different experiences in everyday routines, such as walking into a store. John gets instant attention from the same sales staff that ignores Glenn, even though he has been waiting five minutes. When Glenn is locked out of his car, passersby ignore him, while John receives many offers of help. At an employment agency, Glenn is lectured on laziness and told he will be monitored "real close"; John is encouraged.

What accounts for these differences in the everyday

life experiences of two men? Very simply, John is White and Glenn is Black. The two were part of an experiment, conducted by the television newsmagazine *Primetime Live,* to assess the impact of race on the day-to-day lives of residents in a typical U.S. city. Over a three-week period reporters closely monitored the two men, who had been trained to present themselves in an identical manner. Not once or twice, but "every single day," said program host Diane Sawyer, John and Glenn were treated differently (ABC News 1992).

Prejudice often leads to ***discrimination,*** the denial of opportunities and equal rights to individuals and groups based on some type of arbitrary bias. Say that a White

A sign in a shop window in Los Angeles advertises the proprietor's prejudice against immigrants. According to the functionalist perspective, open displays of racial and ethnic bigotry are an attempt to maintain the power of the dominant group in society.

accept low wages, capitalists can restrict the wages of *all* members of the proletariat. Workers from the dominant group who demand higher wages can always be replaced by minorities who have no choice but to accept low-paying jobs.

The conflict view of race relations seems persuasive in a number of instances. Japanese Americans were the object of little prejudice until they began to enter jobs that brought them into competition with Whites. The movement to keep Chinese immigrants out of the United States became most fervent during the latter half of the nineteenth century, when Chinese and Whites fought over dwindling work opportunities. Both the enslavement of Blacks and the extermination and removal westward of Native Americans were, to a significant extent, economically motivated.

However, the exploitation theory is too limited to explain prejudice in its many forms. Not all minority groups have been economically exploited to the same extent. In addition, many groups (such as the Quakers and the Mormons) have been victimized by prejudice for other than economic reasons. Still, as Gordon Allport (1979:210) concludes, the exploitation theory correctly "points a sure

finger at one of the factors involved in prejudice, . . . rationalized self-interest of the upper classes."

Interactionist Perspective

A Hispanic woman is transferred from a job on an assembly line to a similar position working next to a White man. At first, the White man is patronizing, assuming that she must be incompetent. She is cold and resentful; even when she needs assistance, she refuses to admit it. After a week, the growing tension between the two leads to a bitter quarrel. Yet, over time, each slowly comes to appreciate the other's strengths and talents. A year after they begin working together, these two workers become respectful friends. This is an example of what interactionists call the *contact hypothesis* in action.

The **contact hypothesis** states that interracial contact between people of equal status in cooperative circumstances will cause them to become less prejudiced and to abandon previous stereotypes. People begin to see one another as individuals and discard the broad generalizations characteristic of stereotyping. Note the factors of *equal status* and *cooperative circumstances*. In the example above, if the two workers had been competing for one vacancy as a supervisor, the racial hostility between them might have worsened (Allport 1979; Schaefer 2000b; Sigelman et al. 1996).

As Latinos and other minorities slowly gain access to better-paying and more responsible jobs in the United States, the contact hypothesis may take on even greater significance. The trend in our society is toward increasing contact between individuals from dominant and subordinate groups. This may be one way of eliminating—or at least reducing—racial and ethnic stereotyping and prejudice. Another may be the establishment of interracial coalitions, an idea suggested by sociologist William Julius Wilson (1999b). To work, such coalitions would obviously need to be built on an equal role for all members.

Contact between individuals occurs on the micro-level. We turn now to a consideration of intergroup relations on a macro-level.

Patterns of Intergroup Relations

Racial and ethnic groups can relate to one another in a wide variety of ways, ranging from friendships and intermarriages to genocide, from behaviors that require mutual approval to behaviors imposed by the dominant group.

One devastating pattern of intergroup relations is **genocide**—the deliberate, systematic killing of an entire people or nation. This term describes the killing of 1 million Armenians by Turkey beginning in 1915 (Melson 1986). It is most commonly applied to Nazi Germany's extermination of 6 million European Jews, as well as gays, lesbians, and the Romani people ("Gypsies"), during World War II. The term *genocide* is also appropriate in describing the United States' policies toward Native Americans in the nineteenth century. In 1800, the Native American (or American Indian) population of the United States was about 600,000; by 1850, it had been reduced to 250,000 through warfare with the cavalry, disease, and forced relocation to inhospitable environments.

The *expulsion* of a people is another extreme means of acting out racial or ethnic prejudice. In 1979, Vietnam expelled nearly 1 million ethnic Chinese, partly as a result of centuries of hostility between Vietnam and neighboring China. In a more recent example of expulsion (which had aspects of genocide), Serbian forces began a program of "ethnic cleansing" in 1991 in the newly independent states of Bosnia and Herzegovina. Throughout the former nation of Yugoslavia, the Serbs drove more than 1 million Croats and Muslims from their homes. Some were tortured and killed, others abused and terrorized, in an attempt to "purify" the land for the remaining ethnic Serbs. In 1999, Serbs were again the focus of worldwide con-

Ethnic Albanian women mourn the death of a man killed by Serbs in the province of Kosovo. Such "ethnic cleansings" have met with worldwide condemnation.

demnation as they sought to "cleanse" the province of Kosovo of ethnic Albanians.

Genocide and expulsion are extreme behaviors. More typical intergroup relations as they occur in North America and throughout the world follow four identifiable patterns: (1) amalgamation, (2) assimilation, (3) segregation, and (4) pluralism. Each pattern defines the dominant group's actions and the minority group's responses. Intergroup relations are rarely restricted to only one of the four patterns, although invariably one does tend to dominate. Therefore, think of these patterns primarily as ideal types.

Amalgamation

Amalgamation happens when a majority group and a minority group combine to form a new group. Through intermarriage over several generations, various groups in the society combine to form a new group. This can be expressed as A + B + C → D, where A, B, and C represent different groups present in a society, and D signifies the end result, a unique cultural-racial group unlike any of the initial groups (Newman 1973).

The belief in the United States as a "melting pot" became very compelling in the first part of the twentieth century, particularly since that image suggested that the nation had an almost divine mission to amalgamate various groups into one people. However, in actuality many residents were not willing to have Native Americans, Jews, African Americans, Asian Americans, and Irish Roman Catholics as a part of the melting pot. Therefore, this pattern does not adequately describe dominant–subordinate relations existing in the United States.

Assimilation

Many Hindus in India complain about Indian citizens who copy the traditions and customs of the British. In Australia, Aborigines who have become part of the domi-

"Ho, ho, ho" apparently works in any language. As Japanese Americans assimilated the norms and values of mainstream U.S. culture, they created their own "Shogun Santa." This one can be found in the Little Tokyo neighborhood of Los Angeles.

nant society refuse to acknowledge their darker-skinned grandparents on the street. In the United States, some Italian Americans, Polish Americans, Hispanics, and Jews have changed their ethnic-sounding family names to names typically found among White, Protestant families.

Assimilation is the process by which a person forsakes his or her own cultural tradition to become part of a different culture. Generally, it is practiced by a minority group member who wants to conform to the standards of the dominant group. Assimilation can be described as an ideology in which A + B + C → A. The majority A dominates in such a way that members of minorities B and C imitate A and attempt to become indistinguishable from the dominant group (Newman 1973).

Assimilation can strike at the very roots of a person's identity as he or she seeks to blend in with the dominant group. Alphonso D'Abuzzo, for example, changed his name to Alan Alda. This process is not unique to the United States: the British actress Joyce Frankenberg changed her name to Jane Seymour. Name changes, switches in religious affiliation, and dropping of native languages can obscure one's roots and heritage. Moreover, assimilation does not necessarily bring acceptance for the minority group individual. A Chinese American may speak flawless English, attend a Protestant church faithfully, and know the names of all members of the Baseball Hall of Fame. Yet he or she is still *seen* as different and may therefore be rejected as a business associate, a neighbor, or a marriage partner.

Segregation

Separate schools, separate seating sections on buses and in restaurants, separate washrooms, even separate drinking fountains—these were all part of the lives of African Americans in the South when segregation ruled earlier in the twentieth century. ***Segregation*** refers to the physical separation of two groups of people in terms of residence, workplace, and social events. Generally, a dominant group imposes it on a minority group. Segregation is rarely complete, however. Intergroup contact inevitably occurs even in the most segregated societies. Elijah Anderson's (1990, 1999) participant observation research reflects the social tensions that arise from such strained circumstances. pp. 28—29

From 1948 (when it received its independence) to 1990, the Republic of South Africa severely restricted the movement of Blacks and other non-Whites by means of a wide-ranging system of segregation known as ***apartheid.*** Apartheid even included the creation of homelands where Blacks were expected to live. However, decades of local resistance to apartheid, combined with international pressure, led to marked political changes in the 1990s. In

1994, a prominent Black activist, Nelson Mandela, was elected as South Africa's president, the first election in which Blacks (the majority of the nation's population) were allowed to vote. Mandela had spent almost 28 years in South African prisons for his anti-apartheid activities. His election was widely viewed as the final blow to South Africa's oppressive policy of apartheid.

Until civil rights laws came into play in the latter half of this century, segregation was the rule in many parts of the United States. Housing practices still often force subordinate racial and ethnic groups into certain neighborhoods, usually undesirable ones. While members of a minority group may voluntarily seek to separate themselves from the dominant majority, this is not the primary factor contributing to segregation. The central causes of residential segregation in the United States appear to be the prejudices of Whites and the resulting discriminatory practices in the housing and lending markets. Data consistently show that Blacks, Hispanics, and (to a somewhat lesser extent) Asians face segregation in the nation's metropolitan areas. Such housing segregation is evident around the world: Studies in Sweden, for example, document that migrants from Chile, Greece, and Turkey are confined to segregated areas of Swedish cities (Andersson-Brolin 1988; Doig et al. 1993).

Pluralism

In a pluralistic society, a subordinate group does not have to forsake its lifestyle and traditions. **Pluralism** is based on mutual respect among various groups in a society for one another's cultures. It allows a minority group to express its own culture and still to participate without prejudice in the larger society. Earlier, we described amalgamation as A + B + C → D, and assimilation as A + B + C → A. Using this same approach, we can conceive of pluralism as A + B + C → A + B + C. All the groups are able to coexist in the same society (Newman 1973).

In the United States, pluralism is more of an ideal than a reality. There are distinct instances of pluralism: the ethnic neighborhoods in major cities, such as Koreatown, Little Tokyo, Andersonville (Swedish Americans), and Spanish Harlem. Yet there are also limits to such cultural freedom. In order to survive, a society must promote a certain consensus among its members regarding basic ideals, values, and beliefs. Thus, if a Romanian migrating to the United States wants to move up the occupational ladder, he or she cannot avoid learning the English language.

Switzerland exemplifies a modern pluralistic state. The absence both of a national language and of a dominant religious faith leads to a tolerance for cultural diversity. In addition, various political devices safeguard the interests of ethnic groups in a way that has no parallel in the United States. By contrast, Great Britain has found it difficult to achieve cultural pluralism in a multiracial society. East Indians, Pakistanis, and Blacks from the Caribbean and Africa are experiencing prejudice and discrimination within the dominant White British society. There is pressure to cut off all Asian and Black immigration and a few in Britain even call for expelling those non-Whites currently living there (see the social policy section in this chapter).

Race and Ethnicity in the United States

Few societies have a more diverse population than the United States; the nation is truly a multiracial, multiethnic society. Of course, this has not always been the case. The population of what is now the United States has changed dramatically since the arrival of European settlers in the 1600s, as Figure 9-1 (p. 226) showed. Immigration, colonialism, and in the case of Blacks, slavery determined the racial and ethnic makeup of our present-day society. (See Figure 9-4 for where various racial and ethnic minorities are concentrated in the United States.)

The diversity of the United States is evident in statistics on the general population, especially in the urban centers. But one would not necessarily know that Americans are a diverse people from watching television. In 1977 the U.S. Civil Rights Commission reported that minorities were underrepresented on TV, and tended to be cast in crime-based series set in urban areas. Remarkably, a generation later the situation has not changed much. A token African American doctor or ethnic family may appear in the afternoon soap operas, but nighttime TV programs are overwhelmingly White (see Box 9-2). In the following sections we will attempt to paint a truer picture of United States society than the one seen on television.

Racial Groups

The largest racial minorities in the United States include African Americans, Native Americans, and Asian Americans.

African Americans

"I am an invisible man," wrote Black author Ralph Ellison in his novel *Invisible Man* (1952:3). "I am a man of substance, of flesh and bone, fiber and liquids—and I might even be said to possess a mind. I am invisible, understand, simply because people refuse to see me."

Over four decades later, many African Americans still feel invisible. Despite their large numbers, they have long been treated as second-class citizens. Currently, by the standards of the federal government, more than 1 out of

FIGURE 9-4

Four Images of Diversity

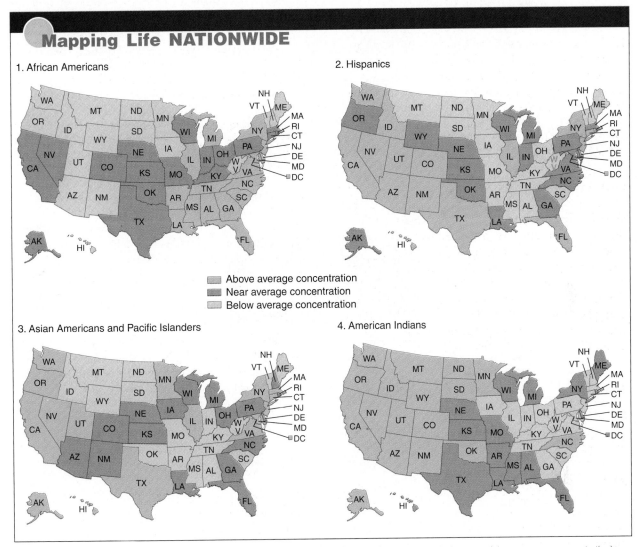

Note: The 50 states and District of Columbia are divided into the 17 with the highest proportion of the particular group (above average concentration) as of 1999 estimates released in 2000 and the 17 with the lowest proportion (below average concentration).

Source: Developed by author based on Bureau of the Census 2000d.

every 4 Blacks—as opposed to 1 out of every 11 Whites—is poor.

Contemporary institutional discrimination and individual prejudice against African Americans are rooted in the history of slavery in the United States. While many other subordinate groups have had little wealth and income, as sociologist W. E. B. Du Bois (1909) and others have noted, enslaved Blacks were in an even more oppressive situation because, by law, they could not own property and could not pass on the benefits of their labor to their children. In bondage, the Africans were forced to assimilate and were stripped of much of their African tribal heritage. Yet the destruction of African cultures was not complete; some aspects survived in oral literature, religious customs, and music. Black resistance to slavery included many slave revolts, such as those led by Denmark Vesey in South Carolina in 1822 and Nat Turner in Virginia in 1831. Still, most Blacks remained subject to the arbitrary and often cruel actions of their White owners (Herskovits 1941, 1943).

The end of the Civil War did not bring genuine freedom and equality for Blacks. The Southern states passed "Jim Crow" laws to enforce official segregation, and they were upheld as constitutional by the Supreme Court in

9-2 The Color of Network TV

In late spring 1999, as the television networks prepared their schedules for the 1999–2000 season, an article in the *Los Angeles Times* hit the broadcasting industry like a bombshell. In every new prime-time series—26 of them—set to debut in the coming season, the *Times* reported, all the leading characters, as well as the vast majority of the supporting casts, would be White. The public response was immediate. The NAACP, alarmed by the "virtual whitewash in programming," threatened a lawsuit, and a national coalition of Latino groups urged viewers to boycott network TV (Braxton 1999:F10).

Incredibly, network executives seemed surprised by the news of the all-White season. It wasn't deliberate, explained director–actor Edward James Olmos; network executives simply weren't aware of the problem. In the aftermath of the article's publication, producers, writers, executives, and advertisers blamed one another for the oversight. Television programming was dictated by advertisers, a former executive claimed; if advertisers said they wanted blatantly biased programming, the networks would provide it. Jery Isenberg, chairman of the Caucus for Producers, Writers & Directors, blamed the networks, saying that writers would produce a series about three-headed Martians if the networks told them to.

Beyond these lame excuses, real reasons can be found for the departure from the diversity of past shows and seasons. In recent years the rise of both cable TV and the Internet has fragmented the broadcast entertainment market, siphoning viewers away from the general-audience sitcoms and dra-

> The NAACP, alarmed by the "virtual whitewash in programming," threatened a lawsuit.

mas of the past. With the proliferation of cable channels such as Black Entertainment Television (BET) and the Spanish-language Univision, and websites that cater to every imaginable taste, there no longer seems a need for broadly popular series such as *The Cosby Show*, whose tone and content appealed to Whites as well as Blacks in a way the newer series do not. The result of these sweeping technological changes has been a sharp divergence in viewer preferences. In current lists of the top 10 network shows among Blacks, Whites, and Latinos, the only show that appeals to all three groups is *Monday Night Football*.

While BET and Univision were grabbing minority audiences and offering new outlets for minority talent, network executives and writers remained overwhelmingly White. Not surprisingly, these mainstream writers and producers, most of whom live far from ethnically and racially diverse inner-city neighborhoods, tend to write and prefer stories about people like themselves. Marc Hirschfeld, an NBC executive, claims some White producers have told him they don't know how to write for Black characters. Steven Bochco, producer of *NYPD Blue*, is a rare exception. Bochco's series, *City of Angels*, has a cast that is mostly non-White, like the people Bochco grew up with in an inner-city neighborhood.

The networks' first response to the bad press was to move some token Black or ethnic characters into the casts of the all-White series set for the fall season. By January 2000, 13 percent of prime-time characters were African American and another 3 percent were from other minority groups. But in the minds of many

Sources: Braxton 1999; Hoffman 1997; Lowry et al. 1999; Wood 2000.

1896. In addition, Blacks faced the danger of lynching campaigns, often led by the Ku Klux Klan, during the late nineteenth and early twentieth centuries. From a conflict perspective, Whites maintained their dominance formally through legalized segregation and informally by means of vigilante terror and violence (Franklin and Moss 2000).

A turning point in the struggle for Black equality came in 1954 with the unanimous Supreme Court decision in the case of *Brown v. Board of Education of Topeka, Kansas.* The Court outlawed segregation of public school students, ruling that "separate educational facilities are inherently unequal." In the wake of the *Brown* decision, there was a surge of activism on behalf of Black civil rights, including boycotts of segregated bus companies and sit-ins at restaurants and lunch counters that refused to serve Blacks.

During the decade of the 1960s, a vast civil rights movement emerged, with many competing factions and strategies for change. The Southern Christian Leadership Conference (SCLC), founded by Dr. Martin Luther King, Jr., used nonviolent civil disobedience to oppose segregation. The National Association for the Advancement of Colored People (NAACP) favored use of the courts to press for equality for African Americans. But many younger Black leaders, most notably Malcolm X, turned toward an ideology of Black power. Proponents of **Black power** rejected the goal of assimilation into White, middle-class society. They defended the beauty and dig-

industry professionals, that measure fell short of the mark. Jesse L. Martin, an African American actor featured on *Ally McBeal*, told a reporter that in his opinion, adding a few Black faces to an all-White cast would not be enough. Sharon D. Johnson of the Writers Guild of America agreed. She doubted the networks would take the more meaningful step of hiring Black writers, though, because writers simply aren't as visible to the public as actors.

In the long run, industry observers believe, the networks will need to integrate their ranks before they achieve true diversity in programming. Adonis Hoffman, director of the Corporate Policy Institute, has urged network executives to throw open their studios and boardrooms to minorities. Hoffman thinks such a move would empower Black writers and producers to present a true-to-life portrait of African Americans. There are some signs of agreement from the networks. According to Doug Herzog, president of Fox Entertainment, incorporating diversity into network programming requires a well-conceived long-term strategy. Real progress, he says, means incorporating diversity from within.

Why should it matter that minority

groups aren't visible on network television, if they are well represented on BET and Univision? The answer is that if they are not, Whites as well as minorities will see a distorted picture of their society every time they turn on network TV. In Hoffman's words, "African Americans, Latinos and Asians, while portrayed as such, are not merely walk-ons in our society—they are woven into the fabric of what has made this country great." (Hoffman 1997:M6)

Let's Discuss

1. Do you watch network TV? If so, how well do you think it reflects the diversity of American society?
2. Have you seen a movie or TV show recently that portrayed members of a minority group in a sensitive and realistic way—as real people rather than stereotypes or token walk-ons? If so, describe the show.

nity of Black and African cultures and supported the creation of Black-controlled political and economic institutions (Ture and Hamilton 1992).

Despite numerous courageous actions to achieve Black civil rights, Black and White citizens are still separate, still unequal. From birth to death, Blacks suffer in pp. 202–05 terms of their life chances. Life remains difficult for millions of poor Blacks, who must attempt to survive in ghetto areas shattered by high unemployment and abandoned housing. The economic position of Blacks is shown in Table 9-1. At the close of the century, the median household income of Blacks was only 62 percent that of Whites, and the unemployment rate among Blacks was more than twice that of Whites.

There have been economic gains for *some* African Americans—especially middle-class men and women—over the last 40 years. For example, data compiled by the Department of Labor show that the number of African Americans in management areas of the labor market increased nationally from 2.4 percent of the total in 1958 to 7.2 percent in 1998. Yet Blacks still represent only 5 percent or less of all physicians, engineers, scientists, lawyers, judges, and marketing managers. In another area important for developing role models, African Americans and Hispanics together account for only 12 percent of all editors and reporters in the United States (Bureau of the Census 1999a:424).

In many respects, the civil rights movement of the

Table 9-1	Relative Economic Positions of African Americans and Whites, 1999–2000	
Characteristic	**African Americans**	**Whites**
Four-year college education, people 25 and over	14.2%	30.6%
Median family income	$31,778	$51,224
Unemployment rate	7.3%	3.4%
People below the poverty line	23.6%	7.7%

Note: Data, where available, are for White non-Hispanics.

Sources: Bureau of the Census 2000d:B8; Bureau of Labor Statistics 2000; Dalaker and Proctor 2000:vi; McKinnon et al. 2000.

1960s left institutionalized discrimination against African Americans untouched. Consequently, in the 1970s and 1980s, Black leaders worked to mobilize African American political power as a force for social change. Between 1970 and 1997, the number of African American elected officials increased by almost sixfold. Even so, Blacks remain significantly *underrepresented*. This underrepresentation is especially distressing in view of the fact that sociologist W. E. B. Du Bois observed over 90 years ago that Blacks could not expect to achieve equal social and economic opportunities without first gaining political rights (Bureau of the Census 1999a:298; Green and Driver 1978).

Native Americans

There are approximately 2 million Native Americans. They represent a diverse array of cultures, distinguishable by language, family organization, religion, and livelihood. The outsiders who came to the United States—European settlers and their descendants—came to know the native people as "American Indians." By the time the Bureau of Indian Affairs (BIA) was organized as part of the *War* Department in 1824, Indian–White relations had already included three centuries of mutual misunderstanding. Many bloody wars during the nineteenth century wiped out a significant part of the nation's Indian population. By the end of the nineteenth century, schools for Indians operated by the BIA or church missions prohibited the practice of Native American cultures. Yet, at the same time, such schools did little to make the children effective competitors in White society.

Today, life remains difficult for members of the 554 tribal groups in the United States, whether they live in cities or on reservations. For example, one Native American teenager in six has attempted suicide—a rate four times higher than the rate for other teenagers. Traditionally, some Native Americans chose to assimilate and abandon all vestiges of their tribal cultures to escape certain forms of prejudice. However, by the 1990s, an increasing number of people in the United States were openly claiming an identity as Native American. Since 1960, the federal government's count of Native Americans has tripled, to an estimated 2.4 million. According to the 1990 census, there has been a 16 percent increase in Native Americans during the 1990s. Demographers believe that more and more Native Americans who previously concealed their identity are no longer pretending to be White (Bureau of the Census 1999a).

The introduction of gambling on Indian reservations threatens to become still another battleground between Native Americans and the dominant White society. By 1998, one-third of all tribes were operating off-track betting, casino tables for such games as blackjack and roulette, slot machines, high-stakes bingo, sports betting,

Like many racial and ethnic minority groups in the United States, Native Americans keep certain aspects of their traditional culture (such as the cradle board) while adopting some customs and practices from the dominant culture (such as the stroller).

world's largest concentration of Jews. Like the Japanese, many Jewish immigrants came to this country and became white-collar professionals in spite of prejudice and discrimination.

Anti-Semitism—that is, anti-Jewish prejudice—in the United States has often been vicious, although rarely so widespread and never so formalized as in Europe. In many cases, Jews have been used as scapegoats for other people's failures. This was clearly indicated in a study of World War II veterans. The researchers found that men who had experienced downward mobility (for example, job failure) were more likely to blame their setbacks on Jewish Americans than on their own shortcomings (Bettelheim and Janowitz 1964).

Jews have not achieved equality in the United States. Despite high levels of education and professional training, they are still conspicuously absent from the top management of large corporations (except for the few firms founded by Jews). Until the late 1960s, many prestigious universities maintained restrictive quotas that limited Jewish enrollment. Private social clubs and fraternal groups frequently limit membership to gentiles (non-Jews), a practice upheld by the Supreme Court in the 1964 case of *Bell v. Maryland*.

The Anti-Defamation League (ADL) of B'nai B'rith, founded in 1913, makes an annual survey of reported anti-Semitic incidents. Although the number has fluctuated, the 1994 tabulation reached the highest level in the 17 years that the ADL has been recording such incidents. It dropped slightly the next three years, but still the total of harassment, threats, episodes of vandalism, and assaults came to 1,571 incidents reported in 1997. Some incidents were inspired and carried out by neo-Nazi skinheads—groups of young people who champion racist and anti-Semitic ideologies. Particularly disturbing has been the number of reported anti-Semitic incidents on college campuses. In 1997, 104 incidents were reported on 80 campuses. Anti-Jewish graffiti, anti-Semitic speakers, and swastikas affixed to predominantly Jewish fraternities were among the documented incidents (Anti-Defamation League 1998). Such threatening behavior only intensifies the fears of many Jewish Americans, who find it difficult to forget the Holocaust—the extermination of 6 million Jews by the Nazi Third Reich during the late 1930s and 1940s.

As is true for other minorities discussed in this chap-

For practicing Jews, the Hebrew language is an important part of religious instruction. This teacher is showing flashcards of Hebrew alphabetic characters to deaf students.

ter, Jewish Americans face the choice of maintaining ties to their long religious and cultural heritage or becoming as indistinguishable as possible from gentiles. Many Jews have tended to assimilate, as is evident from the rise in marriages between Jews and Christians. A study conducted for the Council of Jewish Federations reported that since 1985, slightly more than half of Jews who married chose to marry a non-Jew. Moreover, of those children of intermarriages who receive religious instruction, 72 percent are reared in faiths other than Judaism. These trends worry Jewish leaders, some of whom fear for the long-term future of the Jewish people (*Religion Watch* 1991).

White Ethnics

A significant segment of the population of the United States is made up of White ethnics whose ancestors have come from Europe within the last 100 years. The nation's White ethnic population includes about 58 million people who claim at least partial German ancestry, 39 million Irish Americans, 15 million Italian Americans, and 9 million Polish Americans, as well as immigrants from other European nations. Some of these people continue to live in close-knit ethnic neighborhoods, while others have largely assimilated and left the "old ways" behind (Bureau of the Census 1999a:56).

To what extent are White ethnics found among the nation's elite? Sociologists Richard Alba and Gwen Moore (1982) conducted interviews with 545 people who held important positions in powerful social, economic, and political institutions. They found that White Anglo-Saxon Protestants were overrepresented among the nation's elite, while White ethnics were underrepresented (although not so dramatically as were African Americans, Hispanics, Asian Americans, and Native Americans). Some ethnic minorities appeared to have risen to key positions in particular areas of the elite structure. For example, Irish Catholics were well represented among labor leaders.

White ethnics and racial minorities have often been antagonistic to one another because of economic competition—an interpretation in line with the conflict approach to sociology. As Blacks, Hispanics, and Native Americans emerge from the lower class, they will initially be competing with working-class Whites for jobs, hous-

ing, and educational opportunities. In times of high unemployment or inflation, any such competition can easily generate intense intergroup conflict.

In many respects, the plight of White ethnics raises the same basic issues as that of other subordinate people in the United States. How ethnic can people be—how much can they deviate from an essentially White, Anglo-Saxon, Protestant norm—before society punishes them for a willingness to be different? Our society does seem to reward people for assimilating. Yet, as we have seen, assimilation is no guarantee of equality or freedom from discrimination. In the social policy section that follows, we will focus on immigrants, people who inevitably face the question of whether to strive for assimilation.

SOCIAL POLICY AND RACE AND ETHNICITY

Global Immigration

The Issue

Worldwide immigration is at an all-time high. Each year, two to four million people move from one country to another. As of the mid-1990s, immigrants totaled about 125 million, representing 2 percent of the global population (Martin and Widgren 1996). Their constantly increasing numbers and the pressure they put on job opportunities and welfare capabilities in the countries they enter raise troubling questions for many of the world's economic powers. Who should be allowed in? At what point should immigration be curtailed?

The Setting

The migration of people is not uniform across time or space. At certain times, wars or famines may precipitate large movements of people either temporarily or permanently. Temporary dislocations occur when people wait until it is safe to return to their home areas. However, more and more migrants who cannot make adequate livings in their home nations are making permanent moves to developed nations. Figure 9-5 shows the destinations of the major migration streams: into North America, the oil-rich areas of the Middle East, and the industrial economies of western Europe and Asia. Currently, seven of the world's wealthiest nations (including Germany, France, the United Kingdom, and the United States) shelter about one-third of the world's migrant population, but less

than one-fifth of the total world population. As long as there are disparities in job opportunities among countries, there is little reason to expect this international migration trend to end.

Countries like the United States that have long been a destination for immigrants have a history of policies to determine who has preference to enter. Often, clear racial and ethnic biases are built into these policies. In the 1920s, U.S. policy gave preference to people from western Europe, while making it difficult for residents of southern and eastern Europe, Asia, and Africa to enter the country. During the late 1930s and early 1940s, the federal government refused to lift or loosen restrictive immigration quotas in order to allow Jewish refugees to escape the terror of the Nazi regime. In line with this policy, the *S.S. St. Louis,* with more than 900 Jewish refugees on board, was denied permission to land in the United States in 1939. This ship was forced to sail back to Europe, where it is estimated that at least a few hundred of its passengers later died at the hands of the Nazis (Morse 1967; G. Thomas and Witts 1974).

Since the 1960s, policies in the United States have encouraged immigration of people with relatives here as well as of people who have needed skills. This change has significantly altered the pattern of sending nations. Previously, Europeans dominated, but for the last 40 years, immigrants have come primarily from Latin America and Asia (see Figure 9-6). This means that an ever-growing proportion of the United States will be Asian or Hispanic. To a

FIGURE 9-5

Major Migration Patterns of the 1990s

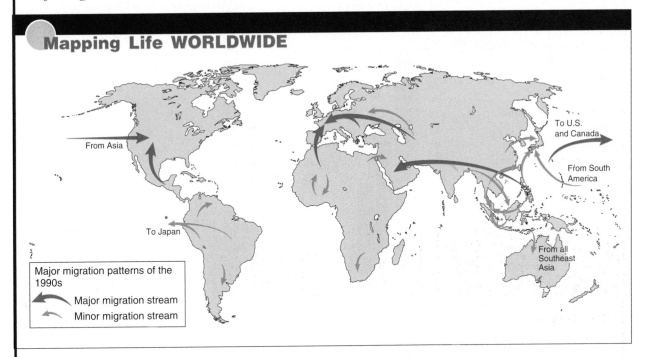

Mapping Life WORLDWIDE

From Asia

To U.S. and Canada

From South America

To Japan

From all Southeast Asia

Major migration patterns of the 1990s

Major migration stream

Minor migration stream

Source: Martin and Widgren 1996:21.

large degree, fear and resentment of this growing racial and ethnic diversity is a key factor in opposition to immigration. In many nations, people are very concerned that the new arrivals do not reflect the cultural and racial heritage of the nation.

Sociological Insights

Despite people's fears about it, immigration provides many valuable functions. For the receiving society, it alleviates labor shortages, such as in the areas of health care and technology in the United States. In 1998, Congress debated not whether individuals with technological skills should be allowed into the country, but just how much to increase the annual number. For the sending nation, migration can relieve economies unable to support large numbers of people. Often overlooked is the large amount of money that immigrants send *back* to their home nations. For example, worldwide immigrants from Portugal alone send more than $4 billion annually back to their home country (World Bank 1995).

There has been considerable research, particularly in the United States, on the impact of immigration on a nation's economy. Studies generally show that it has a positive impact on the economy, although areas experiencing high concentrations of immigrants may find it difficult to meet short-term social service needs. When migrants with skills or educational potential leave developing countries, it can be dysfunctional for those nations. No amount of payments back home can make up for the loss of valuable human resources from poor nations (Martin and Midgley 1999).

Conflict theorists note how much of the debate over immigration is phrased in economic terms. But this debate is intensified when the arrivals are of different racial and ethnic background from the host population. For example, Europeans often refer to "foreigners," but the term does not necessarily mean one of foreign birth. In Germany, "foreigners" refers to people of non-German ancestry, even if they were born in Germany; it does not refer to people of German ancestry born in another country who may choose to come to their "mother country." Fear and dislike of "new" ethnic groups divide countries throughout the world. In 1998, the One Nation Party of Australia sought office on a platform of removing all illegal immigrants and seizing their property to cover deportation costs (Martin and Widgren 1996; *Migration News* 1998b).

FIGURE 9-6

Immigration in the United States, 1820s–1990s

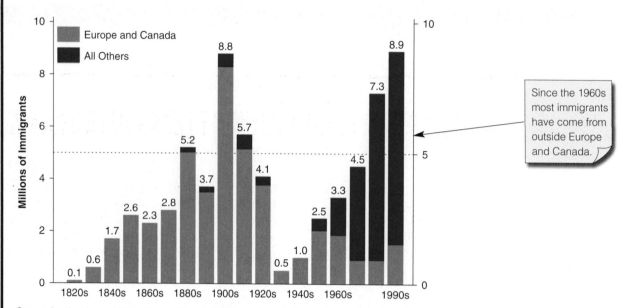

Source: Immigration and Naturalization Service 1999a, 1999b. Projection for the 1990s by the author based on Immigration and Naturalization data.

Policy Initiatives

The long border with Mexico provides ample opportunity for illegal immigration into the United States. Throughout the 1980s, there was a growing perception that the United States had lost control of its borders. Feeling public pressure for immigration control, Congress ended a decade of debate by approving the Immigration Reform and Control Act of 1986. The act marked a historic change in immigration policy. For the first time, hiring of illegal aliens was outlawed, and employers caught violating the law became subject to fines and even prison sentences. Just as significant a change was the extension of amnesty and legal status to many illegal immigrants already living in the United States. More than a decade later, however, the 1986 immigration law appears to have had mixed results. Substantial numbers of illegal immigrants continue to enter the country each year, with an estimated 5 million present at any given time (Martin and Midgley 1999).

In part because the 1986 immigration law failed to end illegal immigration, there has been increasing pressure in several states for further governmental action. Most dramatically, in November 1994, California's voters overwhelmingly approved Proposition 187, a controversial initiative that (among other provisions) calls for withholding social services and schooling opportunities from illegal immigrants. Constitutional challenges to the law resulted in blocking of all the measure's provisions.

The entire world feels the overwhelming impact of economic globalization on immigration patterns. Europe is also wrestling with policy initiatives. The European Union agreement of 1997 gives the governing commission authority to propose Europewide legislation on immigration beginning in 2002. However, the policies must be accepted unanimously, which seems unlikely. An EU policy that would allow immigrants to live and work in one EU country would allow them to work anywhere. The immigration issue is expected to complicate efforts by the sending nations (such as Turkey) to become members of the EU (Light 1999; Sassen 1999).

The intense debate over immigration reflects deep value conflicts in the culture of many nations. One strand of our culture, for example, has traditionally emphasized egalitarian principles and a desire to help people in their time of need. At the same time, however, hostility to potential immigrants and refugees—whether Chinese in the 1880s, European Jews in the 1930s and 1940s, or Mexicans, Haitians, and Arabs today—reflects not only racial, ethnic, and religious prejudice, but also a desire to maintain the dominant culture of the in-group by keeping out those viewed as outsiders.

Let's Discuss

1. Did you or your parents or grandparents immigrate to the United States from another nation? If so, when and where did your family come from, and why? Did they face discrimination?

2. Do you live, work, or study with recent immigrants to the United States? If so, are they well accepted in your community, or do they face prejudice and discrimination?

3. What is your opinion of the backlash against illegal immigrants in California?

Chapter Resources

Summary

The social dimensions of race and ethnicity are important factors in shaping people's lives in the United States and other countries. In this chapter, we examine the meaning of race and ethnicity and study the major racial and ethnic minorities of the United States.

1. A *racial group* is set apart from others by obvious physical differences, whereas an *ethnic group* is set apart primarily because of national origin or distinctive cultural patterns.

2. When sociologists define a *minority group,* they are primarily concerned with the economic and political power, or powerlessness, of the group.

3. In a biological sense, there are no "pure races" and no physical traits that can be used to describe one group to the exclusion of all others.

4. The meaning that people give to the physical differences between races gives social significance to race, leading to *stereotypes* and *self-fulfilling prophecy.*

5. *Prejudice* often leads to *discrimination,* but the two are not identical, and each can be present without the other.

6. *Institutional discrimination* results from the normal operations of a society.

7. Functionalists point out that discrimination is both functional and dysfunctional in society. Conflict theorists explain racial subordination by *exploitation theory.* Interactionists focus on the microlevel of race relations, posing *contact hypothesis* as a means of reducing prejudice and discrimination.

8. Four patterns describe typical intergroup relations in North America and elsewhere: *amalgamation, assimilation, segregation,* and *pluralism.*

9. In the United States, the most highly rewarded pattern of intergroup relations is assimilation. Pluralism remains more of an ideal than a reality.

10. Contemporary prejudice and discrimination against African Americans are rooted in the history of slavery in the United States.

11. Asian Americans are commonly viewed as a "model minority," a stereotype not necessarily beneficial to members of this group.

12. The various groups included under the general term *Hispanics* represent the largest ethnic minority in the United States.

13. The increase of immigration worldwide has raised questions in individual nations about how to control the process.

Critical Thinking Questions

1. How is institutional discrimination even more powerful than individual discrimination? How would functionalists, conflict theorists, and interactionists examine institutional discrimination?
2. The text states that "in the United States, pluralism is more of an ideal than a reality." Can the community in which you grew up and the college you attend be viewed as genuine examples of pluralism?

Examine the relations between dominant and subordinate racial and ethnic groups in your hometown and your college.

3. What are some of the similarities and differences in the position of African Americans and Hispanics as minorities in the United States? What are some of the similarities and differences in the position of Asian Americans and Jewish Americans?

Key Terms

Affirmative action   Positive efforts to recruit minority group members or women for jobs, promotions, and educational opportunities (page 233)

Amalgamation   The process by which a majority group and a minority group combine through intermarriage to form a new group. (236)

Anti-Semitism   Anti-Jewish prejudice. (247)

Apartheid   The policy of the South African government designed to maintain the separation of Blacks and other non-Whites from the dominant Whites. (237)

Assimilation   The process by which a person forsakes his or her own cultural tradition to become part of a different culture. (237)

Black power   A political philosophy promoted by many younger Blacks in the 1960s that supported the creation of Black-controlled political and economic institutions. (240)

Contact hypothesis   An interactionist perspective which states that interracial contact between people of equal status in cooperative circumstances will reduce prejudice. (235)

Discrimination   The process of denying opportunities and equal rights to individuals and groups because of prejudice or other arbitrary reasons. (230)

Ethnic group   A group that is set apart from others because of its national origin or distinctive cultural patterns. (225)

Ethnocentrism   The tendency to assume that one's own culture and way of life represent the norm or are superior to all others. (229)

Exploitation theory   A Marxist theory that views racial subordination in the United States as a manifestation of the class system inherent in capitalism. (234)

Genocide   The deliberate, systematic killing of an entire people or nation. (236)

Glass ceiling   An invisible barrier that blocks the promotion of a qualified individual in a work environment because of the individual's gender, race, or ethnicity. (232)

Institutional discrimination   The denial of opportunities and equal rights to individuals and groups that results from the normal operations of a society. (232)

Issei   The early Japanese immigrants to the United States. (244)

Minority group   A subordinate group whose members have significantly less control or power over their own lives than the members of a dominant or majority group have over theirs. (225)

Nisei   Japanese born in the United States who were descendants of the Issei. (244)

Pluralism   Mutual respect between the various groups in a society for one another's cultures, which allows minorities to express their own cultures without experiencing prejudice. (238)

Prejudice   A negative attitude toward an entire category of people, such as a racial or ethnic minority. (229)

Racial group   A group that is set apart from others because of obvious physical differences. (225)

Racism   The belief that one race is supreme and all others are innately inferior. (229)

Segregation   The act of physically separating two groups; often imposed on a minority group by a dominant group. (237)

Self-fulfilling prophecy   The tendency of people to respond to and act on the basis of stereotypes, leading to validation of false definitions. (227)

Stereotypes   Unreliable generalizations about all members of a group that do not recognize individual differences within the group. (227)

Additional Readings

O'Hearn, Claudine Chiawei, ed. 1998. *Half and Half: Writers on Growing Up Biracial and Bicultural.* New York: Parthenon Books. Eighteen essayists address the difficulties of fitting into, and the benefits of being part of, two worlds.

Pollard, Kevin M., and William P. O'Hare. 1999. *America's Racial and Ethnic Minorities. Population Bulletin* 54. This brief publication (48 pages) provides an overview of contemporary racial and ethnic groups, as well as a discussion of changing definitions of race.

Schaefer, Richard T. 2002. *Racial and Ethnic Groups.* 9th ed. Upper Saddle River, NJ: Prentice Hall. Comprehensive in its coverage of race and ethnicity, this text also discusses women as a subordinate minority and examines dominant–subordinate relations in Canada, Northern Ireland, Israel and the Palestinian territory, Mexico, and South Africa.

Sniderman, Paul S., and Edward G. Carmines. 1997. *Reaching Beyond Race.* Cambridge, MA: Harvard University Press. Using surveys, two political scientists intensively examine White attitudes on race and measure opposition to affirmative action and other policies.

Internet Connection

Note: While all the URLs listed were current as of the printing of this book, these sites often change. Please check our website (http://www.mhhe.com/schaefer4) for updates.

1. Historically, the social and political connections between Cuba and the United States have oscillated between cooperation and tension. Explore the most recent state of this relationship at Yahoo! News (**http://fullcoverage.yahoo.com/fc/world/Cuba**). Visit "News Stories" and "Related Web Sites" in order to answer the following questions:
   (a) How would you describe the current relationship between the Cuban and United States governments? What current events show that relations are improving or worsening?
   (b) Who is Fidel Castro? Who were Jose Marti and Fulgencio Batista? What roles have each played in Cuban history according to the various websites?
   (c) What restrictions currently exist for U.S. citizens who wish to travel to Cuba? What is the Helms-Burton Act (also known as the Libertad Act)?
   (d) How has U.S. policy toward Cuba affected the economic, political, family, and daily lives of Cuban Americans and Cuban citizens?
   (e) According to groups such as Amnesty International, what is the current state of human rights in Cuba? How do Cuban officials respond to these findings?
   (f) What is your opinion of the final decision in the Elian Gonzalez case? What decision would you have made, if different? Why?
   (g) Use the links provided and links from other pages to discover the cultural diversity of Cuba. What contributions have Cubans and Cuban Americans made to the arts, sports, and science?

2. Sometimes referred to as "The Other" or "Forgotten" Holocaust, the conflicts in Nanking, China, starting in 1937, have recently become the subject of historical debate and interest. Masato Kajimoto offers an online documentary entitled *The Nanking Atrocities* (**http://web.missouri.edu/~jschool/nanking/index.htm**). On the site, visitors will find text, photographs, and videos to explore.
   (a) What historical and social forces played a part in the "Nanking Atrocities"? Which groups and individuals were involved?
   (b) What were some of the experiences of Chinese citizens living in Nanking at that time under Japanese military authority? What was the Chinese "scorched earth policy" and how did that affect citizens?
   (c) How many people died during these times described on the site? Why is it hard for researchers to agree upon a precise figure?
   (d) What role did members of the media play before and after these events, according to the site?
   (e) What was the IMTFE? When and where did the postwar trials occur? What arguments were presented by the prosecution and the defense? Ultimately, who was found responsible and what were the punishments?
   (f) Had you ever heard of these events before visiting the site? How did the stories and images impact you?
   (g) How can the sociological theories in this chapter add to our understanding of the causes and consequences of this tragic form of intergroup relations?

3. The Civil Rights Movement has been a defining sociological event in modern U.S. history. Stanford University helps to preserve this important time in history through a virtual presentation of the words

and life of Dr. Martin Luther King, Jr., in the Martin Luther King, Jr. Papers Project (**http://www.stanford.edu/group/King/index.htm**). On this site, you can read, see, and hear speeches and events.

(a) Click on the "Biography" and "Chronology" sections. What early relationships and experiences shaped Dr. King's later life and philosophy? What important contributions to civil rights did Dr. King make through his actions and beliefs? Where, when, and how did Dr. King die?

(b) After examining the "Speeches" and "Sermons" links, how would you summarize Dr. King's views on how best to achieve racial justice?

(c) What patterns of "intergroup relations" was Dr. King trying to end? What patterns was he trying to promote?

(d) Do you believe that the United States is fulfilling the hope symbolized in Dr. King's "I Have A Dream" speech? In your opinion, are race relations and equity improving or declining? What facts and evidence support your position?

 Interactive e-Source with Making the Grade

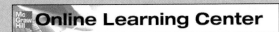 Online Learning Center   www.mhhe.com/schaefer4

 PowerWeb

 SocCity

STRATIFICATION BY GENDER AND AGE

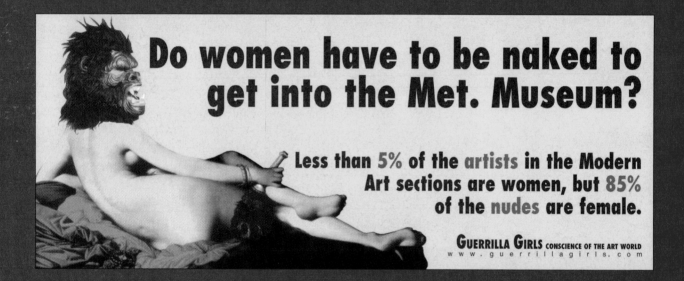

In 1989 a militant group called the Guerrilla Girls called attention to sexism in the art world with this poster, which protests the underrepresentation of female artists at the world-famous Metropolitan Museum of Art in New York City. This poster and others dealing with sexism in the arts can be viewed at www.guerrillagirls.com.

At last, after a long silence, women took to the streets. In the two decades of radical action that followed the rebirth of feminism in the early 1970s, Western women gained legal and reproductive rights, pursued higher education, entered the trades and the professions, and overturned ancient and revered beliefs about their social role. A generation on, do women feel free?

The affluent, educated, liberated women of the First World, who can enjoy freedoms unavailable to any women ever before, do not feel as free as they want to. And they can no longer restrict to the subconscious their sense that this lack of freedom has something to do with—with apparently frivolous issues, things that really should not matter. Many are ashamed to admit that such trivial concerns—to do with physical appearance, bodies, faces, hair, clothes—matter so much. But in spite of shame, guilt, and denial, more and more women are wondering if . . . something important is indeed at stake that has to do with the relationship between female liberation and female beauty.

The more legal and material hindrances women have broken through, the more strictly and heavily and cruelly images of female beauty have come to weigh upon us. . . .

During the past decade, women breached the power structure; meanwhile, eating disorders rose exponentially and cosmetic surgery became the fastest-growing medical specialty. During the past five years, consumer spending doubled, pornography became the main media category, ahead of legitimate films and records combined, and thirty-three thousand American women told researchers that they would rather lose ten to fifteen pounds than achieve any other goal. More women have more money and power and scope and legal recognition than we have ever had before; but in terms of how we feel about ourselves *physically,* we may actually be worse off than our unliberated grandmothers. Recent research consistently shows that inside the majority of the West's controlled, attractive, successful working women, there is a secret "underlife" poisoning our freedom; infused with notions of beauty, it is a dark vein of self-hatred, physical obsessions, terror of aging, and dread of lost control. *(Wolf 1992:9–10)* ∎

In this excerpt from Naomi Wolf's book *The Beauty Myth*, a feminist confronts the power of a false ideal of womanhood. In recent decades, American women have broken legal and institutional barriers that once limited their educational opportunities and career advancement. But, Wolf writes, psychologically they are still enslaved by unrealistic standards of appearance. The more freedom women have gained, in fact, the more obsessed they seem to have become with the ideal of the ultra-thin supermodel—an ideal that few women can ever hope to attain without jeopardizing their health or resorting to expensive cosmetic surgery.

Wolf implies that the Beauty Myth is a societal control mechanism that is meant to keep women in their place—as subordinates to men at home and on the job. But men too are captive to unrealistic expectations regarding their physical appearance. In hopes of attaining a brawny, muscular physique, more and more men are now taking steroids or electing to undergo cosmetic surgery. And now people who are aging have to face down their own form of "beauty myth." Today's media bombards us with images of looking good and masking our age—in ads hawking every-thing from nutrition supplements to hair color formulas that will cover the gray (Thomas and Owens 2000).

The Beauty Myth is but one example of how cultural norms may lead to differentiation based on gender or age. Such differentiation is evident in virtually every human society about which we have information. We saw in Chapters 8 and 9 that most societies establish hierarchies based on social class, race, and ethnicity. This chapter will examine the ways in which societies stratify their members on the basis of gender and age.

We begin by looking at how various cultures, including our own, assign women and men to particular social roles. Then we will consider sociological explanations for gender stratification. Next, the chapter will focus on the unique situation of women as an oppressed majority, analyzing the social, economic, and political aspects of women's subordinate position. We'll then look at theoretical explanations of the aging process and consider what it means to be an aging member of society today. The chapter also examines the emergence of a collective consciousness among both women and the elderly. Finally, the social policy section will analyze the intense and continuing controversy over abortion. ■

Social Construction of Gender

How many air passengers do you think feel a start when the captain's voice from the cockpit belongs to a female? Or what do we make of a father who announces that he will be late for work because his son has a routine medical checkup? Consciously or unconsciously, we are likely to assume that flying a commercial plane is a *man's* job and that most parental duties are, in fact, *maternal* duties. Gender is such a routine part of our everyday activities that we typically take it for granted and only take notice when someone deviates from conventional behavior and expectations.

Although a few people begin life with an unclear sexual identity, the overwhelming majority begin with a definite sex and quickly receive societal messages about how to behave. Many societies have established social distinctions between females and males that do not inevitably result from biological differences between the sexes (such as women's reproductive capabilities).

In studying gender, sociologists are interested in the gender-role socialization that leads females and males to behave differently. In Chapter 5, **gender roles** were defined as expectations regarding the proper behavior, attitudes, and activities of males and females. The application of tra-ditional gender roles leads to many forms of differentiation between women and men. Both sexes are physically capable of learning to cook and sew, yet most Western societies determine that women should perform these tasks. Both men and women are capable of learning to weld and fly airplanes, but these functions are generally assigned to men.

Gender roles are evident not only in our work and behavior but in how we react to others. We are constantly "doing gender" without realizing it. If the father discussed above sits in the doctor's office with his son in the middle of a workday, he will probably receive approving glances from the receptionist and from other patients. "Isn't he a wonderful father?" runs through their minds. But if the boy's mother leaves *her* job and sits with the son in the doctor's office, she will not receive such silent applause.

We socially construct our behavior so that male–female differences are either created or exaggerated. For example, men and women come in a variety of heights, sizes, and ages. Yet traditional norms regarding marriage and even casual dating tell us that in heterosexual couples, the man should be older, taller, and wiser than the woman. As we will see throughout this chapter, such social norms help to reinforce and legitimize patterns of male dominance.

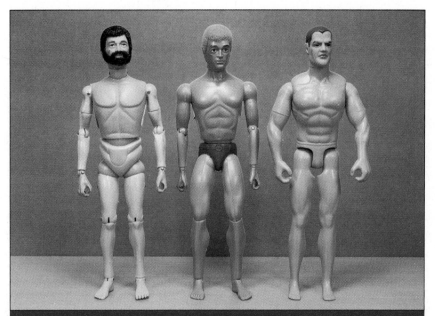

Society often exaggerates male–female differences in appearance and behavior. In 1964, the G.I. Joe doll (left) had a realistic appearance, but by 1992 (middle) it had begun to acquire the exaggerated muscularity characteristic of professional wrestlers (right). The change intensified the contrast with ultra-thin female figures, like the Barbie doll (Angier 1998).

since many people stereotypically associate male homosexuality with femininity and lesbianism with masculinity. Consequently, men and women who deviate from traditional expectations about gender roles are often presumed to be gay. Despite the advances made by the gay liberation movement, the continuing stigma attached to homosexuality in our culture places pressure on all males (whether gay or not) to exhibit only narrow "masculine" behavior and on all females (whether lesbian or not) to exhibit only narrow "feminine" behavior (Seidman 1994; see also Lehne 1995).

It is *adults,* of course, who play a critical role in guiding children into those gender roles deemed appropriate in a society. Parents are normally the first and most crucial agents of socialization. But other adults, older siblings, the p. 91 mass media, and religious and edu-

In recent decades, women have increasingly entered occupations and professions previously dominated by men. Yet our society still focuses on "masculine" and "feminine" qualities as if men and women must be evaluated in these terms. Clearly, we continue to "do gender," and this social construction of gender continues to define significantly different expectations for females and males in the United States (Lorber 1994; L. Rosenbaum 1996; C. West and Zimmerman 1987).

Gender Roles in the United States

Gender-Role Socialization

Male babies get blue blankets, while females get pink ones. Boys are expected to play with trucks, blocks, and toy soldiers; girls are given dolls and kitchen goods. Boys must be masculine—active, aggressive, tough, daring, and dominant—whereas girls must be feminine—soft, emotional, sweet, and submissive. These traditional gender-role patterns have been influential in the socialization of children in the United States.

An important element in traditional views of proper "masculine" and "feminine" behavior is fear of homosexuality. In Chapter 5, we defined **homophobia** as fear of and prejudice against homosexuality. Homophobia contributes significantly to rigid gender-role socialization,

When Fannie Barnes first took the controls of a San Francisco cable car, she probably raised a few eyebrows. No female before had ever been a "gripman" in the cable car system.

cational institutions also exert an important influence on gender-role socialization in the United States and elsewhere.

It is not hard to test how rigid gender-role socialization can be. Just try transgressing some gender norms—say, by smoking a cigar in public if you are female or carrying a purse if you are male. That was exactly the assignment given sociology students at the University of Colorado and Luther College in Iowa. The teachers asked the students to behave in ways that they thought violated norms of how a man or woman should act. The students had no trouble coming up with gender norm "transgressions" (see Table 10-1), and they kept careful notes on how others reacted to their behavior, ranging from amusement to disgust (Nielsen et al. 2000).

Women's Gender Roles

How does a girl come to develop a feminine self-image whereas a boy develops one that is masculine? In part, they do so by identifying with females and males in their families and neighborhoods and in the media. If a young girl regularly sees female characters on television working as defense attorneys and judges, she may believe that she herself can become a lawyer. And it will not hurt if women that she knows—her mother, sister, parents' friends, or neighbors—are lawyers. By contrast, if this young girl sees women portrayed in the media only as models,

nurses, and secretaries, her identification and self-image will be quite different. Even if she does become a professional, she may secretly regret falling short of the media stereotype—a shapely, sexy young woman in a bathing suit (Wolf 1992).

Television is far from being alone in stereotyping women. Studies of children's books published in the United States in the 1940s, 1950s, and 1960s found that females were significantly underrepresented in central roles and illustrations. Virtually all female characters were portrayed as helpless, passive, incompetent, and in need of a strong male caretaker. By the 1980s, there was somewhat less stereotyping in children's books, with some female characters shown to be active. Nevertheless, boys were still shown engaged in active play three times as often as girls (Kortenhaus and Demarest 1993).

Social research on gender roles reveals some persistent differences between men and women in North America and Europe. Women experience a mandate to both marry and be a mother. Often, marriage is viewed as the true entry into adulthood. And women are expected not only to become mothers but to *want* to be mothers. Obviously, men play a role in these events, but they do not appear to be as critical in identifying the life course for a man. Society defines men's roles by economic success. While women may achieve recognition in the labor force, it is not as important to their identity as it is for men (Doyle and Paludi 1998; Russo 1976).

Traditional gender roles have most severely restricted females. Throughout this chapter, we will see how women have been confined to subordinate roles within the political and economic institutions of the United States. Yet it is also true that gender roles have restricted males.

Men's Gender Roles

During the game I always played the outfield. Right field. Far right field. And there I would stand in the hot sun wishing I was anyplace else in the world (Fager et al. 1971).

This is the childhood recollection of a man who, as a boy, disliked sports, dreaded gym classes, and had particular problems with baseball. Obviously, he did not conform to the socially constructed male gender role and no doubt paid the price for it.

Men's roles are socially constructed in much the same way as women's roles are. Family, peers, and

Table 10-1 An Experiment of Gender Norm Violations by College Students

Norm Violations by Women	Norm Violations by Men
Send men flowers	Wear fingernail polish
Spit in public	Needlepoint in public
Use men's bathroom	Throw Tupperware party
Buy jock strap	Cry in public
Buy/chew tobacco	Have pedicure
Talk knowledgeably about cars	Apply to babysit
Open doors for men	Shave body hair

Based on class projects, sociology students were asked to behave in ways that might be regarded as violating gender norms. This is a sample of their actual choices over a seven-year period. Do you agree that these actions test the boundaries of conventional gender behavior?

Source: Nielsen et al. 2000:287.

the media all influence how a boy or a man comes to view his appropriate role in society. Robert Brannon (1976) and James Doyle (1995) have identified five aspects of the male gender role:

- Antifeminine element—show no "sissy stuff," including any expression of openness or vulnerability.
- Success element—prove one's masculinity at work and sports.
- Aggressive element—use force in dealing with others.
- Sexual element—initiate and control all sexual relations.
- Self-reliant element—keep cool and unflappable.

No systematic research has established all these elements as a common aspect among boys and men, but specific studies have confirmed individual elements.

Being antifeminine is basic to men's gender roles. Males who do not conform to the socially constructed gender role face constant criticism and even humiliation both from children when they are boys and from adults as men. It can be agonizing to be treated as a "chicken" or a "sissy"—particularly if such remarks come from one's father or brothers. At the same time, boys who successfully adapt to cultural standards of masculinity may grow up to be inexpressive men who cannot share their feelings with others. They remain forceful and tough—but as a result they are also closed and isolated (Faludi 1999; McCreary 1994; G. Sheehy 1999).

In the last 35 years, inspired in good part by the contemporary feminist movement (examined later in the chapter), increasing numbers of men in the United States have criticized the restrictive aspects of the traditional male gender role. Some men have taken strong public positions in support of women's struggle for full equality and have even organized voluntary associations such as the National Organization for Men Against Sexism (NOMAS), founded in 1975 to support positive changes for men. Nevertheless, the traditional male gender role remains well entrenched as an influential element of our culture (Messner 1997; National Organization for Men Against Sexism 1999).

Cross-Cultural Perspective

To what extent do actual biological differences between the sexes contribute to the cultural differences associated with gender? This question brings us back to the debate over "nature versus nurture." In assessing the alleged and pp. 81–84 real differences between men and women, it is useful to examine cross-cultural data. The research of anthropologist Margaret Mead

points to the importance of cultural conditioning—as opposed to biology—in defining the social roles of males and females. In *Sex and Temperament,* Mead (1963, original edition 1935; 1973) describes typical behaviors of each sex in three different cultures in New Guinea:

> In one [the Arapesh], both men and women act as we expect women to act—in a mild parental responsive way; in the second [the Mundugumor], both act as we expect men to act—in a fierce initiating fashion; and in the third [the Tchambuli], the men act according to our stereotypes for women—are catty, wear curls, and go shopping— while the women are energetic, managerial, unadorned partners. (Preface to 1950 ed.)

If biology determined all differences between the sexes, then cross-cultural differences, such as those described by Mead, would not exist. Her findings confirm the influen-

Cultural conditioning is important in the development of gender role differences. This sister and brother from Sudest Island in Papua New Guinea expect women to be the honorary heads of the family.

tial role of culture and socialization in gender-role differentiation. There appears to be no innate or biological reason to designate completely different gender roles for men and women.

In any society, gender stratification requires not only individual socialization into traditional gender roles within the family, but also the promotion and support of these traditional roles by other social institutions such as religion and education. Moreover, even with all major institutions socializing the young into conventional gender roles, every society has women and men who resist and successfully oppose these stereotypes: strong women who become leaders or professionals, gentle men who care for children, and so forth. It seems clear that differences between the sexes are not dictated by biology. Indeed, the maintenance of traditional gender roles requires constant social controls—and these controls are not always effective.

Explaining Stratification by Gender

Cross-cultural studies indicate that societies dominated by men are much more common than those in which women play the decisive role. Sociologists have turned to all the major theoretical perspectives to understand how and why these social distinctions are established. Each approach focuses on culture, rather than biology, as the primary determinant of gender differences. Yet, in other respects, there are wide disagreements between advocates of these sociological perspectives.

The Functionalist View

Functionalists maintain that gender differentiation has contributed to overall social stability. Sociologists Talcott Parsons and Robert Bales (1955) argued that to function most effectively, the family requires adults who will specialize in particular roles. They viewed the traditional arrangement of gender roles as arising out of this need to establish a division of labor between marital partners.

Parsons and Bales contended that women take the expressive, emotionally supportive role and men the instrumental, practical role, with the two complementing each other. *Instrumentality* refers to emphasis on tasks, focus on more distant goals, and a concern for the external relationship between one's family and other social institutions. *Expressiveness* denotes concern for maintenance of harmony and the internal emotional affairs of the family. According to this theory, women's interest in expressive goals frees men for instrumental tasks, and vice versa. Women become "anchored" in the family as wives, mothers, and household managers; men are anchored in the occupational world outside the home. Of course, Par-

sons and Bales offered this framework in the 1950s, when many more women were full-time homemakers than is true today. These theorists did not explicitly endorse traditional gender roles, but they implied that dividing tasks between spouses was functional for the family unit.

Given the typical socialization of women and men in the United States, the functionalist view is initially persuasive. However, it would lead us to expect girls and women with no interest in children to become babysitters and mothers. Similarly, males who love spending time with children might be "programmed" into careers in the business world. Such differentiation might harm the individual who does not fit into prescribed roles, while also depriving society of the contributions of many talented people who are confined by gender stereotyping. Moreover, the functionalist approach does not convincingly explain why men should be categorically assigned to the instrumental role and women to the expressive role.

The Conflict Response

Viewed from a conflict perspective, this functionalist approach masks underlying power relations between men and women. Parsons and Bales never explicitly presented the expressive and instrumental tasks as unequally valued by society, yet this inequality is quite evident. Although social institutions may pay lip service to women's expressive skills, it is men's instrumental skills that are most highly rewarded—whether in terms of money or prestige. Consequently, according to feminists and conflict theorists, any division of labor by gender into instrumental and expressive tasks is far from neutral in its impact on women.

Conflict theorists contend that the relationship between females and males has traditionally been one of unequal power, with men in a dominant position over women. Men may originally have become powerful in preindustrial times because their size, physical strength, and freedom from childbearing duties allowed them to dominate women physically. In contemporary societies, such considerations are not so important, yet cultural beliefs about the sexes are long established, as anthropologist Margaret Mead and feminist sociologist Helen Mayer Hacker (1951, 1974) both stressed. Such beliefs support a social structure that places males in controlling positions.

Thus, conflict theorists see gender differences as a reflection of the subjugation of one group (women) by another group (men). If we use an analogy to Marx's analysis of class conflict, we can say that males are like the bourgeoisie, or capitalists; they pp. 11–12, 193 ◀ control most of the society's wealth, prestige, and power. Females are like the proletarians, or workers; they can acquire valuable resources only by following the dictates of

Conflict theorists emphasize that men's work is uniformly valued, while women's work (whether unpaid labor in the home or wage labor) is devalued. These women are making tents in a factory in Binghamton, New York.

their "bosses." Men's work is uniformly valued, while women's work (whether unpaid labor in the home or wage labor) is devalued.

The Feminist Perspective

A significant component of the conflict approach to gender stratification draws on feminist theory. While use of that term is comparatively recent, the critique of women's position in society and culture goes back to some of the earliest works that have influenced sociology. Among the most important are Mary Wollstonecraft's *A Vindication of the Rights of Women* (originally published in 1792), John Stuart Mill's *The Subjection of Women* (originally published in 1869), and Friedrich Engels's *The Origin of Private Property, the Family, and the State* (originally published in 1884).

Engels, a close associate of Karl Marx, argued that women's subjugation coincided with the rise of private property during industrialization. Only when people moved beyond an agrarian economy could males "enjoy" the luxury of leisure and withhold rewards and privileges from women. Drawing on the work of Marx and Engels, contemporary feminist theorists often view women's subordination as part of the overall exploitation and injustice that they see as inherent in capitalist societies. Some radical feminist theorists, however, view the oppression of women as inevitable in *all* male-dominated societies, whether they be labeled "capitalist,"

"socialist," or "communist" (Feuer 1959; Tuchman 1992).

Feminist sociologists would find little to disagree with in the conflict theorists' perspective but are more likely to embrace a political action agenda. Also, the feminist perspective would argue that the very discussion of women and society, however well meaning, has been distorted by the exclusion of women from academic thought, including sociology. In Chapter 1 we noted the many accomplishments of Jane Addams, but she generally worked outside the discipline. Her work focused on what we would now call applied sociology and social work. At the time, her efforts, while valued as humanitarian, were seen as unrelated to the research and conclusions being reached in academic circles, which, of course, were male academic circles (M. Andersen 1997; J. Howard 1999).

For most of the history of sociology, studies were conducted on male subjects or about male-led groups and organizations, and the findings were generalized to all people. For example, for many decades studies of urban life focused on street corners, neighborhood taverns, and bowling alleys—places where men typically congregated. While the insights were valuable, they did not give a true impression of city life because they overlooked the areas where women were likely to gather, such as at playgrounds with their children or at grocery stores (L. Lofland 1975).

Since men and women have had different life experiences, the issues they approach are different, and even when they have similar concerns, they approach them from different perspectives. For example, women who enter politics today typically do so for different reasons from men. Men often embark on a political career to make business contacts or build on them, a natural extension of their livelihood; women generally become involved because they want to help. This difference in interests is relevant to the likelihood of their future success. The areas in which women achieve political recognition revolve around such social issues as day care, the environment, education, and child protection—areas that do not attract a lot of big donors. Men focus on tax policies, business regulation, and trade agreements—issues that excite big donors. Sometimes women do become concerned with these issues, such as former Representative Pat

comes and investments—the institution will discriminate against women in state after state. It will do so even at bank branches in which loan officers hold no personal biases concerning women, but are merely "following orders." We will examine institutional discrimination against women within the educational system in Chapter 12.

Our society is run by male-dominated institutions, yet with the power that flows to men come responsibility and stress. Men have higher reported rates of certain types of mental illness than women do and greater likelihood of death due to heart attack or strokes (see Chapter 14). The pressure on men to succeed—and then to remain on top in a competitive world of work—can be especially intense. This is not to suggest that gender stratification is as damaging to men as it is to women. But it is clear that the power and privilege men enjoy are no guarantee of well-being.

The Status of Women Worldwide

The Hindu society of India makes life especially harsh for widows. When Hindu women marry, they join their husband's family. If the husband dies, the widow is the "property" of that family. In many cases, she ends up working as an unpaid servant; in others she is simply abandoned and left penniless. Ancient Hindu scriptures portray widows as "inauspicious" and advise that "a wise man should avoid her blessings like the poison of a snake" (J. Burns 1998:10). Such attitudes die slowly in the villages, where most Indians live.

It is estimated that women grow half the world's food, but they rarely own land. They constitute one-third of the world's paid labor force but are generally found in the lowest-paying jobs. Single-parent households headed by women—which appear to be on the increase in many nations—are typically found in the poorest sections of the population. The feminization of poverty has become a global phenomenon. As in the United States, women worldwide are underrepresented politically.

A detailed overview of the status of the world's women, issued by the United Nations in 1995, noted that "too often, women and men live in different worlds—worlds that differ in access to education and work opportunities, and in health, personal security, and leisure time." While acknowledging that much has been done in the last 20 years to sharpen people's awareness of gender inequities, the report identified a number of areas of continuing concern:

- Despite advances in higher education for women, women still face major barriers when they attempt to use their educational achievements to advance in the workplace. For example, women rarely hold more than 1 to 2 percent of top executive positions.
- Women almost always work in occupations with lower status and pay than men. In both developing and developed countries, many women work as unpaid family laborers. (Figure 10-1 shows the paid labor force participation of women in seven industrialized countries.)
- Despite social norms regarding support and protection, many widows around the world find that they have little concrete support from extended family networks.
- In many African and a few Asian nations, traditions mandate the cutting of female genitals, typically by practitioners who fail to use sterilized instruments. This can lead to immediate and serious complications from infection or to long-term health problems.
- While males outnumber females as refugees, refugee women have unique needs, such as protection against physical and sexual abuse (United Nations 1995:xvi, xvii, xxii, 11, 46, 70).

Moreover, according to a *World Development Report* issued by the World Bank in 2000, there are twice as many illiterate women in developing countries as illiterate men. Some societies do not allow women to attend school. Of 1.2 billion people living on less than a dollar a day around the world, 70 percent are female (World Bank 2000c; 23, 277).

What conclusions can we make about women's equality worldwide? First, as anthropologist Laura Nader (1986:383) has observed, even in the relatively more egalitarian nations of the West, women's subordination is "institutionally structured and culturally rationalized, exposing them to conditions of deference, dependency, powerlessness, and poverty." While the situation of women in Sweden and the United States is significantly better than in Saudi Arabia and Bangladesh, women nevertheless remain in a second-class position in the world's most affluent and developed countries.

Second, there is a link between the wealth of industrialized nations and the poverty of the developing countries. Viewed from a conflict perspective, pp. 207–12 the economies of developing nations are controlled and exploited by industrialized countries and multinational corporations based in those countries. Much of the exploited labor in developing nations, especially in the nonindustrial sector, is performed by women. Women workers typically toil long hours for low pay, but contribute significantly to their families' incomes. The affluence of Western industrialized nations has come, in part, at the expense of women in Third World countries (Jacobson 1993).

FIGURE 10-1

Percentage of Adult Women in the Paid Labor Force by Country, 1960s and 1990s

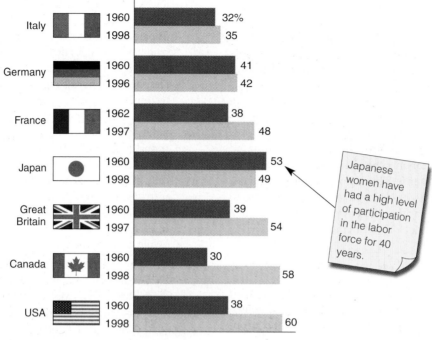

Source: Bureau of Labor Statistics 1999a.

Women in the Workforce of the United States

"Does your mother work?" "No, she's just a housewife." This familiar exchange reminds us of women's traditional role in the United States, and it reminds us that women's work has generally been viewed as unimportant. The U.S. Commission on Civil Rights (1976:1) concluded that the passage in the Declaration of Independence proclaiming that "all men are created equal" has been taken too literally for too long. This is especially true with respect to opportunities for employment.

A Statistical Overview

Women's participation in the paid labor force of the United States increased steadily throughout the twentieth century (see Figure 10-2). No longer is the adult woman associated solely with the role of homemaker. Instead, millions of women—married and single, with and without children—are working in the labor force. In 1998, more than 60 percent of adult women in the United States held jobs outside the home, as compared with 38 percent in 1960. A majority of women are now members of the paid labor force, not full-time homemakers. Among new mothers, 55 percent return to the labor force within a year of giving birth. As recently as 1971, only 31 percent went back to work (Bureau of Labor Statistics 1999a; Fiore 1997).

Yet women entering the job market find their options restricted in important ways. Particularly damaging is occupational segregation, or confinement to sex-typed "women's jobs." For example, in 1997, women accounted for 99 percent of all secretaries, 97 percent of all dental assistants, and 81 percent of all librarians. Entering such sex-typed occupations places women in "service" roles that parallel the traditional gender-role standard under which housewives "serve" their husbands.

Women are *underrepresented* in occupations historically defined as "men's jobs," which often carry much greater financial rewards and prestige than women's jobs. For example, in 1997, women accounted for approximately 46 percent of the paid labor force of the United States. Yet they constituted only 10 percent of all engineers, 17 percent of all dentists, 26 percent of all physicians, and 29 percent of all computer systems analysts (see Table 10-2). In Box 10-1, we consider unique situations that run *against* sex-typing: male nurses and female hockey players.

Women from all groups and men from minority groups sometimes encounter attitudinal or organizational bias that prevents them from reaching their full potential. As we saw in Chapter 9, the term **glass ceiling** refers to an invisible barrier that blocks the promotion of a qualified individual in a work environment because of

FIGURE 10-2

Trends in U.S. Women's Participation in the Paid Labor Force, 1890–1998

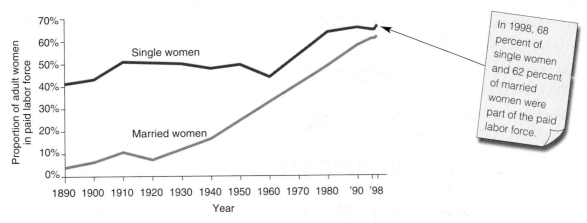

In 1998, 68 percent of single women and 62 percent of married women were part of the paid labor force.

Sources: Bureau of the Census 1975; 1999a:417.

the individual's gender, race, or ethnicity. A recent study of the *Fortune* 1,000 largest corporations in the United States showed that only 9 percent of the seats on their boards of directors were held by women. Indeed, 16 percent of these corporations still did not have even one woman on the board (Catalyst 1999).

One response to the "glass ceiling" and other gender bias in the workplace is to start your own business and work for yourself. This route to success, traditionally taken by men from immigrant and racial minority groups, has become more common among women as they have increasingly sought paid employment outside the home. According to data released in 1998, women own an impressive 8 million businesses in the United States. Yet, according to an earlier study, while women own about one-third of all business firms, they account for only 11 percent of all business revenues. In good part, this is because they typically form small businesses. In fact, 81 percent of all businesses owned by women have no employees (Bureau of the Census 1996a; Dickerson 1998).

The workplace patterns described here have one crucial result: Women earn much less money than men in the paid labor force of the United States. In 1998, the median weekly earnings of full-time female

workers were about 76 percent of those for full-time male workers. Given these data, it is hardly surprising to learn that many women are living in poverty, particularly when they must function as heads of households. In the discussion of poverty in Chapter 8, we noted that female heads of households and their children accounted for most of the nation's poor people living in families. Yet not all

Table 10-2 U.S. Women in Selected Occupations, 1998
Women as Percentage of All Workers in the Occupation

Underrepresented		Overrepresented	
Airline pilots	3%	High school teachers	57%
Firefighters	3	Social workers	68
Engineers	11	Cashiers	78
Clergy	12	File clerks	80
Police	16	Librarians	83
Dentists	19	Elementary teachers	84
Physicians	27	Registered nurses	93
Computer systems analysts	27	Receptionists	96
Mail carriers	30	Child care workers	97
College teachers	42	Secretaries	98
Pharmacists	44	Dental hygienists	99

Source: Bureau of the Census 1999a:424–426.

Research in Action

10-1 Female Ice Hockey Players and Male Nurses

When you sit down to watch ice hockey, you expect to watch men playing. When you are being assisted by a nurse, you expect it to be a woman. And in almost every case you would be correct, but not always.

Nationwide, about 7.5 percent of all nurses are male. Sociologist E. Joel Heikes (1991) wondered what characteristics male nurses exhibit when entering a traditionally female occupation, so he conducted in-depth interviews with male registered nurses employed in hospital settings in Austin, Texas. Heikes reports that male nurses in Austin felt more visible than female nurses and typically responded by overachieving. Although they did not feel polarized from the female nurses, they did feel socially isolated as "tokens" in the workplace. Typically, they were excluded from traditionally female gatherings, such as female nurses' baby and bridal showers. Such social isolation did not reduce the male nurses' skills training, but it excluded

them from informal interactions in which they could have "networked" with female nurses and learned more about the day-to-day workings of the hospital.

Stereotyping was also evident. Male nurses were commonly mistaken for physicians. Even though being mis-

> Like male nurses, female hockey players are rare specimens, although they have actually been around almost as long as male players.

taken for someone of higher status may appear to be advantageous, it can often have negative connotations for the male nurse. It is a constant reminder of his deviant position in a traditionally female occupation. The implicit message is that men should be doctors rather than nurses. When correctly

identified as nurses, men face a much more serious form of stereotyping. Because of the persistence of traditional gender roles, it is assumed that all male nurses must be gay. Many male nurses told Heikes that they felt a need to deny this stigmatized identity.

Sociologist Christine Williams (1992, 1995) examined the underrepresentation of men in four predominantly female professions: nursing, elementary school teaching, librarianship, and social work. Drawing on in-depth interviews with 99 men and women in these professions in four cities in the United States, Williams found that the experience of tokenism is very different for women and men. While men in these traditionally female professions commonly experience negative stereotyping, they nevertheless benefit from hidden *advantages* stemming from their status as men, such as receiving early and disproportionate encouragement to become administrators. By contrast, women in traditionally male

Sources: Bureau of the Census 1999a; DeSimone 2000; Elliot 1997; Heikes 1991; Lillard 1998; Theberge 1997; Zimmer 1988.

women are in equal danger of experiencing poverty. Women who are members of racial and ethnic minorities suffer from "double jeopardy": stratification by race and ethnicity as well as by gender (Bureau of Labor Statistics 1999b).

Social Consequences of Women's Employment

"What a circus we women perform every day of our lives. It puts a trapeze artist to shame." These words by the writer Anne Morrow Lindbergh attest to the lives of women today who try to juggle their work and family lives. This situation has many social consequences. For one thing, it puts pressure on child care facilities and on public financing of day care and even on the fast food industry, which provides many of the meals that women used to prepare during the day. For another, it raises questions about what responsibility male wage earners have in the household.

Who does do the housework when women become productive wage earners? Studies indicate that there continues to be a clear gender gap in the performance of housework, although the differences are narrowing. Still, as shown in Figure 10-3, the most recent study finds women doing more housework and spending more time on child care than men, whether it be on a workday or when off work. Taken together, then, a woman's workday on and off the job is much longer than a man's. A recent development over the last 20 years is women's involvement in elder care. According to a Department of Labor (1998) study, 72 percent of these caregivers are women, typically spending around 18 hours per week caring for a parent.

Sociologist Arlie Hochschild (1989, 1990) has used the phrase "second shift" to describe the double burden—work outside the home followed by child care and housework—that many women face and few men

professions often find that their advancement is limited and their token status is hardly an asset.

Like male nurses, female hockey players are rare specimens, although they have actually been around almost as long as male players. A photograph of the daughter of Lord Stanley, founder of the coveted Stanley Cup given to the champions in professional hockey, shows her playing the sport in 1890. A rivalry between U.S. and Canadian women's teams goes back to 1916. But women were never taken very seriously as hockey players—until quite recently. Since 1990, the number of female hockey players registered on U.S. hockey teams has increased eightfold. By the end of the decade the number of women's teams had risen from 149 in 1990 to 1,268. And in 1998, women made their first appearance on the rink in the Olympics, where the U.S. team took a gold medal.

While increasing numbers of women have come into their own in ice hockey, they still are put down for not being as "tough and strong" as male hockey players. Hockey rules do not allow women to body check, which calls for shoving an opponent hard into the boards on the side of the rink. Their game relies more on finesse than strength.

Using both observation and interviews, sociologist Nancy Theberge (1997) studied a female Canadian league. She found that while the players generally acknowledge that the game is more skill-oriented without body checking, they favor including body checking in women's hockey to make the sport more professional. They reason that if they can make a living at the sport, then they should accept the risk of injury that comes with "hard checks." Ironically, their willingness to accept a more intense level of the game comes at a time when many people feel that men's professional hockey has become too physical and too violent; hard body checking leads to the fights that accompany many games.

Theberge found that even without body checking, injury and pain were routine features of the lives of female hockey players. She notes, "For these athletes, overcoming injury and pain is a measure of both ability and commitment." Some observers, however, find it troubling that as women's involvement in ice hockey grows, the pressure increases to develop a system that normalizes injury and pain in the sport.

Let's Discuss

1. Have you ever played a sport or worked in a job that was stereotyped as being more appropriate for the opposite sex? If so, how comfortable were you with your role?

2. Do you think women's hockey rules should be amended to allow body checking? Why or why not? Should men's hockey rules be amended to discourage checking?

share equitably. On the basis of interviews with and observations of 52 couples over an eight-year period, Hochschild reports that the wives (and not their husbands) drive home from the office while planning domestic schedules and play dates for children—and then begin their second shift. Drawing on national studies, she concludes that women spend 15 fewer hours in leisure activities each week than their husbands do. In a year, these women work an extra month of 24-hour days because of the "second shift"; over a dozen years, they work an extra year of 24-hour days. Hochschild found that the married couples she studied were fraying at the edges, and so were their careers and their marriages. Juggling so many roles means that more things can go wrong for women, which contributes to stress. A study by a Harvard sociologist found that married women are 50 percent more likely than married men to complain of being in a bad mood (Kessler 1998).

With such reports in mind, many feminists have advocated greater governmental and corporate support for child care, more flexible family leave policies, and other reforms designed to ease the burden on the nation's families. pp. 97–99

Most studies of gender, child care, and housework focus on the time actually spent by women and men performing these duties. However, sociologist Susan Walzer (1996) was interested in whether there are gender differences in the amount of time that parents spend *thinking* about the care of their children. Drawing on interviews with 25 couples, Walzer found that mothers are much more involved than fathers in the invisible, mental labor associated with taking care of a baby. For example, while involved in work outside the home, mothers are more likely to think about their babies and to feel guilty if they become so consumed with the demands of their jobs that they *fail* to think about their babies.

FIGURE 10-3

Gender Differences in Child Care and Housework, 1997

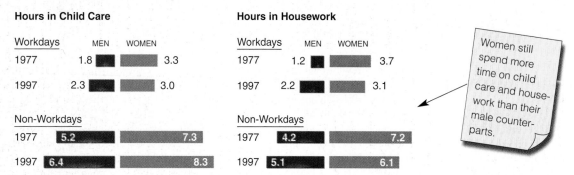

Source: Bond, Galinsky, and Swanberg 1998:40–41, 44–45.

Women: Emergence of a Collective Consciousness

The feminist movement of the United States was born in upstate New York, in a town called Seneca Falls, in the summer of 1848. On July 19, the first women's rights convention began, attended by Elizabeth Cady Stanton, Lucretia Mott, and other pioneers in the struggle for women's rights. This first wave of *feminists*, as they are currently known, battled ridicule and scorn as they fought for legal and political equality for women. They were not afraid to risk controversy on behalf of their cause; in 1872, Susan B. Anthony was arrested for attempting to vote in that year's presidential election.

Ultimately, the early feminists won many victories, among them the passage and ratification of the Nineteenth Amendment to the Constitution, which granted women the right to vote in national elections beginning in 1920. But suffrage did not lead to other reforms in women's social and economic position, and the women's movement became a much less powerful force for social change in the early and middle twentieth century.

The second wave of feminism in the United States emerged in the 1960s and came into full force in the 1970s. In part, the movement was inspired by three pioneering books arguing for women's rights: Simone de Beauvoir's *The Second Sex,* Betty Friedan's *The Feminine Mystique,* and Kate Millett's *Sexual Politics.* In addition, the general political activism of the 1960s led women—many of whom were working for Black civil rights or against the war in Vietnam—to reexamine their own powerlessness as women. The sexism often found within allegedly progressive and radical political circles made many women decide that they needed to establish their own movement for "women's liberation" (Evans 1980; Firestone 1970; J. Freeman 1973, 1975).

More and more women became aware of sexist attitudes and practices—including attitudes they themselves had accepted through socialization into traditional gender roles—and began to challenge male dominance. A sense of "sisterhood," much like the class consciousness that Marx hoped would emerge in the proletariat, became evident. Individual women identified their interests with those of the collectivity *women.* No longer were they "happy" in submissive, subordinate roles ("false consciousness" in Marxist terms).

National surveys today, however, show that while women generally endorse feminist positions, they do not necessarily accept the label of "feminist." Close to 40 percent of women considered themselves feminists in 1989; the proportion dropped to about 20 percent in 1998. Feminism as a unified political cause, requiring one to accept a similar stance on everything from abortion to sexual harassment to pornography to welfare, has fallen out of favor. Both women and men prefer to express their views on these complex issues individually rather than under a convenient umbrella like "feminism." Still, feminism is very much alive in the growing acceptance of women in nontraditional roles and even the basic acknowledgment that a married mother not only can be working outside the home but also perhaps belongs in the labor force. A majority of women say that given the choice, they would prefer to work outside the home rather than stay home and take care of a house and family, and about one-quarter of women prefer Ms. to Miss or Mrs. (Bellafante 1998; P. Geyh 1998).

Aging and Society

The Sherpas—a Tibetan-speaking, Buddhist people in Nepal—live in a culture that idealizes old age. Almost all elderly members of the Sherpa culture own their homes, and most are in relatively good physical condition. Typi-

Taking Sociology to Work

STACEY KARP:
President of San Francisco Chapter of NOW (National Organization for Women)

Stacey Karp got involved with NOW when she took a semester off from the University of Wisconsin to work with the San Francisco chapter. After graduating in 1996, she moved to the Bay Area and continued to volunteer for NOW—and soon found herself in the president's position. The work is unpaid for the most part, but Karp feels the experience she is gaining is invaluable.

"My job is to oversee the entire chapter, with its 1,200 members; to set policies; and to be the spokesperson for those policies." In the course of a day, Karp will typically write press releases, attend government hearings, lobby elected officials, talk to constituents, and, if necessary, organize a protest of some sort. One protest Karp participated in was directed against the Promise Keepers, an organization dedicated to having men take responsibility for their families. According to Karp, "in reality the PK is about having men be in *control* of their families—having men make all the decisions and having women be submissive."

Karp chose sociology as her major because she's always been interested in people. "It was a great way to be able to study people, to understand what statistics mean, and to learn how to take action to involve people." A sociology of gender course got Karp interested in women's issues, which then led her to minor in women's studies.

Karp's advice to students: If you are interested in sociology, don't be concerned about what kind of career your degree will lead to. "Pretty much *everything* has to do with sociology. It's all about the study of people and how our society works."

Let's Discuss

1. How do you think sociology studies would prepare you to head a large lobbying organization like NOW?
2. Stacey Karp got involved with the San Francisco chapter of NOW in an internship while still in college. What kinds of internships might you be interested in pursuing that would tap your interests and abilities?

---

cally, older Sherpas value their independence and prefer not to live with their children. Among the Fulani of Africa, however, older men and women move to the edge of the family homestead. Since this is where people are buried, the elderly sleep over their own graves, for they are already viewed as socially dead. Like gender stratification, age stratification varies from culture to culture. One society may treat older people with great reverence, while another sees them as unproductive and "difficult" (M. C. Goldstein and Beall 1981; Stenning 1958; Tonkinson 1978).

It is understandable that all societies have some system of age stratification and associate certain social roles with distinct periods in one's life (see Box 10-2). Some of this age differentiation seems inevitable; it would make little sense to send young children off to war or to expect most older citizens to handle physically demanding tasks such as loading goods at shipyards. However, as is the case with stratification by gender, age stratification in the United States goes far beyond the physical constraints of human beings at different ages.

"Being old" is a master status that commonly overshadows all others in the United States. The insights of labeling theory help us analyze the consequences p. 172 of aging. Once people are labeled "old," this designation has a major impact on how others perceive them and even on how they view themselves. Negative stereotypes of the elderly contribute to their position as a

This elderly Sherpa living in Nepal is honored among his people for his age. Not all old people are so lucky—in many cultures being old is considered next to dead.

10-2 Aging Worldwide: Issues and Consequences

An electric water kettle is wired so that people in another location can determine if it has been used in the previous 24 hours. This may seem a zany bit of modern technology, but it symbolizes a change taking place around the globe—the growing needs of an aging population. Welfare Network Ikebukuro Honcho has installed these wired hot pots in Japan so that volunteers can monitor if the elderly have used the devices to prepare their morning tea. An unused pot initiates contacts to see if the older person needs help. This technological monitoring system is an indication of the tremendous growth of Japan's elderly population and, of particular social significance, the increasing numbers who live *alone*.

Around the world, there are more than 419 million people aged 65 or over; they represent about 7 percent of the world's population. In an important sense, the aging of the world's population represents a major success story that has unfolded during the later stages of the twentieth century. Through the efforts of both national governments and international agencies, many societies have drastically reduced the incidence of diseases and their rates of death. Consequently, these nations—especially the industrialized countries of Europe and North America—have increasingly higher proportions of older members.

The overall population of Europe is older than that of any other continent. As the proportion of older people in Europe continues to rise, many governments that have long prided themselves on their social welfare programs are examining ways to shift a larger share of the costs of caring for the elderly to the private sector and charities. Germany and France have instituted or are

> An unused pot initiates contacts to see if the older person needs help.

weighing plans to raise the age at which retirees will qualify for pensions.

In most developing countries, people over 60 are likely to be in poorer health than their counterparts in industrialized nations. Yet few of these nations are in a position to offer extensive financial support to the elderly. Ironically, modernization in the developing world, while bringing with it many social and economic advances, has undercut the traditionally high status of the elderly. In many cultures, the earning power of younger adults now exceeds that of older family members.

In 1996, the United Nations cosponsored an international conference that examined social and economic policies dealing with the "Oldest Old"—those people age 80 and over. This rapidly increasing group deserves special attention. First, the oldest old in both industrialized and developing countries will probably have to depend for their security on a declining proportion of the population that is of working age. Second, in their search for support systems from either family or government, the oldest old may be forced to migrate, which will affect the immigration policies of many nations. Finally, the needs of the oldest old may intensify the pressures on their children (older workers) to postpone retirement for 5 or 10 additional years.

Let's Discuss

1. For an older person, how might life in Pakistan differ from life in France?
2. Do you know an aged person who lives alone? What arrangements have been made (or should be made) for care in case of emergency?

Sources: Crossette 1996a; Hani 1998; Haub and Cornelius 1999; Longworth 1996; M. Specter 1998a; Strom 2000a.

minority group subject to discrimination, as we'll see later in the chapter.

The model of five basic properties of a minority or subordinate group (introduced in Chapter 9) can be applied to older people in the United States to clarify their subordinate status: p. 225

1. The elderly experience unequal treatment in employment and may face prejudice and discrimination.
2. The elderly share physical characteristics that distinguish them from younger people. In addition, their cultural preferences and leisure-time activities often differ from those of the rest of society.
3. Membership in this disadvantaged group is involuntary.
4. Older people have a strong sense of group solidarity, as is reflected in the growth of senior citizens' centers, retirement communities, and advocacy organizations.
5. Older people generally are married to others of comparable age.

There is one crucial difference between older people and other subordinate groups, such as racial and ethnic minorities or women: *All* of us who live long enough will eventually assume the ascribed status of being an older person (M. Barron 1953; J. Levin and Levin 1980; Wagley and Harris 1958).

Explaining the Aging Process

Aging is one important aspect of socialization—the lifelong process through which an individual learns the cultural norms and values of a particular society. There are no clear-cut definitions for different periods of the aging cycle in the United States. *Old age* has typically been regarded as beginning at 65, which corresponds to the retirement age for many workers, but not everyone in the United States accepts this definition. With life expectancy being extended, writers are beginning to refer to people in their 60s as the "young old" to distinguish them from those in their 80s and beyond (the "old old").

The particular problems of the elderly have become the focus for a specialized area of research and inquiry known as gerontology. *Gerontology* is the scientific study of the sociological and psychological aspects of aging and the problems of the aged. It originally developed in the 1930s, as an increasing number of social scientists became aware of the plight of the elderly.

Gerontologists rely heavily on sociological principles and theories to explain the impact of aging on the individual and society. They also draw on the disciplines of psychology, anthropology, physical education, counseling, and medicine in their study of the aging process. Two influential views of aging—disengagement theory and activity theory—can be best understood in terms of the sociological perspectives of functionalism and interactionism, respectively. The conflict perspective also contributes to our sociological understanding of aging.

Functionalist Approach: Disengagement Theory

Elaine Cumming and William Henry (1961) introduced *disengagement theory* to explain the impact of aging during one's life course. This theory, based on a study of elderly people in good health and relatively comfortable economic circumstances, contends that society and the aging individual mutually sever many of their relationships. In keeping with the functionalist perspective, disengagement theory emphasizes that passing social roles on from one generation to another ensures social stability.

According to this theory, the approach of death forces people to drop most of their social roles—including those of worker, volunteer, spouse, hobby enthusiast, and even reader. Younger members of society then take on these functions. The aging person, it is held, withdraws into an increasing state of inactivity while preparing for death. At the same time, society withdraws from the elderly by segregating them residentially (retirement homes and communities), educationally (programs designed solely for senior citizens), and recreationally (senior citizens' social centers). Implicit in disengagement theory is the view that society should *help* older people to withdraw from their accustomed social roles.

Since it was first outlined more than three decades ago, disengagement theory has generated considerable controversy. Some gerontologists have objected to the implication that older people want to be ignored and "put away"—and even more to the idea that they should be encouraged to withdraw from meaningful social roles. Critics of disengagement theory insist that society *forces* the elderly into an involuntary and painful withdrawal from the paid labor force and from meaningful social relationships. Rather than voluntarily seeking to disengage, older employees find themselves pushed out of their jobs—in many instances, even before they are entitled to maximum retirement benefits (Boaz 1987).

Although functionalist in its approach, disengagement theory ignores the fact that postretirement employment has been *increasing* in recent decades. In the United States, fewer than half of all employees actually retire from their career jobs. Instead, most move into a "bridge job"—employment that bridges the period between the end of a person's career and his or her retirement. Unfortunately, the elderly can easily be victimized in such "bridge jobs." Psychologist Kathleen Christensen (1990), warning of "bridges over troubled water," emphasizes that older employees do not want to end their working days as minimum-wage jobholders engaged in activities unrelated to their career jobs (Doeringer 1990; Hayward et al. 1987).

Interactionist Approach: Activity Theory

Ask Ruth Vitow if she would like to trade in her New York City custom lampshade business for a condo in Florida, and you will get a quick response: "Deadly! I'd hate it." Vitow is in her nineties and vows to give up her business "when it gives me up." James Russell Wiggins has been working at a weekly newspaper in Maine since 1922. At age 95 he is now the editor. Vitow and Wiggins are among the 3.7 percent of people age 90 or above still in the nation's workforce (Mehren 1999:A21).

How important is staying actively involved for older people, whether at a job or in other pursuits? A tragic disaster in Chicago in 1995 showed that it can be a matter of life and death. An intense heat wave lasting more than a week—with a heat index exceeding 115 degrees on two consecutive days—resulted in 733 heat-related deaths. About three-fourths of the deceased were 65 and older.

Subsequent analysis showed that older people who lived alone had the highest risk of dying, suggesting that support networks for the elderly literally help save lives. Older Hispanics and Asian Americans had lower death rates from the heat wave than did other racial and ethnic groups. Their stronger social networks probably resulted in more regular contact with family members and friends during this critical time (Schaefer 1998a).

Often seen as an opposing approach to disengagement theory, *activity theory* argues that the elderly person who remains active and socially involved will be best-adjusted. Proponents of this perspective acknowledge that a 70-year-old person may not have the ability or desire to perform various social roles that he or she had at age 40. Yet they contend that old people have essentially the same need for social interaction as any other group.

The improved health of older people—sometimes overlooked by social scientists—has strengthened the arguments of activity theorists. Illness and chronic disease are no longer quite the scourge of the elderly that they once were. The recent emphasis on fitness, the availability of better medical care, greater control of infectious diseases, and the reduction of fatal strokes and heart attacks have combined to mitigate the traumas of growing old. Accumulating medical research also points to the importance of remaining socially involved. Among those who decline in their mental capacities later in life, deterioration is most rapid in old people who withdraw from social relationships and activities (Liao et al. 2000; National Institute on Aging 1999b).

Admittedly, many activities open to the elderly involve unpaid labor, for which younger adults may receive salaries. Such unpaid workers include hospital volunteers (versus aides and orderlies), drivers for charities such as the Red Cross (versus chauffeurs), tutors (as opposed to teachers), and craftspeople for charity bazaars (as opposed to carpenters and dressmakers). However, some companies have recently initiated programs to hire retirees for full-time or part-time work. For example, about 130 of the 600 reservationists at the Days Inn motel chain are over 60 years of age.

Disengagement theory suggests that older people find satisfaction in withdrawal from society. Functionally speaking, they conveniently recede into the background and allow the next generation to take over. Proponents of activity theory view such withdrawal as harmful for both the elderly and society and focus on the potential contributions of older people to the maintenance of society. In their opinion, aging citizens will feel satisfied only when they can be useful and productive in society's terms—primarily by working for wages (Civic Ventures 1999; Dowd 1980; Quadagno 1999).

The Days Inn motel chain hires many retirees to work full- or part-time as reservationists. *Activity theory* argues that the elderly person who remains active will be best-adjusted.

The Conflict Approach

Conflict theorists have criticized both disengagement theory and activity theory for failing to consider the impact of social structure on patterns of aging. Neither approach, they say, attempts to question why social interaction "must" change or decrease in old age. In addition, these perspectives, in contrast to the conflict perspective, often ignore the impact of social class on the lives of the elderly.

The privileged position of the upper class generally leads to better health and vigor and to less likelihood of dependency in old age. Affluence cannot forestall aging indefinitely, but it can soften the economic hardships faced in later years. Although pension plans, retirement packages, and insurance benefits may be developed to assist older people, those whose wealth allows them access to investment funds can generate the greatest income for their later years.

By contrast, working-class jobs often carry greater hazards to health and a greater risk of disability; aging will be particularly difficult for those who suffer job-related injuries or illnesses. Working-class people also depend more heavily on Social Security benefits and private pension programs. During inflationary times, their relatively fixed incomes from these sources barely keep pace with escalating costs of food, housing, utilities, and other necessities (Atchley 1985).

Conflict theorists have noted that the transition from agricultural economies to industrialization and capitalism has not always been beneficial for the elderly. As a society's production methods change, the traditionally valued role of older people within the economy tends to erode. Their wisdom is no longer relevant.

According to the conflict approach, the treatment of older people in the United States reflects the many divisions in our society. The low status of older people is seen in prejudice and discrimination against them, age segregation, and unfair job practices—none of which are directly addressed by either disengagement or activity theory.

The three perspectives considered here take different views of the elderly. Functionalists portray them as socially isolated with reduced social roles; interactionists see older people as involved in new networks of people in a change of social roles; conflict theorists regard older people as victimized by social structure, with their social roles relatively unchanged but devalued. Table 10-3 summarizes these perspectives.

Age Stratification in the United States

The "Graying of America"

When Lenore Schaefer, a ballroom dancer, tried to get on the *Tonight Show,* she was told she was "too young": she was in her early 90s. When she turned 101, she made it. But even at that age, Lenore is no longer unusual in our society. Today, people over 100 constitute, proportionately, the country's fastest-growing age group. They are part of the increasing proportion of the population of the United States composed of older people (Krach and Velkoff 1998; Rimer 1998).

Table 10-3 **Theories of Aging**

Sociological Perspective	View of Aging	Social Roles	Portrayal of Elderly
Functionalist	Disengagement	Reduced	Socially isolated
Interactionist	Activity	Changed	Involved in new networks
Conflict	Competition	Relatively unchanged	Victimized, organized to confront victimization

As Figure 10-4 shows, men and women aged 65 and over constituted only 4 percent of the nation's population in the year 1900, but by 2001 this figure had reached 14 percent. It is currently projected to level off by the year 2050. However, the "old old" segment of the population (that is, people 85 years old and over) is growing at an ever-faster rate.

In 1990, 14 percent of Whites were over the age of 65, compared with 8 percent of African Americans, 6 percent of Asian Americans, and 5 percent of Hispanics. These differences reflect the shorter life spans of these latter groups, as well as immigration patterns among Asians and Hispanics, who tend to be young when they enter the country. Yet people of color are increasing their presence

FIGURE 10-4

Actual and Projected Growth of the Elderly Population of the United States

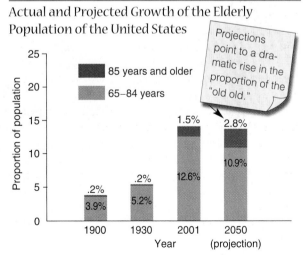

Sources: Bureau of the Census 1975; Bureau of the Census data in Yax 1999.

among the elderly population of the United States. In 1995, 15 percent of all people 65 years and older were people of color; by the year 2050, this figure is projected to rise to 34 percent (Treas 1995).

The highest proportion of older people are found in Florida, Pennsylvania, Rhode Island, Iowa, West Virginia, and Arkansas. However, many more states are undergoing an aging trend. In 1996, Florida was the state most populated by the elderly, with 18.5 percent of the population over the age of 65. Yet, as Figure 10-5 shows, in about 25 years, more than half of the states will have a greater proportion of elderly than Florida does now.

While the United States is noticeably graying, the nation's older citizens are in a sense getting younger, owing to improved health and nutrition. Researchers at the National Institute on Aging (1999b) have found a decrease in chronic disability in every age category. From the perspective of activity theory, this welcome change should be encouraged (Horn and Meer 1987).

The graying of the United States is a phenomenon that can no longer be ignored—either by social scientists or by government policymakers. Advocacy groups on behalf of the elderly have emerged and spoken out on a wide range of issues (as we will see later in the chapter). Politicians court the votes of older people, since they are the age group most likely to register and most likely to vote. In fact, they are the only age group that has actually increased their voter turnout rate over the last 25 years (L. Feldman 1999; LaGanga 2000).

Wealth and Income

There is significant variation in wealth and poverty among the nation's older people. Some individuals and couples find themselves poor in part because of fixed pensions and skyrocketing health care costs (see Chapter 14). Nevertheless, as a group, older people in the United States are neither homogeneous nor poor. The typical elderly person enjoys a standard of living that is much higher than at any point in the nation's past. Class differences among the elderly remain evident but tend to narrow somewhat: Those older people who enjoyed middle-class incomes while younger tend to remain better off after retirement than those who previously had lower incomes, but the financial gap lessens a bit (Arber and Ginn 1991; Duncan and Smith 1989).

To some extent, older people owe their overall improved standard of living to a greater accumulation of wealth—in the form of home ownership, private pensions, and other financial assets. But much of the improvement is due to more generous Social Security benefits. While modest when compared with other countries' pension programs, Social Security nevertheless provides 38 percent of all income received by older people in the United States. Currently, about one-eighth of the nation's elderly population lives below the poverty line; without Social Security, that figure would rise to half. At the extreme end of poverty are those groups who were more likely to be poor at earlier points in the life cycle: female-headed households and racial and ethnic minorities (Duncan and Smith 1989; Hess 1990).

Women account for 59 percent of people in the United States 65 years old and over and 72 percent of those 85 and over. Older women experience a double burden: They are female in a society that favors males, and they are elderly in a society that values youth. The social inequities that women experience throughout their lifetimes, as noted earlier in the chapter, only intensify as they age. As a result, in 1990 about half of older women living alone received some form of public assistance—whether Medicaid, food stamps, or subsidized or public housing.

Viewed from a conflict perspective, it is not surprising that older women experience a double burden; the same is true of elderly members of racial and ethnic minorities. For

FIGURE 10-5

26 Floridas by 2025

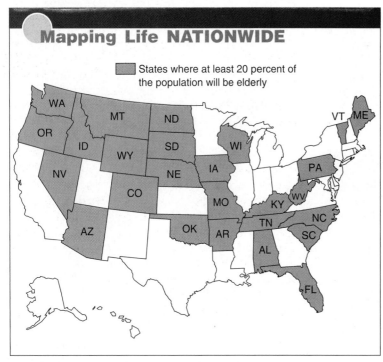

Mapping Life NATIONWIDE

States where at least 20 percent of the population will be elderly

Source: Bureau of the Census in Yax 1999.

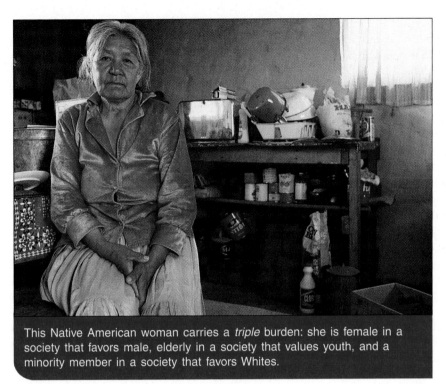

This Native American woman carries a *triple* burden: she is female in a society that favors male, elderly in a society that values youth, and a minority member in a society that favors Whites.

tional organization dedicated to the fight against age discrimination. Later in this chapter, we'll look at other successful efforts of the elderly to organize (R. Thomas 1995).

With ageism all too common in the United States, it is hardly surprising that older people are barely visible on television. A content analysis of 1,446 fictional television characters in the early 1990s revealed that only 2 percent were age 65 and over—even though this age group accounted for about 13 percent of the nation's population. A second study found older women particularly underrepresented on television (Robinson and Skill 1993; Vernon et al. 1990).

Competition in the Labor Force

In the United States in the year 1900, fully two-thirds of men aged 65 and over were found in the paid labor force, working either full-time or part-time. As recently as 1950, 46 percent of older men were in the labor force, but by 1990 this figure had dropped to 16 percent. Even among the "young old" (those 65 to 69 years of age), labor force participation has declined from 60 percent in 1950 to less than 30 percent in 1990 (Taeuber 1992). Despite these falling percentages, younger adults continue to view older workers as "job stealers," a biased judgment similar to that directed against illegal immigrants. This mistaken belief not only intensifies age conflict but leads to age discrimination. p. 249

While firing people simply because they are old violates federal laws, courts have upheld the right to lay off older workers for economic reasons. Critics contend that later the same firms hire young, cheaper workers to replace the experienced, older workers. Norman Matloff (1998), a computer science professor at the University of California, finds rampant age discrimination in the computer software industry, supposedly an understaffed field. Employers shunt aside mid-career programmers because they command higher salaries than recent college graduates. Companies defend their actions on the grounds that the older workers lack skills in the latest software programs.

A controlled experiment conducted in 1993 by the AARP confirmed that older people often face discrimination when applying for jobs. Comparable résumés for two applicants—one 57 years old and the other 32 years old—were sent to 775 large firms and employment agencies around the United States. In situations for which positions

example, in 1999 the proportion of older Hispanics with incomes below the poverty line (20.4 percent) was more than twice as large as the proportion of older Whites (8.3 percent). Moreover, 26 percent of older African Americans were below the federal government's poverty line (Dalaker and Naifeh 2000:3–5).

Economic inequality is not a static condition, for people move in and out of poverty. Race and ethnicity, however, are ascribed characteristics. And while people may move up and down the social ladder, those who *begin* life with greater resources have more opportunities to acquire additional resources. Women and minorities, and especially minority women, are less likely to accumulate savings or even have adequate pension plans for their older years.

Ageism

It "knows no one century, nor culture, and is not likely to go away any time soon." This is how physician Robert Butler (1990:178) described prejudice and discrimination against the elderly, which he called *ageism.* Ageism reflects a deep uneasiness among young and middle-aged people about growing old. For many, old age symbolizes disease, disability, and death; seeing the elderly serves as a reminder that *they* may someday become old and infirm. Ageism was popularized by Maggie Kuhn, a senior citizen who took up the cause of elderly rights after she was forced to retire from her position at the United Presbyterian Church. Kuhn formed the Gray Panthers in 1971, a na-

were actually available, the younger applicant received a favorable response 43 percent of the time. By contrast, the older applicant received favorable responses less than half as often (only 17 percent of the time). One *Fortune* 500 corporation asked the younger applicant for more information, while it informed the older applicant that no appropriate positions were open (Bendick et al. 1993).

In contrast to the negative stereotypes, researchers have found that older workers can be an *asset* for employers. According to a study issued in 1991, older workers can be retrained in new technologies, have lower rates of absenteeism than younger employees, and are often more effective salespeople. The study focused on two corporations based in the United States (the hotel chain Days Inns of America and the holding company Travelers Corporation of Hartford) and a British retail chain—all of which have long-term experience in hiring workers age 50 and over. An official of the private fund that commissioned the study concluded, "We have here the first systematic hard-nosed economic analysis showing older workers are good investments" (Telsch 1991:A16).

The Elderly: Emergence of a Collective Consciousness

During the 1960s, students at colleges and universities across the country, advocating "student power," collectively demanded a role in the governance of educational institutions. In the following decade, the 1970s, many older people became aware that *they* were being treated as second-class citizens and also turned to collective action.

The largest organization representing the nation's elderly is the AARP, founded in 1958 by a retired school principal who was having difficulty getting insurance because of age prejudice. Many of AARP's services involve discounts and insurance for its 31.5 million members, but the organization also functions as a powerful lobbying group. Recognizing that many elderly are still gainfully employed, it has dropped its full name, American Association of *Retired* Persons.

The potential power of AARP is enormous; it is the third-largest voluntary association in the United States (behind only the Roman Catholic church and the American Automobile Association) and represents one out of every four registered voters in the United States. The AARP has endorsed voter registration campaigns, nursing home reforms, and pension reforms. As an acknowledgment of its difficulties in recruiting members of racial and ethnic minority groups, AARP began a Minority Affairs Initiative. The spokeswoman of this initiative, Margaret Dixon, became AARP's first African American president in 1996 (Rosenblatt 2000).

People grow old in many different ways. Not all the elderly face the same challenges or enjoy the same resources. While the AARP lobbies to protect the elderly in general, other groups work in more specific ways. For example, the National Committee to Preserve Social Security and Medicare, founded in 1982, successfully lobbied Congress to keep Medicare benefits for the ailing poor elderly. Other large special interest groups represent retired federal employees, retired teachers, and retired union workers (Quadagno 1999).

Still another manifestation of the new awareness of older people is the formation of organizations for elderly homosexuals. One such group, Senior Action in a Gay Environment (SAGE), was established in New York City in 1978 and now oversees a nationwide network of local community groups. Like more traditional senior citizens' groups, SAGE sponsors workshops, classes, dances, and food deliveries to the homebound. At the same time, SAGE must deal with special concerns. Many gay couples find that nursing homes won't allow them to share a room. In addition, nearly 90 percent of gay seniors today have no children, and more than two-thirds live alone—

Members of SAGE, Senior Action in a Gay Environment, take part in a gay pride demonstration in New York City. This nationwide organization focuses on the special needs of gay seniors.

New technology has sparked a demand for testing services to determine who is and who is not the father of a child. When billboards advertising these services appeared in the United States in 1997, some people found them amusing while others perceived them as further evidence of the problems confronting the family.

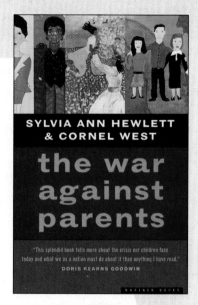

From the time of the breakdown of my marriage to Cliff's mother in 1979 to my marriage to Elleni in 1990, I was forced to deal with a difficult but nonetheless standard set of problems. My ex-wife was awarded custody of two-year-old Cliff and then decided to move to Atlanta. I had no recourse, legal or otherwise. And yet in my struggle to build a close relationship with my son, I now had to cope with an almost impossible set of barriers. Hundreds of miles separated me from Cliff, and I had limited visitation rights—a few specified weekends during the year plus three months in the summer. Besides which, what would I do with my son during our precious time together? My bachelor homes did not provide a supportive context for a four-year-old or a nine-year-old—there were no kids on the block, no basketball hoop in the back yard. But I wrestled with these problems and over time developed a strategy that worked, albeit imperfectly.

I hit upon this great solution for the summers. I would take Cliff back to Sacramento, back to the loving, child-centered home that had been so good to me and my siblings a generation ago. It required a lot of stretching and bending of the rules, but I organized life so that I really could take two and a half months out of the year. It meant postponing book deadlines and taming an almost impossible travel schedule, but it was well worth it. Those summers in Sacramento stand out like jewels in my memory. My parents' home turned out to be a profoundly healing place in which Cliff and I could reach out to one another. It provided the deeply needed (and yet so hard to contrive) rhythms and routines of normal family life. Three meals a day; regular bedtimes; clean clothes; a bevy of cousins—Kahnie, Phillip and Phyllis, Cornel and Erika—just around the corner, on tap for casual play; bicycles and baseball gear in the garage all ready to be put to use whenever a grownup was available. And hovering in the backgrounds, loving, eagle-eyed grandparents. . . . The evening meal was particularly important, as all three generations gathered for a cookout in the back yard. Conversation and laughter flowed, advice was sought and help was freely offered, jokes and stories were traded, and the children, spellbound, hung on the edges, absorbing the spirit and the meaning of family life.

The rest of the year was a struggle. I maintained regular telephone contact with Cliff, calling him several times a week just to hear his voice and shoot the breeze. But in the rushed, tantalizing visits around Thanksgiving, Christmas, and Easter, it was always hard not to lapse into the role of being a "good-time dad," showering gifts on him in an attempt to make up for real time or a deeper agenda. *(Hewlett and West 1998:21–22)* ∎

I n this excerpt from *The War Against Parents* philosophy scholar Cornel West underscores how deeply family life has been altered by divorce, one of many social factors that have gradually but inevitably turned the traditional nuclear family on its head. The family of today is not what it was a century ago or even a generation ago. New roles, new gender distinctions, new child-rearing patterns have all combined to create new forms of family life. Today, for example, we are seeing more and more women take the breadwinner's role, whether married or as a single parent. Blended families—the result of divorces and remarriages—are almost the norm. And many people are seeking intimate relationships outside marriage, whether it be in gay partnerships or in cohabiting arrangements.

This chapter addresses family and intimate relationships in the United States as well as in other parts of the world. As we will see, family patterns differ from one culture to another and even within the same culture. A *family* can be defined as a set of people related by blood, marriage (or some other agreed-upon relationship), or adoption who share the primary responsibility for reproduction and caring for members of society.

In this chapter, we will see that the family is universal—found in every culture—however varied in its organization. We will look at the family and intimate relationships from the functionalist, conflict, and interactionist points of view and at the variations in marital patterns and family life, including different family forms of child rearing. We'll pay particular attention to the increasing number of people in dual-income or single-parent families. We will examine divorce in the United States and consider such diverse lifestyles as cohabitation, remaining single, lesbian and gay relationships, and marriage without children. The social policy section will look at controversial issues surrounding the use of reproductive technology. ■

Global View of the Family

Among Tibetans, a woman may be simultaneously married to more than one man, usually brothers. This system allows sons to share the limited amount of good land. A Hopi woman may divorce her husband by placing her belongings outside the door. A Trobriand Island couple signals marriage by sitting in public on a porch eating yams provided by the bride's mother. She continues to provide cooked yams for a year while the groom's family offers in exchange such valuables as stone axes and clay pots (W. Haviland 1999).

As these examples illustrate, there are many variations in "the family" from culture to culture. Yet the family as a social institution is present in all cultures. Moreover, certain general principles concerning its composition, kinship patterns, and authority patterns are universal.

Composition: What Is the Family?

If we were to take our information on what a family is from what we see on television, we might come up with some very strange scenarios (see Box 11-1). The media don't always help us get a realistic view of the family. Moreover, many people still think of the family in very narrow terms—as a married couple and their unmarried children living together, like the family in the old *Cosby Show* or *Family Ties* or *Growing Pains*. However, this is but one type of family, what sociologists refer to as a **nuclear family**. The term nuclear family is well chosen, since this type of family

In wedding ceremonies in Sumatra, Indonesia, the bride's headdress indicates her village and her social status—the more elaborate the headdress, the higher her status. After she is married, the bride and her husband live with her maternal family, and all property passes from mother to daughter.

Eye on the Media 11-1 The Family in TV Land

Put an alien creature from outer space in front of a television, and it would have no idea of what family life is like in the United States. It would conclude that most adults are men, most adults are not married, almost no one is over age 50, very few adults have children, most mothers don't work for pay, and child care is simply not an issue. When parents are depicted, they are either not around for the most part or they are clueless. The baby boomers in *Everybody Loves Raymond* treat their parents like meddling invaders, which is also how the teenage generation treats their boomer parents in *Dawson's Creek*. Even the cartoon show *Rugrats*, aimed at young children, portrays talking babies as making their way in the world on their own.

The fact is that *Friends, Third Rock from the Sun, Frasier, Will and Grace, Ally McBeal*, and similar programs present lives that most households find fascinating, but not exactly true to their own lives. Eight out of 10 adults in the United States think that almost no TV family is like their own; nearly half find no TV family like theirs.

These conclusions come out of a content analysis of prime-time TV programming conducted by Katharine Heintz-Knowles, a communications professor at the University of Washington and the mother of three children, who knows first-hand what a work–family conflict looks like. She has had to deal with finding sitters on short notice, taking children to work with her when a sitter was unavailable, and missing meetings to tend to a sick child. In fact, she acknowledges that her "life today is one big work–family conflict" (Gardner 1998:13). But when she watched television, she didn't see much of her life reflected on the screen.

Television Reality versus Social Reality		
	Adult TV Characters	**U.S. Adult Population**
Women	38%	51%
Over age 50	14%	38%
Parents of minor children	15%	32%

Her study, called "Balancing Acts: Work/Family Issues on Prime-Time TV," carried out content analysis of 150 episodes of 92 different programs on commercial networks over a two-week period. She found that of the 820 TV characters studied, only 38 percent were women, only 15 percent could be identified as parents of minor children, and only 14 percent were over age 50 (see the table for how these percentages compare to the adult U.S. population). Only 3

> **Eight out of 10 adults in the United States think that almost no TV family is like their own.**

percent of the TV characters faced recognizable conflicts between work and family, and no TV family made use of a child care center. Commenting on this study, TV personality Rosie O'Donnell (1998) noted, "Television may bring the realities of violence and natural disaster into our lives, but it rarely captures the reality of work and family life. . . . And heaven forbid a person over the age of 30 and bigger than a size four ever showed up on *Melrose Place*."

Because television is the major storyteller in our lives today, its programs can shape our attitudes and beliefs. Unfortunately, television gives a distorted view of family life in the United States, not only to our hypothetical alien, but also to viewers at home and in other societies on planet Earth. If very few shows depict real-life challenges in family life and possible solutions, then viewers may well go away thinking their own problems are unique and insoluble. By confronting these issues, television could call attention to what needs to be changed—both on an individual level and on a societal level—and offer hope for solutions. It appears, however, that most TV programmers offer up a fantasy world in order to satisfy people who seek entertainment and escape from their everyday lives.

Let's Discuss

1. How well does television portray the social reality of your family life?

2. Take the role of a television producer. What kind of show would you create to reflect family life today?

Sources: Blanco 1998; National Partnership for Women and Families 1998; O'Donnell 1998.

FIGURE 11-1

Types of Family Households in the United States, 1980, 1997, and 2010

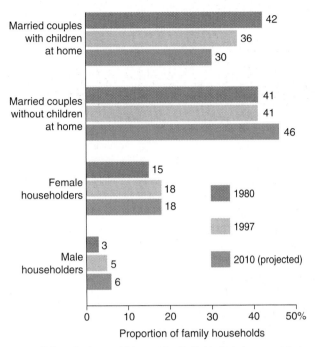

Note: "Children" refers to children under 18. Not included are unrelated people living together with no children present. Because of rounding, numbers may not total 100 percent.

Source: Bureau of the Census 1998c:61, 62.

serves as the nucleus, or core, upon which larger family groups are built. Most people in the United States see the nuclear family as the preferred family arrangement. Yet, as Figure 11-1 shows, by 1997 only about a third of the nation's family households fit this model.

The proportion of households in the United States composed of married couples with children at home has decreased steadily over the last 30 years, and this trend is expected to continue. At the same time, there have been increases in the number of single-parent households (see Figure 11-1). Similar trends are evident in other industrialized nations, including Canada, Great Britain, and Japan (see Figure 11-2).

A family in which relatives—such as grandparents, aunts, or uncles—live in the same home as parents and their children is known as an **extended family.** While not common, such living arrangements do exist in the United States. The structure of the extended family offers certain advantages over that of the nuclear family. Crises such as death, divorce, and illness put less strain on family members, since there are more people who can provide assistance and emotional support. In addition, the extended family constitutes a larger economic unit than the nuclear family. If

the family is engaged in a common enterprise—a farm or a small business—the additional family members may represent the difference between prosperity and failure.

In considering these differing family types, we have limited ourselves to the form of marriage that is characteristic of the United States—monogamy. The term **monogamy** describes a form of marriage in which one woman and one man are married only to each other. Some observers, noting the high rate of divorce in the United States, have suggested that "serial monogamy" is a more accurate description of the form that monogamy takes in the United States. Under **serial monogamy,** a person may have several spouses in his or her life but only one spouse at a time.

Some cultures allow an individual to have several husbands or wives simultaneously. This form of marriage is known as **polygamy.** In fact, most societies throughout the world, past and present, have preferred polygamy to monogamy. Anthropologist George Murdock (1949, 1957) sampled 565 societies and found that more than 80 percent had some type of polygamy as their preferred form. While polygamy steadily declined through most of the twentieth century, in at least five countries in Africa 20 percent of men are still in polygamous marriages (Population Reference Bureau 1996).

There are two basic types of polygamy. According to Murdock, the most common—endorsed by the majority of cultures he sampled—was **polygyny.** Polygyny refers to the marriage of a man to more than one woman at the same time. The various wives are often sisters, who are expected to hold similar values and have already had experience sharing a household. In polygynous societies, relatively few men actually have multiple spouses. Most individuals live in typical monogamous families; having multiple wives is viewed as a mark of status.

The other principal variation of polygamy is **polyandry,** under which a woman can have more than one husband at the same time. This is the case in the culture of the Todas of southern India. Polyandry, however, tends to be exceedingly rare in the world today. It has been accepted by some extremely poor societies that practice female infanticide (the killing of baby girls) and thus have a relatively small number of women. Like many other societies, polyandrous cultures devalue the social worth of women.

Kinship Patterns: To Whom Are We Related?

Many of us can trace our roots by looking at a family tree or listening to elderly family members tell us about their lives—and about the lives of ancestors who died long before we were even born. Yet a person's lineage is more than simply a personal history; it also reflects societal patterns that govern descent. In every culture, children encounter

FIGURE 11-2

The Nuclear Family in Industrialized Nations, 1960 and 1990

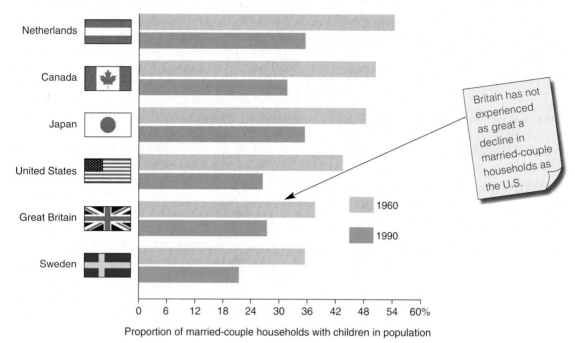

Source: Bureau of Labor Statistics data in Sorrentino 1990 and author's estimate.

relatives to whom they are expected to show an emotional attachment. The state of being related to others is called **kinship.** Kinship is culturally learned and is not totally determined by biological or marital ties. For example, adoption creates a kinship tie that is legally acknowledged and socially accepted.

The family and the kin group are not necessarily the same. While the family is a household unit, kin do not always live together or function as a collective body on a daily basis. Kin groups include aunts, uncles, cousins, in-laws, and so forth. In a society such as the United States, the kinship group may come together only rarely, as for a wedding or funeral. However, kinship ties frequently create obligations and responsibilities. We may feel compelled to assist our kin and feel free to call upon relatives for many types of aid, including loans and baby-sitting.

How do we identify kinship groups? The principle of descent assigns people to kinship groups according to their relationship to an individual's mother or father. There are three primary ways of determining descent. The United States follows the system of **bilateral descent,** which means that both sides of a person's family are regarded as equally important. For example no higher value is given to the brothers of one's father as opposed to the brothers of one's mother.

Most societies—according to George Murdock, 64 percent—give preference to one side of the family or the other in tracing descent. **Patrilineal** (from Latin *pater,* "father") **descent** indicates that only the father's relatives are important in terms of property, inheritance, and emotional ties. Conversely, in societies that favor **matrilineal** (from Latin *mater,* "mother") **descent,** only the mother's relatives are significant.

New forms of reproductive technology (discussed in the policy section) will force a new way of looking at kinship. Today a combination of biological and social processes can "create" a family member, requiring that more distinctions be made about who is related to whom (C. Cussins 1998).

Authority Patterns: Who Rules?

Imagine that you have recently married and must begin to make decisions about the future of your new family. You and your spouse face many questions. Where will you live? How will you furnish your home? Who will do the cooking, the shopping, the cleaning? Whose friends will be invited to dinner? Each time a decision must be made, an issue is raised: Who has the power to make the decision? In simple terms, who rules the family? The conflict perspective examines these questions in the context of traditional gender stratification, under which men have held a dominant position over women.

p. 263

Smile—it's family reunion time! The state of being related to others is called kinship. Kin groups include aunts, uncles, cousins, and so forth, as shown in this family from Slovakia.

Societies vary in the way that power within the family is distributed. If a society expects males to dominate in all family decision making, it is termed a ***patriarchy.*** Frequently, in patriarchal societies, such as Iran, the eldest male wields the greatest power, although wives are expected to be treated with respect and kindness. A woman's status in Iran is typically defined by her relationship to a male relative, usually as a wife or daughter. In many patriarchal societies women find it more difficult to obtain a divorce than a man does (G. Farr 1999). By contrast, in a ***matriarchy,*** women have greater authority than men. Matriarchies, which are very uncommon, emerged among Native American tribal societies and in nations in which men were absent for long periods of time for warfare or food gathering.

A third type of authority pattern, the ***egalitarian family,*** is one in which spouses are regarded as equals. This does not mean, however, that each decision is shared in such families. Wives may hold authority in some spheres, husbands in others. Many sociologists believe the egalitarian family has begun to replace the patriarchal family as the social norm in the United States.

Studying the Family

Do we really need the family? A century ago, Friedrich Engels (1884), a colleague of Karl Marx, described the family as the ultimate source of social inequality be-
cause of its role in the transfer of power, property, and privilege. More recently, conflict theorists have argued that the family contributes to societal injustice, denies opportunities to women that are extended to men, and limits freedom in sexual expression and selection of a mate. By contrast, the functionalist perspective focuses on the ways in which the family gratifies the needs of its members and contributes to the stability of society. The interactionist view considers more intimate, face-to-face relationships.

Functionalist View

There are six paramount functions performed by the family, first outlined more than 65 years ago by sociologist William F. Ogburn (Ogburn and Tibbits 1934):

1. **Reproduction.** For a society to maintain itself, it must replace dying members. In this sense, the family contributes to human survival through its function of reproduction.

2. **Protection.** Unlike the young of other animal species, human infants need constant care and economic security. The extremely long period of dependency for children places special demands on older family members. In all cultures, it is the family that assumes ultimate responsibility for the protection and upbringing of children.

3. **Socialization.** Parents and other kin monitor a child's behavior and transmit the norms, values, and language of a culture to the child (see Chapters 3 and 4). p. 91

4. **Regulation of sexual behavior.** Sexual norms are subject to change over time (for instance, changes in customs for dating) and across cultures (Islamic Saudi Arabia compared with more permissive Denmark). However, whatever the time period or cultural values in a society, standards of sexual behavior are most clearly defined within the family circle. The structure of society influences these standards. In male-dominated societies, for example, formal and informal norms generally permit men to express and enjoy their sexual desires more freely than women may.

5. **Affection and companionship.** Ideally, the family provides members with warm and intimate

relationships and helps them feel satisfied and secure. Of course, a family member may find such rewards outside the family—from peers, in school, at work—and may perceive the home as an unpleasant place. Nevertheless, unlike other institutions, the family is obligated to serve the emotional needs of its members. We *expect* our relatives to understand us, to care for us, and to be there for us when we need them.

6. **Providing of social status.** We inherit a social position because of the "family background" and reputation of our parents and siblings. The family unit presents the newborn child with an ascribed status of race and ethnicity that helps to determine his or her place within a society's stratification system. Moreover, family resources affect children's ability to pursue certain opportunities such as higher education and specialized lessons.

The family has traditionally fulfilled a number of other functions, such as providing religious training, education, and recreational outlets. Ogburn argued that other social institutions have gradually assumed many of these functions. Although the family once played a major role in religious life—Bible reading and hymn singing commonly took place at home—this function has largely shifted to churches, synagogues, and other religious organizations. Similarly, education once took place at the family fireside; now it is the responsibility of professionals working in schools and colleges. Even the family's traditional recreational function has been transferred to outside groups such as Little Leagues, athletic clubs, and Internet chat rooms.

Conflict View

Conflict theorists view the family not as a contributor to social stability, but as a reflection of the inequality in wealth and power found within the larger society. Feminist theorists and conflict theorists note that the family has traditionally legitimized and perpetuated male dominance. Throughout most of human history—and in a very wide range of societies—husbands have exercised overwhelming power and authority within the family. Not until the "first wave" of contemporary feminism in the United States in the mid-1800s was there a substantial challenge to the historic status of wives and children as the legal property of husbands.

p. 15

While the egalitarian family has become a more common pattern in the United States in recent decades—owing in good part to the activism of feminists beginning in the late 1960s and early 1970s—male dominance within the family has hardly disappeared.

Sociologists have found that women are significantly more likely to leave their jobs when their husbands find better employment opportunities than men are when their wives receive desirable job offers (Bielby and Bielby 1992). And unfortunately, many husbands reinforce their power and control over wives and children through acts of domestic violence. (Box 11-2 considers cross-cultural findings about violence within the home.)

Conflict theorists also view the family as an economic unit that contributes to societal injustice. The family is the basis for transferring power, property, and privilege from one generation to the next. The United States is widely viewed as a "land of opportunity," yet social mobility is restricted in important ways. Children "inherit" the privileged or less-than-privileged social and economic status of their parents (and, in some cases, of earlier generations as well). As conflict theorists point out, the social class of their parents significantly influences children's socialization experiences and the protection they receive. This means that the socioeconomic status of a child's family will have a marked influence on his or her nutrition, health care, housing, educational opportunities, and, in many respects, life chances as an adult. For that reason, conflict theorists argue that the family helps to maintain inequality.

p. 205

Interactionist View

Interactionists focus on the microlevel of family and other intimate relationships. They are interested in how individuals interact with one another, whether they are cohabiting partners or long-time married couples. For example, a study of both Black and White two-parent households found that when fathers are more involved with their children (such as reading, helping with homework, restricting television viewing) children have fewer behavior problems, get along better with others, and are more responsible (Mosley and Thomson 1995).

Another interactionist study might examine the role of the stepparent. The increased number of single parents who remarry has sparked an interest in those who are helping to raise other people's children. While no young girl or boy may dream about one day becoming a stepmom or stepdad, this is hardly an unusual occurrence today. Studies have found that stepmothers are more likely to accept the blame for bad relations with their stepchildren, whereas stepfathers are less likely to accept responsibility. Interactionists theorize that stepfathers (like most fathers) may simply be unaccustomed to interaction directly with children when the mother isn't there (Bray and Kelly 1999; Furstenberg and Cherlin 1991).

Sociology in the Global Community

11-2 Domestic Violence

"It's the same every Saturday night. The husband comes home drunk and beats her." This is how Tania Kucherenko describes her downstairs neighbors in Moscow after turning a deaf ear to the screams of terror and the sounds of furniture being overthrown and glass breaking. "There's nothing we can do. It's best not to interfere." Contempt for women runs deep in Russia, where women who dare to leave their husbands risk losing their legal status, a place to live, and the right to work (Bennett 1997:A1).

Wife battering, child abuse, abuse of the elderly, and other forms of domestic violence are an ugly reality of family life across the world. In Japan, Tanzania, and Chile, more than half the women report physical abuse by a partner. While estimates are difficult to find on a topic so hidden from public view, one recent study concluded that around the world one-third of all women have been beaten, or coerced into sex, or otherwise physically abused in their lifetime.

Drawing on studies conducted throughout the world, we can make the following generalizations:

- Women are most at risk of violence from the men they know.
- Violence against women is evident in all socioeconomic groups.
- Family violence is at least as dangerous as assaults committed by strangers.
- Though women sometimes exhibit violent behavior toward men, most acts of violence that cause injury are perpetrated by men against women.
- Violence within intimate relationships tends to escalate over time.

This billboard in Poland featuring the bruised face of a child reads, "Because he had to let off steam." It is a reminder to Poles that domestic violence is a serious problem in their country, affecting both wives and children.

- Emotional and psychological abuse can be at least as debilitating as physical abuse.
- Use of alcohol exacerbates family violence but does not cause it.

Using the conflict and feminist models, researchers have found that in relationships where the inequality is greater between men and women, the likelihood of assault on wives increases

> **The situation of battered women is so intolerable that it has been compared to that of prison inmates.**

dramatically. This suggests that much of the violence between intimates, even when sexual in nature, is about power rather than sex.

The situation of battered women is so intolerable that it has been compared to that of prison inmates. Criminologist Noga Avni (1991) interviewed battered women at a shelter in Israel and found that their day-to-day lives with their hus-

bands or lovers shared many elements of life in an oppressive total institution, as described by Erving Goffman (1961). Physical barriers are imposed on these women; by threatening further violence, men are able to restrict women to their homes, damaging both their self-esteem and their ability to cope with repeated abuse. Moreover, as in a total institution, p. 89 these battered women are cut off from external sources of physical and emotional assistance and moral support. In Avni's view, society could more effectively aid victims of domestic violence if it better understood the essential imprisonment of these women. Women in these situations have few economic alternatives, and they fear that their children may also be victimized if they don't submit to the abuse.

The family can be a dangerous place not only for women but also for children and the elderly. In 1996, public agencies in the United States received more than three million reports of child abuse and/or neglect. That means reports were filed on about 1 out of every 25 children. Another national study found that approximately 450,000 elderly persons, or 1 in every 90, were abused or neglected in that same year.

Let's Discuss

1. How does the degree of equality in a relationship correlate to the likelihood of domestic violence? How might conflict theorists explain this?
2. Do you know of a family that experienced domestic violence? Did the victim(s) seek outside help, and was that help effective?

Sources: American Bar Association 1999; American Humane Association 1999; Gelles and Cornell 1990; Heise et al. 1999; National Center on Elder Abuse 1998; Straus 1994.

Marriage and Family

Currently, close to 90 percent of all men and women in the United States marry at least once during their lifetimes. Historically, the most consistent aspect of family life in this country has been the high rate of marriage. In fact, despite the high rate of divorce, there are indications of a miniboom in marriages in the United States of late, fueled by a strong economy and a return to traditional values (Parker 1998).

In this part of the chapter, we will examine various aspects of love, marriage, and parenthood in the United States and contrast them with cross-cultural examples. We're used to thinking of romance and mate selection as strictly a matter of individual preference. Yet, sociological analysis tells us that social institutions and distinctive cultural norms and values also play an important role.

When fathers interact regularly with their children, it's a win/win situation. The fathers get close to their offspring, and studies show that the children end up with fewer behavior problems.

Courtship and Mate Selection

"My rugby mates would roll over in their graves," says Tom Buckley of his online courtship and subsequent marriage to Terri Muir. But Tom and Terri are hardly alone these days in turning to the Internet for matchmaking services. By the end of 1999 more than 2,500 websites were helping people find mates. You could choose from oneandonly.com or 2ofakind.com or cupidnet.com, among others. One service alone claimed 2 million subscribers. Tom and Terri carried on their romance via e-mail for a year before they met. According to Tom, "E-mail made it easier to communicate because neither one of us was the type to walk up to someone in the gym or a bar and say, 'You're the fuel to my fire' " (B. Morris 1999:D1).

Internet romance is only the latest courtship practice. In the central Asian nation of Uzbekistan and many other traditional cultures, courtship is defined largely through the interaction of two sets of parents. They arrange spouses for their children. Typically, a young Uzbekistani woman will be socialized to eagerly anticipate her marriage to a man whom she has met only once, when he is presented to her family at the time of the final inspection of her dowry. In the United States, by contrast, courtship is conducted primarily by individuals who may have a romantic interest in each other. In our culture, courtship often requires these individuals to rely heavily on intricate games, gestures, and signals. Despite such differences, courtship—whether in the United States, Uzbekistan, or elsewhere—is influenced by the norms and values of the larger society (C. J. Williams 1995).

Take our choice of a mate. Why are we drawn to a particular person in the first place? To what extent are these judgments shaped by the society around us?

Aspects of Mate Selection

Many societies have explicit or unstated rules that define potential mates as acceptable or unacceptable. These norms can be distinguished in terms of endogamy and exogamy. *Endogamy* (from the Greek *endon,* "within") specifies the groups within which a spouse must be found and prohibits marriage with others. For example, in the United States, many people are expected to marry within their own racial, ethnic, or religious group and are strongly discouraged or even prohibited from marrying outside the group. Endogamy is intended to reinforce the cohesiveness of the group by suggesting to the young that they should marry someone "of our own kind."

By contrast, *exogamy* (from the Greek *exo,* "outside") requires mate selection outside certain groups, usually one's own family or certain kinfolk. The *incest taboo,* a social norm common to virtually all societies, prohibits sexual relationships between certain culturally specified

The love expressed by this mother and her two children testifies to successful parenting. Even though parenthood is a crucial social role, society generally provides few clear guidelines.

the period of pregnancy itself. Third, the transition to parenthood is quite abrupt. Unlike adolescence, it is not prolonged; unlike socialization for work, you cannot gradually take on the duties of caregiving. Finally, in Rossi's view, our society lacks clear and helpful guidelines for successful parenthood. There is little consensus on how parents can produce happy and well-adjusted offspring—or even on what it means to be "well-adjusted." For these reasons, socialization for parenthood involves difficult challenges for most men and women in the United States.

One recent development in family life in the United States has been the extension of parenthood, as adult children continue to (or return to) live at home. In 1995, more than half of all children ages 18 to 24 and one out of eight of those ages 25 to 34 lived with their parents. Some of these adult children are still pursuing an education, but in many instances, financial difficulties are at the heart of these living arrangements. While rents and real estate prices skyrocketed in the 1990s, salaries for younger workers did not keep pace, and many found themselves unable

to afford their own homes. Moreover, with many marriages now ending in divorce—most commonly in the first seven years of marriage—divorced sons and daughters are returning to live with their parents, sometimes with their own children (Bureau of the Census 1997a:58).

Is this living arrangement a positive development for family members? Social scientists have just begun to examine this phenomenon, sometimes called the "boomerang generation" or the "full-nest syndrome" in the popular press. One survey in Virginia seemed to show that neither the parents nor their adult children were happy about continuing to live together. The children often felt resentful and isolated, but the parents also suffered: Learning to live without children in the home is an essential stage of adult life and may even be a significant turning point for a marriage (*Berkeley Wellness Letter* 1990; Mogelonsky 1996).

As life expectancy increases in the United States, more and more parents are becoming grandparents and even great-grandparents. After interviewing many grandparents, sociologists Andrew Cherlin and Frank Furstenberg Jr. (1992) identified three principal styles of grandparenting:

1. More than half (55 percent) of grandparents surveyed functioned as "specialists in recreational care-giving." They enriched their grandchildren's lives through recreational outings and other special activities.
2. More than one-fourth (29 percent) carried on a "ritualistic" (primarily symbolic) relationship with their grandchildren. In some instances, this was because the grandparents lived far away from their grandchildren and could see them only occasionally.
3. About one-sixth (16 percent) of grandparents surveyed were actively involved in everyday routine care of their grandchildren and exercised substantial authority over them.

Adoption

In a legal sense, **adoption** is a "process that allows for the transfer of the legal rights, responsibilities, and privileges of parenthood" to a new legal parent or parents (E. Cole 1985:638). In many cases, these rights are transferred from a biological parent or parents (often called birth parents) to an adoptive parent or parents.

Viewed from a functionalist perspective, government has a strong interest in encouraging adoption. Policymakers, in fact, have both a humanitarian and a financial stake in the process. In theory, adoption offers a stable family environment for children who otherwise might not receive satisfactory care. Moreover, government data show that unwed mothers who keep their babies tend to be of lower socioeconomic status and often require public assistance to support their children. Government can lower its social welfare expenses if children are transferred

A. DAVID ROBERTS:
Social Worker

Dave Roberts admits to being a "people person," a trait that sociology courses fostered by showing how "everybody has differences; there are little bits of different cultures in all of us." He also had the benefit of "a lot of great teachers" at Florida State University, including Dr. Jill Quadagno in an "Aging" course. It was this class that sparked his interest in aging issues, which led to a certificate in gerontology in addition to a sociology degree in 1998. He realized that there was a good job market in working with the aging baby boom generation.

Volunteer work with the Meals on Wheels program steered him toward working with the elderly. Today Roberts is a social worker in a nursing home, where he is responsible for patients' care plans. In the course of this work, he meets regularly with patients, family members, and medical residents. Roberts finds that the concept of teamwork he learned in group projects in college has helped him in this job. Also, the projects he had to do in school taught him to work on a schedule. Perhaps most importantly, sociology has helped him "to grow as a person to explore different angles, different theories. . . . I'm a better person."

His advice for sociology students: "Just give it a chance; they throw everything into an intro course. Don't get overwhelmed; take it as it comes."

Let's Discuss

1. In view of the fact that people today are living longer and staying more active, what sorts of job opportunities do you think will open up for serving senior citizens' needs?

2. If you were to create a business to cater to the senior population, what would it be? Where do your own interests lie, and how might they be applied to older people?

---

to economically self-sufficient families. From a conflict perspective, however, such financial considerations raise the ugly specter of adoption as a means whereby affluent (often infertile) couples "buy" the children of the poor (C. Bachrach 1986).

The largest single category of adoption in the United States is adoption by relatives. In most cases, a stepparent adopts the children of a spouse. There are two legal methods of adopting an unrelated person: adoptions arranged by licensed agencies and private agreements sanctioned by the courts (M. Groves 1999).

In some cases the adopters are not married. An important court decision in 1995 in New York held that a couple does not have to be married to adopt a child. Under this ruling, unmarried heterosexual couples, lesbian couples, and gay male couples can all legally adopt children in New York. Writing for the majority, Chief Justice Judith Kaye argued that by expanding the boundaries of who can be legally recognized as parents, the state may be able to assist more children in securing "the best possible home." With this ruling, New York became the third state (after Vermont and Massachusetts) to recognize the right of unmarried couples to adopt children (Dao 1995).

Dual-Income Families

The idea of a family consisting of a wage-earning husband and a wife who stays at home has largely given way to the *dual-income household.* Among married people between the ages of 25 and 34, 96 percent of the men and 72 percent of the women are in the labor force. Why has there been such a rise in the number of dual-income couples? A major factor is economic need. In 1999, the median income for households with both partners employed was 86 percent more than in households in which only one person was working outside the home ($59,699, compared with $31,948). Of course, not all of a family's second wage is genuine additional income because of such work-related costs as child care. Other factors contributing to the rise of the dual-income model include the nation's declining birthrate (see Chapter 14), the increase in the proportion of women with a college education, the shift in the economy of the United States from manufacturing to service industries, and the impact of the feminist movement in changing women's consciousness (Bureau of the Census 1999a:416; 2000d:6).

Single-Parent Families

In the United States of the late nineteenth century, immigration and urbanization made it increasingly difficult to maintain *Gemeinschaft* communities where everyone knew one another and shared responsibility for unwed mothers and their children. In 1883, the Florence Crittenton Houses were founded in New York City—and subsequently established around the nation—as refuges for prostitutes (then stigmatized as "fallen women"). Within a few years, the Crittenton homes began accepting unwed mothers as residents. By the early 1900s, sociologist W. E. B. Du Bois (1911) had noted that the institutionalization of unwed mothers was occurring in segregated facilities.

Dad takes breakfast duty while Mom rushes off to work in this "dual-income" family. An increasing proportion of couples in the United States reject the traditional nuclear family model of husband as breadwinner and wife as homemaker.

Why might low-income teenage women wish to have children and face the obvious financial difficulties of motherhood? Viewed from an interactionist perspective, these women tend to have low self-esteem and limited options; a child may provide a sense of motivation and purpose for a teenager whose economic worth in our society is limited at best. Given the barriers that many young women face because of their gender, race, ethnicity, and class, many teenagers may believe that they have little to lose and much to gain by having a child.

According to a widely held stereotype, "unwed mothers" and "babies having babies" in the United States are predominantly African American. However, this view is not entirely accurate. African Americans account for a disproportionate share of births to unmarried women and to teenagers, but the majority of all babies born to unmarried teenage mothers are born to White adolescents. Moreover, since 1990, birthrates among Black teenagers have declined more than any other group (Ventura and Bachrach 2000).

While 76 percent of single parents in the United States are mothers, the number of households headed by single fathers has more than quadrupled over the period 1980 to 1998. The stereotypes of single fathers are that they raise only boys or older children. In fact, about 44 percent of children living in such households are girls; almost one-third of single fathers care for preschoolers. Whereas single mothers often develop social networks,

At the time that he was writing, there were seven homes of various types nationwide for unwed Black mothers as well as one Crittenton home reserved for that purpose.

In recent decades, the stigma attached to "unwed mothers" and other single parents has significantly diminished. **Single-parent families,** in which there is only one parent present to care for the children, can hardly be viewed as a rarity in the United States. In 1998, a single parent headed about 19 percent of White families with children under 18, 34 percent of Hispanic families with children, and 54 percent of African American families with children (Bureau of the Census 1999a:62).

The lives of single parents and their children are not inevitably more difficult than life in a traditional nuclear family. It is as inaccurate to assume that a single-parent family is necessarily "deprived" as it is to assume that a two-parent family is always secure and happy. Nevertheless, life in a single-parent family can be extremely stressful, in both economic and emotional terms.

A family headed by a single mother faces especially difficult problems when the mother is a teenager. Drawing on two decades of social science research, sociologist Kristin Luker (1996:11) observes:

> The short answer to why teenagers get pregnant and especially to why they continue those pregnancies is that a fairly substantial number of them just don't believe what adults tell them, be it about sex, contraception, marriage, or babies. They don't believe in adult conventional wisdom.

Most households in the United States do not consist of two parents living with their unmarried children.

single fathers are typically more isolated. In addition, they must deal with schools and social service agencies more accustomed to women as custodial parents (Bureau of the Census 1999a:62; D. Johnson 1993).

What about single fathers who do not head the household? This is typically an understudied group for sociological purposes, but a study of low-income unmarried fathers in Philadelphia came up with some unexpected findings. When asked what their lives would be like without having children, many responded that they would be dead or in jail. This was true even of those fathers who had very little to do with their children. Apparently, the mere fact of fathering children prompts men to get jobs, stay in the community, and stay healthy. Many of these men were upset that they have to hand over money without having a say in how it is spent or in some cases even having legal access to their offspring (P. Cohen 1998).

Stepfamilies

Approximately one-third of all people in the United States will marry, divorce, and then remarry. The rising rates of divorce and remarriage have led to a noticeable increase in stepfamily relationships. In 1980, 9 percent of all family households with children present included a stepparent; by 1990, that figure had almost tripled to 24 percent (Bureau of the Census 1995:64; Cherlin and Furstenberg 1994).

Stepfamilies are an exceedingly complex form of family organization. Here is how one 13-year-old boy described his family.

> Tim and Janet are my stepbrother and sister. Josh is my stepdad. Carin and Don are my real parents, who are divorced. And Don married Anna and together they had Ethan and Ellen, my half-sister and brother. And Carin married Josh and had little Alice, my half-sister (Bernstein 1988).

The exact nature of these blended families has social significance for adults and children alike. Certainly resocialization is required when an adult becomes a stepparent or a child becomes a stepchild and stepsibling. Moreover, an important distinction must be made between first-time stepfamilies and households where there have been repeated divorces, breakups, or changes in custodial arrangements.

In evaluating the rise of stepfamilies, some observers have assumed that children would benefit from remarriage because they would be gaining a second custodial parent and potentially would enjoy greater economic security. However, after reviewing many studies on stepfamilies, sociologist Andrew Cherlin (1999:421) concluded that "the well-being of children in stepfamily households is no better, on average, than the well-being of children in divorced, single-parent households." Step-

parents can play valuable and unique roles in their stepchildren's lives, but their involvement does not guarantee an improvement. In fact, standards may decline. Some studies conducted by a Princeton economist found that children raised in families with stepmothers are likely to have less health care, education, and money spent on their food than children raised by biological mothers. The measures are also negative for children raised by a stepfather but only half as negative as in the case of stepmothers. This doesn't mean that stepmothers are "evil"— it may be that the stepmother steps back out of concern of seeming too intrusive or relies mistakenly on the biological father to carry out these parental duties (Lewin 2000).

Divorce

"Do you promise to love, honor, and cherish . . . until death do you part?" Every year, people of all social classes and racial and ethnic groups make this legally binding agreement. Yet an increasing number of these promises shatter in divorce. While rates may vary among states, divorce is a nationwide phenomenon.

Statistical Trends in Divorce

Just how common is divorce? Surprisingly, this is not a simple question; divorce statistics are difficult to interpret.

The media frequently report that one out of every two marriages ends in divorce. But this figure is misleading, since many marriages last for decades. It is based on a comparison of all divorces that occur in a single year (regardless of when the couples were married) against the number of new marriages in the same year.

Divorce in the United States, and many other countries, began to increase in the late 1960s but then started to level off and even decline since the late 1980s (see Figure 11-5). Partly this is due to the aging of the baby boomer population and the corresponding decline in the proportion of people of marriageable age. But the trend also indicates an increase in marital stability in recent years (National Marriage Project 2000).

Getting divorced obviously does not sour people on marriage. About two-thirds of divorced women and three-fourths of divorced men eventually remarry. Women are less likely than men to remarry because many retain custody of children after a divorce, which complicates establishing a new adult relationship (Bianchi and Spain 1996).

Some people regard the nation's high rate of remarriage as an endorsement of the institution of marriage, but it does lead to the new challenges of a remarriage kin network composed of current and prior marital relationships. This network can be particularly complex if children are involved or if an ex-spouse remarries.

FIGURE 11-5

Trends in Marriage and Divorce, 1940–1999

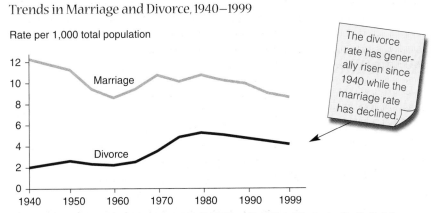

Rate per 1,000 total population

The divorce rate has generally risen since 1940 while the marriage rate has declined.

Sources: Bureau of the Census 1970:60, 1981:80, 1999a:110; National Center for Health Statistics 2000.

Factors Associated with Divorce

Perhaps the most important factor in the increase in divorce throughout the twentieth century has been the greater social *acceptance* of divorce. It's no longer considered necessary to endure an unhappy marriage. Most importantly, various religious denominations have relaxed negative attitudes toward divorce, and most religious leaders no longer treat it as a sin. The growing acceptance of divorce is a worldwide phenomenon. In 1998, a few months after a highly publicized divorce by pop superstar Seiko Matsuda, the prime minister of Japan released a survey showing that 54 percent of those polled supported uncontested divorce, compared to 20 percent in 1979 (Kyodo News International 1998a).

A few other factors deserve mention:

- Many states have adopted more liberal divorce laws in the last two decades. No-fault divorce laws, allowing a couple to end their marriage without fault on either side (such as specifying adultery), accounted for an initial surge in the divorce rate after they were introduced in the 1970s, although they appear to have had little effect beyond that.
- Divorce has become a more practical option in newly formed families, since they now tend to have fewer children than in the past.
- A general increase in family incomes, coupled with the availability of free legal aid for some poor people, has meant that more couples can afford costly divorce proceedings.
- As society provides greater opportunities for women, more and more wives are becoming less dependent on their husbands—both economically and emotionally. They may then feel more able to leave if the marriage seems hopeless.

Impact of Divorce on Children

Divorce is traumatic for all involved, as Cornel West made clear in the excerpt that opened this chapter. But it has special meaning for the more than 1 million children whose parents divorce each year. Of course, for some of these children, divorce signals the welcome end to being witness to a very dysfunctional relationship. A national sample conducted by sociologists Paul Amato and Alan Booth (1997) found that in about a third of divorces, the children benefit from parental separation because it lessens their exposure to conflict. But in about 70 percent of all divorces, they found that the parents engaged in a low level of conflict; in these cases, the realities of divorce appear to be harder for the children to bear than living with the marital unhappiness. Other researchers, using differing definitions of conflict, have found greater unhappiness for children living in homes with marital differences. Still, it would be simplistic to assume that children are automatically better off following the breakup of their parents' marriage. The interests of the parents do not necessarily serve children well.

Divorce can obviously be a painful experience for children, but we should avoid labeling young people as "children of divorce," as if this *parental* experience is the singular event defining the life of a girl or boy. Large-scale studies in the United States and Great Britain have shown that some of the alleged negative effects of divorce actually resulted from conditions (such as poverty) that existed *before* the parental separation. Moreover, if divorce does not lower children's access to resources and does not increase stress, its impact on children may be neutral or even positive. Divorce does not ruin the life of every child it touches, though its effect on a child is not always benign (Cherlin 1999; Wallerstein et al. 2000).

In recent years, concern about the high rate of divorce in the United States and its impact on children has led policymakers to reconsider existing divorce laws. Louisiana's "covenant marriages" have received considerable publicity. Beginning in 1997, couples in that state have had the option of entering a legal union that requires premarital counseling and sets strict limits on divorce; for example, a marriage can dissolve only after a two-year separation or after documented adultery or abuse. It is too early to assess the impact of this system on marital longevity. Seventeen states have considered a similar arrangement, but only Arizona has adopted even a modified form of the procedure. Yet even if few states take up

Louisiana's initiative, the nation appears willing to enter into a discussion of what educational and parenting programs can reduce marital breakup (Nock et al. 1999).

Diverse Lifestyles

Marriage is no longer the presumed route from adolescence to adulthood. In fact, it has lost much of its social significance as a rite of passage. The nation's marriage rate has dipped by 43 percent since 1960 because people are postponing marriage until later in life and more couples, including same-sex couples, are deciding to form partnerships without marriage (Popenoe and Whitehead 1999).

Cohabitation

Saint Paul once wrote, "It is better to marry than to burn." However, as journalist Tom Ferrell (1979) has suggested, more people than ever "prefer combustible to connubial bliss." One of the most dramatic trends of recent years has been the tremendous increase in male–female couples who choose to live together without marrying, thereby engaging in what is commonly called **cohabitation.**

The number of such households in the United States rose sixfold in the 1960s and increased another 48 percent just between 1990 and 1998. According to a 1999 Census Bureau report, at any given time, about 1 out of 10 opposite-sex couples are unmarried. Half of all people between the ages of 25 and 40 have cohabited. If current

This young couple in England are cohabiting, an increasingly popular alternative to marriage in many countries today.

trends continue, that will soon be true of half of all people in the United States between the ages of 25 and 50 (Bureau of the Census 1999a:60; Clark and Fields 1999).

We can also find increases in cohabitation in Canada, France, Sweden, Denmark, and Australia. Data released in Great Britain indicate that more than 12 percent of people ages 18 to 24 are cohabiting. One report notes that in Sweden it is almost universal for couples to live together before marriage. Demographers in Denmark call the practice of living together *marriage without papers.* In Australia, these couples are known as *de factos* (Blanc 1984; Levinson 1984; O'Donnell 1992; Thomson and Colella 1992).

Some countries have governmental policies that do not encourage marriage. For example, Sweden offers no married-couple allowance for tax purposes, no tax deduction for raising children, and no way for couples to jointly file their income taxes. Not surprisingly, many Swedish couples choose to cohabit rather than to marry. About half of the babies in Sweden are born to unmarried mothers—although there are proportionately many fewer unmarried *teenage* mothers in Sweden than in the United States (*The Economist* 1995).

People commonly associate cohabitation only with college campuses or sexual experimentation. But according to a study in Los Angeles, working couples are almost twice as likely to cohabit as college students are. And census data show that in 1997, 36 percent of unmarried couples had one or more children present in the household. These cohabitants are more like spouses than dating partners. Moreover, in contrast to the common perception that people who cohabit have never been married, researchers report that about half of all people involved in cohabitation in the United States have been previously married. Cohabitation serves as a temporary or permanent alternative to matrimony for many men and women who have experienced their own divorces or the inability of their parents to remain married (Popenoe and Whitehead 1999).

Recent research has documented significant increases in cohabitation among older people in the United States. For example, census data indicate that in 1980, there were 340,000 opposite-sex couples who were unmarried, living together, and over the age of 45. By 1998, there were 985,000 such couples—nearly three times as many. Older couples may choose cohabitation rather than marriage for many reasons: because of religious differences, to preserve the full Social Security benefits they receive as single people, out of fear of commitment, to avoid upsetting children from previous marriages, because one partner or both are not legally divorced, or because one or both have lived through a spouse's illness and death and do not want to experience that again. But some older couples simply see no need for marriage and report being happy living together as they are (Bureau of the Census 1999a:60).

Remaining Single

Looking at TV programs today, as Box 11-1 pointed out, you would be justified in thinking most households are composed of singles. While this is not the case, it is true that more and more people in the United States are *postponing* entry into first marriages. In 1998, 70 percent of all women 20 to 24 years of age had never married, compared with only 36 percent in 1970. As of 1998, one out of every four households in the United States (accounting for over 26 million people) was a single-member household. Even so, fewer than 5 percent of women and men in the United States are likely to remain single throughout their lives (Bureau of the Census 1999a:60).

The trend toward maintaining a single lifestyle for a longer period of time is related to the growing economic independence of young people. This is especially significant for women. In 1890, women accounted for only one-sixth of the paid labor force; they are now more than two-thirds of

p. 268 ◄ it. Freed from financial needs, women don't necessarily have to marry to enjoy a satisfying life.

There are many reasons why a person may choose not to marry. (Just ask *Ally McBeal's* Renee, Fish, Elaine, Cage, and, of course, Ally.) Singleness is an attractive option for those who do not want to limit their sexual intimacy to one lifetime partner. Also, some men and women do not want to become highly dependent on any one person—and do not want anyone depending heavily on them. In a society that values individuality and self-fulfillment, the single lifestyle can offer certain freedoms that married couples may not enjoy.

Remaining single represents a clear departure from societal expectations; indeed, it has been likened to "being single on Noah's Ark." A single adult must confront the inaccurate view that he or she is always lonely, is a workaholic, and is immature. These stereotypes help support the traditional assumption in the United States and most other societies that to be truly happy and fulfilled, a person must get married and raise a family. To help counter these societal expectations, singles have formed numerous support groups, such as Alternative to Marriage Project (www.unmarried.org).

Lesbian and Gay Relationships

We were both raised in middle-class families, where the expectation was we would go to college, we would become educated, we'd get a nice white-collar job, we'd move up and own a nice house in the suburbs. And that's exactly what we've done (*New York Times* 1998:B2).

Sound like an average family? The only break with traditional expectations in this case is that the "we" described here is a gay couple.

The lifestyles of lesbians and gay men vary greatly. Some live in long-term, monogamous relationships. Some couples live with children from former heterosexual marriages or adopted children. Some live alone, others with roommates. Others remain married and do not publicly acknowledge their homosexuality. Researchers for the National Health and Social Life Survey—who interviewed more than 3,400 adults in the United States in 1992—found that 2.8 percent of the men and 1.4 percent of the women reported some level of homosexual or bisexual identity (Laumann et al. 1994b:293).

Census data collected in 1998 in preparation for Census 2000 indicated that about 2 percent of all households consisted of same-sex couples. In half of these households, the census respondents chose to classify themselves as "married," despite state laws that preclude legal same-sex marriage. This means that out of more than 2 million same-sex households, a million couples view themselves as married, not merely living together (Clark and Fields 1999; Fields and Clark 1999).

The contemporary lesbian and gay rights movement has given an increasing number of lesbians and gay men the support to proclaim their sexual and affectional orientation. Gay activists were distressed in 1986 when a divided Supreme Court ruled, by a 5–4 vote, that the Constitution does not protect homosexual relations between consenting adults, even within the privacy of their own homes. Nevertheless, as of 2000, 10 states, the District of Columbia, and more than 165 cities and counties in the United States had adopted civil rights laws protecting lesbians and gay men against discrimination in such areas as employment, housing, and public accommodations (American Civil Liberties Union 2000).

Recognition of same-sex partnerships is not uncommon in Europe, including Denmark, Holland, Switzerland, France, Belgium, and parts of Germany, Italy, and Spain. In 2001 the Netherlands converted their "registered same-sex partnerships" into full-fledged marriages, with divorce provisions (S. Daley 2000).

Gay activist organizations emphasize that despite the passage of state and local laws protecting the civil rights of lesbians and gay men, lesbian couples and gay male couples are prohibited from marrying—and therefore from gaining traditional partnership benefits—in all 50 states of the United States. With such inequities in mind, 18 municipalities have passed legislation allowing for registration of domestic partnerships and 49 cities provide employee benefits that extend to domestic partnerships. Under such policies, a ***domestic partnership*** may be defined as two unrelated adults who reside together, agree to be jointly responsible for their dependents, basic living expenses, and other common necessities, and share a mutually caring relationship. Domestic partnership benefits

Lesbian and gay couples are pushing for domestic partnership legislation, which would allow them the traditional partnership benefits enjoyed by married couples.

can apply to such areas as inheritance, parenting, pensions, taxation, housing, immigration, workplace fringe benefits, and health care. While the most passionate support for domestic partnership legislation has come from lesbian and gay male activists, the majority of those eligible for such benefits would be cohabiting heterosexual couples (American Civil Liberties Union 1999a).

Domestic partnership legislation, however, faces strong opposition from conservative religious and political groups. In the view of opponents, support for domestic partnership undermines the historic societal preference for the nuclear family. Advocates of domestic partnership counter that such relationships fulfill the same functions for the individuals involved and for society as the traditional family and should enjoy the same legal protections and benefits. The gay couple quoted at the beginning of this section consider themselves a family unit, just like the nuclear family that lives down the street in their West

Hartford, Connecticut, suburb. They cannot understand why they have been denied a family membership at their municipal swimming pool and why they have to pay more than a married couple (*New York Times* 1998).

In 2000 a national survey showed that only 34 percent of the general public in the United States think gays and lesbians should be allowed to be legally married; 51 percent oppose such an arrangement, and 14 percent are unsure (Associated Press 2000).

Marriage without Children

There has been a modest increase in childlessness in the United States. According to data from the census, about 19 percent of women in 1998 will complete their childbearing years without having borne any children, compared to 10 percent in 1980. As many as 20 percent of women in their 30s expect to remain childless (Bachu 1999).

Childlessness within marriage has generally been viewed as a problem that can be solved through such means as adoption and artificial insemination. More and more couples today, however, choose not to have children and regard themselves as child-free, not childless. They do not believe that having children automatically follows from marriage, nor do they feel that reproduction is the duty of all married couples. Childless couples have formed support groups (with names like "No Kidding") and set up websites on the Internet (Terry 2000).

Economic considerations have contributed to this shift in attitudes; having children has become quite expensive. According to a government estimate in 1998, the average middle-class family will spend $148,450 to feed, clothe, and shelter a child from birth to age 17. If the child attends college, that amount could double, depending on the college chosen. Aware of the financial pressures, some couples are having fewer children than they otherwise might, and others are weighing the advantages of a child-free marriage (Bureau of the Census 1999a:470).

As more couples are childless, they are beginning to question current practices in the workplace. While applauding employers' efforts to provide child care and flexible work schedules, some couples p. 97 nevertheless express concern about tolerance of employees who leave early to take children to doctors, ballgames, or after-school classes. As more dual-career couples enter the paid labor force and struggle to balance career and familial responsibilities, there may be increasing conflicts with employees who have no children (Burkett 2000).

Meanwhile, many childless couples who desperately want children are willing to try any means necessary to get pregnant. The social policy section that follows explores the controversy surrounding recent advances in reproductive technology.

CHAPTER

12

RELIGION AND EDUCATION

Additional Readings

Coontz, Stephanie. 1997. *The Way We Really Are: Coming to Terms with America's Changing Families.* New York: Basic Books. A family historian considers how much and how little family organization has changed in the United States.

Luker, Kristin. 1996. *Dubious Conceptions: The Politics of Teenage Pregnancy.* Cambridge, MA: Harvard University Press. A sociologist analyzes attitudes toward unwed mothers in the United States, including the current "demonization" of these young women.

Mindel, Charles H., Robert W. Habenstein, and Roosevelt Wright, Jr., eds. 1999. *Ethnic Families in America: Patterns and Variations.* 4th ed. Upper Saddle River, NJ: Prentice Hall. This collection of 19 essays covers family as a social institution in a variety of ethnic contexts, including Cuban American, Asian Indian, Native American, and the Amish.

Wallerstein, Judith S., Julia M. Lewis, and Sandra Blaeslee. 2000. *The Unexpected Legacy of Divorce.* New York: Hyperion. A study that tracks children for 25 years after their parents' divorce and examines the impact of this event on their lives.

Technology Resources

Internet Connection

Note: While all the URLs listed were current as of the printing of this book, these sites often change. Please check our website (http://www.mhhe.com/schaefer4) for updates.

1. The Internet is fast becoming a place for families to share information with relatives and the general public. For a virtual look at real families, log onto (**http://www.yahoo.com/Society_and_Culture/ People/Personal_Home_Pages/Families/ Complete_Listing/**). Choose three families that have uploaded their home pages and answer the following questions:

    (a) What family composition or variety does each represent (nuclear, extended, single-parent, dual-career, domestic partnerships)?

    (b) Do any of the families fall into more than one of these categories?

    (c) What social functions do the three family structures serve?

    (d) What demographic characteristics (race/ ethnicity, religion, gender, age, and social class) do you notice?

    (e) How do your chosen families compare with the demographic patterns mentioned in this chapter?

2. Sociologists who study families examine both the positive and negative aspects of family life. Domestic violence is an example of the dark side of relationships, an issue that, as this chapter demonstrates, is a worldwide problem. To learn more about this social problem, log onto famvi.com, designed by Gary Templeton (**http://www.famvi.com/**). Visit the section on "Facts & Stats" to gain an appreciation of the general issues. Visit the sections on "Comments" and "Writings" to understand how family violence affects the individual.

    (a) What myths about family violence does the site address?

    (b) What five statistics from the site reveal the most about the extent of the problem? Why did you choose these facts over others? What general themes do your selections show about violence in the family?

    (c) Which poems and stories had the greatest impact on you? What lessons about violence do the "Writings" give?

    (d) Describe the logo used by famvi.com. Engage your interactionist skills to discuss what this logo symbolizes. What message does it convey?

3. The National Adoption Information Clearinghouse at (**http://www.calib.com/naic**) represents a joint effort of various administrations and government departments to provide online information. Imagine that you have been assigned to write an article for your college newspaper on adoption and answer the following questions:

    (a) Which agencies and departments helped create the site? What services do these agencies provide?

    (b) What new laws, programs, and policies have been created regarding adoption? What are the goals of these new initiatives?

    (c) After examining the statistics on "Single Adoptive Parents," summarize your findings. Has the number of single-parent adoptions increased or decreased in recent decades? What social and economic trends might account for this change?

    (d) Summarize the data presented in the "Intercountry Adoption" link. From which other nations do most U.S. citizens adopt? Why do you think so many adoptions currently come from Russia and China?

    (e) Are more male or female children adopted from other nations? Why might this be so?

    (f) What rights do adopted persons have to records in your state? Do you agree with the current policies and laws regarding this matter? Why or why not?

    (g) Considering all you have learned in the book and from the site, what are some of the most important challenges facing both adoptees and the adopted?

Interactive e-Source with Making the Gra

Online Learning Center   www.mhhe.com/s

PowerWeb

SocCity

In this billboard distributed by Volkswagen of France, the figure of Jesus at the Last Supper says to his apostles, "Rejoice, my friends, for a new Golf is born." While an image of Jesus is sacred for Christians, it is used here in a secular manner—to advertise cars.

Growing up in a small mixed-blood community of seven hundred on the eastern edge of the Pine Ridge Reservation in South Dakota, I uncritically accepted the idea that the old Dakota religion and Christianity were both "true" and in some mysterious way compatible with each other. There were, to be sure, Christian fundamentalists with their intolerance and the old traditional Indians who kept their practices hidden, but the vast majority of the people in the vicinity more or less assumed that a satisfactory blend had been achieved that guaranteed our happiness.

Although my father was an Episcopal priest with a large number of chapels in a loosely organized Episcopal missionary district known (to Episcopalians) as "Corn Creek," he was far from an orthodox follower of the white man's religion. I always had the feeling that within the large context of "religion," which in a border town meant the Christian milieu, there was a special area in his spiritual life in which the old Dakota beliefs and practices reigned supreme. He knew thirty-three songs; some of them social, some ancient, and several spiritual songs used in a variety of ceremonial contexts. Driving to his chapels to hold Christian services he would open the window of the car and beat the side of the door with his hand for the drum beat and sing song after song. . . .

When I went to college I was exposed to a much larger canvas of human experience upon which various societies had left their religious mark. My first reaction was the belief that most of the religious traditions were simply wrong, that a few of them had come close to describing religious reality, but that it would take some intensive study to determine which religious traditions would best assist human beings in succeeding in the world. It was my good fortune to have as a religion and philosophy professor a Christian mystic who was trying to prove the deepest mysteries of the faith. He also had some intense personal problems which emerged again and again in his beliefs, indicating to me that religion and the specific individual path of life were always intertwined.

Over several years and many profound conversations he was able to demonstrate to me that each religious tradition had developed a unique way to confront some problems and that they had something in common if only the search for truth and the elimination of many false paths. But his solution, after many years, became untenable for me. I saw instead religion simply as a means of organizing a society, articulating some reasonably apparent emotional truths, but ultimately becoming a staid part of social establishments that primarily sought to control human behavior and not fulfill human individual potential. It seemed as if those religions that placed strong emphasis on certain concepts failed precisely in the areas in which they claimed expertise. Thus religions of "love" could point to few examples of their efficacy; religions of "salvation" actually saved very few. The more I learned about world religions, the more respect I had for the old Dakota ways. *(Deloria 1999:273–75)* ■

n this excerpt from *For This Land,* Vine Deloria—a Standing Rock Sioux—reveals his deep personal ties to the religion of his ancestors, undiluted by the overlays of missionary Christian theology. Even though his father is an Episcopal priest, Deloria is keenly aware of how tribal beliefs intrude and color his father's religious sensibility. He is also aware of the fact that Native American rites and customs have been appropriated by a generation of non-Indians seeking a kind of New Age "magic." For Deloria, Indian spiritual beliefs are an integral part of the Native American culture and help to define that culture. Mixing those beliefs with the beliefs of other religions or systems of thought threatens to undermine the strength of the culture.

Religion plays a major role in people's lives, and religious practices of some sort are evident in every society. That makes religion a **cultural universal,** along with other general practices found in every culture such as dancing, food preparation, the family, and personal names. At present, an estimated 4 billion people belong to the world's many religious faiths (see Figure 12-1).

p. 56

When religion's influence on other social institutions in a society diminishes, the process of **secularization** is said to be underway. During this process, religion will survive in the private sphere of individual and family life (as in the case of many Native American families); it may even thrive on a personal level. But, at the same time, other social institutions—such as the economy, politics, and education—maintain their own sets of norms independent of religious guidance (Stark and Iannaccone 1992).

Education, like religion, is a *cultural universal.* As such it is an important aspect of socialization—the lifelong process of learning the attitudes, values, and behavior considered appropriate to members of a particular culture, as we saw in Chapter 4. When learning is explicit and formalized—when some people consciously teach, while others adopt the role of learner—the process of socialization is called **education.**

This chapter first looks at religion as it has emerged in modern industrial societies. It begins with a brief overview of the approaches that Émile Durkheim first introduced and those that later sociologists have used in studying religion. We will explore religion's role in societal integration, social support, social change, and social control. We'll examine three important dimensions of religious behavior—belief, ritual, and experience—as well as the basic forms of religious organization. We will pay particular attention to the emergence of new religious movements.

The second part of this chapter focuses on the formal systems of education that characterize modern industrial societies, beginning with a discussion of three theoretical perspectives on education: functionalist, conflict, and interactionist. As we will see, education can both perpetuate the status quo and foster social change. An examination of schools as formal organizations—as bureaucracies and subcultures of teachers and students—follows. Two types of education that are becoming more common in the United States today, adult education and home schooling, merit special mention. The chapter closes with a social policy discussion of the controversy over religion in public schools. ■

Durkheim and the Sociological Approach to Religion

If a group believes that it is being directed by a "vision from God," sociologists will not attempt to prove or disprove this revelation. Instead, they will assess the effects of the religious experience on the group. What sociologists are interested in is the social impact of religion on individuals and institutions (M. McGuire 1981:12).

Émile Durkheim was perhaps the first sociologist to recognize the critical importance of religion in human societies. He saw its appeal for the individual, but—more important—he stressed the *social* impact of religion. In Durkheim's view, religion is a collective act and includes many forms of behavior in which people interact with others. As in his work on suicide, Durkheim was not so interested in the personalities of religious believers as he was in understanding religious behavior within a social context.

p. 8

Durkheim defined **religion** as a "unified system of beliefs and practices relative to sacred things." In his view, religion involves a set of beliefs and practices that are uniquely the property of religion—as opposed to other social institutions and ways of thinking. Durkheim (1947, original edition 1912) argued that religious faiths distinguish between certain events that transcend the ordinary and the everyday world. He referred to these realms as the *sacred* and the *profane.*

The **sacred** encompasses elements beyond everyday life that inspire awe, respect, and even fear. People become

FIGURE 12-1

Religions

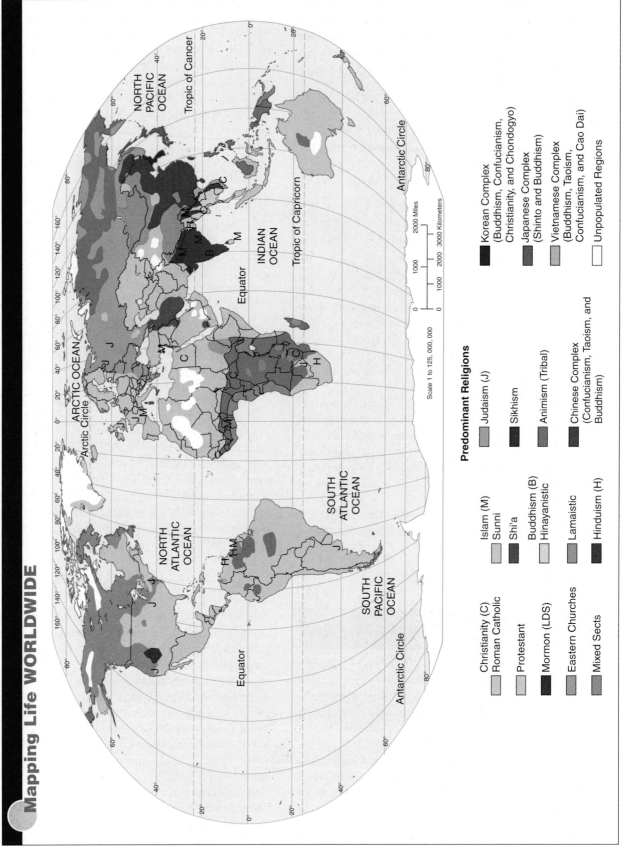

Mapping Life WORLDWIDE

Predominant Religions

Christianity (C)
Roman Catholic

Protestant

Mormon (LDS)

Eastern Churches

Mixed Sects

Islam (M)
Sunni

Shi'a

Buddhism (B)
Hinayanistic

Lamaistic

Hinduism (H)

Judaism (J)

Sikhism

Animism (Tribal)

Chinese Complex
(Confucianism, Taoism, and Buddhism)

Korean Complex
(Buddhism, Confucianism, Christianity, and Chondogyo)

Japanese Complex
(Shinto and Buddhism)

Vietnamese Complex
(Buddhism, Taoism, Confucianism, and Cao Dai)

Unpopulated Regions

Scale 1 to 125,000,000

Source: Allen 1996:12–13.

a part of the sacred realm only by completing some ritual, such as prayer or sacrifice. Believers have faith in the sacred; this faith allows them to accept what they cannot understand. By contrast, the **profane** includes the ordinary and commonplace. It can get confusing, however, because the same object can be either sacred or profane depending on how it is viewed. A normal dining room table is profane, but it becomes sacred to Christians if it bears the elements of a communion. A candelabra becomes sacred for Jews when it is a menorah. For Confucians and Taoists, incense sticks are not mere decorative items; they are highly valued offerings to the gods in religious ceremonies marking new and full moons.

Following the direction established by Durkheim almost a century ago, contemporary sociologists view religions in two different ways. They study the norms and values of religious faiths through examination of their substantive religious beliefs. For example, it is possible to

Young Buddhists in Thailand symbolically shave away the "earthly afflictions" represented by their hair.

compare the degree to which Christian faiths literally interpret the Bible, or Muslim groups follow the Qur'an (or Koran), the sacred book of Islam. At the same time, sociologists examine religions in terms of the social functions they fulfill, such as providing social support or reinforcing the social norms. By exploring both the beliefs and the functions of religion, we can better understand its impact on the individual, on groups, and on society as a whole.

The Role of Religion

Since religion is a cultural universal, it is not surprising that it plays a basic role in human societies. In sociological terms, these include both manifest and latent functions. Among its *manifest* (open and stated) functions, religion defines the spiritual world p. 14 and gives meaning to the divine. Religion provides an explanation for events that seem difficult to understand, such as what lies beyond the grave.

The *latent* functions of religion are unintended, covert, or hidden. Even though the manifest function of church services is to offer a forum for religious worship, they might at the same time fulfill a latent function as a meeting ground for unmarried members.

Functionalists and conflict theorists both evaluate religion's impact as a social institution on human societies. We'll consider a functionalist view of religion's role in integrating society, in social support, and in promoting social change, and then look at religion as a means of social control from the conflict perspective. Note that, for the most part, religion's impact is best understood from a macro-level viewpoint, oriented toward the larger society. The social support function is an exception: it is best viewed on the micro-level, directed toward the individual.

The Integrative Function of Religion

Émile Durkheim viewed religion as an integrative power in human society—a perspective reflected in functionalist thought today. Durkheim sought to answer a perplexing question: "How can human societies be held together when they are generally composed of individuals and social groups with diverse interests and aspirations?" In his view, religious bonds often transcend these personal and divisive forces. Durkheim acknowledged that religion is not the only integrative force—nationalism or patriotism may serve the same end.

How does religion provide this "societal glue"? Religion, whether it be Buddhism, Islam, Christianity, or Judaism, offers people meaning and purpose for their lives. It gives them certain ultimate values and ends to hold in common. Although subjective and not always fully accepted, these values and ends help a society to function as an integrated social system. For example, funerals, weddings, bar and bat mitzvahs, and confirmations serve to integrate people into larger communities by providing shared beliefs and values about the ultimate questions of life.

The integrative power of religion can be seen in the role that churches, synagogues, and mosques have traditionally played and continue to play for immigrant groups in the United States. For example, Roman Catholic immigrants may settle near a parish church that offers services in their native language, such as Polish or Spanish. Similarly, Korean immigrants may join a Presbyterian church with many Korean American members and with religious practices like those of churches in Korea. Like other religious organizations, these Roman Catholic and Presbyterian churches help to integrate immigrants into their new homeland.

Yet another example of the integrative impact of reli-

The first "gay-proud" service at a church in Detroit, Michigan, in 1996. This ecumenical Christian ministry is intended to provide a spiritual home for the gay community and to educate the straight community about homosexuals.

gion is provided by the Universal Fellowship of Metropolitan Community Churches. It was established in the United States in 1968 to offer a welcoming place of worship for lesbians and gay men. This spiritual community is especially important today, given the many organized religions openly hostile to homosexuality. The Metropolitan Community Church has 42,000 members in its local churches in 15 countries. As part of its effort to support lesbian and gay rights, the Metropolitan Community Church performs same-sex marriages, which it calls "holy union ceremonies" (L. Stammer 1999).

In some instances, religious loyalties are *dysfunctional;* they contribute to tension and even conflict between groups or nations. During the Second World War, the German Nazis attempted to exterminate the Jewish people; approximately 6 million European Jews were killed. In modern times, nations such as Lebanon (Muslims versus Christians), Israel (Jews versus Muslims as well as Orthodox versus secular Jews), Northern Ireland (Roman Catholics versus Protestants), and India (Hindus versus Muslims and, more recently, Sikhs) have been torn by clashes that are in large part based on religion.

Religious conflict (though on a less violent level) has been increasingly evident in the United States as well. Sociologist James Davison Hunter (1991) has referred to the "cultural war" taking place in the United States. Christian fundamentalists, conservative Catholics, and Orthodox Jews have joined forces in many communities in a battle against their liberal counterparts for control of the secular culture. The battlefield is an array of familiar social issues, among them multiculturalism, child care (Chapter 4), abortion (Chapter 10), home schooling, gay rights, and government funding for the arts.

pp. 97, 281 ◄

Religion and Social Support

Most of us find it difficult to accept the stressful events of life—death of a loved one, serious injury, bankruptcy, divorce, and so forth. This is especially true when something "senseless" happens. How can family and friends come to terms with the death of a talented college student, not even 20 years old, from a terminal disease?

Through its emphasis on the divine and the supernatural, religion allows us to "do something" about the calamities we face. In some faiths, adherents can offer sacrifices or pray to a deity in the belief that such acts will change their earthly condition. At a more basic level, religion encourages us to view our personal misfortunes as relatively unimportant in the broader perspective of human history—or even as part of an undisclosed divine purpose. Friends and relatives of the deceased college student may see this death as being "God's will" and as having some ultimate benefit that we cannot understand now. This perspective may be much more comforting than the terrifying feeling that any of us can die senselessly at any moment—and that there is no divine "answer" as to why one person lives a long and full life, while another dies tragically at a relatively early age.

Faith-based community organizations have taken on more and more responsibilities in the area of social assistance. In fact, as part of an effort to cut back on government-funded welfare programs, government leaders have advocated shifting the social "safety net" to private organizations in general and to churches and religious charities in particular. Sociologist William Julius Wilson (1999b) has singled out faith-based organizations in 40 communities from California to Massachusetts as models of social reform. These organizations identify experienced leaders and assemble them into nonsectarian coalitions devoted to community development (K. Starr 1999).

Religion and Social Change

The Weberian Thesis

When someone seems driven to work and succeed we often attribute the "Protestant work ethic" to that person. The term comes from the writings of Max Weber, who carefully examined the connection between religious allegiance and capitalist development. His findings appeared in his pioneering work *The Protestant Ethic and the Spirit of Capitalism* (1958a, original edition 1904).

Weber noted that in European nations with both Protestant and Catholic citizens, an overwhelming number of business leaders, owners of capital, and skilled workers were Protestant. In his view, this was no mere coincidence. Weber pointed out that the followers of John Calvin (1509–1564), a leader of the Protestant Reformation, emphasized a disciplined work ethic, this-worldly concerns, and a rational orientation to life that have become known as the **Protestant ethic.** One by-product of the Protestant ethic was a drive to accumulate savings that could be used for future investment. This "spirit of capitalism," to use Weber's phrase, contrasted with the moderate work hours, leisurely work habits, and lack of ambition that he saw as typical of the times (Winter 1977; Yinger 1974).

Few books on the sociology of religion have aroused as much commentary and criticism as Weber's work. It has been hailed as one of the most important theoretical works in the field and as an excellent example of macrolevel analysis. Like Durkheim, Weber demonstrated that religion is not solely a matter of intimate personal beliefs. He stressed that the collective nature of religion has social consequences for society as a whole.

Weber provides a convincing description of the ori-

gins of European capitalism. But this economic system has subsequently been adopted by non-Calvinists in many parts of the world. Contemporary studies in the United States show little or no difference in achievement orientation between Roman Catholics and Protestants. Apparently, the "spirit of capitalism" has become a generalized cultural trait rather than a specific religious tenet (Greeley 1989).

Conflict theorists caution that Weber's theory—even if it is accepted—should not be regarded as an analysis of mature capitalism as reflected in the rise of multinational corporations that cross national boundaries. p. 209 Marxists would disagree with Max Weber not on the origins of capitalism but on its future. Unlike Marx, Weber believed that capitalism could endure indefinitely as an economic system. He added, however, that the decline of religion as an overriding force in society opened the way for workers to express their discontent more vocally (R. Collins 1980).

Liberation Theology

Sometimes the clergy can be found in the forefront of social change. Many religious activists, especially in the Roman Catholic church in Latin America, support **liberation theology**—the use of a church in a political effort to eliminate poverty, discrimination, and other forms of injustice evident in a secular society. Advocates of this religious movement sometimes sympathize with Marxism. Many believe that radical change, rather than economic development in itself, is the only acceptable solution to the desperation of the masses in impoverished developing countries. Activists associated with liberation theology believe that organized religion has a moral responsibility to take a strong public stand against the oppression of the poor, racial and ethnic minorities, and women (C. Smith 1991).

The term *liberation theology* dates back to the 1973 publication of the English translation of *A Theology of Liberation.* This book was written by a Peruvian priest, Gustavo Gutierrez, who lived in a slum area of Lima during the early 1960s. After years of exposure to the vast poverty around him, Gutierrez concluded that "in order to serve the poor, one had to move into political action" (R. M. Brown 1980:23; Gutierrez 1990).

Politically committed Latin American theologians came under the influence of social scientists who viewed the domination of capitalism and multinational corporations as central to the hemisphere's problems. One result was a new approach to theology that rejected the models developed in Europe and the United States and instead built on the cultural and religious traditions of Latin America.

While many worshippers support liberation theology,

religious leaders in the Roman Catholic church are not happy with the radical movement. The official position of Pope John Paul II and others in the church hierarchy is that clergy should adhere to traditional pastoral duties and keep a distance from radical politics. The Pope specifically came out against church activists in his 1999 visit to Mexico City (S. Pagani 1999).

Liberation theology may possibly be dysfunctional, however. Some Roman Catholics have come to believe that by focusing on political and governmental injustice, the clergy are no longer addressing their personal and spiritual needs. Partly as a result of such disenchantment, some Catholics in Latin America are converting to mainstream Protestant faiths or to Mormonism.

Religion and Social Control: A Conflict View

Liberation theology is a relatively recent phenomenon and marks a break with the traditional role of churches. It was this traditional role that Karl Marx opposed. In his view, religion *impeded* social change by encouraging oppressed people to focus on other-worldly concerns rather than on their immediate poverty or exploitation. Marx described religion as an "opiate" particularly harmful to oppressed peoples. He felt that religion often drugged the masses into submission by offering a consolation for their harsh lives on earth: the hope of salvation in an ideal afterlife. For example, during the period of slavery in the United States, White masters forbade Blacks to practice native African religions, while encouraging them to adopt the Christian religion. Christianity taught the slaves that obedience would lead to salvation and eternal happiness in the hereafter. Viewed from a conflict perspective, Christianity may have pacified certain slaves and blunted the rage that often fuels rebellion (M. McGuire 1992; Yinger 1970).

Marx acknowledged that religion plays an important role in propping up the existing social structure. The values of religion, as already noted, reinforce other social institutions and the social order as a whole. From Marx's perspective, however, religion's promotion of stability within society only helps to perpetuate patterns of social inequality. According to Marx, the dominant religion reinforces the interests of those in power (Harap 1982).

Consider, for example, India's traditional caste system. It defined the social structure of that society, at least among the Hindu majority. The caste system was almost

p. 191 certainly the creation of the priesthood, but it also served the interests of India's political rulers by granting a certain religious legitimacy to social inequality.

Contemporary Christianity, like the Hindu faith, reinforces traditional patterns of behavior that call for the

When Raedora Steward-Dodd found out that the American Baptist Church ordains women, she decided to exchange her Texas police officer badge for the robes of a Baptist minister. Female clergy don't often have an easy time, however. They are more likely to serve in subsidiary pastoral roles and to wait longer for desirable assignments than male clergy.

subordination of the less powerful. The role of women in the church is an example of uneven distribution of power. Assumptions about gender roles leave women in a subservient position both within Christian churches and at home. In fact, women find it as difficult to achieve leadership positions in many churches as they do in large corporations. In 1997, 86 percent of all clergy in the United States were male. Female clergy are more likely to serve in subsidiary pastoral roles and to wait longer for desirable assignments. While women play a significant role as volunteers in community churches, men continue to make the major theological and financial judgments for nationwide church organizations. Like Marx, conflict theorists argue that to whatever extent religion actually does influence social behavior, it reinforces existing patterns of dominance and inequality (Bureau of the Census 1998c:417; J. Dart 1997).

From a Marxist perspective, religion functions as an "agent of de-politicization" (J. Wilson 1973). In simpler terms, religion keeps people from seeing their lives and societal conditions in political terms—for example, by obscuring the overriding significance of conflicting economic interests. Marxists suggest that by inducing a "false consciousness" among the disadvantaged, religion **p. 193** lessens the possibility of collective political action that can end capitalist oppression and transform society.

Religious Behavior

All religions have certain elements in common, yet these elements are expressed in the distinctive manner of each faith. The patterns of religious behavior, like other patterns of social behavior, are of great interest to sociologists, since they underscore the relationship between religion and society.

Religious beliefs, religious rituals, and religious experience all help to define what is sacred and to differentiate the sacred from the profane. Let us now examine these three dimensions of religious behavior.

Belief

Some people believe in life after death, in supreme beings with unlimited powers, or in supernatural forces. ***Religious beliefs*** are statements to which members of a particular religion adhere. These views can vary dramatically from religion to religion.

The Adam and Eve account of creation found in Genesis, the first book of the Old Testament, is an example of a religious belief. Many people in the United States strongly adhere to this biblical explanation of creation and even insist that it be taught in public schools. These people, known as *creationists,* are worried by the secularization of society and oppose teaching that directly or indirectly questions biblical scripture.

Ritual

Religious rituals are practices required or expected of members of a faith. Rituals usually honor the divine power (or powers) worshipped by believers; they also remind adherents of their religious duties and responsibilities. Rituals and beliefs can be interdependent; rituals generally involve the affirmation of beliefs, as in a public or private statement confessing a sin (Roberts 1995). Like any social institution, religion develops distinctive nor-

mative patterns to structure people's behavior. Moreover, there are sanctions attached to religious rituals, whether rewards (Bar Mitzvah gifts) or penalties (expulsion from a religious institution for violation of norms).

In the United States, rituals may be very simple, such as saying grace at a meal or observing a moment of silence to commemorate someone's death. Yet certain rituals, such as the process of canonizing a saint, are quite elaborate. Most religious rituals in our culture focus on services conducted at houses of worship. Attendance at a service, silent and spoken prayers, and singing of spiritual hymns and chants are common forms of ritual behavior that generally take place in group settings. From an interactionist perspective, these rituals serve as important face-to-face encounters in which people reinforce their religious beliefs and their commitment to their faith.

For Muslims, a very important ritual is the *hajj*, a pilgrimage to the Grand Mosque in Mecca, Saudi Arabia. Every Muslim who is physically and financially able is expected to make this trip at least once. Each year 2 million pilgrims go to Mecca during the one-week period indicated by the Islamic lunar calendar. Muslims from all over the world make the *hajj*, including those in the United States, where many tours are arranged to facilitate this ritual.

Some rituals induce an almost trancelike state. The Plains Indians eat or drink peyote, a cactus containing the powerful hallucinogenic drug mescaline. Similarly, the ancient Greek followers of the god Pan chewed intoxicating leaves of ivy in order to become more ecstatic during their celebrations. Of course, artificial stimulants are not necessary to achieve a religious "high." Devout believers, such as those who practice the pentecostal Christian ritual of "speaking in tongues," can reach a state of ecstasy simply through spiritual passion.

Experience

In sociological study of religion, the term ***religious experience*** refers to the feeling or perception of being in direct contact with the ultimate reality, such as a divine being, or of being overcome with religious emotion. A religious experience may be rather slight, such as the feeling of exaltation a person receives from hearing a choir sing Handel's "Hallelujah Chorus." But many religious experiences are more profound, such as a Muslim's experience on a *hajj*. In his autobiography, the late African American activist Malcolm X (1964:338) wrote of his *hajj* and how deeply moved he was by the way that Muslims in Mecca came together across lines of race and color. For Malcolm X, the color blindness of the Muslim world "proved to me the power of the One God."

Still another profound religious experience is being "born again"—that is, at a turning point in one's life

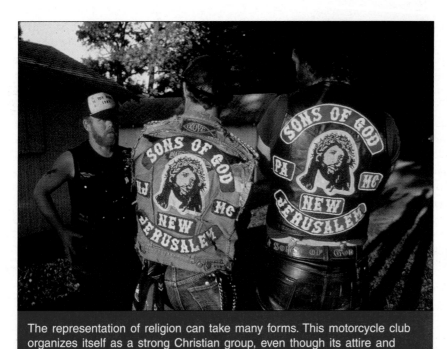

The representation of religion can take many forms. This motorcycle club organizes itself as a strong Christian group, even though its attire and lifestyle may be objectionable to many Christians.

making a personal commitment to Jesus. According to a 1999 national survey, 46 percent of people in the United States claimed that they had a born-again Christian experience at some time in their lives. An earlier survey found that Baptists (61 percent) were the most likely to report such experiences; by contrast, only 18 percent of Catholics and 11 percent of Episcopalians stated that they had been born again. The collective nature of religion, as emphasized by Durkheim, is evident in these statistics. The beliefs and rituals of a particular faith can create an atmosphere either friendly or hostile to this type of religious experience. Thus, a Baptist would be encouraged to come forward and share such experiences with others, whereas an Episcopalian who claimed to have been born again would receive much less support (Princeton Religions Research Center 2000a).

Religious Organization

The collective nature of religion has led to many forms of religious association. In modern societies, religion has become increasingly formalized. Specific structures such as churches and synagogues are constructed for religious worship; individuals are trained for occupational roles within various fields. These developments make it possible to distinguish clearly between the sacred and secular parts of one's life—a distinction that could not be made in earlier societies in which religion was largely a family activity carried out in the home.

Sociologists find it useful to distinguish between four basic forms of organization: the ecclesia, the denomination, the sect, and the new religious movement or cult. We can see differences among these types of organizations in such factors as size, power, degree of commitment expected from members, and historical ties to other faiths.

Ecclesiae

An **ecclesia** (plural, *ecclesiae*) is a religious organization that claims to include most or all of the members of a society and is recognized as the national or official religion. Since virtually everyone belongs to the faith, membership is by birth rather than conscious decision. Examples of ecclesiae include the Lutheran church in Sweden, the Catholic church in Spain, Islam in Saudi Arabia, and Buddhism in Thailand. However, there can be significant differences even within the category of *ecclesia*. In Saudi Arabia's Islamic regime, leaders of the ecclesia hold vast power over actions of the state. By contrast, the Lutheran church in contemporary Sweden has no such power over the Riksdag (parliament) or the prime minister.

Generally, ecclesiae are conservative in that they do not challenge the leaders of a secular government. In a society with an ecclesia, the political and religious institutions often act in harmony and mutually reinforce each other's power over their relative spheres of influence. Within the modern world, ecclesiae tend to be declining in power.

Denominations

A **denomination** is a large, organized religion not officially linked with the state or government. Like an ecclesia, it tends to have an explicit set of beliefs, a defined system of authority, and a generally respected position in society. Denominations claim as members large segments of a population. Generally, children accept the denomination of their parents and give little thought to membership in other faiths. Denominations also resemble ecclesiae in that generally few demands are made on members. However, there is a critical difference between these two forms of religious organization. Although the denomination is considered respectable and is not viewed as a challenge to the

Critical Thinking Questions

1. From a conflict point of view, explain how religion could be used to bring about social change.
2. What role do new religious movements (or cults) play in the organization of religion? Why are they so often controversial?

3. What are the functions and dysfunctions of tracking in schools? Viewed from an interactionist perspective, how would tracking of high school students influence the interactions between students and teachers? In what ways might tracking have positive and negative impacts on the self-concepts of various students?

Key Terms

Correspondence principle The tendency of schools to promote the values expected of individuals in each social class and to prepare students for the types of jobs typically held by members of their class. (page 337)

Creationism A literal interpretation of the Bible regarding the creation of humanity and the universe used to argue that evolution should not be presented as established scientific fact. (344)

Cultural universal General practices found in every culture. (321)

Denomination A large, organized religion not officially linked with the state or government. (328)

Ecclesia A religious organization that claims to include most or all of the members of a society and is recognized as the national or official religion. (328)

Education A formal process of learning in which some people consciously teach while others adopt the social role of learner. (321)

Hidden curriculum Standards of behavior that are deemed proper by society and are taught subtly in schools. (336)

Liberation theology Use of a church, primarily Roman Catholicism, in a political effort to eliminate poverty, discrimination, and other forms of injustice evident in a secular society. (325)

Megachurches Large worship centers affiliated only loosely, if at all, with existing denominations. (329)

New religious movement (NRM) or **cult** A generally small, secretive religious group that represents either a new religion or a major innovation of an existing faith. (331)

Profane The ordinary and commonplace elements of life, as distinguished from the sacred. (323)

Protestant ethic Max Weber's term for the disciplined work ethic, this-worldly concerns, and rational orientation to life emphasized by John Calvin and his followers. (325)

Religion A unified system of beliefs and practices relative to sacred things. (321)

Religious beliefs Statements to which members of a particular religion adhere. (327)

Religious experience The feeling or perception of being in direct contact with the ultimate reality, such as a divine being, or of being overcome with religious emotion. (327)

Religious rituals Practices required or expected of members of a faith. (327)

Sacred Elements beyond everyday life that inspire awe, respect, and even fear. (321)

Sect A relatively small religious group that has broken away from some other religious organization to renew what it views as the original vision of the faith. (330)

Secularization The process through which religion's influence on other social institutions diminishes. (321)

Teacher-expectancy effect The impact that a teacher's expectations about a student's performance may have on the student's actual achievements. (337)

Tracking The practice of placing students in specific curriculum groups on the basis of test scores and other criteria. (336)

Additional Readings

Lee, Martha F. 1996. *The Nation of Islam: An American Millenarium Movement.* Syracuse, NY: Syracuse University Press. A political scientist examines the origins of the organized religion commonly known as the "Black Muslims" and changes in this faith over the last half-century.

Ravitch, Diane. 2000. *Left Back: A Century of Failed School Reforms.* New York: Simon and Schuster. A respected scholar on education considers the failure of several massive efforts to improve public schools in the United States.

Zellner, William W., and Marc Petrowky, eds. 1999. *Sects, Cults, and Spiritual Communities: A Sociological Analysis.* Westport, CT: Praeger. A collection of essays profiling religious groups outside the mainstream of American spiritual organizations. Included are treatments of the Jesus People, Santería, and Scientology.

Technology Resources

 ## Internet Connection

Note: While all the URLs listed were current as of the printing of this book, these sites often change. Please check our website (http://www.mhhe.com/schaefer4) for updates.

1. Visit the search engine Omniseek (**http://www. omniseek.com/dir/Lifestyle/Religion+and+ Spirituality/Faiths+and+Practices/**), which provides an extensive list of "Faiths and Practices" sites. Select two groups and link to sites providing more information. Compare and contrast the two belief systems by answering the following questions:
   (a) What are the dimensions of behavior for these groups (beliefs, rituals, and experiences)? What differences and similarities can you find between your two selections?
   (b) How is each of the groups organized?
   (c) Which of the following best describes the two groups: ecclesia, denomination, sect, or new religious movement—or possibly some combination of these (see Table 12-1)?
   (d) In light of Durkheim's perspective on religion, what social functions do you believe these groups serve?
   (e) If possible, make special note of any demographic information provided on the sites. How do the groups compare in this regard?

2. The Research in Action box in this chapter (see Box 12-2) details some of the social facts regarding violence in schools. In order to address this problem, organizations have begun to emerge and are utilizing the Internet as a tool for communication. Visit the Center for the Prevention of school Violence (**http://www.ncsu.edu/cpsv/**) and explore the information and links to other sites provided.
   (a) Why did the Center form? What are the goals of the Center?
   (b) What is the "Safe Schools Pyramid" and how does it represent the philosophy and goals of the Center?
   (c) What is "S.A.V.E," why was it formed, and what techniques does it use to help alleviate school violence? Using your interactionist training, discover and describe what the "Official Colors of S.A.V.E." symbolize.
   (d) Which of the statistics on the site and in your textbook surprised you the most?
   (e) Do you believe that stronger gun laws will help reduce school violence? Why or why not? What else can educators, legislators, parents, and students do to help?

3. The formation of student subcultures is one of the latent functions of education. Personal relationships, academic advancement, and occupational networking can all be pursued through such groups. Conduct your own "Cyber Student Organization Fair" by logging onto Yahoo! (**http://dir.yahoo.com/Education/Organizations/ Student/**). Choose three different organizations listed, focusing on university/college students. For each, answer the following questions:

GOVERNMENT AND THE ECONOMY

(a) What is the name of the group?

(b) What are the goals and purposes of the group?

(c) What are the demographics of the membership?

(d) What kind of events does the group sponsor? How do those events help the organization achieve its goals?

(e) Which ideal type of student subculture does each organization most resemble—collegiate,

academic, vocation

page 341)? Why did

tion? Could the org

bination of these id

(f) What are some of th join this organizatio

(g) Which of the three o most like to join? Wh

Interactive e-Source with Making the Grade

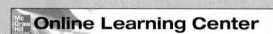

Online Learning Center   www.mhhe.com/schaefer

PowerWeb

SocCity

Voter turnout in the United States is low compared to other Western democracies. A clothing store offered this public service advertisement to encourage citizens to vote.

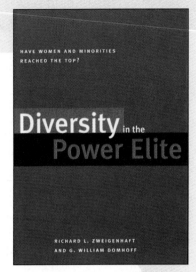

HAVE WOMEN AND MINORITIES
REACHED THE TOP?

Diversity in the
Power Elite

RICHARD L. ZWEIGENHAFT
AND G. WILLIAM DOMHOFF

T he power elite and Congress are more diverse than they were before the social movements that emerged in the 1960s brought pressure to bear on corporations, politicians, and government. Although the power elite is still composed primarily of Christian white men, there are now Jews, women, blacks, Latinos, and Asian Americans on the boards of the country's largest corporations; presidential cabinets are far more diverse than was the case forty years ago; and the highest ranks of the military are no longer filled solely by white men. In the case of elected officials in Congress, the trend toward diversity is even greater for women and all of the minority groups that we have studied. . . .

Ultimately we suggest that the increase in diversity at the top contains several ironies, the most important of which is related to what is perhaps the major unresolved tension in American life, between liberal individualism and the class structure. The diversification of the power elite has been celebrated, but this celebration ignores the continuing importance of the class structure. The movements that led to diversity in the power elite have succeeded to some extent, especially for women and minorities from privileged social backgrounds, but there has been no effect on the way the power elite functions or on the class structure itself. . . .

The power elite has been strengthened because diversity has been achieved primarily by the selection of women and minorities who share the prevailing perspectives and values of those already in power. The power elite is not "multicultural" in any full sense of the concept, but only in terms of ethnic or racial origins. This process has been helped along by those who have called for the inclusion of women and minorities without any consideration of criteria other than sex, race, or ethnicity. Because the demand was strictly for a woman on the Supreme Court, President Reagan could comply by choosing a conservative upper-class corporate lawyer, Sandra Day O'Connor. When pressure mounted to have more black justices, President Bush could respond by appointing Clarence Thomas, a conservative black Republican with a law degree from Yale University. It is yet another irony that appointments like these served to undercut the liberal social movements that caused them to happen. . . .

We therefore have to conclude on the basis of our findings that the diversification of the power elite did not generate any changes in an underlying class system. . . . The values of liberal individualism embedded in the Declaration of Independence, the Bill of Rights, and the civic culture were renewed by vigorous and courageous activists, but despite their efforts the class structure remains a major obstacle to individual fulfillment for the overwhelming majority of Americans. This fact is more than an irony. It is a dilemma. It combines with the dilemma of race to create a nation that celebrates equal opportunity but is, in reality, a bastion of class privilege and conservatism. *(Zweigenhaft and Domhoff 1998:176–77, 192, 194)* ■

Half a century ago C. Wright Mills (1959), the originator of the phrase *the sociological imagination,* studied the political process in the United States and articulated the concept of the power elite. In doing so, Mills stimulated a discussion about how society's most important decisions are made. Mills made a point of stating that the power elite was composed of men. That was no accident; at the time Mills wrote, no women made life-and-death decisions on society's behalf.

Four decades after Mills opened discussion of the subject, psychologist Richard L. Zweigenhaft and sociologist G. William Domhoff returned to the question of who rules America. As the excerpt from their book *Diversity in the Power Elite* (1998) shows, they found only modest changes in the nation's power structure. Today, a few privileged women occupy positions in the power elite, but the majority of the nation's decision makers are still men, and virtually all of them are White.

The power elite operates within the framework of the existing political system, be it local, state, national, or international. By **political system,** sociologists mean the social institution that is founded on a recognized set of procedures for implementing and achieving society's goals, such as the allocation of valued resources. Like religion and the family, the political system is a cultural universal: It is found in every society. In the United States, the political system holds the ultimate responsibility for addressing the social policy issues examined in this textbook: child care, the AIDS crisis, sexual harassment, welfare reform, and so forth.

The term **economic system** refers to the social institution through which goods and services are produced, distributed, and consumed. As with social institutions such as the family, religion, and government, the economic system shapes other aspects of the social order and is, in turn, influenced by them. Throughout this textbook, you have been reminded of the economy's impact on social behavior—for example, individual and group behavior in factories and offices. You have studied the work of Karl Marx and Friedrich Engels, who emphasized that the economic system of a society can promote social inequality. And you learned that foreign investment in developing countries can intensify inequality among residents. p. 11 p. 211

It is difficult to imagine two social institutions more intertwined than government and the economy. In addition to being a large employer in any nation, government at all levels regulates commerce and entry into many occupations. At the same time, the economy generates the revenue to support government services. While government and the economy are distinctive institutions, the interrelationship between the two makes it useful to consider them together while noting characteristics unique to each.

This chapter will present a sociological analysis of the impact of government and the economy on people's lives. We begin with macro-level analysis of capitalism and socialism as ideal types of economic systems. Next we examine the sources of power in a political system and the three major types of authority. We will see how politics works in the United States, with particular attention to political socialization, citizens' participation in politics, the changing role of women in politics, and the influence of interest groups on political decision making. We'll also look at two models of power in the United States: the elite and the pluralist models. Then we take a look at the changing nature of the U.S. economy and the global economy as we enter the twenty-first century. Finally, the social policy section explores the controversy over affirmative action, an issue that focuses on unequal opportunities. ■

Economic Systems

The sociocultural evolution approach developed by Gerhard Lenski categorizes preindustrial societies according to the way in which the economy is organized. The principal types of preindustrial societies, as you recall, are hunting-and-gathering societies, horticultural societies, and agrarian societies. p. 211

As noted in Chapter 5, the *industrial revolution*—which took place largely in England during the period 1760 to 1830—brought about changes p. 122 in the social organization of the workplace. People left their homesteads and began working in central locations such as factories. As the industrial revolution proceeded, a new form of social structure emerged: the **industrial society,** a society that depends on mechanization to produce its goods and services.

Two basic types of economic systems distinguish contemporary industrial societies: capitalism and socialism. As described in the following sections, capitalism and socialism serve as ideal types of economic systems. No nation precisely fits either model. Instead, the economy of each individual state represents a mixture of capitalism and socialism, although one type or the other is generally useful in describing a society's economic structure. China's economy, for example, is primarily socialistic, while the U.S. economy is much more capitalistic.

Capitalism

In preindustrial societies, land functioned as the source of virtually all wealth. The industrial revolution changed all that. It required that certain individuals and institutions be willing to take substantial risks in order to finance new inventions, machinery, and business enterprises. Eventually, bankers, industrialists, and other holders of large sums of money replaced landowners as the most powerful economic force. These people invested their funds in the hope of realizing even greater profits and thereby became owners of property and business firms.

The transition to private ownership of business was accompanied by the emergence of the capitalist economic system. *Capitalism* is an economic system in which the means of production are largely in private hands and the main incentive for economic activity is the accumulation of profits. In practice, capitalist systems vary in the degree to which the government regulates private ownership and economic activity (Rosenberg 1991).

Immediately following the industrial revolution, the prevailing form of capitalism was what is termed *laissez-faire* ("let them do"). Under the principle of laissez-faire, as expounded and endorsed by British economist Adam Smith (1723–1790), people could compete freely with minimal government intervention in the economy. Business retained the right to regulate itself and essentially operated without fear of government regulation (Smelser 1963).

Two centuries later, capitalism has taken on a somewhat different form. Private ownership and maximization of profits still remain the most significant characteristics of capitalist economic systems. However, in contrast to the era of laissez-faire, capitalism today features extensive government regulation of economic relations. Without restrictions, business firms can mislead consumers, endanger the safety of their workers, and even defraud the companies' investors—all in the pursuit of greater profits. That is why the government of a capitalist nation often monitors prices, sets safety standards for industries, protects the rights of consumers, and regulates collective bargaining between labor unions and management. Yet, under capitalism as an ideal type, government rarely takes over ownership of an entire industry.

Contemporary capitalism also differs from laissez-faire in another important respect: It tolerates monopolistic practices. A *monopoly* exists when a single business firm controls the market. Domination of an industry allows the firm to effectively control a commodity by dictating pricing, standards of quality, and availability. Buyers have little choice but to yield to the firm's decisions; there is no other place to purchase the product or service. Monopolistic practices violate the ideal of free competition cherished by Adam Smith and other supporters of laissez-faire capitalism.

Some capitalistic nations, such as the United States, outlaw monopolies through antitrust legislation. Such laws prevent any business from taking over so much of the competition in an industry that it gains control of the market. The U.S. federal government allows monopolies to exist only in certain exceptional cases, such as the utility and transportation industries. Even then, regulatory agencies scrutinize these officially approved monopolies and protect the public. The protracted legal battle between the Justice department and Microsoft points to the uneasy relationship between government and private monopolies in capitalistic countries.

Conflict theorists point out that while *pure* monopolies are not a basic element of the economy of the United States, competition is much more restricted than one might expect in what is called a *free enterprise system*. In numerous industries, a few companies largely dominate the field and keep new enterprises from entering the marketplace.

Socialism

Socialist theory was refined in the writings of Karl Marx and Friedrich Engels. These European radicals were disturbed by the exploitation of the working class as it emerged during the industrial revolution. In their view, capitalism forced large numbers of people to exchange their labor for low wages. The owners of an industry profit from the labor of their workers, primarily because they pay workers less than the value of the goods produced.

As an ideal type, a socialist economic system attempts to eliminate such economic exploitation. Under *socialism,* the means of production and distribution in a society are collectively rather than privately owned. The basic objective of the economic system is to meet people's needs rather than to maximize profits. Socialists reject the laissez-faire philosophy that free competition benefits the general public. Instead, they believe that the central government, acting as the representative of the people, should make basic economic decisions. Therefore, government ownership of all major industries—including steel production, automobile manufacturing, and agriculture—is a major feature of socialism as an ideal type.

In practice, socialist economic systems vary in the extent to which they tolerate private ownership. For example, in Great Britain, a nation with certain aspects of both a socialist and a capitalist economy, passenger airline service is concentrated in the government-owned corporation British Airways. Yet private airline companies are allowed to compete with it.

Socialist societies differ from capitalist nations in their commitment to social service programs. For example, the U.S. government provides health care and health insurance for the elderly and poor through the Medicare and Medicaid programs. By contrast, socialist countries typically offer government-financed medical care for *all* citizens. In theory, the wealth of the people as a collectivity is used to provide health care, housing, education, and other key services for each individual and family.

Marx believed that each socialist state would eventually "wither away" and evolve into a *communist* society. As an ideal type, **communism** refers to an economic system under which all property is communally owned and no social distinctions are made on the basis of people's ability to produce. In recent decades, the Soviet Union, the People's Republic of China, Vietnam, Cuba, and nations in Eastern Europe were popularly thought of as examples of communist economic systems. However, this represents an incorrect usage of a term with sensitive political connotations. All nations known as communist in the twentieth century have actually fallen far short of the ideal type.

By the early 1990s, Communist parties were no longer ruling the nations of Eastern Europe. The first major challenge to Communist rule came in 1980 when Poland's Solidarity movement—led by Lech Walesa and backed by many workers—questioned the injustices of that society. While martial law initially forced Solidarity underground, it eventually negotiated the end of Communist party rule in 1989. Over the next two years, dominant Communist parties were overthrown after popular uprisings in the Soviet Union and throughout Eastern Europe. The former Soviet Union, Czechoslovakia, and Yugoslavia were subdivided to accommodate the ethnic, linguistic, and religious differences within these areas. As of 1998, China, Cuba, and Vietnam remained socialist societies ruled by Communist parties. However, even in these countries capitalism was making inroads. For example, by 1995, 60 percent of Vietnam's economic output and 25 percent of China's came from the private sector (Steinfeld 1999; World Bank 1996:15).

Cuba, in particular, is adjusting to a dual economy. While the Communist government leader Fidel Castro remains firmly committed to Marxism, the centrally controlled economy has been in ruins following the end

Soon after the U.S. government lifted its trade embargo against Vietnam in 1994, Coca-Cola and Pepsi rushed in to corner the market. Coca-Cola made its "biggest" statement on the steps of the Opera House in Hanoi.

of Soviet aid and the continued trade embargo by the United States. Reluctantly, Castro has allowed small-scale family-managed businesses, such as restaurants and craft shops, to operate and accept dollars rather than the heavily devalued Cuban peso. This leads to an ironic situation in which government-employed teachers and doctors earn less than the small business operators, taxi drivers, and hotel workers who have access to foreign currency. This situation underscores how difficult it is to understand any nation's economy without considering its position in the global economy (J. McKinley 1999).

As we have seen, capitalism and socialism serve as ideal types of economic systems. In reality, the economy of each industrial society—including the United States, Great Britain, and Japan—includes certain elements of both capitalism and socialism. Whatever the differences, whether they more closely fit the ideal type of capitalism or socialism, all industrial societies rely chiefly on mechanization in the production of goods and services.

Politics and Government

An economic system does not exist in a vacuum. Someone or some group makes important decisions about how to use resources and how to allocate goods, whether it be a tribal chief or a parliament or a dictator. A cultural universal common to all economic systems, then, is the exercise of power and authority. The struggle for power and authority inevitably involves *politics,* which political scientist Harold Lasswell (1936) tersely defined as "who gets what, when, and how." In their study of politics and government, sociologists are concerned with social interactions among individuals and groups and their impact on the larger political and economic order.

Power

pp. 193—94 Power is at the heart of a political system. According to Max Weber, *power* is the ability to exercise one's will over others. To put it another way, whoever can control the behavior of others is exercising power. Power relations can involve large organizations, small groups, or even people in an intimate association.

There are three basic sources of power within any political system—force, influence, and authority. *Force* is the actual or threatened use of coercion to impose one's will on others. When leaders imprison or even execute political dissidents, they are applying force; so, too, are terrorists when they seize or bomb an embassy or assassinate a political leader. *Influence,* on the other hand, refers to the exercise of power through a process of persuasion. A citizen may change his or her position regarding a Supreme Court nominee because of a newspaper editorial, the expert testimony of a law school dean before the Senate Judiciary Committee, or a stirring speech at a rally by a political activist. In each case, sociologists would view such efforts to persuade people as examples of influence. Now let's take a look at the third source of power, *authority.*

Types of Authority

The term *authority* refers to power that has been institutionalized and is recognized by the people over whom it is exercised. Sociologists commonly use the term in connection with those who hold legitimate power through elected or publicly acknowledged positions. A person's authority is limited by the constraints of a particular social position. Thus, a referee has the authority to decide whether a penalty should be called during a football game but has no authority over the price of tickets to the game.

Max Weber (1947, original edition 1913) developed a classification system regarding authority that has become one of the most useful and frequently cited contributions of early sociology. He identified three ideal types of authority: traditional, legal-rational, and charismatic. Weber did not insist that only one type applies to a given society or organization. All can be present, but their relative importance will vary. Sociologists have found Weber's typology valuable in understanding different manifestations of legitimate power within a society.

Traditional Authority

Until the middle of this century, Japan was ruled by a revered emperor, whose power was absolute and passed down from generation to generation. In a political system based on *traditional authority,* legitimate power is conferred by custom and accepted practice. A king or queen is accepted as ruler of a nation simply by virtue of inheriting the crown; a tribal chief rules because that is the accepted practice. The ruler may be loved or hated, competent or destructive; in terms of legitimacy, that does not matter. For the traditional leader, authority rests in custom, not in personal characteristics, technical competence, or even

King Bhumibol Adulyadoj of Thailand reviews the Royal Honor Guard during a ceremony honoring his birthday. In a political system based on traditional authority, power is conferred according to accepted custom—in this case, on the basis of royal birth.

written law. People accept this authority because "this is how things have always been done." Traditional authority is absolute when the ruler has the ability to determine laws and policies.

Legal-Rational Authority

The U.S. Constitution gives Congress and our president the authority to make and enforce laws and policies. Power made legitimate by law is known as **legal-rational authority.** Leaders derive their legal-rational authority from the written rules and regulations of political systems, such as a constitution. Generally, in societies based on legal-rational authority, leaders are thought to have specific areas of competence and authority, but are not thought to be endowed with divine inspiration, as in certain societies with traditional forms of authority.

Charismatic Authority

Joan of Arc was a simple peasant girl in medieval France, yet she was able to rally the French people and lead them in major battles against English invaders. How was this possible? As Weber observed, power can be legitimized by the *charisma* of an individual. The term **charismatic authority** refers to power made legitimate by a leader's exceptional personal or emotional appeal to his or her followers. Charisma lets a person lead or inspire without relying on set rules or traditions. In fact, charismatic authority is derived more from the beliefs of followers than from the actual qualities of leaders. So long as people *perceive* a leader as having qualities setting him or her apart from ordinary citizens, that leader's authority will remain secure and often unquestioned.

Unlike traditional rulers, charismatic leaders often become well known by breaking with established institutions and advocating dramatic changes in the social structure and the economic system. Their strong hold over their followers makes it easier to build protest movements that challenge the dominant norms and values of a society. Thus, charismatic leaders such as Jesus, Joan of Arc, Mahatma Gandhi, Malcolm X, and Martin Luther King all used their power to press for changes in accepted social behavior. But so did Adolf Hitler, whose charismatic appeal turned people toward violent and destructive ends in Nazi Germany.

Observing from an interactionist perspective, sociologist Carl Couch (1996) points out that the growth of the electronic media has facilitated the development of charismatic authority. During the 1930s and 1940s, the heads of state of the United States, Great Britain, and Germany all used radio to issue direct appeals to citizens. In recent decades, television has allowed leaders to "visit" people's homes and communicate with them. Time and again, Saddam Hussein has rallied the Iraqi people through shrewd use of television appearances. In both Taiwan and South Korea in 1996, troubled political leaders facing reelection campaigns spoke frequently to national audiences and exaggerated military threats from neighboring China and North Korea, respectively.

As was noted earlier, Weber used traditional, legal-rational, and charismatic authority as ideal types. In reality, particular leaders and political systems combine elements of two or more of these forms. Presidents Franklin D. Roosevelt, John F. Kennedy, and Ronald Reagan wielded power largely through the legal-rational basis of their authority. At the same time, they were unusually charismatic leaders who commanded the personal loyalty of large numbers of citizens.

Political Behavior in the United States

Citizens of the United States take for granted many aspects of their political system. They are accustomed to living in a nation with a Bill of Rights, two major political parties, voting by secret ballot, an elected president, state and local governments distinct from the national government, and so forth. Yet, of course, each society has its own ways of governing itself and making decisions. Just as U.S. residents expect Democratic and Republican candidates to compete for public offices, residents of the People's Republic of China and Cuba are accustomed to one-party rule by the Communist party. In this section, we will examine a number of important aspects of political behavior within the United States.

Political Socialization

Do your political views coincide with those of your parents? Did you vote in the last election? Did you register to vote, or do you plan to do so? The process by which you acquire political attitudes and develop patterns of political behavior is known as **political socialization.** This involves not only learning the prevailing beliefs of a society but also coming to accept the political system, whatever its limitations and problems.

Chapter 6 identified five functional prerequisites that a society must fulfill to survive. One of these was the need to teach recruits to accept the values and customs of the group. In a political sense, this function is crucial; each succeeding generation must be encouraged to accept a society's basic political values and its particular methods of decision making. The principal institutions of political socialization are those that also socialize us to other cultural norms: the family, schools, and the media.

Many observers see the family as playing a particularly significant role in the process. Parents pass on their political attitudes and evaluations to their sons and daughters through discussions at the dinner table and also through the example of their political involvement or apathy. Early socialization does not always determine a person's political orientation; there are changes over time and between generations. Yet research on political socialization continues to show that parents' views have an important impact on their children's outlook (M. Jennings and Niemi 1981).

Schools provide young people with information and analysis of the political world. Unlike the family and peer groups, schools are easily susceptible to centralized and uniform control. That is why totalitarian societies commonly use educational institutions to indoctrinate the students in certain political beliefs. Even in democracies, where local schools are not under the pervasive control of the national government, political education will generally reflect the norms and values of the prevailing political order.

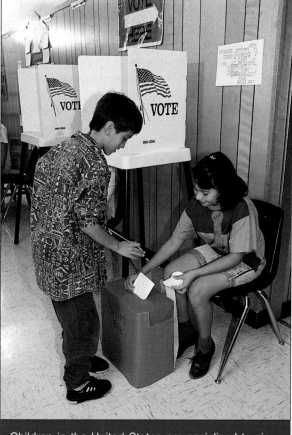

Children in the United States are socialized to view representative democracy as the best form of government. One part of this process is encouraging schoolchildren to vote in mock elections.

In the view of conflict theorists, students in the United States learn much more than factual information about their political and economic way of life. They are socialized to view capitalism and representative democracy as the "normal" and most desirable ways of organizing a nation, a form of dominant ideology. At the same time, schools often present p. 65—66 competing values and forms of government in a negative fashion or simply ignore them. From a conflict perspective, this type of political education serves the interests of the powerful and ignores the significance of the social divisions found within the United States.

Political socialization can take different forms in different types of societies. Using observation research, sociologist Benigno Aguirre (1984) concluded that the Cuban government encouraged certain types of crowd behavior to reinforce its legitimacy. The Committees for the Defense of the Revolution—which functioned much as the Communist party did when it ruled the Soviet Union—mobilized Cubans for parades, celebrations, protests, and testimonials on behalf of deceased revolutionary leaders. Through these mobilizations, Cuba's rulers hoped to convey the political message that Fidel Castro's communist government had and deserved widespread popular support.

Participation and Apathy

In theory, a representative democracy will function most effectively and fairly if an informed and active electorate communicates its views to government leaders. Unfortunately, this is hardly the case in the United States. Virtually all citizens are familiar with the basics of the political process, and most tend to identify to some extent with a political party (see Table 13-1), but only a small minority (often members of the higher social classes) actually participate in political organizations on a local or national level. Studies reveal that only 8 percent of the people in the United States belong to a political club or organization. Not more than one in five has *ever* contacted an official of national, state, or local government about a political issue or problem (Orum 2001).

The failure of most citizens to become involved in political parties diminishes the democratic process. Within the political system of the United States, the political party serves as an intermediary between people and government. Through competition in regularly scheduled elections, the two major parties provide for challenges to public policies and for an orderly transfer of power. An individual dissatisfied with the state of the nation or a local community can become involved in the political party process in many ways, such as by joining a political club supporting candidates for public office or working to

Table 13-1 Political Party Preferences in the United States

Party Identification	Percentage of Population
Strong Democrat	13
Not very strong Democrat	22
Independent, close to Democrat	13
Independent	17
Independent, close to Republican	9
Not very strong Republican	18
Strong Republican	9

Note: Data are for 1998. Numbers do not add to 100 percent due to rounding.

Source: J. Davis and Smith 1999:83.

change the party's position on controversial issues. If, however, people do not take an interest in the decisions of major political parties, public officials in a "representative" democracy will be chosen from two unrepresentative lists of candidates.

By the 1980s, it became clear that many people in the United States were beginning to be turned off by political parties, politicians, and big government. The most dramatic indication of this growing alienation comes from voting statistics. Voters of all ages and races appear to be less enthusiastic than ever about elections, even presidential contests. For example, almost 80 percent of eligible voters in the United States went to the polls in the presidential election of 1896. Yet by the 1996 election, turnout had fallen to less than 49 percent of all eligible voters. Obviously, even modestly higher voter turnout could dramatically change election outcomes, as we saw in the razor-thin margin in the 2000 presidential election.

While a few nations still command high voter turnout, it is increasingly common to hear national leaders of other countries complain of voter apathy. Japan typically enjoyed 70 percent turnout in its Upper House elections in the 1950s through mid-1980s, but by 1998 turnout was closer to 58 percent. In the 1998 British general elections, there was only a 34 percent turnout in London and 28 percent in the rest of England (A. King 1998; Masaki 1998).

Political participation makes government accountable to the voters. If participation declines, government can operate with less of a sense of accountability to society. This issue is most serious for the least powerful individuals and groups within the United States. Voter turnout has been particularly low among members of racial and ethnic minorities. According to a 1996 postelection survey, only 50.6 percent of *registered* Black voters and 26.7 percent of *registered* Hispanics reported that they had actually voted (see Table 13-2). Many more potential voters failed to register to vote. The poor—whose focus understandably is on survival—are traditionally underrepresented among voters as well. The low turnout found among these groups is explained, at least in part, by their common feeling of powerlessness. Yet these low statistics encourage political power brokers to continue to

Table 13-2 Surveys of Voter Participation in the Presidential Elections of 1972 and 1996

Group	1972 (Nixon–McGovern)		1996 (Clinton–Dole–Perot)	
	Percent Registered	Percent Who Voted	Percent Registered	Percent Who Voted
Total U.S. Population	72.3	63.0	65.9	54.2
Whites	73.4	64.5	67.7	56.0
Blacks	65.5	52.1	63.5	50.6
Hispanics	44.4	37.5	35.7	26.7

Source: Casper and Bass 1998.

Research in Action 13-1 Why Don't Young People Vote?

n 1971, there was great optimism. All through the 1960s, young people in the United States had actively participated in a range of political issues—from pushing civil rights to protesting the Vietnam War. They were especially disturbed by the fact that young men were barred from voting but were being drafted to serve in the military and dying for their country. In response to these concerns, the 26th Amendment to the Constitution was ratified in 1971, lowering the voting age from 21 to 18 in federal, state, and local elections.

Now, 30 years later, we can consider the available research and see what happened. Frankly, what is remarkable is what did *not* happen. First, young voters (those between 18 and 21) have not united in any particular political sentiment. We can see in how the young vote the same divisions of race, ethnicity, and gender that are apparent among older age groups.

Second, while the momentum for lowering the voting age came from college campuses, the majority of young voters are not students at all. Many are already part of the workforce and

either live with their parents or have established their own households.

Third, and particularly troubling, is their low voter turnout. In the 1996 presidential election, only 46 percent of the voting age population ages 18–20 was even registered. Among these young people, only 31 percent bothered to show up at the polls. This is an even

> While the momentum for lowering the voting age came from college campuses, the majority of young voters are not students at all.

lower turnout than among non–high school graduates or the unemployed.

What is behind this voter apathy among the young? The popular explanation is that people, especially young people, are alienated from the political system, turned off by the shallowness and negativity of candidates and campaigns. True, studies document that young voters are susceptible to cynicism and distrust, but these are not

necessarily associated with voter apathy. Numerous studies show the relationship between how people perceive the candidates and issues and their likelihood of voting is a very complex one. Communication scholars Erica Weintraub Austin and Bruce Pinkleton completed a survey of less experienced eligible voters and found that those who believe that they can see through the "lies" told by politicians via the media are *more* apt to think their participation can make a difference. In any event, young people do vote as they age. Any disaffection with the voting booth is certainly not permanent.

Other explanations for the lower turnout among the young seem more plausible. First, the United States is virtually alone in requiring citizens to, in effect, vote twice. They must first *register* to vote, often at a time when issues are not on the front burner and candidates haven't even declared. Then they must vote on election day. Young people, who tend to be mobile and to lead hectic lives, find it difficult to track voting requirements (which vary by state) and be present where they are legally eligible to vote. Time constraints are the single

Sources: Austin and Pinkleton 1995; Bureau of the Census 1998f; Casper and Bass 1998; Clymer 2000; Cook 1991; Landers 1988; Leon 1996; Shogan 1998.

---

ignore the interests of the less affluent and the nation's minorities. The segment of the voting population that has shown the *most* voter apathy—the young—is highlighted in Box 13-1.

Women in Politics

Women continue to be dramatically underrepresented in the halls of government. In 1999, there were only 67 women in Congress. They accounted for 58 of the 435 members of the House of Representatives and 9 of the 100 members of the Senate. Only two states other than Arizona had female governors—New Hampshire and New Jersey (Center for the American Woman and Politics 1999).

Sexism has been the most serious barrier to women interested in holding office. p. 266 Women were not even allowed to vote in national elections until 1920, and subsequent female candidates have had to overcome the prejudices of both men and women regarding women's fitness for leadership. Not until 1955 did a majority of people state that they would vote for a qualified woman for president. Moreover, women often encounter prejudice, discrimination, and abuse after they are elected. Despite these problems, more women are being elected to political office, and more of them are identifying themselves as feminists.

But while women politicians may be enjoying more electoral success now than in the past, there is evidence that the media cover them differently from men. A content

The face of the workforce is changing as more women and minorities make their appearance. Women are also showing up in the executive suites, as exemplified by Carly Fiorina, the CEO of Hewlett-Packard.

changes, 75 percent of businesses have instituted some type of cultural diversity training programs as of 2000 (Melia 2000).

Deindustrialization

What happens when a company decides it is more profitable to move its operations out of a long-established community to another part of the country or out of the country altogether? People lose jobs; stores lose customers; the local government's tax base declines and it cuts services. This devastating process has occurred again and again in the last decade or so.

p. 205 changing labor force is not merely statistical. A more diverse workforce means that relationships between workers are more likely to cross gender, racial, and ethnic lines. Interactionists note that people will find themselves supervising and being supervised by people very different from themselves. In response to these

The term **deindustrialization** refers to the systematic, widespread withdrawal of investment in basic aspects of productivity such as factories and plants. Giant corporations that deindustrialize are not necessarily refusing to invest in new economic opportunities. Rather, the targets and locations of investment change. First, there may be a relocation of plants from the nation's central cities to the suburbs. The next step may be relocation from suburban areas of the Northeast and Midwest to southern states,

FIGURE 13-3

Racial and Ethnic Composition of the Labor Force, 1986 and 2008 (projection)

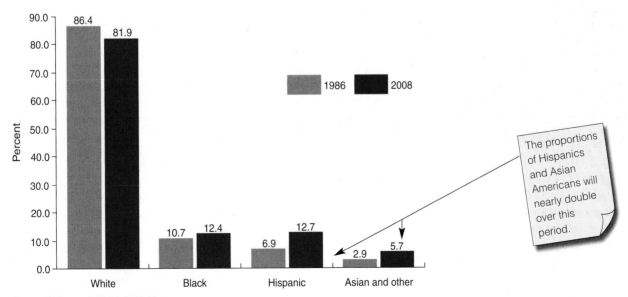

The proportions of Hispanics and Asian Americans will nearly double over this period.

Source: Fullerton 1997:24, 1999:20.

When U.S. plants deindustrialize at home, they often move their investment in manufacturing outside the country to take advantage of low wages. Shown here is an AT&T telephone repair plant located across the border in Nuevo Laredo, Mexico.

where labor laws place more restrictions on unions. Finally, a corporation may simply relocate *outside* the United States to a country with a lower rate of prevailing wages. General Motors, for example, decided to build a multibillion-dollar plant in Spain rather than in Kansas City (Bluestone and Harrison 1982; Rifkin 1995a).

While deindustrialization often involves relocation, in some instances it takes the form of corporate restructuring, as companies seek to reduce costs in the face of growing worldwide competition. When such restructuring occurs, the impact on the bureaucratic hierarchy of formal organizations can be significant. A large corporation may choose to sell off or entirely abandon less productive divisions and eliminate layers of management viewed as unnecessary. Wages and salaries may be frozen and fringe benefits cut—all in the name of "restructuring." Increasing reliance on automation also spells the end of work as we have known it.

The term **downsizing** was introduced in 1987 to refer to reductions in a company's workforce. According to the Department of Labor, about 75 percent of "downsized" employees find new jobs, while 14 percent are forced into retirement and 11 percent do not find new jobs. Among workers laid off from their jobs, 19 percent of Hispanics and 18 percent of African Americans were still unemployed two years later, compared with 11 percent of Whites.

Viewed from a conflict perspective, the unprece-dented attention given to downsizing in the mid-1990s reflected the continuing importance of social class in the United States. Conflict theorists note that job loss, affecting factory workers in particular, has long been a feature of industrialization. But when large numbers of middle-class managers and other white-collar employees with substantial incomes began to be laid off, suddenly there was great concern in the media over downsizing. By mid-2000, downsizing was even being applied to dot-com companies, the sector of the economy that flew high in the 1990s (Richtel 2000; Safire 1996; R. Samuelson 1996a, 1996b).

Trade unions are organizations that seek to improve the material status of their members, all of whom perform a similar job or work for a common employer. They constitute a significant part of the workforce in many industrial nations. In the United States, however, in 1999 only 9.4 percent of the private workforce was unionized, compared to 21.2 percent in 1979. In the 1990s, labor unions and their members were somewhat reluctant to fight downsizing since they recognized that increased international competition caused plant closings. As a result, many union–management negotiations now deal less with preventing layoffs than with establishing retirement plans for existing workers, benefits for part-time workers, company commitment to retraining programs, and equitable severance arrangements (Clawson and Clawson 1999; S. Franklin 2000).

The social costs of deindustrialization and downsizing cannot be minimized. Plant closings lead to substantial unemployment in a community, which can have a devastating impact on both the micro- and macrolevel. On the micro-level, the unemployed person and his or her family must adjust to a loss of p. 207 spending power. Both marital happiness and family cohesion may suffer as a result. Although many dismissed workers eventually reenter the paid labor force, they often must accept less desirable positions with lower salaries and fewer benefits. Unemployment and underemployment are tied into many of the social problems discussed throughout this textbook, among them the need for child care, the pp. 97, 214 controversy over welfare, and the issue of health care reform (which will be discussed in Chapter 14).

BINTI HARVEY:
CBS Online Reporter

Binti Harvey writes for the Online Business News Service, a financial news network that is accessed by the web. She covers technology stocks in the two columns she writes daily. In the course of her work, she often talks with the chief financial officers of multinational technology firms.

Harvey finds that her sociology degree, earned at UCLA in 1996, has been of tremendous value in her job. The first aspect is in "writing, writing, writing! Sociology gave me a really strong grasp of the fundamentals of writing. It has helped me with deadlines and to put together a comprehensive yet concise story quickly." Sociology has also helped her to take a broader look at issues and make connections. Finally, and perhaps most importantly, it has played a big role in helping her to understand others. "I'm in a lot of situations with business people who aren't comfortable with a young Black female. My sociological background has helped me un-

derstand where they're coming from, their perspective. It has helped me to help them to see me as a reporter." In Harvey's view, sociology allows people who would normally not have power to empower themselves.

Her advice to sociology students is to learn the terms but put more emphasis on learning the concepts and how to apply them to everyday life. "It's one of the few subjects that you'll encounter in college that you can apply to your daily life."

Let's Discuss

1. In what ways do you think an understanding of sociology would enhance a reporter's interviewing skills?

2. If someone's goal is to be an online financial journalist, what topics and courses in the field of sociology might be useful to study?

On the societal, or macro, level, the impact of a plant closing on a community can be as difficult as it is for an individual worker and his or her family. As noted earlier, the community will experience a significant loss of tax revenues, thereby straining its ability to support police and fire protection, schools, parks, and other public services. Moreover, rising unemployment in a community leads to a reduced demand for goods and services. Sales by retail firms and other businesses fall off, and this can lead to further layoffs.

The impact of deindustrialization is evident not only in the United States but also in Asia and western Europe. In an effort to remain competitive within a global economy, many European companies have laid off workers. French sociologist Loic Wacquant (1993) has studied urban rioting in the United States and Europe and suggests that most communities that are the scene of riots share a common sociological profile. They typically are former working-class communities that were sustained by factories that formed the heart of a manufacturing economy. As their countries' economies shifted to the service- and information-based economy of postindustrial society, the local factories closed, leaving these working-class communities behind. In Europe, right-wing politicians and political movements have exploited the difficulties of these communities by scapegoating immigrants (rather than deindustrialization) as the cause of a loss of jobs (Tagliabue 1996).

E-Commerce

Another development following close on the heels of deindustrialization is the emergence of e-commerce, as online businesses replace bricks-and-mortar establishments. *E-commerce* refers to the numerous ways that people with access to the Internet can do business from their computer. Amazon.com, for example, began in 1995 as a supplier of book titles but soon became the prototype for online businesses, branching into selling a variety of merchandise, including toys and hardware equipment. By 2000 Amazon.com boasted 20 million customers in 160 countries. The growth of e-commerce means jobs in a new line of industry as well as growth for related industries, such as warehousing, packing, and shipping.

E-commerce has brought new social dynamics to the retail trade. Consider the impact on traditional retail outlets and on face-to-face interaction with local storeowners. Even established companies like Nike, Timex, Levi's, and Mattel are establishing their own online "stores," bypassing the retail outlets that they have courted for years to directly reach customers with their merchandise. Megamalls once replaced personal ties to stores for many shoppers; the growth of e-commerce with its "cybermalls" is just the latest change in the economy.

Some observers note that e-commerce offers more opportunities to consumers in rural areas and to those with disabilities. To its critics, however, e-commerce signals more social isolation, more alienation, and greater

disconnect for the poor and disadvantaged who are not a part of the new information technology (Amazon.com 2000; Drucker 1999; Hansell 1999; Stoughton and Walker 1999).

The Contingency Workforce

In the past, the term "temp" typically conjured up images of a replacement receptionist or a worker covering for someone on vacation. However, in association with the deindustrialization and downsizing described above, a "contingency workforce," in which workers are hired only for as long as they are needed, has emerged in the United States, and we have witnessed what has been called the "temping of America."

Unemployed workers and entrants to the paid labor force accept positions as temporary or part-time workers. Some do so for flexibility and control over their work time, but others accept these jobs because they are the only ones available. Young people are especially likely to fill temporary positions. Employers find it attractive and functional to shift toward a contingency workforce because it allows them to respond more quickly to workforce demands—as well as to hire employees without having to offer the fringe benefits that full-time employees enjoy. All around the United States, large firms have come to rely on part-time or temporary workers, most of whom work part-time involuntarily. Many of these workers feel the effects of deindustrialization and shifts in the global economy. They lost their full-time jobs when companies moved operations to developing nations (Cooper 1994; Francis 1999).

It is difficult to estimate the size of the contingency workforce of the United States. Heidi Hartmann of the Institute for Women's Policy Research notes that there is no agreement among social scientists as to how to define a "contingent worker" or how many there are. According to one estimate, however, contingent workers constitute about one-fourth of the nation's paid labor force. In 1998, for example, about 28 percent of Microsoft's workforce was temporary. This included a large number of long-term temporaries (those who work more than one year), who have come to refer to their awkward status as "permatemps" (S. Greenhouse 1998).

During the 1970s and 1980s, temporary workers typically held low-skill positions at fast-food restaurants, telemarketing firms, and other service industries. Today, the contingent workforce is evident at virtually *all* skill levels and in *all* industries. Clerical "temps" handle word processing and filing duties, managers are hired on a short-term basis to reorganize departments, freelance

An accountant studies a ledger in an office. Increasing numbers of educated, white-collar professionals (such as accountants) have joined low-level "temp" workers in the contingency workforce.

writers prepare speeches for corporate executives, and blue-collar workers are employed for a few months when a factory receives an unusually high number of orders. A significant minority of temporary employees are contract workers who are being "rented" for specific periods of time by the companies that previously downsized them—and are now working at lower salary levels without benefits or job security (Kirk 1995; Uchitelle 1996).

Workers in the United States generally blame forces outside their control—indeed, outside the nation—for the problems they experience as a result of deindustrialization and the rise of a contingency workforce. The relocation of factories to other countries has unquestionably contributed to job loss in the United States. But there are growing indi-cations that automation is substantially reducing the need for human labor in both manufacturing and service industries. By the year 2020, it is projected that less than 2 percent of the entire global labor force will be engaged in factory work. In Chapter 16, we will look at the role of technology in promoting social and economic change (Rifkin 1996).

In the struggles of part-time workers and the unemployed to make ends meet, we find government and the economy intertwined, as the government steps in with assistance, whether it be unemployment compensation, government-funded child care, or welfare. In the social policy section that follows, we examine affirmative action, a controversial issue that provides another example of the link between government and the economy.

SOCIAL POLICY AND THE ECONOMY

Affirmative Action

www.mhhe.com/schaefer4

The Issue

Jessie Sherrod began picking cotton in the fields of Mississippi when she was eight years old, earning $1.67 each time she worked a 12-hour day. Today, at 45, she is a Harvard-educated pediatrician who specializes in infectious diseases. But the road from the cotton fields to the medical profession was hardly an easy one. "You can't make up for 400 years of slavery and mistreatment and unequal opportunity in 20 years," she says angrily. "We had to ride the school bus for five miles . . . and pass by a white school to get to our black elementary school. Our books were used books. Our instructors were not as good. We didn't have the proper equipment. How do you make up for that?" (Stolberg 1995:A14). Some people think it should be done through affirmative action programs.

The term *affirmative action* first appeared in an executive order issued by President John F. Kennedy in 1961. That order called for contractors to "take affirmative action to ensure that applicants are employed, and that employees are treated during employment, without regard to their race, creed, color, or national origin." In 1967, the order was amended by President Lyndon Johnson to also prohibit discrimination on the basis of sex, but affirmative action remained a vague concept. Currently, **affirmative action** refers to positive efforts to recruit minority group members or women for jobs, promotions, and educational opportunities. But many people feel that affirmative action programs constitute re-verse discrimination against qualified Whites and males. Does government have a responsibility to make up for past discrimination? If so, how far should it take it?

The Setting

A variety of court decisions and executive branch statements have outlawed certain forms of job discrimination based on race, sex, or both, including (1) word-of-mouth recruitment among all-White or all-male workforces, (2) recruitment exclusively in schools or colleges that are limited to one sex or are predominantly White, (3) discrimination against married women or forced retirement of pregnant women, (4) advertising in male and female "help wanted" columns when gender is not a legitimate occupational qualification, and (5) job qualifications and tests that are not substantially related to the job. Also, the lack of minority (African American, Asian, American Indian, or Hispanic) or female employees may in itself represent evidence of unlawful exclusion (Commission on Civil Rights 1981).

In the late 1970s, a number of bitterly debated cases on affirmative action reached the Supreme Court. In 1978, in the *Bakke* case, by a narrow 5–4 vote, the Supreme Court ordered the medical school of the University of California at Davis to admit Allen Bakke, a White engineer who originally had been denied admission. The justices ruled that the school had violated Bakke's constitutional rights by establishing a fixed quota system for minority students. The Court added, however, that it was constitutional for universities to adopt flexible admissions programs that use race as one factor in decision making.

Sociological Insights

Sociologists—and especially conflict theorists—view affirmative action as a legislative attempt to reduce inequality embedded in the social structure by increasing opportunities of groups such as women and African Americans that have been deprived in the past. The gap in earning power between White males and other groups (see Figure 13-4) is one indication of the inequality that needs to be addressed.

Even if they acknowledge the disparity in earnings between White males and others, many people in the United States doubt that everything done in the name of affirmative action is desirable. By 1996, a national survey suggested that the nation was fairly evenly split on this controversial issue. Forty-five percent of respondents agreed that most governmental affirmative action programs should be continued, while 43 percent contended that such programs should be abolished (Bennet 1996).

Much less documented than economic inequality are the social consequences of affirmative action policies on everyday life. Interactionists focus on situations in which some women and minorities in underrepresented professions and schools are often mistakenly viewed as products of affirmative action. Fellow students and workers may stereotype them as less qualified and see them as beneficiaries of preference over more qualified White males. Obviously, this is not necessarily the case, but such labeling may well affect social relationships. Sociologist Orlando Patterson (1998) has noted that workplace isolation experienced by minority workers inhibits their advancement up the corporate ladder; yet if efforts to increase their representation are scaled back, these problems in advancement will persist.

Has affirmative action actually helped to alleviate employment inequality on the basis of race and gender? Sociologists In Soo Son, Suzanne Model, and Gene Fisher (1989) studied income data and occupational mobility among Black male and White male workers in the period 1974 to 1981 to examine possible class polarization among Blacks. The researchers found that while Black college graduates made substantial gains as a result of affirmative action, less advantaged Blacks apparently did not benefit from it. The researchers (1989:325) conclude that the "racial parity achieved by young college-educated blacks in the 1970s will be maintained only if the government's commitment to affirmative action does not slacken."

Policy Initiatives

By the early 1990s, affirmative action had emerged as an increasingly important issue in state and national political campaigns. Generally, discussion focused on the use of quotas (or the "Q word," as it came to be known) in hiring practices. Supporters of affirmative action argue that hiring goals (or

FIGURE 13-4

Median Income by Race, Ethnicity, and Gender, 1999

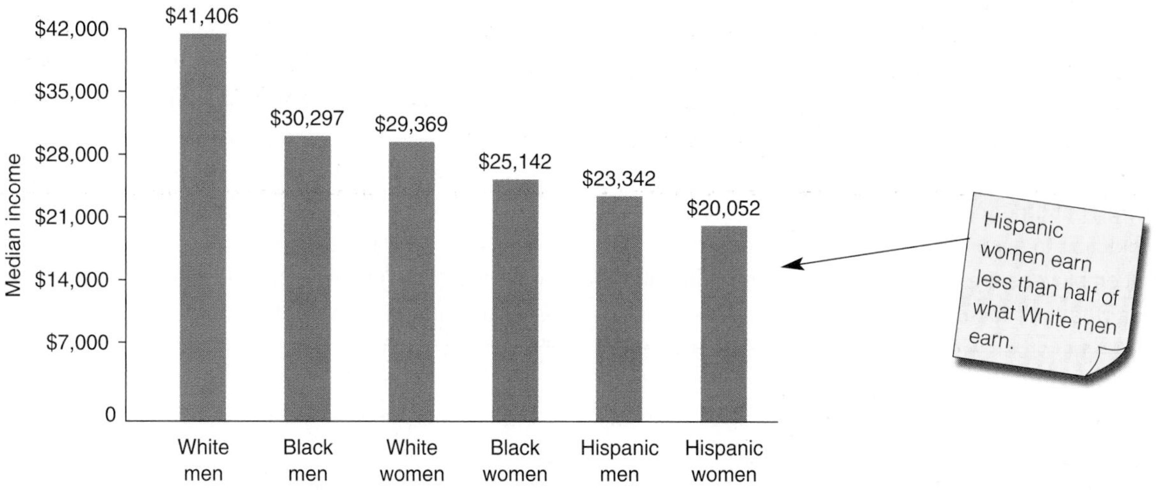

Note: Median income includes all financial sources and is limited to year-round, full-time workers over 15 years of age. "White" refers to non-Hispanic.

Source: Bureau of the Census 2000d:33,35.

targets) establish floors for minority inclusion but do not exclude truly qualified candidates from any group. Opponents insist that these "targets" are, in fact, quotas that lead to reverse discrimination. However, affirmative action has caused very few claims of reverse discrimination by White people. Fewer than 100 of the more than 3,000 discrimination opinions in federal courts from 1990 to 1994 even raised the issue of reverse discrimination, and reverse discrimination was actually established in only six cases (*New York Times* 1995).

In the 1996 elections, California's voters approved by a 54 to 46 percent margin the California Civil Rights Initiative, also known as Proposition 209. This measure amends the state constitution to *prohibit* any program that gives preference to women and minorities in college admissions, hiring, promotion, or government contracts. In other words, it aims to abolish affirmative action programs. In 1997, the Supreme Court turned down a request to put an immediate halt to the initiative. This ruling suggests the Court is unlikely to overturn the measure.

The approval of Proposition 209 by California voters has encouraged opponents of affirmative action across the nation. In early 1997, the American Civil Rights Institute was established to aggressively lobby for federal and state legislation that will abolish all preferential treatment based on race and sex in employment, government contracts, and admissions. In 1998, voters in Washington State passed an anti-affirmative action measure known as Initiative 200, and other states were considering similar measures (Wickham 1998).

The United States is not alone in its effort to compensate for generations of inequality between racial groups. After dismantling the system of apartheid that favored Whites economically and socially, the Republic of South Africa is now trying to level the playing field. Inequality is stark: 88 percent of the nation's population is non-White, yet this group accounts for only 4 percent of

the managerial ranks. The South African government has chosen the term "affirmative action" for its policy to encourage the hiring of Blacks in management positions where none existed before. Because the gaps are much greater than in the United States, there has been a virtual hiring frenzy in the limited pool of black South African managers and professionals. The subject of affirmative action in this nation almost always splits along racial lines: Blacks are infuriated that there is so much injustice to make up for, while Whites are reluctant to embrace the program meant to redress inequality. The specifics may be different from the United States, but the concerns and impatience seen in South Africa are familiar (Daley 1997).

Let's Discuss

1. Would a conflict theorist support the policy of affirmative action? Why or why not?
2. Do you think claims of reverse discrimination have any validity? What should be done about them?
3. If you were to draft legislation either supporting or abolishing affirmative action, what provisions would it include?

Summary

The *economic system* of a society has an important influence on social behavior and on other social institutions. Each society must have a *political system* to establish procedures for the allocation of valued resources.

1. As the industrial revolution proceeded, a new form of social structure emerged: the *industrial society.*

2. Economic systems of *capitalism* vary in the degree to which the government regulates private ownership and economic activity, but all emphasize the profit motive.

3. The basic objective of a *socialist* economic system is to eliminate economic exploitation and meet people's needs.

4. Marx believed that *communism* would naturally evolve out of the socialism stage.

5. There are three basic sources of *power* within any political system : *force, influence,* and *authority.*

6. Max Weber identified three ideal types of authority: *traditional, legal-rational,* and *charismatic.*

7. The principal institutions of *political socialization* in the United States are the family, schools, and the media.

8. Political participation makes government accountable to its citizens, but there is a great deal of apathy in both the United States and other countries.

9. Women are still underrepresented in office but are becoming more successful at winning elections to public office.

10. Sometimes people band together in *interest groups* to influence public policy.

11. Advocates of the *elite model* of the power structure of the United States see the nation as being ruled by a small group of individuals who share common political and economic interests (a *power elite*), whereas advocates of a *pluralist model* believe that power is more widely shared among conflicting groups.

12. The nature of the U. S. economy is changing. Sociologists are interested in the changing face of the workforce, the effects of *deindustrialization,* increased use of a contingency workforce, and the emergence of e-commerce.

13. Despite numerous recent *affirmative action* programs, White males continue to hold the overwhelming majority of prestigious and high-paying jobs in the United States.

Critical Thinking Questions

1. The United States has long been put forward as the model of a capitalist society. Drawing on material in earlier chapters of the textbook, discuss the values and beliefs that have led people in the United States to cherish a laissez-faire, capitalist economy. To what degree have these values and beliefs changed during the twentieth century? What aspects of socialism are now evident in the nation's economy? Have there been basic changes in our values and beliefs to support certain principles traditionally associated with socialist societies?

2. Who really holds power in the college or university you attend? Describe the distribution of power at your school, drawing on the elite and pluralist models where they are relevant.

3. Imagine that you have joined your state representative's legislative staff as a summer intern. She has assigned you to a committee that is working on solutions to the problem of school violence, particularly school shootings. How could you use what you have learned about sociology to conceptualize the problem? What type of research would you suggest the committee undertake? What legislative solutions might you recommend?

Key Terms

Affirmative action   Positive efforts to recruit minority group members or women for jobs, promotions, and educational opportunities. (page 371)

Authority   Power that has been institutionalized and is recognized by the people over whom it is exercised. (356)

Capitalism   An economic system in which the means of production are largely in private hands, and the main incentive for economic activity is the accumulation of profits. (354)

Charismatic authority   Power made legitimate by a leader's exceptional personal or emotional appeal to his or her followers. (357)

Communism   As an ideal type, an economic system under which all property is communally owned and no social distinctions are made on the basis of people's ability to produce. (355)

Deindustrialization   The systematic, widespread withdrawal of investment in basic aspects of productivity such as factories and plants. (367)

Downsizing   Reductions taken in a company's workforce as part of deindustrialization. (368)

E-commerce   Numerous ways that people with access to the Internet can do business from their computer. (369)

Economic system   The social institution through which goods and services are produced, distributed, and consumed. (353)

Elite model   A view of society as ruled by a small group of individuals who share a common set of political and economic interests. (363)

Force   The actual or threatened use of coercion to impose one's will on others. (356)

Industrial society   A society that depends on mechanization to produce its goods and services. (353)

Influence   The exercise of power through a process of persuasion. (356)

Interest group   A voluntary association of citizens who attempt to influence public policy. (363)

Laissez-faire   A form of capitalism under which people compete freely, with minimal government intervention in the economy. (354)

Legal-rational authority   Power made legitimate by law. (357)

Monopoly   Control of a market by a single business firm. (354)

Pluralist model   A view of society in which many competing groups within the community have access to government so that no single group is dominant. (365)

Political action committee (PAC)   A political committee established by an interest group—say, a national bank, corporation, trade association, or cooperative or membership association—to solicit contributions for candidates or political parties. (363)

Political socialization   The process by which individuals acquire political attitudes and develop patterns of political behavior. (357)

Political system   The social institution that relies on a recognized set of procedures for implementing and achieving the goals of a group. (353)

Politics   In Harold D. Lasswell's words, "who gets what, when, and how." (356)

Power   The ability to exercise one's will over others. (356)

Power elite   A small group of military, industrial, and government leaders who control the fate of the United States. (363)

Socialism   An economic system under which the means of production and distribution are collectively owned. (354)

Trade unions   Organizations that seek to improve the material status of their members, all of whom perform a similar job or work for a common employer. (368)

Traditional authority   Legitimate power conferred by custom and accepted practice. (356)

Additional Readings

Bowen, William G., and Derek Bok. 1998. *The Shape of the River: Long-Term Consequences of Considering Race in College and University Admissions.* Princeton, NJ: Princeton University Press. A detailed statistical analysis of affirmative action leads Bowen and Bok, former presidents of Princeton and Harvard, to conclude that not only do minority students admitted to college under affirmative action policies gain from their experiences, but so do the colleges and the larger society.

Enloe, Cynthia. 1990. *Bananas, Beaches, and Bases: Making Feminist Sense of International Politics.* Berkeley: University of California Press. Enloe studied the lives of women on military bases and of diplomatic wives as part of her examination of the male-dominated agenda of international politics.

Gleick, James. 1999 *Faster: The Acceleration of Just About Everything.* New York: Pantheon Book. A journalistic look at the ever-increasing pace of life in the workplace and throughout the lives of people in industrial nations.

Rogers, Jackie Krasas. 2000. *Temps: The Many Faces of the Changing Workplace.* Ithaca, NY: Cornell University Press. An examination of the growing use of temporary workers in both low- and high-skill jobs.

Technology Resources

Internet Connection

Note: While all the URLs listed were current as of the printing of this book, these sites often change. Please check our website (http://www.mhhe.com/schaefer4) for updates.

1. Rock the Vote (**http://www.rockthevote.org**) is among a growing list of organizations trying to involve youths in the political and voting process. Review the material in Box 13-1 in your text, and then explore the Rock the Vote website to learn more. On the site, visitors can read information, view pictures, and participate in online polls, as well as discover how to register to vote.
   (a) When and why did Rock and Vote form?
   (b) Choose one of the "Issues" detailed on the site. What recent events are occurring in terms of this issue? How do various politicians stand on this issue? What statistics does the site provide? Why is this issue important?
   (c) What are musicians, actors, and politicians doing about the issue that you chose?
   (d) Take some of the "Interactive Polls." How do your opinions compare to others?
   (e) Visit the "Activist Gallery" and view the images. What messages does the art communicate? What symbols are used?
   (f) What do you think can be done to increase the involvement of young voters in the political process?
2. Max Weber's writings have been crucial in expanding sociologists' understanding of the workings of political institutions, government, and bureaucracies. In particular, his work on types of authority helps to frame the relationship of those in power to the people they lead. First, direct your web browser to an Internet search engine such as Lycos® (**http://www.lycos.com**) or Alta Vista (**http://www.altavista.com**). Second, think of a leader from politics, religion, or history that you always wanted to learn more about. If you need an idea, just flip through your textbook and you will find pictures and names of many such leaders. Search for that person's name and visit links dedicated to her or his life.
   (a) Which person did you choose? Why did you select her or him?
   (b) When did this person live? What group or nation did this person lead? What role has this person played in history?
   (c) What type of authority did he or she have over followers? Was it traditional, legal-rational, or charismatic authority, or some combination? What reasons/examples can you give to support your choice?
   (d) Did the person you studied ever use force to exert or maintain power over others? Did the person ever use influence? How so?
   (e) What is your opinion of this leader in light of all you have learned?
3. Sociology emerged, in part, as a way to grasp the dynamic changes in society after the Industrial Revolution. Today, people are living through an-

other social revolution due to the computer, a technology that is changing education, relationships, government, and the economy. One area of alteration involves "where" and "how" people work. To learn more about how the computer has impacted work, visit the About® "Telecommuting" site, "guided by" Catherine A. Roseberry (**http://telecommuting.about.com/**).

(a) Define and describe some of the evolving styles of work, such as "telecommuting," "job-sharing," and "flex time." What do these terms mean? What are the pros and cons (see "Flex Options—Advantages & Disadvantages" on the site) of these newer styles?

(b) What is "Telecommuting Volunteer Work"?

(c) What current government and business news/events are having an impact on telecommuting? Has recent legislation or policies encouraged telecommuting in your opinion? If so, how? If not, why?

(d) What skills will be needed by workers in the new economy?

(e) Considering what you have learned on the site and in your book, would you like to be a telecommuter? Why or why not?

Interactive e-Source with Making the Grade

Online Learning Center — www.mhhe.com/schaefer4

PowerWeb

SocCity

WELCOME TO AMERICA

the only industrialized country besides South Africa without national healthcare

Sociological Perspectives on Health and Illness

From a sociological point of view, social factors contribute to the evaluation of a person as "healthy" or "sick." How, then, can we define health? We can imagine a continuum with health on one end and death on the other. In the preamble to its 1946 constitution, the World Health Organization defined **health** as a "state of complete physical, mental, and social well-being, and not merely the absence of disease and infirmity" (Leavell and Clark 1965:14). With this definition in mind, the "healthy" end of our continuum represents an ideal rather than a precise condition. Along the continuum, people define themselves as "healthy" or "sick" on the basis of criteria established by each individual, relatives, friends, coworkers, and medical practitioners. Because health is relative, we can view it in a

Medical problems are, in part, sometimes a product of the culture. A young woman checks her weight on the bathroom scale. In the United States, an intense fear of becoming obese causes some young women to develop a culture-bound syndrome known as *anorexia nervosa*.

social context and consider how it varies in different situations or cultures (Twaddle 1974; Wolinsky 1980).

Why is it that you may consider yourself sick or well when others do not agree? Who controls definitions of health and illness in our society, and for what ends? What are the consequences of viewing yourself (or being viewed) as ill or disabled? Drawing on four sociological perspectives—functionalism, conflict theory, interactionism, and labeling theory—we can gain greater insight into the social context shaping definitions of health and treatment of illness.

Functionalist Approach

Illness entails at least a temporary disruption in a person's social interactions both at work and at home. Consequently, from a functionalist perspective, "being sick" must be controlled so that not too many people are released from their societal responsibilities at any one time. Functionalists contend that an overly broad definition of illness would disrupt the workings of a society.

"Sickness" requires that one take on a social role, even if temporarily. The **sick role** refers to societal expectations about the attitudes and behavior of a person viewed as being ill. Sociologist Talcott Parsons (1951, 1972, 1975), well known for his contributions to functionalist theory (see Chapter 1), has outlined the behavior required of people considered "sick." They are exempted from their normal, day-to-day responsibilities and generally are not blamed for their condition. Yet they are obligated to try to get well, and this may include seeking competent professional care. Attempting to get well is particularly important in the world's developing countries. In modern automated industrial societies, we can absorb a greater degree of illness or disability, but in horticultural or agrarian societies, the availability of workers is far more critical (Conrad 1997).

According to Parsons's theory, physicians function as "gatekeepers" for the sick role, either verifying a patient's condition as "illness" or designating the patient as "recovered." The ill person becomes dependent on the doctor because the latter can control valued rewards (not only treatment of illness but also excused absences from work and school). Parsons suggests that the doctor–patient relationship is somewhat like that between parent and child. Like a parent, the physician helps the patient to return to society as a full and functioning adult (Segall 1976).

There have been a number of criticisms of the concept of the sick role. First, patients' judgments regarding their own state of health may be related to their gender, age, social class, and ethnic group. For example, younger people may fail to detect warning signs of a dangerous illness while the elderly may focus too much on the

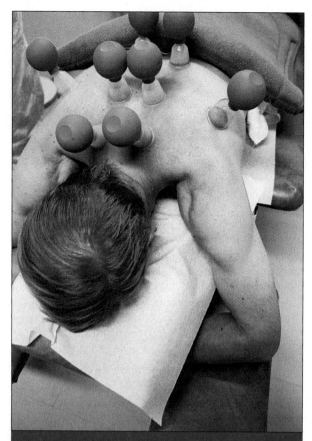

Health care takes many forms around the world. Cupping—a traditional practice used in ancient China, India, Egypt, and Greece—survives in modern Finland (left). Physiotherapists there use suction cups to draw out blood in order to lower patients' blood pressure, improve their circulation, and relieve muscular pain. In the western Pacific (right), the Malaitan people of Laulasi Island, one of the Solomon Islands, believe that a leaf called *raralu* has medicinal properties that reduce swelling. This boy has squeezed a *raralu* leaf to release its juices and used it to bandage his broken finger.

slightest physical malady. Second, the sick role may be more applicable to people experiencing short-term illnesses than to those with recurring, long-term illnesses. Finally, even simple factors, such as whether a person is employed or not, seem to affect willingness to assume the sick role—as does the impact of socialization into a particular occupation or activity. For example, beginning in childhood, athletes learn to define certain ailments as "sports injuries" and therefore do not regard themselves as "sick" (Curry 1993). Nonetheless, sociologists continue to rely on Parsons's model for functionalist analysis of the relationship between illness and societal expectations for the sick.

Conflict Approach

Functionalists seek to explain how health care systems meet the needs of society as well as those of individual patients and medical practitioners, but conflict theorists take issue with this view. They express concern that the profession of medicine has assumed a preeminence that extends well beyond whether to excuse a student from school or an employee from work. Sociologist Eliot Freidson (1970:5) has likened the position of medicine today to that of state religions yesterday—it has an officially approved monopoly of the right to define health and illness and to treat illness. Conflict theorists use the term *medicalization of society* to refer to the growing role of medicine as a major institution of social control (Conrad and Schneider 1992; McKinlay and McKinlay 1977; Zola 1972, 1983).

Social control involves techniques and strategies for regulating behavior in order to enforce the distinctive norms and values of a culture. Typically, we think of informal social control as occurring pp. 159 within families and peer groups, and formal social control as carried out by authorized agents such as police officers, judges, school administrators, and employers. However,

Interactive e-Source with Making the Grade

 www.mhhe.com/schaefer4

 PowerWeb

SocCity

COMMUNITIES AND
THE ENVIRONMENT

In India, pollution is becoming a controversial political issue. This billboard graphically suggests the harmful effect of pollution on public health.

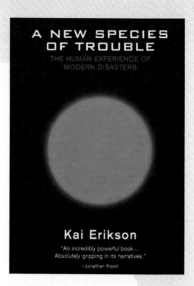

A NEW SPECIES OF TROUBLE

THE HUMAN EXPERIENCE OF MODERN DISASTERS

Kai Erikson

"An incredibly powerful book.... Absolutely gripping in its narratives."
–Jonathan Kozol

Over the past twenty years, research errands of one kind or another have taken me to a number of communities still stunned by the effects of a recent disaster. These include a valley in West Virginia known as Buffalo Creek, devastated by a fearsome flood; an Ojibwa Indian reserve in Canada called Grassy Narrows, plagued by contamination of the waterways along which members of the band had lived for centuries; a town in South Florida named Immokalee, where three hundred migrant farm workers were robbed of the only money most of them had ever saved; a group of houses in Colorado known as East Swallow, threatened by vapors from silent pools of gasoline that had gathered in the ground below; and the neighborhoods surrounding Three Mile Island.

In one respect, at least, these events were altogether different. A flood. An act of larceny. A toxic poisoning. A gasoline spill. A nuclear accident. My assignment in each of those cases was to learn enough about the people who thought they had been damaged by the blow to appear on their behalf in a court of law, so each was a separate research effort, and each resulted in a separate research report.

In another respect, though, it was clear from the beginning that those scenes of trouble had much in common. I was asked to visit them in the first place, obviously, because the persons who issued the invitations thought they could see resemblances there. And just as obviously, I was drawn to them because they touched a corresponding set of curiosities and preoccupations in me. Moreover, common themes seemed to come into focus as I moved from one place to another, so that those separate happenings (and the separate stories told of them) began to fuse into a more inclusive whole. One of the excitements of sociological work in general is to watch general patterns—dim and shapeless at first—emerge from a wash of seemingly unconnected details. . . . *(Erikson 1994:11–12)* ■

n this passage from *A New Species of Trouble*, Kai Erikson explains how he brought his sociological imagination to bear on five seemingly unrelated disasters in five different communities. Each disaster, he realized, had been caused not by natural forces, but by human disregard for the natural world or for other human beings. But while ignorance or negligence is often thought to be at the bottom of such catastrophes, Erikson saw a larger, more sweeping process at work—a "new species of trouble." Consumerism and rapid increases in population, he thought, lay at the bottom of these calamities. The ever-increasing wants and needs of ever-growing numbers of people had begun to outstrip the capacity of the environment to tolerate their encroachments.

As this excerpt shows, communities and their environments are intimately connected. Environmental issues, in fact, can make or break a community because they determine how safe, healthy, and satisfying our living conditions are. This chapter explores the important role that communities of all sorts, from rural towns to suburbs and big-city neighborhoods, play in people's lives. Communities give people the feeling that they are a part of something larger than themselves. In sociological terms, a **community** may be

formally defined as a spatial or political unit of social organization that gives people a sense of belonging. That sense of belonging can be based either on shared residence in a particular city or neighborhood or on a common identity, like that of gays and lesbians (Dotson 1991; see also Hillery 1955).

Anthropologist George Murdock (1949) has observed that there are only two truly universal units of human social organization: the family and the community. This chapter looks at the importance of communities from a sociological perspective. We will begin with the successive development of early communities, preindustrial cities, and industrial and postindustrial cities. We will examine the dramatic urbanization evident around the world in the twentieth century, and contrast two different views of urban growth. Then we'll look at the three types of communities found in the United States—central cities, suburbs, and rural areas. We will also consider a new type of community brought about by technological change: the online community. Later in the chapter, we will examine the environmental problems facing the world as we enter the twenty-first century and will draw on the functionalist and conflict perspectives to better understand environmental issues. Finally, in the social policy section, we will analyze the distressing phenomenon of homelessness in the United States and elsewhere. ■

How Did Communities Originate?

Early Communities

For most of human history, people used very basic tools and knowledge to survive. They satisfied their need for an adequate food supply through hunting, foraging for fruits or vegetables, fishing, and herding. In comparison with later industrial societies, early civilizations were much more dependent on the physical environment and much

p. 121 ←

less able to alter that environment to their advantage. The emergence of horticultural societies, in which people actually cultivated food rather than merely gathering fruits and vegetables, led to many dramatic changes in human social organization.

It was no longer necessary to move from place to place in search of food. Because people had to remain in specific locations to cultivate crops, more stable and enduring communities began to develop. As agricultural techniques became more and more sophisticated, a cooperative division of labor involving both family members

and others developed. It gradually became possible for people to produce more food than they actually needed for themselves. They could give food, perhaps as part of an exchange, to others who might be involved in nonagricultural labor. This transition from subsistence to surplus represented a critical step in the emergence of cities.

Eventually, people produced enough goods to cover both their own needs and those of people not engaged in agricultural tasks. Initially, the surplus was limited to agricultural products, but it gradually evolved to include all types of goods and services. Residents of a city came to rely on community members who provided craft products and means of transportation, gathered information, and so forth (Lenski et al. 1995).

With these social changes came an even more elaborate division of labor, as well as a greater opportunity for differential rewards and privileges. So long as everyone was engaged in the same tasks, stratification was limited to such factors as gender, age, and perhaps the ability to perform the task (a skillful hunter could win unusual respect from the community). However, the surplus

This painting shows twelfth-century traders in a port city on the Mediterranean Sea. Such early settlements represented one type of preindustrial city.

allowed for expansion of goods and services, leading to greater differentiation, a hierarchy of occupations, and social inequality. Therefore, surplus was a precondition not only for the establishment of cities but also for the division of members of a community into social classes (see Chapter 8). The ability to produce goods for other communities marked a fundamental shift in human social organization.

Preindustrial Cities

It is estimated that, beginning about 10,000 B.C., permanent settlements free from dependence on crop cultivation emerged. Yet, by today's standards of population, these early communities would barely qualify as cities. The *preindustrial city,* as it is termed, generally had only a few thousand people living within its borders and was characterized by a relatively closed class system and limited mobility. Status in these early cities was usually based on ascribed characteristics such as family background, and education was limited to members of the elite. All the residents relied on perhaps 100,000 farmers and their own part-time farming to provide them with the needed agricultural surplus. The Mesopotamian city of Ur had a population of about 10,000 and was limited to roughly

220 acres of land, including the canals, the temple, and the harbor.

Why were these early cities so small and relatively few in number? A number of key factors restricted urbanization:

Reliance on animal power (both humans and beasts of burden) as a source of energy for economic production. This limited the ability of humans to make use of and alter the physical environment.

Modest levels of surplus produced by the agricultural sector. Between 50 and 90 farmers may have been required to support one city resident (Davis 1995, originally published in 1949).

Problems in transportation and storage of food and other goods. Even an excellent crop could easily be lost as a result of such difficulties.

Hardships of migration to the city. For many peasants, migration was both physically and economically impossible. A few weeks of travel was out of the question without more sophisticated techniques of food storage.

Dangers of city life. Concentrating a society's population in a small area left it open to attack from outsiders, as well as more susceptible to extreme damages from plagues and fires.

Gideon Sjoberg (1960) examined the available information on early urban settlements of medieval Europe, India, and China. He identified three preconditions of city life: advanced technology in both agricultural and nonagricultural areas, a favorable physical environment, and a well-developed social organization.

For Sjoberg, the criteria for defining a "favorable" physical environment are variable. Proximity to coal and iron helps only if a society knows how to *use* these natural resources. Similarly, proximity to a river is particularly beneficial only if a culture has the means to transport water efficiently to the fields for irrigation and to the cities for consumption.

A sophisticated social organization is also an essential precondition for urban existence. Specialized social roles bring people together in new ways through the exchange of goods and services. A well-developed social organization ensures that these relationships are clearly defined and generally acceptable to all parties. Admittedly, Sjoberg's view of city life is an ideal type, since inequality did not vanish with the emergence of urban communities.

Industrial and Postindustrial Cities

Imagine how life could change by harnessing the energy of air, water, and other natural resources to power soci-

Table 15-2 Comparing Approaches to Urbanization

	Urban Ecology	New Urban Sociology
Theoretical Perspective	Functionalist	Conflict
Primary Focus	Relationship of urban areas to their spatial setting and physical environment	Relationship of urban areas to global, national, and local forces
Key Source of Change	Technological innovations such as new methods of transportation	Economic competition and monopolization of power
Initiator of Actions	Individuals, neighborhoods, communities	Real estate developers, banks and other financial institutions, multinational corporations
Allied Disciplines	Geography, Architecture	Political science, Economics

Types of Communities

Communities vary substantially in the degree to which their members feel connected and share a common identity. Ferdinand Tönnies (1988, original edition 1887) used the term *Gemeinschaft* pp. 119–20 to describe close-knit communities where social interaction among people is intimate and familiar. It is the kind of place where people in a coffee shop will stop talking when anyone enters, because they are sure to know whoever walks through the door. A shopper at the small grocery store in this town would expect to know every employee, and probably every other customer as well. By contrast, the ideal type of *Gesellschaft* describes modern urban life, in which people feel little in common with others and often form social relationships as a result of interactions focused on immediate tasks, such as purchasing a product. Contemporary city life in the United States generally resembles a *Gesellschaft.*

The following sections will examine different types of communities found in the United States, focusing on the distinctive characteristics and problems of central cities, suburbs, and rural communities.

Central Cities

In terms of both land and population, the United States is the fourth-largest nation in the world. Yet three-quarters of the population is concentrated in a mere 1.5 percent of the nation's land area. In 1996, some 212 million people—accounting for 80 percent of the nation's population—lived in metropolitan areas. Even those who live outside central cities, such as residents of suburban and rural communities, find that urban centers heavily influence their lifestyles (Bureau of the Census 1998c:39).

Urban Dwellers

Many urban residents are the descendants of European immigrants—Irish, Italians, Jews, Poles, and others—who came to the United States in the nineteenth and early twentieth centuries. The cities socialized these newcomers to the norms, values, and language of their new homeland and gave them an opportunity to work their way up the economic ladder. In addition, a substantial number of low-income African Americans and Whites came to the cities from rural areas in the period following World War II.

Even today, cities in the United States are the destinations of immigrants from around the world—including Mexico, Ireland, Cuba, Vietnam, and Haiti—as well as migrants from the United States commonwealth of Puerto Rico. Yet, unlike pp. 248–51 those who came to this country 100 years ago, current immigrants are arriving at a time of growing urban decay. This makes it more difficult for them to find employment and decent housing.

Urban life is noteworthy for its diversity, so it would be a serious mistake to see all city residents as being alike. Sociologist Herbert J. Gans (1991) has distinguished between five types of people found in our cities:

1. *Cosmopolites.* These residents remain in cities to take advantage of unique cultural and intellectual benefits. Writers, artists, and scholars fall into this category.
2. *Unmarried and childless people.* Such people choose to live in cities because of the active nightlife and varied recreational opportunities.

Indian American residents of Chicago enjoy an outdoor ethnic festival. Many subordinate racial and ethnic groups in the United States live in close-knit urban neighborhoods.

3. *Ethnic villagers.* These urban residents prefer to live in their own tight-knit communities. Typically, immigrant groups isolate themselves in such neighborhoods to avoid resentment from well-established urban dwellers.

4. *The deprived.* Very poor people and families have little choice but to live in low-rent, and often run-down, urban neighborhoods.

5. *The trapped.* Some city residents wish to leave urban centers but cannot because of their limited economic resources and prospects. Gans includes the "downward mobiles" in this category—people who once held higher social positions but who are forced to live in less prestigious neighborhoods owing to loss of a job, death of a wage earner, or old age. Both elderly individuals living alone and families may feel "trapped" in part because they resent changes in their communities. Their desire to live elsewhere may reflect their uneasiness with unfamiliar immigrant groups who have become their neighbors.

These categories remind us that the city represents a choice (even a dream) for certain people and a nightmare for others. Gans's work underscores the importance of neighborhoods in contemporary urban life. Ernest Burgess, in his study of life in Chicago in the 1920s, had given special attention to the ethnic neighborhoods of that city. Many decades later, residents in such districts as Chinatowns or Greektowns continue to feel attached to

their own ethnic communities rather than to the larger unit of a city. Even outside ethnic enclaves, a special sense of belonging can take hold in a neighborhood.

In a more recent study in Chicago, Gerald Suttles (1972) coined the term ***defended neighborhood*** to refer to people's definitions of their community boundaries. Neighborhoods acquire unique identities because residents view them as geographically separate—and socially different—from adjacent areas. The defended neighborhood, in effect, becomes a sentimental union of similar people. Neighborhood phone directories, community newspapers, school and parish boundaries, and business advertisements all serve to define an area and distinguish it from nearby communities.

In some cases, a neighborhood must literally defend itself. Plans for urban renewal or a superhighway may threaten to destroy an area's unique character and sense of attachment. In resisting such changes, a neighborhood may use the strategies and tactics of community organization developed by pioneering organizer Saul Alinsky (1909–1972). Like many conflict sociologists, Alinsky was concerned with the ways in which society's most powerful institutions protect the privileges of certain groups (such as real estate developers) while keeping other groups (such as slum dwellers) in a subservient position. Alinsky (1946) emphasized the need for community residents to fight for power in their localities. In his view, it was only through the achievement and constructive use of power that people could better themselves (Horwitt 1989).

Of course, a defended neighborhood may maintain its distinctive identity by excluding those who are deemed different or threatening. In 1981, the Supreme Court upheld the right of the city of Memphis, Tennessee, to erect a barrier and close a street connecting an all-White and all-Black neighborhood. White residents requested the closure, claiming that there was too much undesirable traffic coming through their own communities. In a dissenting opinion, Justice Thurgood Marshall, the first African American to serve on the Supreme Court, called the barrier a "badge of slavery." Close to two decades later, however, defended neighborhoods with physical barriers have become more common across the United States because of the growing number of "gated communities" (see Box 15-2).

he poet Robert Frost wrote that "good fences make good neighbors"; locked doors, walls, and fences have been features of shelter in the United States for generations. However, in recent decades, there has been a growing interest in isolating entire communities from those who otherwise would be neighbors. Political scientist Evan McKenzie (1994) uses the term *privatopia* to describe the emergence of a new type of artificial utopia: private communities within cities and suburbs.

In some cases, the communities are gated, sealed off from surrounding neighborhoods. There are three categories of gated communities:

- *Lifestyle communities,* including retirement communities, golf and country club leisure developments, and suburban new towns.
- *Prestige communities,* where gates symbolize distinction and stature, including enclaves of the rich and famous, developments for high-level professionals, and executive home developments for the middle class.
- *Security zones,* motivated by fear of crime and outsiders.

The private developers who build these generally "upscale" communities create homeowners' associations to establish rules and to contract for such services as security, garbage collection, and even education. The associations build community parks, recreation centers, swimming pools, and golf courses—all of which are restricted to association members and their guests.

Some gated communities and homeowners' associations have banned display of the U.S. flag and political signs, prohibited the distribution of newspapers, and barred political meetings or rallies in public areas. Many res-

> **The message is clear: These streets are for members only.**

idents of private communities defend such restrictions as essential for maintaining property values and believe that relinquishing a bit of personal freedom is worthwhile so they may be protected from improper behavior by their neighbors.

From a conflict perspective, there is particular concern about the symbolism of gated communities, which currently house about 4 million people in the United States. The residents of gated communities are overwhelmingly White and affluent. Gated communities are vividly separated from ad-

joining neighborhoods; their gates, walls, and entry doors are monitored 24 hours a day by uniformed private security guards. The message is clear: These streets are for members only.

The emergence of homeowners' associations and gated communities is troubling because it suggests an even sharper segregation of our society, with the "haves" hidden in their private fortresses and walled off from the "have-nots." Moreover, as people become isolated in private communities, they may care less and less about the deterioration of public services *outside* their communities, in nearby cities and counties. With this in mind, Evan McKenzie refers to the shift toward privatopia as "secession by the successful," with affluent individuals and families seceding from the rights and responsibilities of citizenship in a larger society.

Let's Discuss

1. Is there a gated community near you? If so, is it a lifestyle community, a prestige community, or a security zone?
2. What do you think of people who live in gated communities? Would you want to live in one yourself (or if you already do, would you want to stay)?

Sources: Blakely and Snyder 1997; Egan 1995; E. McKenzie 1994; Vanderpool 1995.

Issues Facing Cities

People and neighborhoods vary greatly within any city in the United States. Yet all residents of a central city—regardless of social class, racial, and ethnic differences—face certain common problems. Crime, air pollution, noise, unemployment, overcrowded schools, inadequate public transportation—these unpleasant realities and many more are an increasing feature of contemporary urban life.

Perhaps the single most dramatic reflection of the nation's urban ills has been the apparent "death" of entire neighborhoods. In some urban districts, business activity seems virtually nonexistent. You can walk for blocks and find little more than a devastating array of deteriorating, boarded-up, abandoned, and burned-out buildings. Such urban devastation has greatly contributed to the growing problem of homelessness, discussed in the social policy section.

Residential segregation has also been a persistent problem in cities across the United States. The segregation has resulted from the policies of financial institutions, the business practices of real estate agents, the actions of home sellers, and even urban planning initiatives (for example, in decisions about where to locate public housing).

Developers and bankers are less interested in providing affordable housing than in building new ballparks, preferably with government subsidies. Yet subsidized sports complexes rarely yield the employment opportunities they promise. Baltimore's Camden Yards, shown here, added little to the local economy compared to its cost.

Sociologists Douglas Massey and Nancy Denton (1993) have used the term "American apartheid" to refer to the residential patterns of the nation. In their view, we no longer perceive segregation as a problem but rather accept it as a feature of the urban landscape. For subordinate minority groups, segregation means not only limited housing opportunities but also less access to employment, retail outlets, and medical services.

Another critical problem for the cities has been mass transportation. Since 1950, the number of cars in the United States has multiplied twice as fast as the number of people. Growing traffic congestion in metropolitan areas has led many cities to recognize a need for safe, efficient, and inexpensive mass transit systems. However, the federal government has traditionally given much more assistance to highway programs than to public transportation. Conflict theorists note that such a bias favors the relatively affluent (automobile owners) as well as corporations such as auto manufacturers, tire makers, and oil companies. Meanwhile, low-income residents of metropolitan areas, who are much less likely to own cars than members of the middle and upper classes, face higher fares on public transit along with deteriorating service (Mason 1998).

In 1968, Dr. Martin Luther King Jr. observed that "urban transit systems in most American cities have become a genuine civil rights issue." An overcrowded public bus system in Los Angeles County carries 94 percent of the county's passengers—80 percent of whom are African American, Hispanic, Asian American, or Native American—yet receives less than one-third of the county's mass transit expenditures. At the same time, a lavish commuter rail system that already connects or will connect predominantly White suburbs to the downtown business district of Los Angeles carries only 6 percent of the county's passengers yet receives 71 percent of mass transit funding. Similar inequities in funding for public transportation have been challenged in New York City (Kelley 1996:18).

Ironically, while many communities are insisting that they cannot afford to maintain public services and are shifting them to the private sector, some nevertheless find substantial funds to attract professional sports franchises. According to estimates, at least $11 billion of public money was spent in the United States during the 1990s on 45 stadiums and arenas. Local politicians and business leaders claim that winning a sports franchise boosts the local economy and enhances community spirit. But critics counter that professional sports teams build profits for a wealthy few—and offer tax write-offs to corporations that maintain lavish luxury boxes—without genuinely revitalizing neighborhoods, much less an entire city. These critics refer to the use of significant public funds to attract professional sports franchises as "stadium welfare." Baltimore's highly praised Camden Yards baseball stadium produced a net gain, in terms of new jobs and tax revenue, of only $3 million a year—not much of a return on the $200 million invested (Egan 1999; Noll and Zimbalist 1997).

Suburbs

The term *suburb* derives from the Latin *sub urbe,* meaning "under the city." Until recent times, most suburbs were just that—tiny communities totally dependent on urban centers for jobs, recreation, and even water.

Today, the term *suburb* defies any simple definition. The term generally refers to any community near a large city—or, as the Census Bureau would say, any territory within a metropolitan area that is not included in the central city. By that definition, more than 138 million people, or about 51 percent of the population of the United States, lived in the suburbs in 1999.

BEV has had a positive effect on the town, users in Blacksburg agree. An enhanced sense of community is the most pervasive outcome. Seniors have greeted the new service enthusiastically: The senior center houses 10 computers, and a special service tailored to the needs of elders has 180 subscribers. The strengthening of local bonds has surprised some, perhaps because it runs counter to the conventional wisdom that the Internet will unite people from around the world in a global online community. One retired physicist didn't think BEV would catch on, but was pleasantly surprised by the speed with which residents adopted it.

BEV has also brought some noticeable economic benefits to the town. Some residents, like the proprietor of Green Dreams, an online retailer of homemade vinegars, have seized the opportunity to become online entrepreneurs. And a corporate research center at the edge of town has been attracting more and more startup ventures, bringing new jobs and income to the college town. CEOs of the innovative new companies like the fresh air, low crime rate, and cutting-edge intellectual climate of Blacksburg. One, the head of Blue Ridge Interactive, an online purveyor of magazines, raves about the supportive atmosphere in the town (Clark 1999; Yaukey 1997; Zajac 1999).

The wider implications of the electronic village are only beginning to become clear. If the installation of universal high-speed access to the Internet can draw new companies away from more heavily populated areas like northern Virginia, it may contribute to the decay of older urban areas, worsening the plight of inner-city residents. And BEV users are concerned about the fact that not all families in rural Montgomery County can afford to tap into the network, which requires an in-home computer and a small monthly connection fee. Roger Ehrich, a professor of computer science at Virginia Tech, believes the best way to level the playing field is to provide Internet access to children at school, wherever they live (Zajac 1999).

Finally, the advent of the electronic community has the potential to revolutionize not just communities, but the way sociological research on communities is done. Automatic electronic monitoring of online response rates may someday replace telephone surveys and the distribution, collection, and coding of paper questionnaires. In the future, scholars may be able to visit far-flung electronic communities without leaving the comfort of their offices, and to travel safely through otherwise dangerous villages.

Within all communities, environmental issues play a part in determining the quality of life people enjoy or must endure. We'll turn now to a closer look at these important concerns.

The Environment

In December 1999 Julia Butterfly Hill, a 25-year-old environmental activist, agreed to climb down from the ancient redwood tree she had been living in for the past two years. Hill, who is passionately dedicated to preserving the redwoods of northern California, had braved storms, helicopters, and the privations of camping in the wild to reach a hard-won agreement with Pacific Lumber, the logging company that wanted to cut the tree down. Through the intervention of Senator Dianne Feinstein, the company had finally agreed to spare the tree and a buffer zone around it (Lappé 1999; *New York Times* 1999a).

While most people would consider Hill's protest an extreme one, it demonstrated the lengths to which activists must go to reverse the wave of destruction humans have unleashed on the environment in recent centuries. With each passing year, we are learning more about the environmental damage caused by burgeoning

Julia Butterfly Hill clings to the 200-foot-tall redwood tree she lived in for two years to keep a logging company from cutting it down.

population levels and consumption patterns. Though disasters like the ones sociologist Kai Erikson investigated (see chapter opening) are still comparatively rare, we can see the superficial signs of despoliation almost everywhere. Our air, our water, and our land are being polluted, whether we live in St. Louis, Mexico City, or Lagos, Nigeria.

Environmental Problems: An Overview

In recent decades, the world has witnessed serious environmental disasters. For example, Love Canal, near Niagara Falls in New York State, was declared a disaster area in 1978 because of chemical contamination. In the 1940s and 1950s, a chemical company had disposed of waste products on the site where a housing development and a school were subsequently built. The metal drums that held the chemical wastes eventually rusted out, and toxic chemicals with noxious odors began seeping into the residents' yards and basements. Subsequent investigations revealed that the chemical company knew as early as 1958 that toxic chemicals were seeping into homes and a school playground. After repeated protests in the late 1970s, 239 families living in Love Canal had to be relocated.

In 1986, a series of explosions set off a catastrophic nuclear reactor accident at Chernobyl, a part of Ukraine (in what was then the Soviet Union). This accident killed at least 32,000 people. Some 300,000 residents had to be evacuated, and the area became uninhabitable for 19 miles in any direction. High levels of radiation were found as far as 30 miles from the reactor site, and radioactivity levels were well above normal as far away as Sweden and Japan. According to one estimate, the Chernobyl accident and the resulting nuclear fallout may ultimately result in 100,000 excess cases of cancer worldwide (Shcherbak 1996).

While Love Canal, Chernobyl, and other environmental disasters understandably grab headlines, it is the silent, day-to-day deterioration of the environment that ultimately poses a devastating threat to humanity. It is impossible to examine all our environmental problems in detail, but three broad areas of concern stand out: air pollution, water pollution, and contamination of land.

Air Pollution

More than 1 billion people on the planet are exposed to potentially health-damaging levels of air pollution (World Resources Institute 1998). Unfortunately, in cities around the world, residents have come to accept smog and polluted air as "normal." Air pollution in urban areas is caused primarily by emissions from automobiles and secondarily by emissions from electric power plants and heavy industries. Urban smog not only limits visibility; it can lead to health problems as uncomfortable as eye irri-

tation and as deadly as lung cancer. Such problems are especially severe in developing countries. The World Health Organization estimates that up to 700,000 premature deaths *per year* could be prevented if pollutants were brought down to safer levels (Carty 1999).

We are making strides. Southern California in 1998 had three times the population and four times the number of vehicles as in 1955, yet the air was much safer. The improvement comes primarily from a law requiring new cars to be fitted with air pollution control devices beginning in 1963 and the 1970 Clean Air Act, which established minimum air quality standards for cities and industry. While these advances did require some behavioral changes, they relied for the most part on new technology.

People are capable of changing their behavior, but they are also unwilling to make such changes permanent. For example, during the 1984 Olympics in Los Angeles, residents were asked to carpool and stagger work hours to relieve traffic congestion and improve the quality of air the athletes would breathe. These changes resulted in a remarkable 12 percent drop in ozone levels. However, when the Olympians left, people reverted to their normal behavior and the ozone levels climbed back up (Nussbaum 1998).

Water Pollution

Throughout the United States, dumping of waste materials by both industries and local governments has polluted streams, rivers, and lakes. Consequently, many bodies of water have become unsafe for drinking, fishing, and swimming. Around the world, the pollution of the oceans is an issue of growing concern. Such pollution results regularly from waste dumping and is made worse by fuel leaks from shipping and occasional oil spills. In a dramatic accident in 1989, the oil tanker *Exxon Valdez* ran aground in Prince William Sound, Alaska. The tanker's cargo of 11 million gallons of crude oil spilled into the sound and washed onto the shore, contaminating 1,285 miles of shoreline. About 11,000 people joined in a cleanup effort that cost over $2 billion.

Contamination of Land

Love Canal made it clear that industrial dumping of hazardous wastes and chemicals also seriously contaminates land. In another noteworthy case of contamination, unpaved roads in Times Beach, Missouri, were sprayed to control dust in 1971 with an oil that contained dioxin. This highly toxic chemical is a by-product of the manufacture of herbicides and other chemicals. After the health dangers of dioxin became evident, the entire community of 2,800 people was relocated (at a cost of $33 million) and the town of Times Beach was shut down in 1985.

A significant part of land contamination comes from the tremendous demand for landfills to handle the na-

Fish poisoned by a deadly cyanide spill lie on the bank of the Tisa River in Yugoslavia. Throughout the world, industrial pollutants have rendered many water bodies unsafe for fishing, drinking, or swimming.

What are the basic causes of our growing environmental problems? Neo-Malthusians such as Paul Ehrlich and Anne Erhlich (P. Ehrlich 1968; P. Ehrlich and Ehrlich 1990) see world population growth as the central factor in environmental deterioration. They argue that population control is essential in preventing widespread starvation and environmental decay. Barry Commoner (1971, 1990), a biologist, counters that the primary cause of environmental ills is the increasing use of technological innovations that are destructive to the world's environment—among them plastics, detergents, synthetic fibers, pesticides, herbicides, and chemical fertilizers. In the following sections, we will contrast the functionalist and conflict approaches to the study of environmental issues.

Functionalism and Human Ecology

Earlier, we noted that human ecology is concerned with interrelationships between people and their environment. Environmentalist Barry Commoner (1971:39) has stated that "everything is connected to everything else." Human ecologists, as we've seen, focus on how the physical environment shapes people's lives and also on how people influence the surrounding environment.

In an application of the human ecological perspective, sociologist Riley Dunlap suggests that the natural environment serves three basic functions for humans, as it does for the many animal species (Dunlap 1993; Dunlap and Catton 1983):

1. *The environment provides the resources essential for life.* These include air, water, and materials used to create shelter, transportation, and needed products. If human societies exhaust these resources—for example, by polluting the water supply or cutting down rain forests—the consequences can be dire.
2. *The environment serves as a waste repository.* More so than other living species, humans produce a huge quantity and variety of waste products—bottles, boxes, papers, sewage, garbage, to name just a few. Various types of pollution have become more common because human societies are generating more wastes than the environment can safely absorb.
3. *The environment "houses" our species.* It is our home, our living space, the place where we reside, work, and play. At times we take this for granted, but not when day-to-day living conditions become unpleasant and difficult. If our air is "heavy," if our tap water turns brown, if toxic chemicals seep into our neighborhood, we remember why it is vital to live in a healthful environment.

tion's waste. Recycling programs aimed at reducing the need for landfills are perhaps the most visible aspect of environmentalism. How successful have such programs been? In 1980, about 10 percent of urban waste was recycled; the proportion increased steadily throughout the 1980s, but started to level off at about 29 percent in 1998. Experts are beginning to revise their goals for recycling campaigns, which now appear overambitious. Still, a new way to be green has developed: the Internet. For example, over-the-Net commercial transactions allow the downloading of new software, reducing the need for wasteful packaging and shipping materials, including fuel for delivery trucks. And the availability of e-mail and electronic networking encourages people to work at home rather than contribute to the pollution caused by commuting (Belsie 2000; Booth 2000).

FIGURE 15-3

Global Concern for the Environment

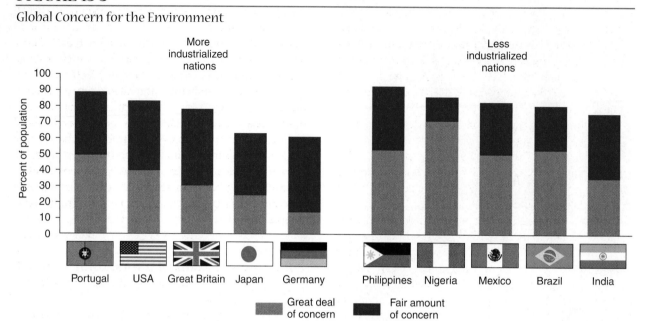

Source: Adapted from R. Dunlap 1993.

Dunlap (1993) points out that these three functions of the environment actually compete with one another. Human use of the environment for one of these functions will often strain its ability to fulfill the other two. For example, with world population continuing to rise, we have an increasing need to raze forests or farmland and build housing developments. But each time we do so, we are reducing the amount of land providing food, lumber, or habitat for wildlife.

The tension between the three essential functions of the environment brings us back to the human ecologists' view that "everything is connected to everything else." In facing the environmental challenges of the twenty-first century, government policymakers and environmentalists must determine how they can fulfill human societies' pressing needs (for example, for food, clothing, and shelter) while at the same time preserving the environment as a source of resources, a waste repository, and our home.

Conventional wisdom holds that concern for environmental quality is limited to the world's wealthy industrialized nations. However, the results of the 1992 Health of the Planet survey conducted in 24 countries by the Gallup International Institute show that there is *widespread* environmental concern around the planet. As Figure 15-3 shows, a higher proportion of people in the Philippines, Nigeria, Mexico, and Brazil said that they had a "great deal" of personal concern about environmental problems than did people in the United States, Great Britain, Japan, and Germany.

Conflict View of Environmental Issues

In Chapter 8, we drew on world systems analysis to show how a growing share of the human and natural resources of the developing countries is being redistributed to the core industrialized nations. This process only intensifies the destruction of natural resources in poorer regions of the world. From a conflict perspective, less affluent nations are being forced to exploit their mineral deposits, forests, and fisheries in order to meet their debt obligations. The poor turn to the only means of survival available to them: They plow mountain slopes, burn plots in tropical forests, and overgraze grasslands (Livernash and Rodenburg 1998).

Brazil exemplifies the interplay between economic troubles and environmental destruction. Each year more than 11,000 square miles of the Amazon rain forest are cleared for crops and livestock through burning. This elimination of the rain forest affects worldwide weather patterns and heightens the gradual warming of the earth in a process known as the *greenhouse effect.* More than 160 nations gathered in Kyoto, Japan, in December 1997 for the Conference of the Parties on Climate Change. The preconference goal was to develop a strategy to reduce production of "greenhouse gases" by the year 2010 to pre-1900 levels. The treaty, known as the Kyoto Protocol, does call for industrial nations to reduce their emissions. However, it set no similar goals for developing countries, which, like Brazil, are struggling to move ahead economically.

These socioeconomic patterns, with harmful environmental consequences, are evident not only in Latin America but also in many regions of Africa and Asia. Conflict theorists are well aware of the environmental implications of land use policies in the Third World, but they contend that such a focus on the developing countries can contain an element of ethnocentrism. Who, they ask, is more to blame for environmental deterioration: the poverty-stricken and "food-hungry" populations of the world or the "energy-hungry" industrialized nations (G. Miller 1972:117)?

Conflict theorists point out that Western industrialized nations account for only 25 percent of the world's population but are responsible for 85 percent of worldwide consumption. Take the United States alone: A mere 6 percent of the world's people consume more than half the world's nonrenewable resources and more than one-third of all the raw materials produced. Such data lead conflict theorists to charge that the most serious threat to the environment comes from "affluent megaconsumers and megapolluters" (Bharadwaj 1992; G. Miller 1972).

Allan Schnaiberg (1994) further refines this analysis by criticizing the focus on affluent consumers as the cause of environmental troubles. In his view, a capitalist system has a "treadmill of production" because of its inherent need to build ever-expanding profits. This treadmill necessitates creating an increasing demand for products, obtaining natural resources at minimal cost, and manufacturing products as quickly and cheaply as possible—no matter what the long-term environmental consequences of this approach.

Environmental Justice

Kennedy Heights, a new subdivision of Houston, attracted buyers in the late 1960s with its tidy brick façade homes and bucolic street names. But what the mostly Black buyers were not told was that the developers had constructed these homes on oil pits abandoned by Gulf Oil decades earlier. After experiencing periodic contaminated water supplies and a variety of illnesses, including large numbers of cancer

and lupus, Kennedy Heights residents filed a class-action suit against Chevron, the company that acquired Gulf Oil. This case of environmental pollution is compounded by charges of "environmental racism," based on Gulf Oil documents in 1967 that targeted the area "for Negro residential and commercial development" (Verhovek 1997).

While the Kennedy Heights residents' case is still making its tortuous way through the courts, there are signs that some headway is being made in establishing *environmental justice,* a legal strategy based on claims that racial minorities are subjected disproportionately to environmental hazards. In 1998, Shintech, a chemical company, dropped plans to build a plastics plant in an impoverished Black community in Mississippi. Opponents of the plant had filed a civil rights complaint with the Environmental Protection Agency (EPA). EPA administrator Carol Browner praised Shintech's decision: "The principles applied to achieve this solution should be incorporated into any blueprint for dealing with environmental justice issues in communities across the nation" (Associated Press 1998a:18).

Following reports from the EPA and other organizations documenting discriminatory locating of hazardous waste sites, President Bill Clinton issued an Executive Order in 1994 that requires all federal agencies to ensure that low-income and minority communities have access to better information about their environment and have an opportunity to participate in shaping government policies that affect their communities' health. Initial efforts to implement the policy have aroused widespread opposition because of the delays it imposes in establishing new industrial sites. Some observers question the wisdom of an order that slows economic development coming to areas in dire need of employment opportunities. On the other hand, there are those who point out that such businesses employ few unskilled or less skilled workers and only make the environment less livable for those left behind (Cushman 1998a; Goldman and Fitton 1994).

SOCIAL POLICY AND COMMUNITIES

Seeking Shelter Worldwide

The Issue

A chance meeting brought two old classmates together. In late 1997, Prince Charles encountered Clive Harold during a tour of the offices of a magazine sold by the homeless in London. But while Prince Charles can call several palaces home, Harold is homeless. This modern-day version of the "The Prince and the Pauper" intrigued many people with its message that "it can happen to

anyone." Harold had been a successful author and journalist until his marriage fell apart and alcohol turned his life inside out (*Chicago Tribune* 1997b).

The issue of inadequate shelter manifests itself in many ways, for all housing problems can be considered relative. For a middle-class family in the United States, it may mean a somewhat smaller house than they need because that is all they can afford. For a single working adult in Tokyo, it

In a story the press dubbed "The Prince and the Pauper," Prince Charles was surprised to run into an old classmate while visiting the office of a magazine sold by the homeless—and was even more surprised to learn that the fellow was himself homeless.

may mean having to commute two hours to a full-time job. For many people worldwide, however, the housing problem consists of merely finding shelter of any kind that they can afford, in a place where anyone would reasonably wish to live. Prince Charles of Buckingham Palace and Clive Harold, homeless person, are extreme examples of a continuum present in all communities in all societies. What can be done to ensure adequate shelter for those who can't afford it?

The Setting

Homelessness is evident in both industrialized and developing countries. According to a 1999 estimate, our nation's homeless population is at least 700,000, and may be as high as 3 million. Given the limited space in public shelters, at a minimum, hundreds of thousands of people in the United States are homeless and without shelter (Kilborn 1999; see also Jencks 1994; Snow and Anderson 1993; Snow et al. 1996).

In Great Britain, some 175,000 people are accepted as homeless by the government and are given housing. An even larger number, perhaps 1 million people, are turned away from government assistance or are sharing a household with relatives or acquaintances but want separate accommodations. While an accurate figure is not available, it is estimated that 1 percent of Western Europeans are homeless; they sleep in the streets, depend on night shelters and hostels, or live in precarious accommodations (B. Lee 1992; Platt 1993; Stearn 1993).

In Japan, the problem of homelessness is just as serious. A single protest drew roughly 6,000 homeless people to Tokyo in 1998. The Japanese usually hide such misfortune, thinking it shameful, but a severe economic downturn had victimized many formerly prosperous citizens, swelling the numbers of the homeless. A chronic space shortage in the heavily populated island nation, together with opposition to the establishment of homeless shelters in residential neighborhoods, compounds the problem (Hara 2000).

In Third World countries, rapid population growth has outpaced the expansion of housing by a wide margin, leading to a rise in homelessness. For example, estimates of homelessness in Mexico City range from 10,000 to 100,000, and these estimates do not include the many people living in caves or squatter settlements (see Box 15-1). By 1998, in urban areas alone, 600 million people around the world were either homeless or inadequately housed (G. Goldstein 1998; Ross 1996).

Sociological Insights

Both in the United States and around the world, being homeless functions as a master status that largely defines a person's position within society. In this case, homelessness tends to mean pp. 110, 167 that in many important respects, the individual is *outside* society. Without a home address and telephone, it is difficult to look for work or even apply for public assistance. Moreover, the master status of being homeless carries a serious stigma and can lead to prejudice and discrimina-

In Japan in 1998, as many as six thousand homeless people marched on the Tokyo Metropolitan Office to protest the lack of shelter facilities. This biting cartoon from the *Japan Times* acknowledges their plight.

tion. Poor treatment of people suspected of being homeless is common in stores and restaurants, and many communities have reported acts of random violence against homeless people.

The profile of homelessness has changed significantly during the last 20 years. In the past, homeless people were primarily older White males living as alcoholics in skid-row areas. However, today's homeless are comparatively younger—with an average age in the low 30s. Overall, an estimated 59 percent of homeless people in the United States are from racial and ethnic minority groups. Moreover, a 26-city survey done in 1999 found that the homeless population is growing faster than the increase in emergency food and shelter space (Burt et al. 1999; U.S. Conference of Mayors 1999).

Changing economic and residential patterns account for much of this increase in homelessness. In recent decades, the process of urban renewal has included a noticeable boom in **gentrification.** This term refers to the resettlement of low-income city neighborhoods by prosperous families and business firms. In some instances, city governments have promoted gentrification by granting lucrative tax breaks to developers who convert low-cost rental units into luxury apartments and condominiums. Conflict theorists note that although the affluent may derive both financial and emotional benefits from gentrification and redevelopment, the poor often end up being thrown out on the street.

There is an undeniable connection between the nation's growing shortage of affordable housing and the rise in homelessness (Elliot and Krivo 1991). Yet sociologist Peter Rossi (1989, 1990) cautions against focusing too narrowly on housing shortage while ignoring structural factors, such as the decline in the demand for manual labor in cities and the increasing prevalence of chronically unemployed young men among the homeless. Rossi contends that structural changes have put everyone in extreme poverty at higher risk of becoming homeless—especially poor people with an accumulation of disabilities (such as drug abuse, bad health, unemployment, and criminal records). Being disabled in this manner forces the individual to rely on family and friends for support, often for a prolonged period. If the strain on this support network is so great that it collapses, homelessness may result. While many researchers accept Rossi's theory, the general public often prefers to "blame the victim" for becoming homeless (B. Lee 1992).

Homeless women often have additional problems that distinguish them from homeless men. Homeless women report more recent injuries or acute illnesses, as well as more chronic health problems, than homeless men. Moreover, these women have experienced more disruption in their families and social networks than homeless men (Liebow 1993).

Sociologists attribute homelessness in developing nations not only to income inequality but also to population growth and an influx of people from rural areas and areas experiencing natural disaster, famine, or warfare. A major barrier to constructing decent, legal, and affordable housing in the urban areas of these developing nations is the political power of large-scale landowners and small-scale land speculators—anyone buying a few lots as investment. In the view of conflict theorists, these groups conspire to enhance their own financial investment by making the supply of legally buildable land scarce. (This problem is not unknown in the cities of North America, but a World Bank survey shows that the increase in the cost of land is twice as great in developing nations as in industrial countries.) In many cases, residents who can afford building materials have no choice but to become squatters. Those who can't are likely to become homeless.

Policy Initiatives

Thus far, policymakers have often been content to steer the homeless toward large, overcrowded, unhealthy shelters. Many neighborhoods and communities have resisted plans to open large shelters or even smaller residences for the homeless, often raising the familiar cry of "Not in my backyard!" The major federal program intended to assist the homeless is the McKinney Homeless Assistance Act, passed in 1987. This act authorizes federal aid for emergency food, shelter, physical and mental health care, job training, and education for homeless children and adults. Approximately $600 to $800 million in funds are distributed annually to about 100 community-based service organizations (Housing and Urban Development 1999).

According to a report by the National Law Center on Homelessness and Poverty (1996), there was a growing trend in the 1990s toward the adoption of anti-homeless public policies and the "criminalization" of homeless people. In 1995 alone, at least 29 cities enacted curbs on panhandling, sitting on sidewalks, standing near banks at automated teller machines, or other behavior sometimes evident among the homeless. At the same time, more and more policymakers—especially conservative officials—advocated cutbacks in government funding for the homeless and argued that voluntary associations and religious organizations should assume a more important role in addressing the problem of homelessness (Morse 1999).

By the late 1990s, the availability of low-rent housing had reached the lowest levels since surveys began in 1970. Despite occasional media spotlights on the homeless and the booming economy, affordable hous-

ing has become harder to find. Two out of three low-income renters receive no housing allowance, and most spend a disproportionately large share of their income to maintain their shelter. Research shows that this worsening of affordable housing stems from a substantial drop in the number of unsubsidized low-cost rental housing units in the private market and a growing number of low-income renter households. Meanwhile, federally funded rental assistance has failed to keep pace with the need (Daskal 1998).

Developing nations have special problems. They have understandably given highest priority to economic productivity as measured by jobs with living wages. Unfortunately, even the most ambitious economic and social programs may be overwhelmed by minor currency fluctuations, a drop in the value of a nation's major export, or an influx of refugees from a neighboring country. Some of the reforms implemented have included promoting private (as opposed to government-controlled) housing markets, allowing dwellings to be places of business as well, and loosening restrictions on building materials.

All three of these short-term solutions have shortcomings. Private housing markets invite exploitation; mixed residential/commercial use may only cause good housing to deteriorate faster; and the use of marginal building materials leaves low-income residential areas more vulnerable to calamities such as floods, fires, and earthquakes. Large-scale rental housing under government supervision, the typical solution in North America and Europe, has been successful only in economically advanced city-states like Hong Kong and Singapore (Strassman 1998).

In sum, homeless people both in the United States and abroad are not getting the shelter they need, and they lack the political clout to corral the attention of policymakers.

Let's Discuss

1. Have you ever worked as a volunteer in a shelter or soup kitchen? If so, were you surprised by the type of people who lived or ate there? Has anyone you know ever had to move into a shelter?

2. Is gentrification of low-income housing a problem where you live? Have you ever had difficulty finding an affordable place to live?

3. What kind of assistance is available to homeless people in the community where you live? Does the help come from the government, from private charities, or both? What about housing assistance for people with low incomes, such as rent subsidies—is it available?

Summary

A *community* is a spatial or political unit of social organization that gives people a sense of belonging. This chapter explains how communities originated and analyzes the process of urbanization from both the functionalist and conflict perspectives. It describes various types of communities, including the central cities, the suburbs, and rural communities, and it introduces the new concept of an electronic community. The functionalist and conflict perspectives are also used to explore environmental issues.

1. Stable communities began to develop when people stayed in one place to cultivate crops; surplus production enabled cities to emerge.
2. Gideon Sjoberg identified three preconditions of city life: advanced technology in both agricultural and nonagricultural areas, a favorable physical environment, and a well-developed social organization.
3. There are important differences between the *preindustrial city,* the *industrial city,* and the *postindustrial city.*
4. Urbanization is evident not only in the United States but throughout the world; by 2000, 45 percent of the world's population lived in urban areas.
5. The *urban ecological* approach is functionalist because it emphasizes that different elements in urban areas contribute to stability.
6. Drawing on conflict theory, *new urban sociology* considers the interplay of a community's political and economic interests as well as the impact of the global economy on communities in the United States and other countries.
7. Many urban residents are immigrants from other nations and tend to live in ethnic neighborhoods.

8. In the last three decades, cities have confronted an overwhelming array of economic and social problems, including crime, unemployment, and the deterioration of schools and public transit systems.
9. Suburbanization was the most dramatic population trend in the United States throughout the twentieth century. In recent decades, suburbs have witnessed increasing diversity in race and ethnicity.
10. Farming, mining, and logging have all been in decline in the rural communities of the United States.
11. Technological advances like electronic information networks are changing the economy, the distribution of population, and even the concept of community.
12. Three broad areas of environmental concern are air pollution, water pollution, and contamination of land.
13. Using the human ecological perspective, sociologist Riley Dunlap suggests that the natural environment serves three basic functions: It provides essential resources, it serves as a waste repository, and it "houses" our species.
14. Conflict theorists charge that the most serious threat to the environment comes from Western industrialized nations.
15. *Environmental justice* is concerned with the disproportionate subjection of minorities to environmental hazards.
16. Soaring housing costs, unemployment, cutbacks in public assistance, and rapid population growth have all contributed to rising homelessness around the world. Most social policy is directed toward sending the homeless to large shelters.

Critical Thinking Questions

1. How can the functionalist and conflict perspectives be used in examining the growing interest among policymakers in privatizing public services presently offered by cities and other communities?
2. How has your home community (your city, town, or neighborhood) changed over the years you have lived there? Have there been significant changes in the community's economic base and in its racial and ethnic profile? Have the community's social

problems intensified or lessened over time? Is unemployment currently a major problem? What are the community's future prospects as it approaches the twenty-first century?
3. Imagine that you have been asked to study the issue of air pollution in the largest city in your state. How might you draw on surveys, observation research, experiments, and existing sources to help you study this issue?

Key Terms

Community   A spatial or political unit of social organization that gives people a sense of belonging, based either on shared residence in a particular place or on a common identity. (page 415)

Concentric-zone theory   A theory of urban growth that sees growth in terms of a series of rings radiating from the central business district. (418)

Defended neighborhood   A neighborhood that residents identify through defined community borders and a perception that adjacent areas are geographically separate and socially different. (424)

Environmental justice   A legal strategy based on claims that racial minorities are subjected disproportionately to environmental hazards. (435)

Gentrification   The resettlement of low-income city neighborhoods by prosperous families and business firms. (437)

Human ecology   An area of study concerned with the interrelationships between people and their spatial setting and physical environment. (418)

Industrial city   A city characterized by relatively large size, open competition, an open class system, and elaborate specialization in the manufacturing of goods. (417)

Megalopolis   A densely populated area containing two or more cities and their surrounding suburbs. (418)

Multiple-nuclei theory   A theory of urban growth that views growth as emerging from many centers of development, each of which may reflect a particular urban need or activity. (421)

New urban sociology   An approach to urbanization that considers the interplay of local, national, and worldwide forces and their effect on local space, with special emphasis on the impact of global economic activity. (421)

Postindustrial city   A city in which global finance and the electronic flow of information dominate the economy. (417)

Preindustrial city   A city with only a few thousand people living within its borders and characterized by a relatively closed class system and limited mobility. (416)

Squatter settlements   Areas occupied by the very poor on the fringes of cities, in which housing is often constructed by the settlers themselves from discarded material. (420)

Suburb   According to the Census Bureau, any territory within a metropolitan area that is not included in the central city. (426)

Urban ecology   An area of study that focuses on the interrelationships between people and their environment in urban areas. (418)

Urbanism   Distinctive patterns of social behavior evident among city residents. (418)

World systems analysis   A view of the global economic system that sees it as divided between certain industrialized nations and the developing countries that they control and exploit. (422)

Zoning laws   Legal provisions stipulating land use and architectural design of housing, sometimes used as a means of keeping racial minorities and low-income people out of suburban areas. (428)

Social change often reflects accessibility to new technology. A recent music innovation is IDM (intelligent dance music), experimental techno music made totally from electronic sources. This pixel painting appears as the cover art of the techno music compilation of England's Warp Records.

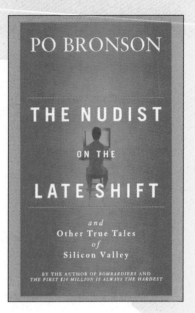

From the moment I met him, Sabeer Bhatia has given credit to the power of the idea. The idea was so powerful that when his friend and coworker Jack Smith, who was driving home to Livermore across the Dunbarton Bridge, called Sabeer on his car phone to brainstorm the pregnant thought that had just occurred to him, Sabeer heard one sentence of it and said, "Oh, my! Hang up that cellular and call me back on a secure line when you get to your house! We don't want anyone to overhear!"

It was so powerful an idea that when Jack did call Sabeer back fifteen minutes later, their minds melded as they talked, completely in sync, leaping from one ramification to the next as simultaneously as the steps of two soldiers marching side by side. It was so powerful that sleep that night was impossible for Sabeer, with the idea now in his head, exploding, autocatalytic, a bonfire of the mind. He stayed up all night, sitting at the glass-topped dining table in his small Bayside Village apartment, writing the business plan, which he took to his day job the next morning, looking so haggard that his boss stopped him and said, "You've got to cut out the partying, Sabeer." . . .

The idea came about this way: Sabeer and Jack had wanted to start a company, and they had been brainstorming possible business ideas for a few months. They wanted to e-mail each other notes, but they had been afraid that their bosses might glean their e-mail and accuse them of spending their working hours on personal projects (an accurate accusation). The budding entrepreneurs had personal America Online accounts, but these couldn't be accessed through the office network. On the evening he was driving home across the Dunbarton Bridge, Jack Smith had been frustrated all day by this problem. Then it occurred to him:

Free e-mail accounts that can be accessed anonymously, over the Web.

In getting over their own obstacle to coming up with a business idea, they came up with just that idea. . . .

It was the kind of idea that inspires legions of entrepreneurs. It was the kind of idea that spurs thousands of young people to give up their lives elsewhere and crash the Valley party. It sent the message and cc'd the entire world: to make it in Silicon Valley, you just have to come up with the right idea. . . .

Nowadays, meet Sabeer at a party and ask what he does, and he will tell you only that he works in high tech, just like hundreds of thousands of other young people in the valley. . . . Push him for more detail about his job, and he'll say he works at Hotmail. Ask if he's an engineer and he'll say no, he's the president. He's not being reclusive or coy, it just hasn't sunk in that he might be special.

What is Hotmail but e-mail on the Web? *(Bronson 1999:78–79, 80)* ∎

Po Bronson specializes in writing about that hotbed of technology known as Silicon Valley. In this excerpt from his book *The Nudist on the Late Shift*, Bronson profiles the inventor of Hotmail and highlights the importance of a good idea—even so simple an idea as accessing e-mail on the Internet. Combining the convenience of e-mail with the global reach of the web, Hotmail allows anyone in the world to communicate instantly with anyone else, as long as both have access to the web. To appreciate the impact of this idea, drop into any cyber café—whether it be in Bangkok, Bali, or Bismarck—and observe the flurry of e-mail being sent and received by backpackers, tourists, students, and businesspeople alike.

The development of the computer as an integral part of the day-to-day life in the United States and other countries is an example of social change. *Social change* has been defined as significant alteration over time in behavior patterns and culture (Moore 1967). Social changes that have had long-term and important consequences include the emergence of slavery as a system of stratification (see Chapter 8), the industrial revolution (Chapter 5), the increased participation of women in the paid labor forces of the United States and Europe (Chapter 10), and the worldwide population explosion (Chapter 14). As we will see, social movements have played an important role in promoting social change.

This chapter examines social movements and the process of social change, with special emphasis on the impact of technological advances. Efforts to explain long-term social changes have led to the development of theories of change; we will consider the evolutionary, functionalist, and conflict approaches to change. We will see how vested interests can block changes that they see as threatening.

We'll also look at various aspects of our technological future through discussion of telecommuting, the Internet, biotechnology, and technological accidents. We will examine the effects of technological advances on culture and social interaction, social control, and stratification and inequality. Taken together, the impact of these technological changes may be approaching a level of magnitude comparable to that of the industrial revolution. Finally, the social policy section will discuss the ways in which technological advances have intensified concerns over privacy and censorship. ■

Social Movements

Although such factors as physical environment, population, technology, and social inequality serve as sources of change, it is the *collective* effort of individuals organized in social movements that ultimately leads to change. Sociologists use the term *social movements* to refer to organized collective activities to bring about or resist fundamental change in an existing group or societey (Benford 1992). Herbert Blumer (1955:19) recognized the special importance of social movements when he defined them as "collective enterprises to establish a new order of life."

In many nations, including the United States, social movements have had a dramatic impact on the course of history and the evolution of social structure. Consider the actions of abolitionists, suffragists, civil rights workers, and activists opposed to the war in Vietnam. Members of each social movement stepped outside traditional channels for bringing about social change and yet had a noticeable influence on public policy. Equally dramatic collective efforts in Eastern Europe helped to topple Communist regimes in a largely peaceful manner, in nations that many observers had felt were "immune" to such social change (Ramet 1991). Social movements imply the existence of conflict, but we can also analyze their activities from a functionalist

perspective. Even when unsuccessful, social movements contribute to the formation of public opinion. Initially, the ideas of Margaret Sanger and other early advocates of birth control were viewed as "radical," yet contraceptives are now widely available in the United States. Moreover, functionalists view social movements as training grounds for leaders of the political establishment. Such heads of state as Cuba's Fidel Castro and South Africa's Nelson Mandela came to power after serving as leaders of revolutionary movements. More recently, Poland's Lech Walesa, Russia's Boris Yeltsin, and Czech playwright Vaclav Havel led protest movements against Communist rule and subsequently became leaders of their countries' governments.

How and why do social movements emerge? Obviously, people are often discontented with the way things are. But what causes them to organize at a particular moment in a collective effort to work for change? Sociologists rely on two explanations for why people mobilize: the relative-deprivation and resource-mobilization approaches.

Relative Deprivation

Those members of a society who feel most frustrated and disgruntled by the social and economic conditions of their lives are not necessarily "worst off" in an objective

Two views on abortion among social movements in France: In the top photo, members of the pro-choice movement take to the streets. One sign states, "A child if I want it, when I want it." In the bottom photo, a member of the pro-life movement wears a T-shirt that states. "To abort is to kill."

other words, things aren't as good as you hoped they would be. Such a state may be characterized by scarcity rather than complete lack of necessities (as we saw in the distinction between absolute and relative poverty in Chapter 8). A relatively deprived person is dissatisfied because he or she feels downtrodden relative to some appropriate reference group. Thus, blue-collar workers who live in two-family houses with little lawn space—though hardly at the bottom of the economic ladder—may nevertheless feel deprived in comparison with corporate managers and professionals who live in lavish and exclusive suburbs.

p. 199

In addition to the feeling of relative deprivation, two other elements must be present before discontent will be channeled into a social movement. People must feel that they have a *right* to their goals, that they deserve better than what they have. For example, the struggle against European colonialism in Africa intensified when growing numbers of Africans decided that it was legitimate for them to have political and economic independence. At the same time, the disadvantaged group must perceive that it cannot attain its goals through conventional means. This belief may or may not be correct. Whichever is the case, the group will not mobilize into a social movement unless there is a shared perception that it can end its relative deprivation only through collective action (Morrison 1971).

p. 207

Critics of this approach have noted that an increase in feelings of deprivation is not always necessary before people are moved to act. In addition, this approach fails to explain why certain feelings of deprivation are transformed into social movements, whereas in other similar situations, there is no collective effort to reshape society. Consequently, in recent years, sociologists have given increasing attention to the forces needed to bring about the emergence of social movements (Alain 1985; Finkel and Rule 1987; Orum 1989).

sense. Social scientists have long recognized that what is most significant is how people *perceive* their situation. Karl Marx pointed out that although the misery of the workers was important in reflecting their oppressed state, so was their position *relative* to the capitalist ruling class (Marx and Engels 1955, original edition 1847).

The term ***relative deprivation*** is defined as the conscious feeling of a negative discrepancy between legitimate expectations and present actualities (J. Wilson 1973). In

Resource Mobilization

It takes more than desire to start a social movement. It helps to have money, political influence, access to the media, and workers. The term ***resource mobilization*** refers to the ways in which a social movement utilizes such resources. The success of a movement for change will depend in good part on what resources it has and how effectively it mobilizes them (see also Gamson 1989; Staggenborg 1989a, 1989b).

Sociologist Anthony Oberschall (1973:199) has argued that to sustain social protest or resistance, there must be an "organizational base and continuity of leadership." As people become part of a social movement, norms develop to guide their behavior. Members of the movement may be expected to attend regular meetings of organizations, pay dues, recruit new adherents, and boycott "enemy" products or speakers. An emerging social movement may give rise to special language or new words for familiar terms. In recent years, social movements have been responsible for such new terms of self-reference as *Blacks* and *African Americans* (used to replace *Negroes*), *senior citizens* (used to replace *old folks*), *gays* (used to replace *homosexuals*), and *people with disabilities* (used to replace *the handicapped*).

Leadership is a central factor in the mobilization of the discontented into social movements. Often, a movement will be led by a charismatic figure, such as Dr. Martin Luther King Jr. As Max Weber described it in 1904, *charisma* is that quality of an individual that sets him or her apart from ordinary people. Of course, charisma can fade abruptly; this helps account for the fragility of certain social movements (Morris 2000).

p. 357

Yet many social movements do persist over long periods of time because their leadership is frequently well organized and ongoing. Ironically, as Robert Michels (1915) noted, political movements fighting for social change eventually take on bureaucratic forms of organization. Leaders tend to dominate the decision-making process without directly consulting followers.

p. 144

Why do certain individuals join a social movement whereas others who are in similar situations do not? Some of them are recruited to join. Karl Marx recognized the importance of recruitment when he called on workers to become *aware* of their oppressed status and develop a class consciousness. In agreement with the contemporary resource-mobilization approach, Marx held that a social movement (specifically, the revolt of the proletariat) would require leaders to sharpen the awareness of the oppressed. They must help workers to overcome feelings of ***false consciousness***, or attitudes that

p. 193

do not reflect workers' objective position, in order to organize a revolutionary movement. Similarly, one of the challenges faced by women's liberation activists of the late 1960s and early 1970s was to convince women that they were being deprived of their rights and of socially valued resources.

Unlike the relative-deprivation approach, the resource-mobilization perspective focuses on strategic difficulties facing social movements. Any movement for fundamental change will almost certainly arouse opposition; effective mobilization will depend in part on how the movement deals with resistance to its activities.

Gender and Social Movements

Sociologists point out that gender is an important element in understanding social movement development. In our male-dominated society, women find it more difficult to assume leadership positions in social movement organizations. And while women often disproportionately serve as volunteers in these movements, their work is not always recognized nor are their voices as easily heard as men's. Moreover, gender bias causes the real extent of women's influence to be overlooked. Traditional examination of the sociopolitical system tends to focus on such male-dominated corridors of power as legislatures and corporate boardrooms to the neglect of more female-dominated domains, such as households, community-based groups, or faith-based networks. But efforts to influence family values, child rearing, relationships between parents and schools, and spiritual values are clearly significant to a culture and society (Ferree and Merrill 2000; Noonan 1995).

Scholars of social movements now realize that gender can affect even the way we view organized efforts to bring about or resist change. For example, an emphasis on using rationality and cold logic to achieve goals helps to obscure the importance of passion and emotion in successful social movements. Calls for a more serious study of the role of emotion are frequently seen as applying only to the women's movement, because emotion is traditionally thought of as feminine. Yet it would be difficult to find any movement from labor battles to voting rights to animal rights where passion was not part of the consensus-building force (Ferree and Merrill 2000; Taylor 1995).

New Social Movements

Beginning in the late 1960s, European social scientists observed that there was a change in both the composition and the targets of emerging social movements. Previously, traditional social movements had focused on economic issues, often led by people sharing the same occupation or by labor unions. However, many social movements that have become active in recent decades—including the contemporary women's movement, the peace movement, and the environmental movement—did not have the social class roots typical of the labor protests in the United States and Europe over the preceding 100 years (Tilly 1993).

The term *new social movements* was introduced to refer to organized collective activities that promote autonomy and self-determination as well as improvements in the quality of life. These movements may be involved in developing collective identities, have complex agendas that go beyond a single issue, and often cross national boundaries. Educated, middle-class people are significantly represented in some of these new social movements, such as the women's movement and the movement for lesbian and gay rights. However, marginalized people are also involved in new social movements; as one example, some homeless people create communities of squatters who take over abandoned buildings and fight efforts to evict them (Buechler 1995).

New social movements generally do not view government as their ally in the struggle for a better society. While they typically do not seek to overthrow the government, they may criticize, protest, or harass public officials. Researchers have found that members of new social movements show little inclination to accept established authority, even scientific or technical authority. This is especially evident in the environmental and anti–nuclear power

movements, where movement activists present their own experts to counter those of government or big business (Garner 1996; A. Scott 1990).

The environmental social movement is one of many new movements that have adopted a worldwide focus. In their efforts to reduce air and water pollution, curtail global warming, and protect endangered animal species, environmental activists have realized that strong regulatory measures within a single country are not sufficient. Similarly, labor union leaders and human rights advocates cannot adequately address exploitative sweatshop conditions in a developing country if a multinational corporation can simply move the factory to another country where it pays workers even less. Whereas traditional views of social movements tended to emphasize resource mobilization on a local level, new social movement theory offers a broader, global perspective on social and political activism. Moreover, today's technology provides new ways to unite groups of people across distances and publicize their concerns. A social movement can even be "virtual," as Box 16-1 on pages 452–53 shows.

Theories of Social Change

A new millennium provides the occasion to offer explanations of social change, but this is clearly a challenge in the diverse and complex world we inhabit today. Nevertheless, theorists from several disciplines have sought to analyze social change. In some instances, they have examined historical events to arrive at a better understanding of contemporary changes. We will review three theoretical approaches to change—evolutionary, functionalist, and conflict theory—and then take a look at global change today.

Evolutionary Theory

Charles Darwin's (1809–1882) pioneering work in biological evolution contributed to nineteenth-century theories of social change. According to his approach, there has been a continuing progression of successive life forms. For example, since human beings came at a later stage of evolution than reptiles, we represent a "higher" form of life. Social theorists sought an analogy to this biological model and originated *evolutionary theory,* which views society as moving in a definite direc-

These homeless "squatters" have taken over abandoned buildings in New York City and have fought efforts to evict them. They are an example of marginalized people who are now involved in *new social movements.*

tion. Early evolutionary theorists generally agreed that society was inevitably progressing to a higher state. As might be expected, they concluded in ethnocentric fashion that their own behavior and culture were more advanced than those of earlier civilizations.

p. 9 August Comte (1798–1857), a founder of sociology, was an evolutionary theorist of change. He saw human societies as moving forward in their thinking from mythology to the scientific method. Similarly, Émile Durkheim (1933, original edition 1893) maintained that society progressed from simple to more complex forms of social organization.

The writings of Comte and Durkheim are examples of **unilinear evolutionary theory.** This approach contends that all societies pass through the same successive stages of evolution and inevitably reach the same end. English sociologist Herbert Spencer (1820–1903) used a p. 10 similar approach: Spencer likened society to a living body with interrelated parts that were moving toward a common destiny. However, contemporary evolutionary theorists such as Gerhard Lenski are more likely to picture social change as multilinear than to rely on the more limited unilinear perspective. **Multilinear evolutionary theory** holds that change can occur in several ways and that it does not inevitably lead in the same direction (Haines 1988; J. Turner 1985).

Multilinear theorists recognize that human culture has evolved along a number of lines. For example, the theory of demographic transition graphically demonstrates that population change in developing nations has not p. 385 necessarily followed the model evident in industrialized nations. Sociologists today hold that events do not necessarily follow in a single or several straight lines but instead are subject to disruptions—a topic we will consider later in the discussion of global social change.

Functionalist Theory

Functionalist sociologists focus on what *maintains* a system, not on what changes it. This might seem to suggest that functionalists can offer little of value to the study of social change. Yet, as the work of sociologist Talcott Parsons demonstrates, functionalists have made a distinctive contribution to this area of sociological investigation.

Parsons (1902–1979), a leading proponent of functionalist theory, viewed society as naturally being in a state of equilibrium. By "equilibrium," he meant that society tends toward a p. 13 state of stability or balance. Parsons would view even prolonged labor strikes or civilian riots as temporary disruptions in the status quo rather than as significant alterations in social structure. Therefore, according to his **equilibrium model,** as changes occur in one part of society, there must be adjustments in other parts. If this does not take place, the society's equilibrium will be threatened and strains will occur.

Reflecting an evolutionary approach, Parsons (1966) maintained that four processes of social change are inevitable. The first, *differentiation,* refers to the increasing complexity of social organization. A change from "medicine man" to physician, nurse, and pharmacist is an illustration of differentiation in the field of health. This process is accompanied by *adaptive upgrading,* whereby social institutions become more specialized in their purposes. The division of labor among physicians into obstetricians, internists, surgeons, and so forth is an example of adaptive upgrading.

The third process identified by Parsons is the *inclusion* of groups into society that were previously excluded because of such factors as gender, race, and social class background. Medical schools have practiced inclusion by admitting increasing numbers of women and African Americans. Finally, Parsons contends that societies experience *value generalization,* the development of new values that tolerate and legitimate a greater range of activities.

African Americans are now accepted in many exclusive golf clubs that were previously restricted, illustrating the process of *inclusion* described by Talcott Parsons. The phenomenal success of pro golfer Tiger Woods has helped the process along.

16-1 Virtual Social Movements

We are accustomed to think of social movements in terms of protest marches and door-to-door petition drives. But the World Wide Web allows for alternative ways of trying to organize people and either bring about fundamental change or resist change. The Internet itself has often been referred to as a "virtual community," and as in any community there are people who seek to persuade others to their point of view. Furthermore, the Internet serves to "bring people together"— say, by transforming the cause of the Mexican Zapatista into an international lobbying effort or linking environmentalists on every continent through Greenpeace International or e-mailing information and news from abroad to dissidents in China.

Being like-minded and in face-to-face contact, critical to conventional social movements, is not necessary on the Internet. Moreover, people can engage in their own virtual community with little impact on their everyday lives. On the Internet, for example, one can mount a petition drive to free a death row inmate without taking days and weekends away from one's job and family. Dissidents can communicate with

one another using computers in Internet cafes, with little concern for being traced or monitored by the government.

Two new studies by Matthew Zook and research by sociologist Roberta Garner examined how many websites express ideological points of view that are contentious or hostile to existing institutions. Garner looked at 542 websites that could be regarded as "ideolog-

> **The Internet itself has often been referred to as a "virtual community," and as in any community there are people who seek to persuade others to their point of view.**

ical postings"; some reflect the interests of a particular group or organization and some are only the opinions of isolated individuals. Among the sites were postings that reflected extreme patriotic views, White racism, attachment to cults, regional separatism and new forms of nationalism, and expression of militant environmentalism.

While the Garner sample was not random and therefore may not be rep-

resentative of all ideological postings, the hundreds of sites did show some consistencies, many of them also noted by Zook:

- Like conventional social movements, these sites serve as an alternative source of information, bypassing mainstream sources of opinions found in newspaper editorials.
- These nonmainstream movements enjoy legitimacy because no gate-keeper keeps them off the web. By virtue of being on a website, even an unsophisticated one, the information has the appearance of being just as legitimate as that found on a website for a *Fortune* 500 corporation or CNN news. And because the information appears on *individual* sites, it seems to be more real and even sincere than messages that come from the mass media of television or radio.
- The sites make little reference to time or specific events, except to historic moments. There is not much sense of movement along an agenda.
- The sites rely heavily on written documents, either in the form of

Sources: Calhoun 1998; Castells 2000; Garner 1999; Rosenthal 2000; Van Slambrouck 1996b; Zook 1996.

The acceptance of preventive and alternative medicine is an example of value generalization; our society has broadened its view of health care. All four processes identified by Parsons stress consensus—societal agreement on the nature of social organization and values (B. Johnson 1975; R. Wallace and Wolf 1980).

Parsons's approach explicitly incorporates the evolutionary notion of continuing progress. However, the dominant theme in his model is balance and stability. Society may change, but it remains stable through new forms of integration. For example, in place of the kinship ties that provided social cohesion in the past, there are laws, judicial processes, and new values and belief systems.

Functionalists assume that social institutions will

not persist unless they continue to contribute to the overall society. This leads functionalists to conclude that altering institutions will threaten societal equilibrium. Critics note that the functionalist approach virtually disregards the use of coercion by the powerful to maintain the illusion of a stable, well-integrated society (Gouldner 1960).

Conflict Theory

The functionalist perspective minimizes change. It emphasizes the persistence of social life and sees change as a means of maintaining the equilibrium (or balance) of a society. By contrast, conflict theorists contend that social institutions and practices persist because powerful groups

- manifestos or established documents such as the Constitution or the Bible. Written testimonials (such as "How I Became a Conservative") also proliferate on these websites.
- The presentations are still fairly unsophisticated. While there are glossy animated websites, most sites look like a printed page.
- Unlike conventional social movements, these virtual sites are generally not geared for action. Despite expressions of concern or foreboding (such as the site "Are You Ready for Catastrophic Natural Disasters?"), there were few calls to do anything. Sites like "Glory to the Cuban Revolution" seek to inform visitors, serve as a resource, and, perhaps, bring people around to their point of view.

Zook as well as Garner and her student researchers found that these sites often seem to define themselves by their choice of links on the web. In other words, with whom do they wish to be associated? This is particularly true of well-established social movements that have expanded to use the Internet. For example, both the leading abortion rights groups and anti-abortion organizations feature links to other groups, but only to those that are like-minded.

The entire process of "links" is very important in the Internet network. How one defines one's ideology determines how a site may be located and who makes links. For example, the website of a female national socialist from Sweden boldly encourages visitors to establish a link from their website to hers as long as they are a part of the "white aryan movement on the Net." Using the term "militia" as opposed to "patriotic" would bring different people to one's site. The terms one uses are important since webpages act as recruiting tools to attract new members to a movement and may, in fact, be the only realistic way that some groups will attract followers.

People in conventional social movements commonly try to infiltrate other groups holding opposing views to learn their strategy or even disrupt their ability to function. There is a parallel to that emerging on the Internet. The term *hactivists* (a merging of "hackers" with "*activists*") refers to people who invade computer systems electronically, placing embarrassing information on their enemies' webpages or, at the very least,

defacing them. During the height of the 1999 NATO attacks on Yugoslavia, movements opposed to the military action bombarded the official NATO website with requests meant to overload it and paralyze its operation.

Research into virtual social movements is still exploratory. Social movement researchers such as Garner and Zook are interested in establishing the relationship between ideological websites and "real" organizations. Do these sites merely reflect a single posting? Or are they the visible manifestation of a broader consensus? And sociologists will be interested in examining a more representative sample of such sites to determine how often they explicitly call for social change.

Let's Discuss

1. What are some of the advantages of having a virtual social movement on the Internet? What might be some disadvantages?
2. If you were to create a webpage designed to attract followers to a social movement, what would it be like?

---

have the ability to maintain the status quo. Change has crucial significance, since it is needed to correct social injustices and inequalities.

Karl Marx accepted the evolutionary argument that societies develop along a particular path. However, unlike Comte and Spencer, he did not view each successive stage as an inevitable improvement over the previous one. History, according to Marx, proceeds through a series of stages, each of which exploits a class of people. Ancient society exploited slaves; the estate system of feudalism exploited serfs; modern capitalist society exploits the working class. Ultimately, through a socialist revolution led by the proletariat, human society will move toward the final stage of development: a classless communist society, or "community of free individuals" as Marx de-

scribed it in *Das Kapital* in 1867 (see Bottomore and Rubel 1956:250).

As we have seen, Karl Marx had an important influence on the development of sociology. His thinking offered insights into such institu- pp. 11–12 tions as the economy, the family, religion, and government. The Marxist view of social change is appealing because it does not restrict people to a passive role in responding to inevitable cycles or changes in material culture. Rather, Marxist theory offers a tool for those who wish to seize control of the historical process and gain their freedom from injustice. In contrast to functionalists' emphasis on stability, Marx argues that conflict is a normal and desirable aspect of social change. In fact, change must be encouraged as a means of eliminating social inequality (Lauer 1982).

One conflict sociologist, Ralf Dahrendorf (1959), has noted that the contrast between the functionalist perspective's emphasis on stability and the conflict perspective's focus on change reflects the contradictory nature of society. Human societies are stable and long-lasting, yet they also experience serious conflict. Dahrendorf found that the functionalist approach and the conflict approach were ultimately compatible despite their many areas of disagreement. Indeed, Parsons spoke of new functions that result from social change, and Marx recognized the need for change so that societies could function more equitably.

Global Social Change

We are at a truly dramatic time in history to consider global social change. Maureen Hallinan (1997), in her presidential address to the American Sociological Association, asked those present to consider just a few of the recent political events: the collapse of communism; terrorism in various parts of the world, including the United States; the dismantling of the welfare system in the United States; revolution and famine in Africa and Eastern Europe; the spread of AIDS; and the computer revolution. Just a few months after her remarks came the first verification of the cloning of a complex animal, Dolly the sheep.

In this era of massive social, political, and economic change on a global scale, is it possible to predict change? Some technological changes seem obvious, but the collapse of communist governments in the former Soviet Union and Eastern Europe took people by surprise in its speed and its unexpectedness. However, prior to the Soviet collapse, sociologist Randall Collins (1986, 1995), a conflict theorist, had observed a crucial sequence of changes that most observers had missed.

In seminars as far back as 1980—and in a book published in 1986—Collins argued that Soviet expansionism in the twentieth century had resulted in an overextension of resources, including disproportionate spending on military forces. Such overextension strains a regime's stability. Moreover, geopolitical theory suggests that nations in the middle of a geographic region (like the Soviet Union) tend to fragment over time into smaller units.

Collins predicted that the coincidence of social crises on several frontiers would precipitate the collapse of the Soviet Union. The success of the Iranian revolution in 1979 led to an upsurge of Islamic fundamentalism in nearby Afghanistan and in Soviet republics with substantial Muslim populations. At the same time, there was growing resistance to communist rule throughout Eastern Europe and within the Soviet Union itself. Collins predicted that the rise of a dissident form of communism within the Soviet Union might facilitate the breakdown of the regime. Beginning in the late 1980s, Soviet leader Mikhail Gorbachev chose not to use military power and other types of repression to crush dissidents in Eastern Europe, offered plans for democratization and social reform of Soviet society, and seemed willing to reshape the Soviet Union into a loose federation of somewhat autonomous states. But, in 1991, six republics on the western periphery declared their independence, and within months the entire Soviet Union had formally disintegrated into Russia and a number of independent nations.

In her address, Hallinan (1997) cautioned that we need to move beyond the restrictive models of social change—the linear view of evolutionary theory and the assumptions about equilibrium within functionalist theory. She and other sociologists have looked to "chaos theory" advanced by mathematicians to consider erratic events as a part of change. Hallinan noted that upheavals and major chaotic shifts do occur and that sociologists must learn to predict their occurrence, as Collins did with the Soviet Union. Imagine the dramatic nonlinear social change that will result from major innovations in the areas of communication and biotechnology, a topic we will discuss later in the chapter.

● Resistance to Social Change

Efforts to promote social change are likely to meet with resistance. In the midst of rapid scientific and technological innovations, many people are frightened by the demands of an ever-changing society. Moreover, certain individuals and groups have a stake in maintaining the existing state of affairs.

Social economist Thorstein Veblen (1857–1929) coined the term *vested interests* to refer to those people or groups who will suffer in the event of social change. For example, the American Medical Association (AMA) has taken strong stands against national health insurance and the professionalization of midwifery. National health insurance could lead to limits on the income of physicians, and a rise in the status of midwives could threaten the preeminent position of doctors as the nation's deliverers of babies. In general, those with a disproportionate share of society's wealth, status, and power, such as members of the American Medical Association, have a vested interest in preserving the status quo (Starr 1982; Veblen 1919).

p. 406 ◄

Economic and Cultural Factors

Economic factors play an important role in resistance to social change. For example, it can be expensive for manufacturers to meet high standards for the safety of products and workers. Conflict theorists argue that, in a capitalist economic system, many firms are not willing to pay the price of meeting strict safety standards. They may resist social change by cutting corners within their plants or by pressuring the government to ease regulations.

Communities, too, protect their vested interests, often in the name of "protecting property values." The abbreviation "NIMBY" stands for "not in my backyard," a cry often heard when people protest landfills, prisons, nuclear power facilities, and even bike trails and group homes for people with developmental disabilities. The targeted community may not challenge the need for the facility but may simply insist that it be located elsewhere. The "not in my backyard" attitude has become so common that it is almost impossible for policymakers to find acceptable locations for such facilities as dump sites for hazardous wastes (J. Jasper 1997).

Like economic factors, cultural factors frequently shape resistance to change. William F. Ogburn (1922) distinguished between material and nonmaterial aspects of culture. *Material culture* includes inventions, artifacts, and technology; *nonmaterial culture* encompasses ideas, norms, communication, and social organization. Ogburn pointed out that one cannot devise methods for controlling and utilizing new technology before the introduction of a technique. Thus, nonmaterial culture typically must respond to changes in material culture. Ogburn introduced the term **culture lag** to refer to

p. 58

the period of maladjustment during which the nonmaterial culture is still adapting to new material conditions. One example is the Internet. Its rapid uncontrolled growth raises questions about whether to regulate it and, if so, how much (see the social policy section in this chapter).

In certain cases, changes in material culture can add strain to the relationships between social institutions. For example, new means of birth control have been developed in recent decades. Large families are no longer economically necessary, nor are they commonly endorsed by social norms. But certain religious faiths, among them Roman Catholicism, continue to extol large families and to disapprove methods of limiting family size such as contraception and abortion. This represents a lag between aspects of material culture (technology) and nonmaterial culture (religious beliefs). Conflicts may emerge between religion and other social institutions, such as government and the educational system, over the dissemination of birth control and family-planning information (M. Riley et al. 1994a, 1994b).

Resistance to Technology

Technological innovations are examples of changes in material culture that have often provoked resistance. The *industrial revolution,* which took place largely in England during the period 1760 to 1830, was a scientific revolution focused on the application of nonanimal sources of power to labor tasks. As this revolution proceeded, societies relied on new inventions that facilitated agricultural and industrial production and on new sources of energy such as steam. In some industries, the introduction of power-driven machinery reduced the need for factory workers and made it easier to cut wages.

p. 417

Strong resistance to the industrial revolution emerged in some countries. In England, beginning in 1811, masked craft workers took extreme measures: They conducted nighttime raids on factories and destroyed some of the new machinery. The government hunted these rebels, known as **Luddites,** and ultimately banished some while hanging others. In a similar effort in France, some angry workers threw their wooden shoes (*sabots*) into factory machinery to destroy it,

"Not in my backyard!" say these demonstrators, objecting to the placement of a new incinerator in a Hartford, Connecticut, neighborhood. The phenomenon of NIMBY has become so common that it is almost impossible for policymakers to find acceptable locations for incinerators, landfills, and dump sites for hazardous wastes.

thereby giving rise to the term *sabotage*. While the resistance of the Luddites and the French workers was short-lived and unsuccessful, they have come to symbolize resistance to technology over the last two centuries.

Are we now in the midst of a second industrial revolution, with a contemporary group of Luddites engaged in resistance? Many sociologists believe that we are now living in a *postindustrial society*. It is difficult to pinpoint exactly when this era began. Generally, it is viewed as having begun in the 1950s, when for the first time the majority of workers in industrial societies became involved in services rather than in the actual manufacturing of goods (D. Bell 1999; Fiala 1992).

p. 122

Just as the Luddites resisted the industrial revolution, people in many countries have resisted postindustrial technological changes. The term *neo-Luddites* refers to those who are wary of technological innovations and who question the incessant expansion of industrialization, the increasing destruction of the natural and agrarian world, and the "throw it away" mentality of contemporary capitalism with its resulting pollution of the environment. Neo-Luddites insist that whatever the presumed benefits of industrial and postindustrial technology, such technology has distinctive social costs and may represent a danger to the future of the human species and our planet (Bauerlein 1996; Rifkin 1995b; Sale 1996; Snyder 1996).

Such concerns are worth remembering as we turn now to examine aspects of our technological future and their possible impact on social change.

Technology and the Future

Technology is information about how to use the material resources of the environment to satisfy human needs and desires. Technological advances—the airplane, the automobile, the television, the atomic bomb, and, more recently, the computer, the fax machine, and the cellular phone—have brought striking changes in our cultures, our patterns of socialization, our social institutions, and our day-to-day social interactions. Technological innovations are, in fact, emerging and being accepted with remarkable speed. For example, scientists at Monsanto estimated in 1998 that the amount of genetic information used in practical applications will double every year. Part of the reason for this explosion in using new technology is that it is becoming cheaper. In 1974, it cost $2.5 million to determine the chemical structure of a single gene; less than 25 years later that cost was $150 (Belsie 1998).

p. 57

The technological knowledge with which we work today represents only a tiny portion of the knowledge that will be available in the year 2050. We are witnessing an information explosion as well: The number of volumes in major libraries in the United States doubles every 14 years. Individuals, institutions, and societies will face unprecedented challenges in adjusting to the technological advances still to come (Cetron and Davies 1991; Wurman 1989).

In the following sections, we will examine various aspects of our technological future and consider their overall impact on social change, including the strains they will bring. We will focus in particular on recent developments in computer technology and biotechnology.

Computer Technology

The last decade has witnessed an explosion of computer technology in the United States and around the world. We will now examine two aspects of the technological and social changes related to computers: telecommuting and the Internet.

Today's version of Luddites are protesting technological innovations that they regard as destructive. This Greenpeace demonstrator in Montreal scales a giant corn "monster" in protest of genetically engineered food (see the discussion later in this chapter).

transformed by the growing availability of electronic forms of communication? Will people turn to e-mail, websites, and faxes rather than telephone conversations and face-to-face meetings? Certainly, the technological shift to telephones reduced the use of letter writing as a means of maintaining kinship and friendship ties. But, while it is sometimes assumed that computers and other forms of electronic communication will be socially isolating, there are indications that computers actually put users in touch with large numbers of people on an interactive basis (L. Miller 1995). And in late 1998, the Internet was the means of putting two people together—a father and a daughter who had not seen each other in 50 years. The daughter had spent 14 years searching for her father through state and federal agencies. But after only three hours on the Internet searching the white pages (telephone directories for the entire nation), she found her father's number in Detroit. An emotional family reunion soon followed at the daughter's home in California.

Two young patients at a New York City hospital communicate electronically with peers at a hospital in California. Electronic communication has proved useful in promoting social interaction among children who are seriously ill. The new technology, known as Starbright World, was developed with the assistance of director Steven Spielberg.

Computer-mediated communication also takes place in chat rooms as well as in the more unconventional multiuser domains (MUDs), which allow people to assume new identities in role-playing games. Sociologist Sherry Turkle (1995, 1999) studied this interaction by anonymously visiting MUDs and other electronic chat rooms over a 10-year period and by conducting face-to-face interviews with more than 1,000 people who communicate by electronic mail and actively participate in MUDs. The interviews were especially important because Turkle wanted to be able to distinguish between the users' on-screen personae and their real identities. Turkle concluded that many MUD users' lives were enhanced by the opportunity to engage in role playing and "become someone else." A new sense of self emerges that is "decentered and multiple," expanding on George Herbert p. 86 Mead's notion of self. At the same time, she warns that some individuals may become so gratified by their online lives that they lose touch with their families, p. 115 friends, and work responsibilities. Indeed, psychologists and therapists are giving increasing attention to what is being called "Internet addiction" (Belluck 1996).

If electronic communication can facilitate social interaction within a community—if it can create ties among people in different communities or even countries who "meet" in chat rooms or MUDs—then is there genuinely a new interactive world known as "cyberspace"? The term *cyberspace* was introduced in 1984 by William Gibson, a Canadian science fiction writer. He came up with this term after he walked by a video arcade and noticed the intensity of the players hunched over their screens. Gibson felt that these video game enthusiasts "develop a belief that there's some kind of actual space behind the screen. Some place that you can't see but you know is there" (Elmer-DeWitt 1995:4; see also Shields 1996; Wellman et al. 1996).

The emergence of cyberspace can be viewed as yet another step away from Ferdinand Tönnies's concept of the familiar, intimate *Gemeinschaft* to the comparatively impersonal *Gesellschaft* and as yet another way in which social cohesion is being eroded in pp. 119–20 contemporary society. Critics of electronic communication question whether nonverbal communication, voice inflections, and other forms of interpersonal interaction will be lost as people turn to e-mail and chat rooms (P. Schaefer 1995; Schellenberg 1996). A 1998 study that used survey analysis found that people in Pittsburgh who spend even a few hours a week online experience higher levels of depression and loneliness than if they had used the computer network less frequently (R. Kraut et al. 1998).

But while some conclude that by opening up the world to interaction, we may have reduced face-to-face interaction, others have reached different conclusions. One study surveyed more than 2,000 households nationwide to assess the impact of the Internet on the everyday lives of its users. It found that parents report that they often surf the web together with their children, and that the Internet has had little effect on their children's interactions with friends. This study concludes that about two-thirds of the population in the United States are using the Internet more than ever and without sacrificing their social lives (Cha 2000).

Social Control

A data entry employee pauses to say hello to a colleague. A checker at the supermarket takes a moment to banter with a customer. A customer service telephone representative takes too much time helping callers. Each of these situations is subject to computer surveillance. Given the absence of strong protective legislation, employees in the United States are subject to increasing and pervasive supervision by computers. Supervisors have always scrutinized the performance of their workers, but with so much work now being handled electronically, the possibilities for surveillance have risen dramatically.

With Big Brother watching and listening in more and more places, computer and video technology has facilitated supervision, control, and even domination by employers or government. There is a danger that electronic monitoring

of employees can become a substitute for effective management and can lead to perceptions of unfairness and intrusiveness. An American Management Association study found that 35 percent of firms keep track of their workers by recording their phone calls and voice mail, looking through their computer files, or videotaping. About a quarter of these firms said they do not inform their employees of these surveillance practices (Grimsley 1997).

In recent years, a new type of corporate surveillance has emerged. A number of Internet sites are highly critical of the operations of various corporations. On McSpotlight, one could find attacks on nutritional practices at McDonald's; on Up Against the Wal, one could study advice on how to fight plans to open new Wal-Mart stores in a community. The Internet sites of such "anticorporate vigilantes" are generally protected by the First Amendment, but powerful corporations are carefully monitoring the sites in an attempt to counteract the activities of their critics (Neuborne 1996).

Technological advances have also created the possibility for a new type of white-collar crime: computer crime. It is now possible to gain access to a computer's inventory without leaving home and p. 175 ◄ to carry out embezzlement or electronic fraud without leaving a trace. One report released in 2000 put cybercrime losses by big businesses at $10 billion in the United States alone. Typically, discussions of computer crime focus on computer theft and on problems caused by computer "hackers," but widespread use of computers has facilitated many new ways of participating in deviant behavior. Consequently, greatly expanded police resources may be needed to deal with online child molesters, prostitution rings, software pirates, con artists, and other types of computer criminals. There is now a Computer Crime and Intellectual Property section of the Justice Department. The consensus of the heads of the section is that these cases are increasing and becoming more difficult (Computer Security Institute 1999; Piller 2000).

Not all the technological advances relevant to social control have been electronic in nature. DNA data banks have given police a powerful weapon in solving crimes; they have also opened the way to free wrongfully convicted citizens. A 1996 Department of Justice report noted that 28 men convicted of rape had been freed from U.S. prisons after DNA testing established their innocence. From 1996 through 1999, five death row inmates were released on the

"Keystroke! ... Keystroke! ... Keystroke!"

basis of DNA evidence. Efforts are under way to make such testing and other forms of DNA evidence as easily available as fingerprinting. As of mid-1996, 26 states had begun to develop DNA data banks that eventually will be linked in a nationwide network by the Federal Bureau of Investigation (FBI). While appropriate safeguards must be devised, the expansion of such DNA data banks has the potential to revolutionize law enforcement in the United States—especially in the area of sex crimes, where biological evidence is telling (Butterfield 1996; DPIC 2000c).

Another connection between technology and social control is the use of computer databases and electronic verification of documents to reduce illegal immigration into the United States. While concerned about the issue of illegal entry, many Hispanics and Asian Americans nevertheless believe that *their* privacy, rather than that of Whites, is most likely to be infringed by government authorities (Brandon 1995). The next section of the chapter looks more fully at how technological changes can intensify stratification and inequality based on race, ethnicity, and other factors.

Stratification and Inequality

"Today we stand at the brink of becoming two societies, one largely white and plugged in and the other black and unplugged." This is how Black historian Henry Lewis Gates Jr. starkly describes today's "digital divide" (Gates 1999: A15). An important continuing theme in sociology is stratification among people. Thus far, there is little evidence to suggest that technology will reduce inequality; in fact, it may only intensify it. Technology is costly, and it is generally impossible to introduce advances to everyone simultaneously. So who gets this access first? Conflict theorists contend that as we travel further and further along the electronic frontier through advances such as telecommuting and the Internet, the disenfranchised poor may be isolated from mainstream society in an "information ghetto," just as racial and ethnic minorities have traditionally been subjected to residential segregation (Ouellette 1993).

Available data show clear differences in use of computers based on class, race, and ethnicity. A national study released in 2000 estimates that only 13 percent of households earning less than $20,000 use the Internet, compared to 78 percent of those with incomes of $75,000 or more. Moreover, 57 percent of Asian American households and 46 percent of White households used the Internet, compared with 24 percent of Hispanic and African American households (National Telecommunications and Information Administration 2000: 13, 31). (See Figure 16-2.)

FIGURE 16-2

Internet Access, 2000

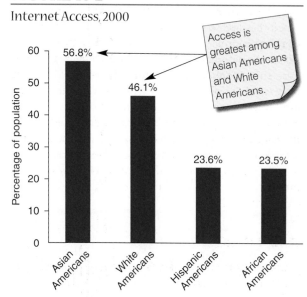

Source: National Telecommunications and Information Administration 2000:13.

This issue goes beyond individual interest or lack of interest in computers. Accessibility is a major concern. According to a study by the Consumer Federation of America and the NAACP (National Association for the Advancement of Colored People), accessibility to computer networks through fiber-optic corridors (the "information superhighway") may bypass poor neighborhoods and minority populations. The researchers concluded that regional telephone companies' plans for these advanced communications networks target affluent areas and may lead to an exclusionary "electronic redlining" similar to discrimination in fields such as banking, real estate, and insurance. Industry executives counter that they have repeatedly stated their intention to deploy the information superhighway to *all* areas. Congress has proposed regulatory legislation to ensure equal access to the information superhighway by mandating the wiring of schools, libraries, and hospitals. Several communities, such as Manchester, New Hampshire, and Oakland, California, have recently arranged for computer hookups in publicly built low-income housing (Lohr 1994; Lieberman 1999).

Technological advances of the present and future may not be equally beneficial to men and women. Feminist sociologists point out that technology is not necessarily gender-neutral. For example, many studies have shown the differential use of computers by boys and girls. Computer games, which often serve as a means of early socialization to computers, typically involve sports or skills associated with traditional male gender roles. As a result, computer camps and video arcades have become predominantly male settings.

A report on "gender gaps" in schools issued by the American Association of University Women in 1998 noted that high school girls lag behind boys in technology. For example, only 17 percent of those who took the advanced placement exam in computer science in 1996 were girls. Moreover, girls tend to limit use of the computer to word processing or data entry, while boys are more likely to use it for solving problems or writing programs, preparing them in better ways for high-tech careers. Internet use is more evenly distributed. By 2000, boys and girls used the Internet equally and adult female users slightly outnumbered male users (Lewin 1998; National Telecommunications and Information Administration 2000; *New York Times* 2000).

The issue of technology and inequality is especially sensitive when viewed in a cross-cultural perspective. Although industrialization has dramatically improved the standard of living of many workers, it has allowed elites to amass untold wealth. Moreover, the activities of multinational corporations have increased the inequality between industrialized core nations (such as the United States, Germany, and Japan) and the periphery of developing countries.

SOCIAL POLICY AND TECHNOLOGY

Privacy and Censorship in a Global Village

The Issue

In 1992, a huge explosion in a Texaco refinery in Wilmington, California, spread fire and caused panic in a nearby Hispanic community. Soon afterward, the Texaco Corporation was hit by close to 5,000 property damage claims and 14,000 claims of personal injury. Texaco promptly hired a private investigator, but not to probe the cause of the explosion. His task was to unearth compromising information about the claimants and their lawyers, whose class action suits could cost Texaco millions of dollars.

One of the claimants was 23-year-old Rossana Rivera. The private investigator didn't just learn her Social Security number, date of birth, every address where she had lived, names and numbers of present and past neighbors, the number of bedrooms in her house, her welfare history, and the employment background of her children's fathers. He also dredged up two delinquent traffic tickets, which he used to threaten her with arrest if she did not come up with damaging information about the lawyers in her case.

How did he arrive at all this information? For the most part, by buying or uncovering data in commercial databases (which most citizens are unaware of) and searching law enforcement computer files (supposedly off-limits to civilians). The Texaco investigator's actions are not at all unusual these days. According to a deputy U.S. attorney in New Jersey, "The buying and selling of information is just a huge business" (Bernstein 1997: A20). The biggest customers are companies involved in litigation or business conflicts or just screening applicants. The suppliers in the information network include investigators, underground information brokers, online databases, governments that sell public records, former law enforcement personnel, even former cold war spies. The means of getting information range from simple payments to computer hacking to electronic surveillance to deception in all forms.

At this point in the United States, privacy laws have so many loopholes and are so patchy that it is often difficult to distinguish between data that are obtained legally and data that are gathered illicitly. The other side of the coin is the fear that government will restrict the flow of electronic information too much, stepping over the border into censorship. Some observers, however, feel the government is fully justified in restricting pornographic information. The whole issue of privacy and censorship in this technological age is another case of culture lag, in which the material culture (the technology) is changing faster than the nonmaterial culture (norms controlling the technology).

The Setting

The typical consumer in the United States is included in at least 25 marketing databases, while some consumers are on upward of 100 databases. Overall, there are more than 15,000 specialized lists available in the United States with a total of some 2 billion consumer names. Christine Varney, former commissioner of the Federal Trade Commission (FTC), has observed, "Vast quantities of data are available easily and cheaply to business to be stored, analyzed, and re-used" (Castelli 1996:52; Horovitz 1995).

These lists may at first seem innocent enough. Does it really matter if companies can buy lists for marketing with our names, addresses, and telephone numbers? Part of the problem is that computer technology has made it increasingly easy for any individual, business firm, or government agency to retrieve more and more information about any of us. For decades, information from motor vehicle offices, voter registration lists, and credit bureaus has been electronically stored, yet the incompatibility of different computer systems used to prevent access from one system to another. Today, having some information about a person has made it much easier to get other and perhaps more sensitive information (Stoll 1995).

The question of how much free expression should be permitted on the Internet relates to the issue of censorship. Pornography websites proliferate, especially after federal legislation to regulate "indecent" words and images was struck down by the Supreme Court in 1997 (as we will see later in this section). Some of the X-rated material is perfectly legal, if inappropriate for children who use the Net. Some of the sites are clearly illegal, such as those that serve the needs of pedophiles and prey on young children. Some are morally and legally elusive, such as the "upskirt" sites that post images taken by video cameras aimed under the skirts of unsuspecting women in public places. This is another area in which we can see the results of culture lag.

Sociological Insights

Functionalists can point to the manifest function of the Internet in its ability to facilitate communications. They also can identify the latent function of providing a forum for groups with few resources to communicate with literally tens of millions of people. Poorly financed groups can range from hate organizations to special interest groups vying against powerful wealthy interests. Thus, the functionalist perspective would see many aspects of technology fostering communication; the issue of censorship depends on how one views the content of the message, and the issue of privacy hinges on how information is used.

Even if computers and other forms of modern technology are peering deeper and deeper into our daily lives, some observers insist that we *benefit* from such innovations and can exist quite well with a bit less privacy. Sociologist Amitai Etzioni (1996:14A) bluntly states, "The genie is out of the bottle. We must either return to the Stone Age (pay cash, use carrier pigeons, and forget insurance) or learn to live with shrunken privacy." Etzioni adds that there are many instances in which preservation of the common good requires giving up some part of our privacy. Amnesty International, the global human rights advocacy group, has applauded the expansion of the Internet. This group sees it as a means to reach a wider audience and, in the case of specific cases of torture or repression, to speedily disseminate information worldwide so that appropriate steps can be taken to end unjust situations (S. Perry 1998a).

Viewed from a conflict perspective, however, there is the ever-present danger that a society's most powerful groups will use technological advances to invade the privacy of the less powerful and thereby maintain or intensify various forms of inequality and injustice. For example, in 1989, the People's Republic of China used various types of technology to identify protestors who had participated in prodemocracy demonstrations at Tiananmen Square and elsewhere. Some protestors identified in this manner received long prison terms because of their activism. During the same period, the Chinese government intercepted the news reports, telephone calls, and facsimile messages of foreign journalists covering the demonstrations. While encouraging e-commerce, the government began in 2000 to undertake a "security certification" of all Internet content and service providers in China. Conflict theorists argue that control of technology in almost any form remains in the hands of those who already wield the most power, usually at the expense of the powerless and poor (Pomfret 2000).

Interactionists view the privacy and censorship debate as one that parallels concerns people have in any social interaction. Just as we may disapprove of some associations that relatives or friends have with other people, we also express concern over controversial websites and attempt to monitor people's social interaction. Obviously, the Internet facilitates interactions with a broad range of people, with minimal likelihood of detection compared to face-to-face interaction. Moreover, one can easily move a website from one country to another, avoiding not only detection but also prosecution.

Policy Initiatives

In 1986, the federal government passed the Electronic Communications Privacy Act. Wire communications—defined as use of the human voice in telephone and cordless calls—are highly protected. They cannot be subjected to surveillance unless a prosecutor obtains authorization from both the U.S. attorney general and a federal judge. By contrast, telegrams, faxes, and e-mail can be monitored simply with the approval of a judge (Eckenwiler 1995).

In 1996, the Communications Decency Act made it a federal crime to transmit "indecent" or "patently offensive" material over the Internet without maintaining safeguards to ensure that children cannot see it. Private e-mail and online chat room communications with anyone under the age of 18 were subjected to the same standard. Violations of the law could lead to up to two years in prison and a $250,000 fine (Fernandez 1996; Lappin 1996).

Civil liberties advocates insisted that such governmental action infringed on private communications between consenting adults and inevitably limited freedom of speech. They noted that at one point America Online even banned use of the term *breast,* thereby preventing any meaningful discussion of breast cancer or breast examinations. Lawsuits challenging the constitutionality of the Communications Decency Act were supported by such organizations as the American Civil Liberties Union (ACLU), the American Library Association, the American Society of Newspaper Editors, and the National Writers Union. In 1997, the Supreme Court declared that major parts of the act were unconstitutional. The Court called government attempts to regulate content on the Internet an attack on the First Amendment guarantee of freedom of speech (Fernandez 1996; A. Harmon 1998).

Censorship and privacy are also issues globally. In Myanmar (or Burma), the government has ruled that fax machines and computer modems are illegal. In Saudi Arabia, access to the Internet was banned until 1999. Now all Internet connections are routed through a government hub where computers block access to thousands of sites cataloged on a rapidly expanding censorship list—for example, all gambling sites, all free-wheeling chat rooms, and all sites critical of the ruling Saudi family. By contrast, the openness of the Internet in other parts of the Middle East allows scattered Palestinian refugees to communicate with one another and establish websites that provide a history of Palestinian settlements. While China encourages expansion of the Internet, it has been wary of facilitating commu-

There are few secrets on the Internet. This naval officer faced dismissal from the Navy for acknowledging his homosexuality on a computer online service. The Navy obtained this confidential information from America Online, raising questions about how private one's online communications can be.

nication that it regards as disruptive. The government has blocked all websites related to the Falun Gong spiritual group, and in 2000 it announced that "state secrets" (very vaguely defined) were banned from the Internet. Meanwhile, the British government is constructing an Internet spy center that is geared to watch all online activity in Great Britain. It will be able to track every website a person visits (Africa News Service 1998; Jehl 1999; MacLeod 2000; Rosenthal 1999b, 2000; T. Wilkinson 1999).

While some people chastise government efforts to curb technology, others decry their *failure* to limit certain aspects of technology. The United States is developing an international reputation of being opposed to efforts to protect people's privacy. For example, the Center for Public Integrity, a nonpartisan research organization, issued a report in 1998 that critiques the U.S. government for failing to approve legislation protecting the confidentiality of medical records. In another case, America Online revealed to a U.S. Navy investigator the identity of a sailor who had described his marital status online as gay. In 1998, both the Navy and America Online were forced to reach settlements for violating the privacy of the sailor. At the same time, the United States has been vocal in opposing efforts by the 15 European Union countries to implement a tough law designed to protect citizens from computer-age invasions of privacy. The U.S. technology industry does not want to have access to information blocked, since information is vital to global commerce. While a compromise is likely, this case illustrates the fine line between safeguarding privacy and stifling the electronic flow of information (Center for Public Integrity 1998; S. Perry 1998b; Shenon 1998).

The conflict over privacy and censorship is far from over. As technology continues to advance in the twenty-first century, there are sure to be new battlegrounds.

Let's Discuss

1. What are some of the ways that people can obtain information about us? Are you aware of any databases that contain information about your personal life?

2. Do you think corporations and employers have a right to monitor employees' e-mail and phone calls? Why or why not?

3. Are you more concerned about government

Chapter Resources

Summary

Social movements are organized collective activities to promote or resist charge. *Social change* is significant alteration over time in behavior patterns and culture, including norms and values. *Technology* is information about how to use the material resources of the environment to satisfy human needs and desires. This chapter examines social movements and their role in social change, sociological theories of social change, resistance to change, and the impact of technology on society and on social change.

1. A group mobilizes into a social movement when there is a shared perception that is *relative deprivation* can be ended only through collective action.
2. The success of social movement will depend in good part on how effectively it mobilizes its resources.
3. *New social movements* tend to focus on more than just economic issues and often cross national boundaries.
4. Early advocates of evolutionary theory of social change believed that society was inevitably progressing to a higher state.
5. Talcott Parsons, a leading advocate of functionalist theory, viewed society as naturally being in a state of equilibrium or balance.
6. Conflict theorists see change as having crucial significance, since it is needed to correct social injustices and inequalities.
7. In general, those with a disproportionate share of society's wealth, status, and power have a vested interest in preserving the status quo and will resist change.
8. The period of maladjustment when the non-material culture is still adapting to new material conditions is known as *culture lag.*

9. In the computer age, *telecommuters* are linked to their supervisors and colleagues through computer terminals, phone lines, and fax machines.
10. Early users of the Internet, the world's largest computer network, established a subculture with specific norms and values and with distinctive argot terms.
11. Advances in biotechnology have raised difficult ethical questions about sex selection of fetuses and genetic engineering.
12. Social scientists focus on human error in the *normal accidents* associated with increasing reliance on technology.
13. The domination of the Internet by the English language is not surprising, since English has largely become the international language of commerce and communication.
14. Computer and video technology has facilitated supervision, control, and even domination by employers or government.
15. Conflict theorists fear that the disenfranchised poor may be isolated from mainstream society in an "information ghetto," just as racial and ethnic minorities have been subjected to residential segregation.
16. Computer technology has made it increasingly easy for any individual, business firm, or government agency to retrieve more and more information about any of us and thereby infringe on our privacy; it is also easy to disseminate pornographic material to millions of people at a time. How much government should restrict access to electronic information is an import policy issue today.

Critical Thinking Questions

1. Select one social movement that is currently working for change in the United States. analyze that movement, drawing on the concepts of relative deprivation, resource mobilization, and false consciousness.
2. In the last few years we have witnessed phenomenal growth in the use of cellular phones in all parts of the world. Analyze this example of material culture from the point of view of culture lag. Consider how

usage, government regulation, and privacy issues are being worked out to keep up with the new technology.
3. In what ways has social interaction in your college community been affected by the kinds of technological advances examined in this chapter? Are there particular subcultures that are more likely or less likely to use new forms of electronic communication?

Key Terms

Culture lag   A period of maladjustment during which the nonmaterial culture is still adapting to new material conditions. (455)

Equilibrium model   A functionalist view of society as tending toward a state of stability or balance. (451)

Evolutionary theory   A theory of social change that holds that society is moving in a definite direction. (450)

False consciousness   A term used by Karl Marx to describe an attitude held by members of a class that does not accurately reflect its objective position. (449)

Luddites   Rebellious craft workers in nineteenth-century England who destroyed new factory machinery as part of their resistance to the industrial revolution. (455)

Multilinear evolutionary theory   A theory of social change that holds that change can occur in several ways and does not inevitably lead in the same direction. (451)

New social movements   Organized collective activities that promote autonomy and self-determination as well as improvements in the quality of life. (450)

Normal accidents   Failures that are inevitable given the manner in which human and technological systems are organized. (461)

Relative deprivation   The conscious feeling of a negative discrepancy between legitimate expectations and present actualities. (448)

Resource mobilization   The ways in which a social movement utilizes such resources as money, political influence, access to the media, and personnel. (449)

Social change   Significant alteration over time in behavior patterns and culture, including norms and values. (447)

Social movements   Organized collective activities to promote or resist change in an existing group or society. (447)

Technology   Information about how to use the material resources of the environment to satisfy human needs and desires. (456)

Telecommuters   Employees who work full-time or part-time at home rather than in an outside office and who are linked to their supervisors and colleagues through computer terminals, phone lines, and fax machines. (457)

Unilinear evolutionary theory   A theory of social change that holds that all societies pass through the same successive stages of evolution and inevitably reach the same end. (451)

Vested interests   Those people or groups who will suffer in the event of social change and who have a stake in maintaining the status quo. (454)

Additional Readings

Castells, Manuel. 1996, 1997. *The Information Age: Economy, Society, and Culture.* Vol. 1: *The Rise of the Network Society.* Vol. 2: *The Power of Identity.* Vol. 3: *End of Millennium.* Cambridge, MA: Blackwell Publishers. This massive work by a noted sociologist describes how global networks of both computers and people are transforming work, politics, and social relationships.

Kotkin, Joel. 2000. *The New Geography.* New York: Random House. An historical examination of how technology changes the social and economic reality of cities, towns, and rural areas. Considers the digital divide within the United States and around the world.

McChesney, Robert W. 1999. *Rich Media, Poor Democracy: Communication Politics in Dubious Times.* Urbana, IL: University of Illinois Press. A look at the increasing concentration of newspapers, television stations, and radio stations in the hands of a few wealthy corporations, making the information age harmful for public life, according to the author.

Miller, David L. 2000. *Introduction to Collective Behavior and Collective Actions.* 2nd ed. Prospect Heights, IL: Waveland. The author, associated with the assembling perspective, covers all the major theoretical approaches of the field. He examines rumors, riots, social movements, immigration, and other forms of collective behavior.

Internet Connection

Note: While all the URLs listed were current as of the printing of this book, these sites often change. Please check our website (http://www.mhhe.com/schaefer4) for updates.

1. "Trust" in technology is at the heart of modern life. Many people "trust" that computers, cars, medical equipment, and cellular phones will work as specified. Sometimes, that "trust" is misplaced, with results that range from annoyance to tragedy. Visit AirDisaster. Com *(http://www.airdisaster.com/)*, which provides an online examination of recent and past airplane accidents and crashes.
   (a) What is the "latest accident" featured on the site?
   (b) Did you hear about this story on television or in the newspapers?
   (c) Does the cause of any of the crashes featured on the site connect to your chapter's discussion of "Technological Accidents" and Charles Perrow's concept of "normal accidents"?
   (d) Choose a "Model" of aircraft or an "Airline" and review the statistics provided. How many "Events" has your choice been involved in? How many flights has the model or the airline made?
   (e) Choose the "Click Here for accident statistics by Year" link in "Statistics." How would you describe the frequency of accidents, fatalities, and departures occurring over time as presented on the site?
   (f) Take the "air safety web poll." How does your answer match up to others who have visited the site?
   (g) What did you find most surprising about the statistics and information presented on the site?

2. Sociologists interested in technological change are currently studying the effects the Internet is having on such aspects of daily life as work, relationships, and health. Another area of interest is in how the web is being utilized in education. Use a search engine such as Lycos® *(http://www.lycos.com/)* and see if your college offers any online courses. If not, or if you cannot access these sites without a password, try examining some of the classes featured on the Illinois Virtual Campus *(http://www.ivc. illinois.edu/)*.
   (a) What kinds of classes are offered online?
   (b) How do the students and teachers interact? What are some of the assignments and how do students turn them in?
   (c) What kinds of classes—if any—do you think should *not* be offered online? Why?
   (d) What are some of the advantages and disadvantages of taking classes over the computer?
   (e) In what ways would the experience of taking an online course be different from taking a "live" course? In what ways would it be the same?
   (f) How might the issues of "global disconnect" and "privacy" play a role in online education?
   (g) In what other ways have you seen technology change education over the course of your academic career?

3. PBS offers an online exploration of the "digital divide" *(http://www.pbs.org/digitaldivide/)*. Visit the site after reading your chapter, taking time to examine the links, viewpoints, and stories presented, and then answer the following:
   (a) What is meant by the term "digital divide"? How does this concept compare to your book's discussion of "global disconnect"?
   (b) How has life in classrooms and at work been changed by technology and computers? In what specific ways might current costs, use patterns, designs, and policies regarding technology perpetuate and even increase gender, racial, and social class inequity and stereotypes?
   (c) What can be done to alleviate the "digital divide"?
   (d) Be sure to participate in the "Interact!" activities on the site. How well did you do on the "gender quiz"? What important facts did you learn about technology and computers through your activities?
   (e) What will the jobs of the next few decades look like, and what skills must we have in order to compete for them?

Interactive e-Source with Making the Grade

 Online Learning Center   www.mhhe.com/schaefer4

 PowerWeb

SocCity

Glos

Numbers following the definitions indicate pages where the terms were identified. Consult the index for further page references.

A

Absolute poverty A standard of poverty based on a minimum level of subsistence below which families should not be expected to exist. (198)

Achieved status A social position attained by a person largely through his or her own efforts. (110, 190)

Activity theory An interactionist theory of aging that argues that elderly people who remain active will be best-adjusted. (276)

Adoption In a legal sense, a process that allows for the transfer of the legal rights, responsibilities, and privileges of parenthood to a new legal parent or parents. (303)

Affirmative action Positive efforts to recruit minority group members or women for jobs, promotions, and educational opportunities. (233, 371)

Ageism A term coined by Robert N. Butler to refer to prejudice and discrimination against the elderly. (279)

Agrarian society The most technologically advanced form of preindustrial society. Members are primarily engaged in the production of food but increase their crop yield through such innovations as the plow. (121)

Alienation The condition of being estranged or disassociated from the surrounding society. (141)

Amalgamation The process by which a majority group and a minority group combine through intermarriage to form a new group. (236)

Anomie Durkheim's term for the loss of direction felt in a society when social control of individual behavior has become ineffective. (10, 168)

Anomie theory of deviance A theory developed by Robert Merton that explains deviance as an adaptation either of socially prescribed goals or of the norms governing their attainment, or both. (169)

Anticipatory socialization Processes of socialization in which a person "rehearses"

social relationships. (..)

Anti-Semitism Anti-Jewish prejudice. (247)

Apartheid The former policy of the South African government designed to maintain the separation of Blacks and other non-Whites from the dominant Whites. (237)

Argot Specialized language used by members of a group or subculture. (67)

Ascribed status A social position "assigned" to a person by society without regard for the person's unique talents or characteristics. (109, 190)

Assimilation The process by which a person forsakes his or her own cultural tradition to become part of a different culture. (237)

Authority Power that has been institutionalized and is recognized by the people over whom it is exercised. (356)

B

Bilateral descent A kinship system in which both sides of a person's family are regarded as equally important. (294)

Bilingualism The use of two or more languages in particular settings, such as workplaces or educational facilities, treating each language as equally legitimate. (70)

Birthrate The number of live births per 1,000 population in a given year. Also known as the *crude birthrate*. (384)

Black power A political philosophy promoted by many younger Blacks in the 1960s that supported the creation of Black-controlled political and economic institutions. (240)

Bourgeoisie Karl Marx's term for the capitalist class, comprising the owners of the means of production. (193)

Bureaucracy A component of formal organization in which rules and hierarchical ranking are used to achieve efficiency. (140)

Bureaucratization The process by which a group, organization, or social movement becomes increasingly bureaucratic. (143)

C

Capitalism An economic system in which the means of production are largely in private hands and the main incentive for economic activity is the accumulation of profits. (193, 354)

Castes Hereditary systems of rank, usually religiously dictated, that tend to be fixed and immobile. (191)

...usal logic The relationship between a condition or variable and a particular consequence, with one event leading to the other. (31)

Census An enumeration, or counting, of a population. (384)

Charismatic authority Max Weber's term for power made legitimate by a leader's exceptional personal or emotional appeal to his or her followers. (357)

Class A term used by Max Weber to refer to a group of people who have a similar level of wealth and income. (193)

Class consciousness In Karl Marx's view, a subjective awareness held by members of a class regarding their common vested interests and need for collective political action to bring about social change. (193)

Classical theory An approach to the study of formal organizations that views workers as being motivated almost entirely by economic rewards. (146)

Class system A social ranking based primarily on economic position in which achieved characteristics can influence mobility. (191)

Closed system A social system in which there is little or no possibility of individual mobility. (205)

Coalition A temporary or permanent alliance geared toward a common goal. (139)

Code of ethics The standards of acceptable behavior developed by and for members of a profession. (39)

Cognitive theory of development Jean Piaget's theory explaining how children's thought progresses through four stages. (88)

Cohabitation The practice of living together as a male–female couple without marrying. (308)

Colonialism The maintenance of political, social, economic, and cultural dominance over a people by a foreign power for an extended period of time. (207)

Communism As an ideal type, an economic system under which all property is communally owned and no social distinctions are made on the basis of people's ability to produce. (355)

Community A spatial or political unit of social organization that gives people a sense of belonging, based either on shared residence in a particular place or on a common identity. (415)

Concentric-zone theory A theory of urban growth that sees growth in terms of a series of rings radiating from the central business district. (418)

Conflict perspective A sociological approach that assumes that social behavior is best understood in terms of conflict or tension between competing groups. (14)

Conformity Going along with one's peers, individuals of a person's own status, who have no special right to direct that person's behavior. (160)

Contact hypothesis An interactionist perspective that states that interracial contact between people of equal status in cooperative circumstances will reduce prejudice. (235)

Content analysis The systematic coding and objective recording of data, guided by some rationale. (38)

Control group Subjects in an experiment who are not introduced to the independent variable by the researcher. (37)

Control theory A view of conformity and deviance that suggests that our connection to members of society leads us to systematically conform to society's norms. (165)

Control variable A factor held constant to test the relative impact of an independent variable. (34)

Correlation A relationship between two variables whereby a change in one coincides with a change in the other. (32)

Correspondence principle A term used by Bowles and Gintis to refer to the tendency of schools to promote the values expected of individuals in each social class and to prepare students for the types of jobs typically held by members of their class. (337)

Counterculture A subculture that deliberately opposes certain aspects of the larger culture. (68)

Creationism A literal interpretation of the Bible regarding the creation of man and the universe used to argue that evolution should not be presented as established scientific fact. (344)

Crime A violation of criminal law for which formal penalties are applied by some governmental authority. (174)

Cult Due to the stereotyping, this term has been abandoned by sociologists in favor of *new religious movements*. (331)

Cultural relativism The viewing of people's behavior from the perspective of their own culture. (69)

Cultural transmission A school of criminology that argues that criminal behavior is learned through social interactions. (171)

Cultural universals General practices found in every culture. (56, 321)

Culture The totality of learned, socially transmitted behavior. (55)

Culture lag Ogburn's term for a period of maladjustment during which the nonmaterial culture is still adapting to new material conditions. (58, 455)

Culture shock The feeling of surprise and disorientation that is experienced when people witness cultural practices different from their own. (68)

D

Death rate The number of deaths per 1,000 population in a given year. Also known as the *crude death rate*. (384)

Defended neighborhood A neighborhood that residents identify through defined community borders and through a perception that adjacent areas are geographically separate and socially different. (424)

Degradation ceremony An aspect of the socialization process within total institutions, in which people are subjected to humiliating rituals. (90)

Deindustrialization The systematic, widespread withdrawal of investment in basic aspects of productivity such as factories and plants. (367)

Demographic transition A term used to describe the change from high birthrates and death rates to relatively low birthrates and death rates. (385)

Demography The scientific study of population. (381)

Denomination A large, organized religion not officially linked with the state or government. (328)

Dependency theory An approach that contends that industrialized nations continue to exploit developing countries for their own gain. (209)

Dependent variable The variable in a causal relationship that is subject to the influence of another variable. (31)

Deviance Behavior that violates the standards of conduct or expectations of a group or society. (165)

Differential association A theory of deviance proposed by Edwin Sutherland that holds that violation of rules results from exposure to attitudes favorable to criminal acts. (171)

Diffusion The process by which a cultural item is spread from group to group or society to society. (57)

Discovery The process of making known or sharing the existence of an aspect of reality. (57)

Discrimination The process of denying opportunities and equal rights to individuals and groups because of prejudice or other arbitrary reasons. (230)

Disengagement theory A functionalist theory of aging introduced by Cumming and Henry that contends that society and the aging individual mutually sever many of their relationships. (275)

Domestic partnership Two unrelated adults who have chosen to share one another's lives in a relationship of mutual caring, who reside together, and who agree to be jointly responsible for their dependents, basic living expenses, and other common necessities. (309)

Dominant ideology A set of cultural beliefs and practices that helps to maintain powerful social, economic, and political interests. (65, 195)

Downsizing Reductions taken in a company's workforce as part of deindustrialization. (368)

Dramaturgical approach A view of social interaction, popularized by Erving Goffman, under which people are examined as if they were theatrical performers. (16, 86)

Dyad A two-member group. (138)

Dysfunction An element or a process of society that may disrupt a social system or lead to a decrease in stability. (14, 141)

E

Ecclesia A religious organization that claims to include most or all of the members of a society and is recognized as the national or official religion. (328)

E-commerce Numerous ways that people with access to the Internet can do business from their computers. (369)

Economic system The social institution through which goods and services are produced, distributed, and consumed. (353)

Education A formal process of learning in which some people consciously teach while others adopt the social role of learner. (321)

Egalitarian family An authority pattern in which the adult members of the family are regarded as equals. (295)

Elite model A view of society as ruled by a small group of individuals who share a common set of political and economic interests. (363)

Endogamy The restriction of mate selection to people within the same group. (298)

Environmental justice A legal strategy based on claims that racial minorities are subjected disproportionately to environmental hazards. (435)

Equilibrium model Talcott Parsons's functionalist view of society as tending toward a state of stability or balance. (451)

Esteem The reputation that a particular individual has earned within an occupation. (196)

Ethnic group A group that is set apart from others because of its national origin or distinctive cultural patterns. (225)

Ethnocentrism The tendency to assume that one's culture and way of life represent the norm or are superior to all others. (69, 229)

Ethnography The study of an entire social setting through extended systematic observation. (36)

Evolutionary theory A theory of social change that holds that society is moving in a definite direction. (450)

Exogamy The requirement that people select mates outside certain groups. (298)

Experiment An artificially created situation that allows the researcher to manipulate variables. (37)

Experimental group Subjects in an experiment who are exposed to an independent variable introduced by a researcher. (37)

Exploitation theory A Marxist theory that views racial subordination in the United States as a manifestation of the class system inherent in capitalism. (234)

Expressiveness A term used by Parsons and Bales to refer to concern for maintenance of harmony and the internal emotional affairs of the family. (263)

Extended family A family in which relatives—such as grandparents, aunts, or uncles—live in the same home as parents and their children. (293)

F

Face-work A term used by Erving Goffman to refer to the efforts of people to maintain the proper image and avoid embarrassment in public. (86)

False consciousness A term used by Karl Marx to describe an attitude held by members of a class that does not accurately reflect its objective position. (193, 449)

Familism Pride in the extended family, expressed through the maintenance of close ties and strong obligations to kinfolk. (301)

Family A set of people related by blood, marriage (or some other agreed-upon relationship), or adoption who share the primary responsibility for reproduction and caring for members of society. (291)

Fertility The amount of reproduction among women of childbearing age. (381)

Folkways Norms governing everyday social behavior whose violation raises comparatively little concern. (62)

Force The actual or threatened use of coercion to impose one's will on others. (356)

Formal norms Norms that generally have been written down and that specify strict rules for punishment of violators. (61)

Formal organization A special-purpose group designed and structured for maximum efficiency. (140)

Formal social control Social control carried out by authorized agents, such as police officers, judges, school administrators, and employers. (163)

Functionalist perspective A sociological approach that emphasizes the way that parts of a society are structured to maintain its stability. (13)

G

Gemeinschaft A term used by Ferdinand Tönnies to describe close-knit communities, often found in rural areas, in which strong personal bonds unite members. (119)

Gender roles Expectations regarding the proper behavior, attitudes, and activities of males and females. (91, 259)

Generalized others A term used by George Herbert Mead to refer to the child's awareness of the attitudes, viewpoints, and expectations of society as a whole that a child takes into account in his or her behavior. (85)

Genocide The deliberate, systematic killing of an entire people or nation. (236)

Gentrification The resettlement of low-income city neighborhoods by prosperous families and business firms. (437)

Gerontology The scientific study of the sociological and psychological aspects of aging and the problems of the aged. (275)

Gesellschaft A term used by Ferdinand Tönnies to describe communities, often urban, that are large and impersonal with little commitment to the group or consensus on values. (120)

Glass ceiling An invisible barrier that blocks the promotion of a qualified individual in a work environment because of the individual's gender, race, or ethnicity. (232, 268)

Goal displacement Overzealous conformity to official regulations within a bureaucracy. (142)

Group Any number of people with similar norms, values, and expectations who interact with one another on a regular basis. (113, 135)

Growth rate The difference between births and deaths, plus the difference between immigrants and emigrants, per 1,000 population. (384)

H

Hawthorne effect The unintended influence that observers or experiments can have on their subjects. (38)

Health As defined by the World Health Organization, a state of complete physical, mental, and social well-being, and not merely the absence of disease and infirmity. (391)

Health maintenance organizations (HMOs) Organizations that provide comprehensive medical services for a preestablished fee. (407)

Hidden curriculum Standards of behavior that are deemed proper by society and are taught subtly in schools. (336)

Holistic medicine A means of health maintenance using therapies in which the health care practitioner considers the person's physical, mental, emotional, and spiritual characteristics. (402)

Homophobia Fear of and prejudice against homosexuality. (125, 260)

Horizontal mobility The movement of an individual from one social position to another of the same rank. (205)

Horticultural societies Preindustrial societies in which people plant seeds and crops rather than subsist merely on available foods. (121)

Human ecology An area of study concerned with the interrelationships between people and their spatial setting and physical environment. (418)

Human relations approach An approach to the study of formal organizations that emphasizes the role of people, communication, and participation within a bureaucracy and tends to focus on the informal structure of the organization. (146)

Hunting-and-gathering society A preindustrial society in which people rely on whatever foods and fiber are readily available in order to live. (121)

Hypothesis A speculative statement about the relationship between two or more variables. (31)

I

Ideal type A construct or model that serves as a measuring rod against which specific cases can be evaluated. (10, 141)

Impression management A term used by Erving Goffman to refer to the altering of the presentation of the self in order to create distinctive appearances and satisfy particular audiences. (86)

Incest taboo The prohibition of sexual relationships between certain culturally specified relatives. (298)

Incidence The number of new cases of a specific disorder occurring within a given population during a stated period of time. (396)

Income Salaries and wages. (190)

Independent variable The variable in a causal relationship that, when altered, causes or influences a change in a second variable. (31)

Industrial city A city characterized by relatively large size, open competition, an open class system, and elaborate specialization in the manufacturing of goods. (417)

Industrial society A society that depends on mechanization to produce its economic goods and services. (122, 353)

Infant mortality rate The number of deaths of infants under one year of age per 1,000 live births in a given year. (384)

Influence The exercise of power through a process of persuasion. (356)

Informal norms Norms that generally are understood but are not precisely recorded. (61)

Informal social control Social control carried out by people casually through such means as laughter, smiles, and ridicule. (163)

In-group Any group or category to which people feel they belong. (136)

Innovation The process of introducing new elements into a culture through either discovery or invention. (57)

Institutional discrimination The denial of opportunities and equal rights to individuals and groups that results from the normal operations of a society. (232, 266)

Instrumentality A term used by Parsons and Bales to refer to emphasis on tasks, focus on more distant goals, and a concern for the external relationship between one's family and other social institutions. (263)

Interactionist perspective A sociological approach that generalizes about fundamental or everyday forms of social interaction. (16)

Interest group A voluntary association of citizens who attempt to influence public policy. (363)

Intergenerational mobility Changes in the social position of children relative to their parents. (205)

Interview A face-to-face or telephone questioning of a respondent to obtain desired information. (36)

Intragenerational mobility Changes in a person's social position within his or her adult life. (205)

Invention The combination of existing cultural items into a form that did not previously exist. (57)

Iron law of oligarchy A principle of organizational life developed by Robert Michels under which even democratic organizations will become bureaucracies ruled by a few individuals. (144)

Issei The early Japanese immigrants to the United States. (244)

K

Kinship The state of being related to others. (294)

L

Labeling theory An approach to deviance that attempts to explain why certain people are viewed as deviants while others engaging in the same behavior are not. (172)

Laissez-faire A form of capitalism under which people compete freely, with minimal government intervention in the economy. (354)

Language An abstract system of word meanings and symbols for all aspects of culture. It also includes gestures and other nonverbal communication. (58)

Latent functions Unconscious or unintended functions; hidden purposes. (14)

Law Governmental social control. (61, 164)

Legal-rational authority Max Weber's term for power made legitimate by law. (357)

Liberation theology Use of a church, primarily Roman Catholicism, in a political effort to eliminate poverty, discrimination, and other forms of injustice evident in a secular society. (325)

Life chances Max Weber's term for people's opportunities to provide themselves with material goods, positive living conditions, and favorable life experiences. (202)

Life expectancy The average number of years a person can be expected to live under current mortality conditions. (384)

Looking-glass self A concept used by Charles Horton Cooley that emphasizes the self as the product of our social interactions with others. (84)

Luddites Rebellious craft workers in nineteenth-century England who destroyed new factory machinery as part of their resistance to the industrial revolution. (455)

M

Machismo A sense of virility, personal worth, and pride in one's maleness. (301)

Macrosociology Sociological investigation that concentrates on large-scale phenomena or entire civilizations. (13)

Manifest functions Open, stated, and conscious functions. (14)

Master status A status that dominates others and thereby determines a person's general position within society. (110)

Material culture The physical or technological aspects of our daily lives. (58)

Matriarchy A society in which women dominate in family decision making. (295)

Matrilineal descent A kinship system that favors the relatives of the mother. (294)

McDonaldization The process by which the principles of the fast-food restaurant have come to dominate certain sectors of society, both in the United States and throughout the world. (135)

Megachurches Large worship centers affiliated only loosely, if at all, with existing denominations. (329)

Megalopolis A densely populated area containing two or more cities and their surrounding suburbs. (418)

Microsociology Sociological investigation that stresses study of small groups and often uses laboratory experimental studies. (13)

Minority group A subordinate group whose members have significantly less control or power over their own lives than the members of a dominant or majority group have over theirs. (225)

Modernization The far-reaching process by which a society moves from traditional or less developed institutions to those characteristic of more developed societies. (211)

Modernization theory A functionalist approach that proposes that modernization and development will gradually improve the lives of people in peripheral nations. (211)

Monogamy A form of marriage in which one woman and one man are married only to each other. (293)

Monopoly Control of a market by a single business firm. (354)

Morbidity rates The incidence of diseases in a given population. (396)

Mores Norms deemed highly necessary to the welfare of a society. (62)

Mortality rate The incidence of death in a given population. (396)

Multilinear evolutionary theory A theory of social change that holds that change can occur in several ways and does not inevitably lead in the same direction. (451)

Multinational corporations Commercial organizations that are headquartered in one country but do business throughout the world. (209)

Multiple-nuclei theory A theory of urban growth that views growth as emerging from many centers of development, each of which may reflect a particular urban need or activity. (421)

N

Natural science The study of the physical features of nature and the ways in which they interact and change. (6)

Negotiated order A social structure that derives its existence from the social interactions through which people define and redefine its character. (109)

Negotiation The attempt to reach agreement with others concerning some objective. (108)

Neocolonialism Continuing dependence of former colonies on foreign countries. (207)

New religious movement (NRM) or **cult** A generally small, secretive religious group that represents either a new religion or a major innovation of an existing faith. (331)

New social movements Organized collective activities that promote autonomy and self-determination as well as improvements in the quality of life. (450)

New urban sociology   An approach to urbanization that considers the interplay of local, national, and worldwide forces and their effect on local space, with special emphasis on the impact of global economic activity. (421)

Nisei   Japanese born in the United States who were descendants of the Issei. (244)

Nonmaterial culture   Cultural adjustments to material conditions, such as customs, beliefs, patterns of communication, and ways of using material objects. (58)

Nonverbal communication   The sending of messages through the use of posture, facial expressions, and gestures. (16)

Normal accidents   Failures that are inevitable, given the manner in which human and technological systems are organized. (461)

Norms   Established standards of behavior maintained by a society. (61)

Nuclear family   A married couple and their unmarried children living together. (291)

O

Obedience   Compliance with higher authorities in a hierarchical structure. (160)

Objective method   A technique for measuring social class that assigns individuals to classes on the basis of criteria such as occupation, education, income, and place of residence. (196)

Observation   A research technique in which an investigator collects information through direct participation in and/or observation of a group, tribe, or community. (36)

Open system   A social system in which the position of each individual is influenced by his or her achieved status. (205)

Operational definition   An explanation of an abstract concept that is specific enough to allow a researcher to measure the concept. (30)

Organized crime   The work of a group that regulates relations between various criminal enterprises involved in the smuggling and sale of drugs, prostitution, gambling, and other activities. (175)

Out-group   A group or category to which people feel they do not belong. (136, 175)

P

Patriarchy   A society in which men dominate family decision making. (295)

Patrilineal descent   A kinship system that favors the relatives of the father. (294)

Personality   In everyday speech, a person's typical patterns of attitudes, needs, characteristics, and behavior. (81)

Peter principle   A principle of organizational life, originated by Laurence J. Peter, according to which each individual within a hierarchy tends to rise to his or her level of incompetence. (143)

Pluralism   Mutual respect between the various groups in a society for one another's cultures, which allows minorities to express their own cultures without experiencing prejudice. (238)

Pluralist model   A view of society in which many competing groups within the community have access to governmental officials so that no single group is dominant. (365)

Political action committee (PAC)   A political committee established by an interest group—say, a national bank, corporation, trade association, or cooperative or membership association—to solicit contributions for candidates or political parties. (363)

Political socialization   The process by which individuals acquire political attitudes and develop patterns of political behavior. (357)

Political system   The social institution that relies on a recognized set of procedures for implementing and achieving the goals of a group. (353)

Politics   In Harold D. Lasswell's words, "who gets what, when, and how." (356)

Polyandry   A form of polygamy in which a woman can have several husbands at the same time. (293)

Polygamy   A form of marriage in which an individual can have several husbands or wives simultaneously. (293)

Polygyny   A form of polygamy in which a husband can have several wives at the same time. (293)

Population pyramid   A special type of bar chart that shows the distribution of the population by gender and age. (387)

Postindustrial city   A city in which global finance and the electronic flow of information dominate the economy. (417)

Postindustrial society   A society whose economic system is primarily engaged in the processing and control of information. (122, 417)

Postmodern society   A technologically sophisticated society that is preoccupied with consumer goods and media images. (122)

Power   The ability to exercise one's will over others. (193, 356)

Power elite   A term used by C. Wright Mills for a small group of military, industrial, and government leaders who control the fate of the United States. (363)

Preindustrial city   A city with only a few thousand people living within its borders and characterized by a relatively closed class system and limited mobility. (416)

Prejudice   A negative attitude toward an entire category of people, such as a racial or ethnic minority. (229)

Prestige   The respect and admiration that an occupation holds in a society. (196)

Prevalence   The total number of cases of a specific disorder that exist at a given time. (396)

Primary group   A small group characterized by intimate, face-to-face association and cooperation. (135)

Profane   The ordinary and commonplace elements of life, as distinguished from the sacred. (323)

Professional criminal   A person who pursues crime as a day-to-day occupation, developing skilled techniques and enjoying a certain degree of status among other criminals. (174)

Proletariat   Karl Marx's term for the working class in a capitalist society. (193)

Protestant ethic   Max Weber's term for the disciplined work ethic, this-worldly concerns, and rational orientation to life emphasized by John Calvin and his followers. (325)

Q

Qualitative research   Research that relies on what is seen in the field or naturalistic settings more than on statistical data. (36)

Quantitative research   Research that collects and reports data primarily in numerical form. (36)

Questionnaire   A printed research instrument employed to obtain desired information from a respondent. (36)

R

Racial group   A group that is set apart from others because of obvious physical differences. (225)

Racism   The belief that one race is supreme and all others are innately inferior. (229)

Random sample   A sample for which every member of the entire population has the same chance of being selected. (32)

Reference group   Any group that individuals use as a standard in evaluating themselves and their own behavior. (137)

Relative deprivation   The conscious feeling of a negative discrepancy between legitimate expectations and present actualities. (448)

Relative poverty   A floating standard of deprivation by which people at the bottom of a society, whatever their lifestyles, are judged to be disadvantaged in comparison with the nation as a whole. (199)

Reliability   The extent to which a measure provides consistent results. (33)

Religion   According to Émile Durkheim, a unified system of beliefs and practices relative to sacred things. (321)

Religious beliefs Statements to which members of a particular religion adhere. (327)

Religious experience The feeling or perception of being in direct contact with the ultimate reality, such as a divine being, or of being overcome with religious emotion. (327)

Religious rituals Practices required or expected of members of a faith. (327)

Representative sample A selection from a larger population that is statistically found to be typical of that population. (32)

Research design A detailed plan or method for obtaining data scientifically. (34)

Resocialization The process of discarding former behavior patterns and accepting new ones as part of a transition in one's life. (89)

Resource mobilization The ways in which a social movement utilizes such resources as money, political influence, access to the media, and personnel. (449)

Rites of passage Rituals marking the symbolic transition from one social position to another. (88)

Role conflict Difficulties that occur when incompatible expectations arise from two or more social positions held by the same person. (112)

Role exit The process of disengagement from a role that is central to one's self-identity and reestablishment of an identity in a new role. (113)

Role strain Difficulties that result from the differing demands and expectations associated with the same social position. (112)

Role taking The process of mentally assuming the perspective of another, thereby enabling one to respond from that imagined viewpoint. (85)

Routine activities theory The notion that criminal victimization increases when there is a convergence of motivated offenders and suitable targets. (171)

S

Sacred Elements beyond everyday life that inspire awe, respect, and even fear. (321)

Sanctions Penalties and rewards for conduct concerning a social norm. (63, 159)

Sapir-Whorf hypothesis A hypothesis concerning the role of language in shaping cultures. It holds that language is culturally determined and serves to influence our mode of thought. (60)

Science The body of knowledge obtained by methods based upon systematic observation. (6)

Scientific management approach Another name for the *classical theory* of formal organizations. (146)

Scientific method A systematic, organized series of steps that ensures maximum objectivity and consistency in researching a problem. (29)

Secondary analysis A variety of research techniques that make use of publicly accessible information and data. (38)

Secondary group A formal, impersonal group in which there is little social intimacy or mutual understanding. (135)

Sect A relatively small religious group that has broken away from some other religious organization to renew what it views as the original vision of the faith. (330)

Secularization The process through which religion's influence on other social institutions diminishes. (321)

Segregation The act of physically separating two groups; often imposed on a minority group by a dominant group. (237)

Self According to George Herbert Mead, the sum total of people's conscious perceptions of their own identity as distinct from others. (84)

Self-fulfilling prophecy The tendency of people to respond to and act on the basis of stereotypes, leading to validation of false definitions. (227)

Serial monogamy A form of marriage in which a person can have several spouses in his or her lifetime but only one spouse at a time. (293)

Sexism The ideology that one sex is superior to the other. (266)

Sexual harassment Behavior that occurs when work benefits are made contingent on sexual favors (as a "quid pro quo") or when touching, lewd comments, or appearance of pornographic material creates a "hostile environment" in the workplace. (148)

Sick role Societal expectations about the attitudes and behavior of a person viewed as being ill. (391)

Significant others A term used by George Herbert Mead to refer to those individuals who are most important in the development of the self, such as parents, friends, and teachers. (86)

Single-parent families Families in which there is only one parent present to care for children. (305)

Slavery A system of enforced servitude in which people are legally owned by others and in which enslaved status is transferred from parents to children. (190)

Small group A group small enough for all members to interact simultaneously, that is, to talk with one another or at least be acquainted. (137)

Social change Significant alteration over time in behavior patterns and culture, including norms and values. (447)

Social constructionist perspective An approach to deviance that emphasizes the role of culture in the creation of the deviant identity. (173)

Social control The techniques and strategies for preventing deviant human behavior in any society. (159)

Social epidemiology The study of the distribution of disease, impairment, and general health status across a population. (396)

Social inequality A condition in which members of a society have different amounts of wealth, prestige, or power. (189)

Social institutions Organized patterns of beliefs and behavior centered on basic social needs. (116)

Social interaction The ways in which people respond to one another. (107)

Socialism An economic system under which the means of production and distribution are collectively owned. (354)

Socialization The process whereby people learn the attitudes, values, and actions appropriate for individuals as members of a particular culture. (81)

Social mobility Movement of individuals or groups from one position of a society's stratification system to another. (205)

Social movements Organized collective activities to bring about or resist fundamental change in an existing group or society. (447)

Social network A series of social relationships that links a person directly to others and therefore indirectly to still more people. (114)

Social role A set of expectations of people who occupy a given social position or status. (110)

Social science The study of various aspects of human society. (6)

Social structure The way in which a society is organized into predictable relationships. (107)

Societal-reaction approach Another name for *labeling theory.* (172)

Society A fairly large number of people who live in the same territory, are relatively independent of people outside it, and participate in a common culture. (55)

Sociobiology The systematic study of the biological bases of social behavior. (84)

Sociocultural evolution The process of change and development in human societies that results from cumulative growth in their stores of cultural information. (120)

Sociological imagination An awareness of the relationship between an individual and the wider society. (5)

Sociology The systematic study of social behavior and human groups. (5)

Squatter settlements Areas occupied by the very poor on the fringes of cities, in which housing is often constructed by the settlers themselves from discarded material. (420)

Status A term used by sociologists to refer to any of the full range of socially defined positions within a large group or society. (109)

Status group A term used by Max Weber to refer to people who have the same prestige or lifestyle, independent of their class positions. (193)

Stereotypes Unreliable generalizations about all members of a group that do not recognize individual differences within the group. (227)

Stigma A label used to devalue members of deviant social groups. (166)

Stratification A structured ranking of entire groups of people that perpetuates unequal economic rewards and power in a society. (189)

Subculture A segment of society that shares a distinctive pattern of mores, folkways, and values that differs from the pattern of the larger society. (67)

Suburb According to the Census Bureau, any territory within a metropolitan area that is not included in the central city. (426)

Survey A study, generally in the form of interviews or questionnaires, that provides sociologists and other researchers with information concerning how people think and act. (35)

Symbols The gestures, objects, and language that form the basis of human communication. (85)

T

Teacher-expectancy effect The impact that a teacher's expectations about a student's performance may have on the student's actual achievements. (337)

Technology Information about how to use the material resources of the environment to satisfy human needs and desires. (57, 120, 456)

Telecommuters Employees who work full-time or part-time at home rather than in an outside office and who are linked to their supervisors and colleagues through computer terminals, phone lines, and fax machines. (147, 457)

Theory In sociology, a set of statements that seeks to explain problems, actions, or behavior. (8)

Total fertility rate (TFR) The average number of children born alive to a woman, assuming that she conforms to current fertility rates. (384)

Total institutions A term coined by Erving Goffman to refer to institutions that regulate all aspects of a person's life under a single authority, such as prisons, the military, mental hospitals, and convents. (89)

Tracking The practice of placing students in specific curriculum groups on the basis of test scores and other criteria. (336)

Trade unions Organizations that seek to improve the material status of their members, all of whom perform a similar job or work for a common employer. (368)

Traditional authority Legitimate power conferred by custom and accepted practice. (356)

Trained incapacity The tendency of workers in a bureaucracy to become so specialized that they develop blind spots and fail to notice obvious problems. (141)

Triad A three-member group. (138)

U

Underclass Long-term poor people who lack training and skills. (200)

Unilinear evolutionary theory A theory of social change that holds that all societies pass through the same successive stages of evolution and inevitably reach the same end. (451)

Urban ecology An area of study that focuses on the interrelationships between people and their environment. (418)

Urbanism Distinctive patterns of social behavior evident among city residents. (418)

V

Validity The degree to which a scale or measure truly reflects the phenomenon under study. (33)

Value neutrality Max Weber's term for objectivity of sociologists in the interpretation of data. (41)

Values Collective conceptions of what is considered good, desirable, and proper—or bad, undesirable, and improper—in a culture. (63)

Variable A measurable trait or characteristic that is subject to change under different conditions. (31)

Verstehen The German word for "understanding" or "insight"; used by Max Weber to stress the need for sociologists to take into account people's emotions, thoughts, beliefs, and attitudes. (10)

Vertical mobility The movement of a person from one social position to another of a different rank. (205)

Vested interests Veblen's term for those people or groups who will suffer in the event of social change and who have a stake in maintaining the status quo. (454)

Victimization surveys Questionnaires or interviews used to determine whether people have been victims of crime. (177)

Victimless crimes A term used by sociologists to describe the willing exchange among adults of widely desired, but illegal, goods and services. (176)

Vital statistics Records of births, deaths, marriages, and divorces gathered through a registration system maintained by governmental units. (384)

W

Wealth An inclusive term encompassing all of a person's material assets, including land and other types of property. (190)

White-collar crime Crimes committed by affluent individuals or corporations in the course of their daily business activities. (175)

World systems analysis Immanuel Wallerstein's view of the global economic system as divided between certain industrialized nations that control wealth and developing countries that are controlled and exploited. (207, 422)

X

Xenocentrism The belief that the products, styles, or ideas of one's society are inferior to those that originate elsewhere. (70)

Z

Zero population growth (ZPG) The state of a population with a growth rate of zero, achieved when the number of births plus immigrants is equal to the number of deaths plus emigrants. (390)

Zoning laws Legal provisions stipulating land use and architectural design of housing sometimes used as a means of keeping racial minorities and low-income people out of suburban areas. (428)

F. Borgatta and Marie L. Borgatta. New York: Macmillan.

Brannon, Robert. 1976. "Ideology, Myth, and Reality: Sex Equality in Israel." *Sex Roles* 6:403–419.

Braxton, Greg. 1999. "A Mad Dash for Diversity." *Los Angeles Times,* August 9, pp. F1, F10.

Bray, James H., and John Kelly. 1999. *Stepfamilies: Love, Marriage, and Parenting in the First Decade.* New York: Broadway Books.

Brewer, Rose M. 1989. "Black Women and Feminist Sociology: The Emerging Perspective." *American Sociologist* 20(Spring):57–70.

Brint, Steven. 1998. *Schools and Societies.* Thousand Oaks, CA: Pine Forge Press.

Bronson, P. 1999. *The Nudist in the Late Shift and Other True Tales of Silicon Valley.* New York: Random House.

Brown, Robert McAfee. 1980. *Gustavo Gutierrez.* Atlanta: John Knox.

Bruni, Frank. 1998. "A Small-But-Growing Sorority Is Giving Birth to Children for Gay Men." *New York Times,* June 25, p. A12.

Bryant, Adam. 1999. "American Pay Rattles Foreign Partners." *New York Times,* January 17, sec. 6, pp. 1, 4.

Buckley, Stephen. 1997. "Left Behind Prosperity's Door." *Washington Post National Weekly Edition,* March 24, pp. 8–9.

Buechler, Steven M. 1995. "New Social Movement Theories." *Sociological Quarterly* 36(3):441–464.

Bulle, Wolfgang F. 1987. *Crossing Cultures? Southeast Asian Mainland.* Atlanta: Centers for Disease Control.

Bunzel, John H. 1992. *Race Relations on Campus: Stanford Students Speak.* Stanford, CA: Portable Stanford.

Bureau of the Census. 1970. *Statistical Abstract of the United States, 1970.* Washington, DC: U.S. Government Printing Office.

———. 1975. *Historical Statistics of the United States, Colonial Times to 1970.* Washington, DC: U.S. Government Printing Office.

———. 1981. *Statistical Abstract of the United States, 1981.* Washington, DC: U.S. Government Printing Office.

———. 1991a. "Marital Status and Living Arrangements: March 1990." *Current Population Reports,* ser. P-20, no. 450. Washington, DC: U.S. Government Printing Office.

———. 1991b. "Half of the Nation's Population Lives in Large Metropolitan Areas." Press release, February 21.

———. 1994. *Statistical Abstract of the United States, 1994.* Washington, DC: U.S. Government Printing Office.

———. 1995. *Statistical Abstract of the United States, 1995.* Washington, DC: U.S. Government Printing Office.

———. 1996a. *1992 Women-Owned Businesses.* Washington, DC: U.S. Government Printing Office.

———. 1996b. *Statistical Abstract of the United States, 1996.* Washington DC: U.S. Government Printing Office.

———. 1997a. *Statistical Abstract of the United States, 1997.* Washington, DC: U.S. Government Printing Office.

———. 1997b. "Geographical Mobility: March 1995 to March 1996." *Current Population Reports,* ser. P-20, no. 497. Washington, DC: U.S. Government Printing Office.

———. 1998a. "Race of Wife by Race of Husband." Internet release of June 10.

———. 1998c. *Statistical Abstract of the United States, 1998.* Washington, DC: U.S. Government Printing Office.

———. 1998d,e. Unpub.Tables—Marital Status and Living Arrangements: March 1998 (Update). Accessed July 26, 1999 (http://www.census.gov/prod/99pubs/p20-514u.pdf).

———. 1998f. Voting and Registration: November 1996. Internet release of October 17, 1997. Accessed July 17, 1998 (http://www.census.gov/population/socdemo/voting/history/vot01.txt).

———. 1999a. *Statistical Abstract of the United States, 1996.* Washington, DC: U.S. Government Printing Office.

———. 1999b. "The Asian and Pacific Islander Population in the United States: March 1998 (Update) (PP1-113). Table 9." *Total Money Income in 1997 of Families.* Accessed August 3, 1999 (http://www.census.gov/population/sucdemo/race/api98/table09.txt).

———. 1999i. "Money Income in the United States." *Current Population Reports,* ser. P-60, no. 206. Washington, DC: U.S. Government Printing Office.

———. 2000a. *Statistical Abstract of the United States, 2000.* Washington, DC: U.S. Government Printing Office.

———. 2000b. "The Hispanic Population in the United States." *Current Population Reports,* ser. P20–527. Washington, DC: U.S. Government Printing Office.

———. 2000c. "National Population Projections." Internet release of January 13. Accessed May 11, 2000 (http://www.census.gov/population/www/projection/natsum-T3html).

———. 2000d. "Money Income in the United States 1999." *Current Population Reports,* ser. P60, no. 209. Washington, DC: U.S. Government Printing Office.

Bureau of Labor Statistics. 1999a. "Comparative Civilian Labor Force Statistics for Ten Countries 1959–1990." Posted April 13, 1999. Accessed October 9, 1999 (ftp://ftp.bls.gov/pub/special.requests/ForeignLabor/flslforc.txt).

———. 1999b. "What Women Earned in 1998." *Issues in Labor Statistics.* Washington, DC: U.S. Government Printing Office.

———. 2000. "Employment Status of the Civilian Population by Race, Sex, Age, and Hispanic Origin." Accessed at http://www.bls.gen/news.release.

Bureau of Primary Health Care. 1999. Home Page. Accessed January 18, 2000 (http://www.bphc.hrsa.gov/bphcfactsheet.htm).

Burgess, Ernest W. 1925. "The Growth of the City." Pp. 47–62 in *The City,* edited by Robert E. Park, Ernest W. Burgess, and Roderick D. McKenzie. Chicago: University of Chicago Press.

Burkett, Elinor. 2000. *The Baby Boom: How Family Friendly America Cheats the Childless.* New York: Free Press.

Burns, John R. 1998. "Once Widowed in India, Twice Scorned." *New York Times,* March 29, p. A1.

Burt, Martha R. et al. 1999. *Homeless: Programs and the People They Save.* Washington, DC: Urban Institute.

Bush, Melanie. 1993. "The Doctor Is Out," *Village Voice* 38, June 22,p. 18.

Butler, Daniel Allen. 1998. *"Unsinkable:" The Full Story.* Mechanicsburg, PA: Stackpole Books.

Butler, Robert N. 1990. "A Disease Called Ageism." *Journal of American Geriatrics Society* 38(February): 178–180.

Butterfield, Fox. 1996. "U.S. Has Plan to Broaden Availability of DNA Testing." *New York Times,* June 14, p. A8.

C

Calhoun, Craig. 1998. "Community Without Propinquity Revisited." *Sociological Inquiry* 68(Summer): 373–397.

Calhoun, David B. 2000. "Learning at Home." P. 193 in *Yearbook of the Encyclopedia Britannica 2000.* Chicago: Encyclopedia Britannica.

Camus, Albert. 1948. *The Plague.* New York: Random House.

Caplan, Ronald L. 1989. "The Commodification of American Health Care." *Social Science and Medicine* 28(11): 1139–1148.

Cardarelli, Luise. 1996. "The Lost Girls: China May Come to Regret Its Preference for Boys." *Utne Reader,* May–June, pp. 13–14.

Carey, Anne R., and Elys A. McLean. 1997. "Heard It Through the Grapevine?" *USA Today,* September 15, p. B1.

———, and Grant Jerding. 1999. "What Workers Want." *USA Today,* August 17, p. B1.

———, and Jerry Mosemak. 1999. "Big on Religion." *USA Today,* April 1, p. D1.

Carty, Win. 1999. "Greater Dependence on Cars Leads to More Pollution in World's Cities." *Population Today* 27(December):1–2.

Casper, Lynne M., and Loretta E. Bass. 1998. "Voting and Registration in the Election of November 1996." *Current Population Reports,* ser. P-20, no. 504. Washington, DC: U.S. Government Printing Office.

Castelli, Jim. 1996. "How to Handle Personal Information." *American Demographics* 18(March):50–52, 57.

Castells, Manuel. 1983. *The City and the Grass Roots.* Berkeley: University of California Press.

———. 1996. *The Information Age: Economy, Society and Culture.* Vol. 1 of *The Rise of the Network Society.* London: Blackwell.

———. 1997. *The Power of Identity.* Vol. 1 of *The Information Age: Economy, Society and Culture.* London: Blackwell.

———. 1998. *End of Millennium.* Vol. 3 of *The Information Age: Economy, Society and Culture.* London: Blackwell.

———. 2000. *The Information Age: Economy, Society and Culture* (3 vols.). 2d. ed. Oxford and Malden, MA: Blackwell.

Catalyst. 1999. *1999 Catalyst Census of Women Board of Directors of the Fortune 1000.* New York: Catalyst.

Cavanagh, John, and Robin Broad. 1996. "Global Reach: Workers Fight the Multinationals." *The Nation* 262(March 18):21–24.

CBS News. 1979. Transcript of *Sixty Minutes* segment, "I Was Only Following Orders." March 31, pp. 2–8.

———. 1998. "Experimental Prison." *Sixty Minutes.* June 30.

Center for the American Woman and Politics. 1999. *Women in Elective Office 1998.* New Brunswick, NJ: CAWP, Rutgers University.

Centers for Disease Control and Prevention. 2000a. "Abortion Surveillance: Preliminary Analysis—United States, 1997." *Morbidity and Mortality Weekly Reports,* January 7, p. 2.

———. 2000b. "Commentary." *HIV/AIDS Surveillance Supplemental Report 5,* January 18, p. 1.

Center for Public Integrity. 1998. *Nothing Sacred: The Politics of Privacy.* Washington, DC: CPI.

Cetron, Marvin J., and Owen Davies. 1991. "Trends Shaping the World." *Futurist* 20(September–October):11–21.

Cha, Ariena Eunjung. 2000. "Painting a Portrait of Dot-Camaraderie." *The Washington Post,* October 26, pp. E1, E10.

Chaddock, Gail Russell. 1998. "The Challenge for Schools: Connecting Adults with Kids." *Christian Science Monitor,* August 4, p. B7.

Chalfant, H. Paul, Robert E. Beckley, and C. Eddie Palmer. 1994. *Religion in Contemporary Society.* 3d ed. Itasca, IL: F. E. Peacock.

Chambliss, William. 1972. "Introduction." Pp. ix–xi in Harry King, *Box Man.* New York: Harper and Row.

———. 1973. "The Saints and the Roughnecks." *Society* 11(November–December):24–31.

Charmaz, Kathy, and Debora A. Paterniti, eds. 1999. *Health, Illness, and Healing: Society, Social Context, and Self.* Los Angeles, CA: Roxbury.

Charter, David, and Jill Sherman. 1996. "Schools Must Teach New Code of Values." *London Times,* January 15, p. 1.

Chase-Dunn, Christopher, and Peter Grimes. 1995. "World-Systems Analysis." Pp. 387–417 in *Annual Review of Sociology, 1995,* edited by John Hagan. Palo Alto, CA: Annual Reviews.

Cheng, Wei-yuan, and Lung-li Liao. 1994. "Women Managers in Taiwan." Pp. 143–159 in *Competitive Frontiers: Women Managers in a Global Economy,* edited by Nancy J. Adler and Dafna N. Izraeli. Cambridge, MA: Blackwell Business.

Cherlin, Andrew J. 1999. *Public and Private Families: An Introduction.* 2d ed. New York: McGraw-Hill.

———, and Frank Furstenberg. 1992. *The New American Grandparent: A Place in the Family, A Life Apart.* Cambridge, MA: Harvard University Press.

———, and ———. 1994. "Stepfamilies in the United States: A Reconsideration." Pp. 359–381 in *Annual Review of Sociology, 1994,* edited by John Hagan. Palo Alto, CA: Annual Reviews.

Chesney-Lind, Meda, and Noelie Rodriguez. 1993. "Women under Lock and Key." *Prison Journal* 63:47–65.

Chicago Tribune. 1997a. "China Aborting Female Fetuses." October 17, p. 13.

———. 1997b. "In London, Prince Meets a Pauper, an Ex-Classmate." December 5, p. 19.

Chin, Ko-lin. 1996. *Chinatown Gangs: Extortion, Enterprise, and Ethnicity.* New York: Oxford University Press.

Chow, Esther Ngan-Ling, and S. Michael Zhao. 1995. "The Impact of the One-Child Policy on Parent-Child Relationships in the People's Republic of China." Presented at the annual meeting of the American Sociological Association, August, Washington, DC.

Christiansen, Kathleen. 1990. "Bridges over Troubled Water: How Older Workers View the Labor Market." Pp. 175–207 in *Bridges to Retirement,* edited by Peter B. Doeringer. Ithaca, NY: IRL Press.

Civic Ventures. 1999. *The New Face of Retirement: Older Americans, Civic Engagement, and the Longevity Revolution.* Washington, DC: Peter D. Hart Research Associates.

Clark, Brian L. 1999. "Internet Life: Our Town. Online." *Money* 28(September):36.

Clark, Burton, and Martin Trow. 1966. "The Organizational Context." Pp. 17–70 in *The Study of College Peer*

Groups, edited by Theodore M. Newcomb and Everett K. Wilson. Chicago: Aldine.

Clark, Candace. 1983. "Sickness and Social Control." Pp. 346–365 in *Social Interaction: Readings in Sociology,* 2d. ed., edited by Howard Robboy and Candace Clark. New York: St. Martin's.

Clark, Charles, and Jason M. Fields. 1999. "First Glance: Preliminary Analysis of Relationship, Marital Status, and Grandparents Items on the Census 2000 Dress Rehearsal." Presented at the annual meeting of the American Sociological Association, August, Chicago.

Clark, Thomas. 1994. "Culture and Objectivity." *The Humanist* 54(August):38–39.

Clarke, Lee. 1999. *Mission Improbable: Using Fantasy Documents to Tame Disaster.* Chicago: University of Chicago Press.

Clawson, Dan, and Mary Ann Clawson. 1999. "What Has Happened to the U.S. Labor Movement? Union Decline and Renewal." Pp. 95–119 in *Annual Review of Sociology,* edited by Karen S. Hook and John Hagan. Palo Alto, CA: Annual Reviews.

Cloud, John. 1998. "Sex and the Law." *Time* 151(March 23):48–54.

Cloward, Richard A. 1959. "Illegitimate Means, Anomie, and Deviant Behavior." *American Sociological Review* 24(April):164–176.

Clymer, Adam. 2000. "College Students Not Drawn to Voting or Politics, Poll Shows." *New York Times,* January 2, p. A14.

Coatney, Caryn. 1998. "Arrest of Abortion Doctors Puts Australia Laws on Spot." *Christian Science Monitor,* March 25, p. 6.

Cockerham, William C. 1998. *Medical Sociology.* 7th ed. Upper Saddle River, NJ: Prentice-Hall.

Coeyman, Marjorie. 1999. "Schools Question the Benefits of Tracking." *Christian Science Monitor,* September 21, p. 20.

Cohen, David, ed. 1991. *The Circle of Life: Ritual from the Human Family Album.* San Francisco: Harper.

Cohen, Lawrence E., and Marcus Felson. 1979. "Social Change and Crime Rate Trends: A Routine Activities Approach." *American Sociological Review* 44:588–608.

Cohen, Patricia. 1998. "Daddy Dearest: Do You Really Matter?" *New York Times,* July 11, p. B7.

Cole, David. 1999. *No Equal Justice: Race and Class in the American Criminal Justice System.* New York: The New Press.

Cole, Elizabeth S. 1985. "Adoption, History, Policy, and Program." Pp. 638–666 in *A Handbook of Child Welfare,* edited by John Laird and Ann Hartman. New York: Free Press.

Cole, Mike. 1988. *Bowles and Gintis Revisited: Correspondence and Contradiction in Educational Theory.* Philadelphia: Falmer.

Colker, David. 1996. "Putting the Accent on World Wide Access." *Los Angeles Times* (May 21), p. E3.

Collins, Gail. 1998. "Why the Women Are Fading Away." *New York Times,* October 25, pp. 54–55.

Collins, Patricia Hill. 1991. *Black Feminist Thought: Knowledge, Consciousness, and the Politics of Empowerment.* New York: Routledge.

Collins, Randall. 1975. *Conflict Sociology: Toward an Explanatory Sociology.* New York: Academic.

———. 1980. "Weber's Last Theory of Capitalism: A Systematization." *American Sociological Review* 45(December):925–942.

———. 1986. *Weberian Sociological Theory.* New York: Cambridge University Press.

———. 1995. "Prediction in Macrosociology: The Case of the Soviet Collapse." *American Journal of Sociology* 100(May):1552–1593.

Commission on Behavioral and Social Sciences Education. 1998. *Protecting Youth at Work.* Washington, DC: National Academy Press.

Commission on Civil Rights. 1976. *A Guide to Federal Laws and Regulations Prohibiting Sex Discrimination.* Washington, DC: U.S. Government Printing Office.

———. 1981. *Affirmative Action in the 1980s: Dismantling the Process of Discrimination.* Washington, DC: U.S. Government Printing Office.

Commoner, Barry. 1971. *The Closing Circle.* New York: Knopf.

———. 1990. *Making Peace with the Planet.* New York: Pantheon.

Computer Security Institute. 1999. "1999 CSI/FBI Computer Crime and Security Survey." *Computer Security Issues and Trends* 5(Winter):1–15.

Conrad, Peter, ed. 1997. *The Sociology of Health and Illness: Critical Perspectives.* 5th ed. New York: St. Martin's.

———, and Joseph W. Schneider. 1992. *Deviance and Medicalization: From Badness to Sickness.* Expanded ed. Philadelphia: Temple University Press.

Cook, P. J., and J. A. Leitzel. 1996. *Perversity, Futility, Jeopardy: An Economic Analysis of the Attack on Gun Control.* Durham, NC: Sanford Institute of Public Policy, Duke University.

Cook, Rhodes. 1991. "The Crosscurrents of the Youth Vote." *Congressional Quarterly Weekly Report* 49(June 29): 1802.

Cooley, Charles H. 1902. *Human Nature and the Social Order.* New York: Scribner.

Cooper, Kenneth J. 1994. "Wrong Turns on the Map?" *Washington Post National Weekly Edition* 12(January 31):14.

Cooper, Richard T. 1998. "Jobs Outside High School Can Be Costly, Report Finds." *Los Angeles Times,* November 6, p. A1.

Coser, Lewis A. 1956. *The Functions of Social Conflict.* New York: Free Press.

———. 1977. *Masters of Sociological Thought: Ideas in Historical and Social Context.* 2d ed. New York: Harcourt, Brace and Jovanovich.

Coser, Rose Laub. 1984. "American Medicine's Ambiguous Progress." *Contemporary Sociology* 13(January): 9–13.

Couch, Carl. 1996. *Information Technologies and Social Orders.* Edited with an introduction by David R. Maines and Shing-Ling Chien. New York: Aldine de Gruyter.

Cox, Craig. 1999. "Prime-Time Activism." *Utne Reader* (September–October), pp. 20–22.

Cox, Oliver C. 1948. *Caste, Class and Race: A Study in Social Dynamics.* Detroit: Wayne State University Press.

Crenshaw, Edward M., Matthew Christenson, and Doyle Ray Oakey. 2000. "Demographic Transition in Ecological Focus." *American Sociological Review* 65(June):371–391.

Cressey, Donald R. 1960. "Epidemiology and Individual Contact: A Case from

Criminology." *Pacific Sociological Review* 3(Fall):47–58.

Cromwell, Paul F., James N. Olson, and D'Aunn Wester Avarey. 1995. *Breaking and Entering: An Ethnographic Analysis of Burglary.* Newbury Park, CA: Sage.

Crossette, Barbara. 1996a. "'Oldest Old,' 80 and Over, Increasing Globally." *New York Times,* December 22, p. 7.

———. 1996b. "Snubbing Human Rights," *New York Times,* April 28, p. E3.

———. 1999. "The Internet Changes Dictatorship's Rules." *New York Times,* August 1, sec. 4, p. 1.

Crouse, Kelly. 1999. "Sociology of the Titanic." *Teaching Sociology Listserv.* May 24.

Cuff, E. C., W. W. Sharrock, and D. W. Francis, eds. 1990. *Perspectives in Sociology.* 3d ed. Boston: Unwin Hyman.

Cullen, Francis T., Jr., and John B. Cullen. 1978. *Toward a Paradigm of Labeling Theory,* ser. 58. Lincoln: University of Nebraska Studies.

Cumming, Elaine, and William E. Henry. 1961. *Growing Old: The Process of Disengagement.* New York: Basic Books.

Currie, Elliot. 1985. *Confronting Crime: An American Challenge.* New York: Pantheon.

———. 1998. *Crime and Punishment in America.* New York: Metropolitan Books.

Curry, Timothy Jon. 1993. "A Little Pain Never Hurt Anyone: Athletic Career Socialization and the Normalization of Sports Injury." *Symbolic Interaction* 26(Fall):273–290.

Curtius, Mary. 1999. "Struggling Town Split Over Wal-Mart Plan." *Los Angeles Times,* July 5, pp. A1, A16–18.

Cushman, John H., Jr. 1998a. "Pollution Policy Is Unfair Burden, States Tell E. P. A." *New York Times,* May 10, pp. 1, 20.

———. 1998b. "Nike Pledges to End Child Labor and Apply U.S. Rules Abroad." *New York Times,* May 13, p. C1.

Cussins, Choris M. 1998. In *Cyborg Babies: From Techno-Sex to Techno-Tots,* edited by Robbie Davis-Floyd and Joseph Dumit. New York: Routledge.

D

Dahl, Robert A. 1961. *Who Governs?* New Haven, CT: Yale University Press.

Dahrendorf, Ralf. 1958. "Toward a Theory of Social Conflict." *Journal of Conflict Resolution* 2(June):170–183.

———. 1959. *Class and Class Conflict in Industrial Sociology.* Stanford, CA: Stanford University Press.

Dalaker, Joseph, and Bernadette D. Proctor. 2000. "Poverty in the United States." *Current Population Reports,* ser. P60, no. 210. Washington, DC: U.S. Government Printing Office.

Daley, Suzanne. 1997. "Reversing Roles in a South African Dilemma." *New York Times,* October 26, sec. WE, p. 5.

———. 2000. "French Couples Take Plunge that Falls Short of Marriage." *New York Times,* April 18, pp. A1, A4.

Dao, James. 1995. "New York's Highest Court Rules Unmarried Couples Can Adopt." *New York Times,* November 3, pp. A1, B2.

Dart, John. 1997. "Lutheran Women Wait Longer for Pastor Jobs, Survey Finds." *Los Angeles Times,* May 3, pp. B1, B5.

Daskal, Jennifer. 1998. *In Search of Shelter: The Growing Shortage of Affordable Rental Housing.* Washington, DC: Center on Budget and Policy Priorities.

Davies, Christie. 1989. "Goffman's Concept of the Total Institution: Criticisms and Revisions." *Human Studies* 12(June):77–95.

Davis, Darren W. 1997. "The Direction of Race of Interviewer Effects Among African-Americans: Donning the Black Mask." *American Journal of Political Science* 41(January):309–322.

Davis, James. 1982. "Up and Down Opportunity's Ladder." *Public Opinion* 5(June–July):11–15, 48–51.

Davis, James Allan, and Tom W. Smith. 1999. *General Social Surveys, 1972–1998.* Storrs, CT: The Roper Center.

———, and ———. 1999. *General Social Surveys, 1972–1998* [MRDF]. Storrs, CT: The Roper Center for Public Opinion Research.

Davis, Kingsley. 1937. "The Sociology of Prostitution." *American Sociological Review* 2(October):744–755.

———. 1940. "Extreme Social Isolation of a Child." *American Journal of Sociology* 45(January):554–565.

———. 1947. "A Final Note on a Case of Extreme Isolation." *American Journal of Sociology* 52(March):432–437.

———. [1949] 1995. *Human Society.* Reprint, New York: Macmillan.

———, and Wilbert E. Moore. 1945. "Some Principles of Stratification." *American Sociological Review* 10(April): 242–249.

Davis, Nanette J. 1975. *Sociological Constructions of Deviance: Perspectives and Issues in the Field.* Dubuque, IA: Wm. C. Brown.

Day, Jennifer Cheeseman. 1993. "Population Projections of the United States by Age, Sex, Race, and Hispanic Origin: 1993–2050," *Current Population Reports,* ser. P-25, no. 1104. Washington, DC: U.S. Government Printing Office.

Daycare Action Council. 2000. Interview, January 5. Chicago: Daycare Action Council of Illinois.

Death Penalty Information Center. 2000a. "The Death Penalty in 1999: Year End Report." Accessed February 13, 2000 (http://www.essential.org/ dpic/yrendrpt99.html).

———. 2000b. "History of the Death Penalty. Part II." Accessed February 13, 2000 (http://www.essential.org/dpic/ history3.html#Innocence).

———. 2000c. "Innocence: Freed From Death Row." Accessed March 20, 2000 (http://www.essential.org/dpic/ Innocent/ist.html.)

Deegan, Mary Jo, ed. 1991. *Women in Sociology: A Bio-Biographical Sourcebook.* Westport, CT: Greenwood.

Deloria, Jr., Vine. 1999. *For This Land: Writings on Religion in America.* New York: Routledge.

Denzin, Norman K., and Yvonna S. Lincoln, eds. 2000. *Handbook of Qualitative Research.* 2d ed. Thousand Oaks, CA: Sage.

DePalma, Anthony. 1999. "Rules to Protect a Culture Make for Confusion." *New York Times,* July 14, pp. B1, B2.

DeParle, Jason. 1998. "Shrinking Welfare Rolls Leave Record High Share of Minorities." *New York Times,* July 27, pp. A1, A12.

Department of Education. 1999. *Report on State Implementation of the Gun-Free Schools Act. School Year 1997–98.* Rockville, MD: Westat.

Department of Health and Human Services. 2000. "Change in TANF Caseloads (January 1993–September

1999)." Accessed August 8, 2000 (http://www.acf.dhhs.gov/news/stats/caseload.htm).

Department of Justice. 1999a. *Uniform Crime Reports, 1998.* Washington, DC: U.S. Government Printing Office.

———. 1999b. *Correctional Populations in the United States, 1996.* Washington, DC: Bureau of Justice Statistics.

Department of Labor. 1995a. *Good for Business: Making Full Use of the Nation's Capital.* Washington, DC: U.S. Government Printing Office.

———. 1995b. *A Solid Investment: Making Full Use of the Nation's Human Capital.* Washington, DC: U.S. Government Printing Office.

———. 1998. "Work and Elder Care: Facts for Caregivers and Their Employers." Accessed November 20 (http://www.dol.gov/dol/wb/public/wb_pubs/elderc.htm).

DeSimone, Bonnie. 2000. "Gold Tendency." *Chicago Tribune Magazine,* February 20, pp. 9–19.

Devine, Don. 1972. *Political Culture of the United States: The Influence of Member Values on Regime Maintenance.* Boston: Little, Brown.

Devitt, James. 1999. *Framing Gender on the Campaign Trail: Women's Executive Leadership and the Press.* New York: Women's Leadership Conference.

Dickerson, Marla. 1998. "Belief in Ideas Inspires Women to Start Businesses." *Los Angeles Times,* February 24, pp. D1, D13.

Dionne, Annette, Cecile, and Yvonne. 1997. "Letter." *Time,* December 1, p. 39.

Doeringer, Peter B., ed. 1990. *Bridges to Retirement: Older Workers in a Changing Labor Market.* Ithaca, NY: ILR Press.

Doig, Stephen, Reynolds Farley, William Frey, and Dan Gillman. 1993. *Blacks on the Block—New Patterns of Residential Segregation in a Multi-Ethnic Country.* Cambridge, MA: Harvard University Press.

Dolbeare, Kenneth M. 1982. *American Public Policy: A Citizen's Guide.* New York: McGraw-Hill.

Domhoff, G. William. 1978. *Who Really Rules? New Haven and Community Power Reexamined.* New Brunswick, NJ: Transaction.

———. 1998. *Who Rules America?* 3d ed. Mountain View, CA: Mayfield.

Domino, John C. 1995. *Sexual Harassment and the Courts.* New York: HarperCollins.

Donohue, Elizabeth, Vincent Schiraldi, and Jason Ziedenberg. 1998. *School House Hype: School Shootings and Real Risks Kids Face in America.* New York: Justice Policy Institute.

Doob, Christopher Bates. 1999. *Racism: An American Cauldron.* 3d ed. New York: Longman.

Dorai, Frances. 1998. *Insight Guide: Singapore.* Singapore: Insight Media, APA Publications.

Doress, Irwin, and Jack Nusan Porter. 1977. *Kids in Cults: Why They Join, Why They Stay, Why They Leave.* Brookline, MA: Reconciliation Associates.

Dornbusch, Sanford M. "The Sociology of Adolescence." Pp. 233–259 in *Annual Review of Sociology, 1989,* edited by W. Richard Scott and Judith Blake. Palo Alto, CA: Annual Reviews.

Dotson, Floyd. 1991. "Community." P. 55 in *Encyclopedic Dictionary of Sociology,* 4th ed. Guilford, CT: Dushkin.

Dougherty, Kevin, and Floyd M. Hammack. 1992. "Education Organization." Pp. 535–541 in *Encyclopedia of Sociology,* vol. 2, edited by Edgar F. Borgatta and Marie L. Borgatta. New York: Macmillan.

Douglas, Jack D. 1967. *The Social Meanings of Swank.* Princeton, NJ: Princeton University Press.

Dowd, James J. 1980. *Stratification among the Aged.* Monterey, CA: Brooks/Cole.

Downie, Andrew. 2000. "Brazilian Girls Turn to a Doll More Like Them." *Christian Science Monitor.* January 20. Accessed January 20, 2000 (http://www.csmonitor.com/durable/2000/01/20/fpls3-csm.shtml).

Doyle, James A. 1995. *The Male Experience.* 3d ed. Dubuque, IA: Brown & Benchmark.

———, and Michele A. Paludi. 1998. *Sex and Gender: The Human Experience.* 4th ed. New York: McGraw-Hill.

DPIC 2000c. (See Death Penalty Information Center. 2000c).

Drucker, Peter F. 1999. "Beyond the Information Revolution." *Atlantic Monthly* 284(October):42–57.

Du Bois, W. E. B. 1909. *The Negro American Family.* Atlanta University.

Reprinted 1970, Cambridge, MA: M.I.T. Press.

———. 1911. "The Girl Nobody Loved," *Social News* 2(November):3.

Duberman, Lucille. 1976. *Social Inequality: Class and Caste in America.* Philadelphia: Lippincott.

Dugger, Celia W. 1999. "Massacres of Low-Born Touch Off a Crisis in India." *New York Times,* March 15, p. A3.

Duncan, Greg J. 1994. "Welfare Can Fuel Upward Mobility." *Profiles* 18(May):6.

———, and Ken R. Smith. 1989. "The Rising Affluence of the Elderly: How Far, How Fair, and How Frail." Pp. 261–289 in *Annual Review of Sociology, 1989,* edited by W. Richard Scott and Judith Blake. Palo Alto, CA: Annual Reviews.

———, and Wei-Jun J. Yeung. 1995. "Extent and Consequences of Welfare Dependence among America's Children." *Children and Youth Service Review* 17(1–3):157–182.

Duneier, Mitchell. 1994a. "On the Job, but Behind the Scenes." *Chicago Tribune,* December 26, pp. 1, 24.

———. 1994b. "Battling for Control." *Chicago Tribune,* December 28, pp. 1, 8.

Dunlap, Riley E. 1993. "From Environmental to Ecological Problems." Pp. 707–738 in *Introduction to Social Problems,* edited by Craig Calhoun and George Ritzer. New York: McGraw-Hill.

———, and William R. Catton, Jr. 1983. "What Environmental Sociologists Have in Common." *Sociological Inquiry* 53(Spring):113–135.

Durkheim, Émile. [1893] 1933. *Division of Labor in Society.* Translated by George Simpson. Reprint, New York: Free Press.

———. [1912] 1947. *The Elementary Forms of the Religious Life.* Reprint, Glencoe, IL: Free Press.

———. [1897] 1951. *Suicide.* Translated by John A. Spaulding and George Simpson. Reprint, New York: Free Press.

———. [1845] 1964. *The Rules of Sociological Method.* Translated by Sarah A. Solovay and John H. Mueller. Reprint, New York: Free Press.

Durning, Alan B. 1990. "Life on the Brink." *World Watch* 3(March–April):22–30.

Dvany, Andres, Elizabeth Plater-Zyberk, and Jeff Speck. 2000. *Surburban Nation: The Rise of Sprawl and the Decline of the American Dream.* New York: Farrar, Straus & Giroux.

Dworkin, Rosalind J. 1982. "A Woman's Report: Numbers Are Not Enough." Pp. 375–400 in *The Minority Report,* edited by Anthony Dworkin and Rosalind Dworkin. New York: Holt.

E

Eayrs, Caroline B., Nick Ellis, and Robert S. P. Jones. 1993. "Which Label? An Investigation into the Effects of Terminology on Public Perceptions of and Attitudes toward People with Learning Difficulties." *Disability, Handicap, and Society* 8(2):111–127.

Ebaugh, Helen Rose Fuchs. 1988. *Becoming an Ex: The Process of Role Exit.* Chicago: University of Chicago Press.

Eckenwiler, Mark. 1995. "In the Eyes of the Law." *Internet World* (August):74, 76–77.

Eckholm, Erik. 1994. "While Congress Remains Silent, Health Care Transforms Itself." *New York Times,* December 18, pp. 1, 34.

The Economist. 1995. "Home Sweet Home." 336(September 9):25–26, 29, 32.

———. 1998. "Cruel and Ever More Unusual." 346(February 14).

Edmonston, Barry, and Jeff Passel. 1999. "How Immigration and Intermarriage Affect the Racial and Ethnic Composition of the U.S. Population" in *Immigration and Opportunity, Race, Ethnicity, and Employment in the United States,* edited by Frank D. Bean and Stephanie Bell-Rose. New York: Russell Sage Foundation.

Edwards, Harry. 1984. "The Black 'Dumb Jock,'" *College Board Review* 131(Spring):8–13.

Efron, Sonni. 1997. "In Japan, Even Tots Must Make the Grade." *Los Angeles Times,* February 16, pp. A1, A17.

———. 1998. "Japanese in Quandary on Fertility." *Los Angeles Times,* July 27, pp. A1, A6.

Egan, Timothy. 1995. "Many Seek Security in Private Communities." *New York Times,* September 3, pp. 1, 22.

———. 1998. "New Prosperity Brings New Conflict to Indian Country." *New York Times,* March 8, pp. 1, 24.

———. 1999. "What Price the Most Expensive Diamond of All?" *New York Times,* July 17, p. A7.

Ehrenreich, Barbara, and Deidre English. 1973. *Witches, Midwives, and Nurses: A History of Women Healers.* Old Westbury, NY: Feminist Press.

Ehrlich, Paul R. 1968. *The Population Bomb.* New York: Ballantine.

———, and Anne H. Ehrlich. 1990. *The Population Explosion.* New York: Simon and Schuster.

Eisenberg, David M. et al. 1998. "Trends in Alternative Medicine Use in the United States, 1990–1997." *Journal of the American Medical Association* 280(November 11):1569–1636.

Ekman, Paul, Wallace V. Friesen, and John Bear. 1984. "The International Language of Gestures." *Psychology Today* 18(May):64–69.

El-Badry, Samira. 1994. "The Arab-American Market." *American Demographics* 16(January):21–27, 30.

Elias, Marilyn. 1996. "Researchers Fight Child Consent Bill." *USA Today,* January 2, p. A1.

Elliott, Helene. 1997. "Having an Olympic Team Is Their Miracle on Ice." *Los Angeles Times,* March 25, Sports section, p. 5.

Elliott, Marta, and Lauren J. Krivo. 1991. "Structural Determinants of Homelessness in the United States." *Social Problems* 38(February):113–131.

Elliott, Michael. 1994. "Crime and Punishment." *Newsweek* 123(April 18):18–22.

Ellis, Virginia, and Ken Ellingwood. 1998. "Welfare to Work: Are There Enough Jobs?" *Los Angeles Times,* February 8, pp. A1, A30.

Ellison, Ralph. 1952. *Invisible Man.* New York: Random House.

Elmer-DeWitt, Philip. 1995. "Welcome to Cyberspace." *Time* 145(Special Issue, Spring):4–11.

El Nasser, Haya. 1999. "Soaring Housing Costs Are Culprit in Suburban Poverty." *USA Today,* April 28, pp. A1, A2.

Ely, Robin J. 1995. "The Power of Demography: Women's Social Construction of Gender Identity at Work." *Academy of Management Journal* 38(3):589–634.

Engardio, Pete. 1999. "Activists Without Borders." *Business Week,* October 4, pp. 144–145, 148, 150.

Engels, Friedrich. 1884. "The Origin of the Family, Private Property and the State." Pp. 392–394, excerpted in *Marx and Engels: Basic Writings on Politics and Philosophy,* edited by Lewis Feuer. Garden City, NY: Anchor, 1959.

England, Paula. 1999. "The Impact of Feminist Thought on Sociology." *Contemporary Sociology* 28(May):263–268.

Entine, Jon, and Martha Nichols. 1996. "Blowing the Whistle on Meaningless 'Good Intentions.'" *Chicago Tribune,* June 20, sec. 1, p. 21.

Epstein, Steven. 1997. *Impure Science: AIDS, Activism, and the Politics of Knowledge.* Berkeley: University of California Press.

Erikson, Kai. 1966. *Wayward Puritans: A Study in the Sociology of Deviance.* New York: Wiley.

———. 1994. *A New Species of Trouble: The Human Experience of Modern Disasters.* New York: Norton.

Espenshade, Edward B., Jr. 1990. *Rand McNally Goode's World Atlas.* 18th ed. Chicago: Rand McNally.

Etzioni, Amitai. 1964. *Modern Organization.* Englewood Cliffs, NJ: Prentice-Hall.

———. 1985. "Shady Corporate Practices." *New York Times,* November 15, p. A35.

———. 1990. "Going Soft on Corporate Crime." *Washington Post,* April 1, p. C3.

———. 1996. "Why Fear Date Rape?" *USA Today,* May 20, p. 14A.

Evans, Peter. 1979. *Dependent Development.* Princeton, NJ: Princeton University Press.

Evans, Sara. 1980. *Personal Politics: The Roots of Women's Liberation in the Civil Rights Movement and the New Left.* New York: Vintage.

F

Fager, Marty, Mike Bradley, Lonnie Danchik, and Tom Wodetski. 1971. *Unbecoming Men.* Washington, NJ: Times Change.

Fahs, Ivan J., Dan A. Lewis, C. James Carr, and Mark W. Field. 1997. "Homelessness in an Affluent Suburb: The Story of Wheaton, Illinois." Paper presented at the annual meeting of the

Illinois Sociological Association, October, Rockford, IL.

Faludi, Susan. 1999. *Stiffed: The Betrayal of the American Man.* New York: William Morrow.

Farhi, Paul, and Megan Rosenfeld. 1998. "Exporting America." *Washington Post National Weekly Edition* 16(November 30):6–7.

Farley, Maggie. 1997. "Loophole Lets More Chinese Have 2 Children." *Los Angeles Times,* October 20, pp. A1, A14–A15.

———. 1998. "Indonesia's Chinese Fearful of Backlash." *Los Angeles Times,* January 31, pp. A1, A8–A9.

Farr, Grant M. 1999. *Modern Iran.* New York: McGraw-Hill.

Feagin, Joe R. 1983. *The Urban Real Estate Game: Playing Monopoly with Real Money.* Englewood Cliffs, NJ: Prentice-Hall.

———. 1989. *Minority Group Issues in Higher Education: Learning from Qualitative Research.* Norman, OK: Center for Research on Minority Education, University of Oklahoma.

———, Harnán Vera, and Nikitah Imani. 1996. *The Agony of Education: Black Students at White Colleges and Universities.* New York: Routledge.

Featherman, David L., and Robert M. Hauser. 1978. *Opportunity and Change.* New York: Aeodus.

Federman, Joel. 1998. *1998 National Television Violence Study: Executive Summary.* Santa Barbara: University of California, Santa Barbara.

Federman, Maya et al. [8 authors]. 1996. "What Does It Mean to Be Poor in America?" *Monthly Labor Review* 119(May):3–17.

Feinglass, Joe. 1987. "Next, the McDRG." *The Progressive* 51(January):28.

Feldman, Linda. 1999. "Control of Congress in Seniors' Hands." *Christian Science Monitor,* June 21, pp. 1–4.

Felson, Marcus. 1998. *Crime and Everyday Life: Insights and Implications for Society.* 2d ed. Thousand Oaks, CA: Pine Forge Press.

Fernandez, John R. 1999. *Race, Gender and Rhetoric.* New York: McGraw-Hill.

Fernández, Sandy. 1996. "The Cyber Cops." *Ms.* 6(May–June):22–23.

Ferree, Myra Marx, and David A. Merrill. 2000. "Hot Movements, Cold Cognition: Thinking about Social Movements in Gendered Frames." *Contemporary Society* 29(May):454–462.

Ferrell, Tom. 1979. "More Choose to Live outside Marriage." *New York Times,* July 1, p. E7.

Feuer, Lewis S., ed. 1959. *Karl Marx and Friedrich Engels: Basic Writings on Politics and Philosophy.* Garden City, NY: Doubleday.

Fiala, Robert. 1992. "Postindustrial Society." Pp. 1512–1522 in *Encyclopedia of Sociology,* vol. 3, edited by Edgar F. Borgatta and Marie L. Borgatta. New York: Macmillan.

Fields, Jason M., and Charles L. Clark. 1999. "Unbinding the Ties: Edit Effects of Marital Status on Same Gender Groups." Paper presented at the annual meeting of the American Sociological Assocation, August, Chicago.

Finder, Alan. 1995. "Despite Tough Laws, Sweatshops Flourish." *New York Times,* January 6, pp. A1, B4.

Findlay, Steven. 1998. "85% of American Workers Using HMOs." *USA Today,* January 20, p. 3A.

Fine, Gary Alan. 1984. "Negotiated Orders and Organizational Cultures." Pp. 239–262 in *Annual Review of Sociology, 1984,* edited by Ralph Turner. Palo Alto, CA: Annual Reviews.

Finkel, Steven E., and James B. Rule. 1987. "Relative Deprivation and Related Psychological Theories of Civil Violence: A Critical Review." *Research in Social Movements* 9:47–69.

Fiore, Faye. 1997. "Full-Time Moms a Minority Now, Census Bureau Finds." *Los Angeles Times,* November 26, pp. A1, A20.

Firestone, David. 1999. "School Prayer Is Revived As an Issue In Alabama." *New York Times,* July 15, p. A14.

Firestone, Shulamith. 1970. *The Dialectic of Sex: The Case for Feminist Revolution.* New York: Bantam.

Firmat, Gustavo Perez. 1994. *Life on Hyphen: The Cuban-American Way.* Austin: University of Texas Press.

Fitzpatrick, Kevin, and Mark LaGray. 2000. *Unhealthy Places: The Ecology of Risk in the Urban Landscape.* New York: Routledge.

Flacks, Richard. 1971. *Youth and Social Change.* Chicago: Markham.

Flavin, Jeanne. 1998. "Razing the Wall: A Feminist Critique of Sentencing Theory, Research, and Policy." Pp. 145–164 in *Cutting the Edge,* edited by Jeffrey Ross. Westport, CT: Praeger.

Fletcher, Connie. 1995. "On the Line: Women Cops Speak Out." *Chicago Tribune Magazine,* February 19, pp. 14–19.

Fornos, Werner. 1997. *1997 World Population Overview.* Washington, DC: The Population Institute.

Fortune. 2000. "The Fortune Global 200." 142(July 24):F1–F24.

Francis, David R. 1999. "Part-time Workers Face Full-time Problems." *Christian Science Monitor,* July 1, p. 11.

Franklin, John Hope, and Alfred A. Moss. 2000. *From Slavery to Freedom: A History of African Americans.* 8th ed. Upper Saddle River, NJ: Prentice-Hall.

Franklin, Stephen. 2000. "Hard Times at End?" *Chicago Tribune,* January 29, section 2, pp. 1–2.

Frazee, Valerie. 1997. "Establishing Relations in Germany." *Workforce* 76(No. 4):516.

Freeman, Jo. 1973. "The Origins of the Women's Liberation Movement." *American Journal of Sociology* 78(January): 792–811.

———. 1975. *The Politics of Women's Liberation.* New York: McKay.

Freeman, Linton C. 1958. "Marriage without Love: Mate Selection in Non-Western Countries." Pp. 20–30 in *Mate Selection,* edited by Robert F. Winch. New York: Harper and Row.

Freidson, Eliot. 1970. *Profession of Medicine.* New York: Dodd, Mead.

Freire, Paulo. 1970. *Pedagogy of the Oppressed.* New York: Herder and Herder.

French, Howard W. 2000. "Women Win a Battle, But Job Bias Still Rules Japan." *New York Times,* February 26, p. A3.

Freudenheim, Milt. 1990. "Employers Balk at High Cost of High-Tech Medical Care." *New York Times,* April 29, pp. 1, 16.

Fridlund, Alan. J., Paul Erkman, and Harriet Oster. 1987. "Facial Expressions of Emotion: Review of Literature 1970–1983." Pp. 143–224 in *Nonverbal Behavior and Communication,* 2d ed., edited by Aron W. Seigman and Stanley Feldstein. Hillsdale, NJ: Lawrence Erlbaum Associates.

Friedan, Betty. 1963. *The Feminine Mystique.* New York: Dell.

Friedland, Jonathon. 2000. "An American in Mexico Champions Midwifery as a Worthy Profession." *Wall Street Monitor,* February 15, pp. A1, A12.

Friedrichs, David O. 1998. "New Directions in Critical Criminology and White Collar Crime." Pp. 77–91 in *Cutting the Edge,* edited by Jeffrey Ross. Westport, CT: Praeger.

Fuller, Bruce, and Xiaoyan Liang. 1993. *The Unfair Search for Child Care.* Cambridge, MA: Preschool and Family Choice Project, Harvard University.

———, and Sharon Lynn Kagan. 2000. *Remember the Children: Mothers Balance Work and Child Care Under Welfare Reform.* Berkeley: Graduate School of Education, University of California.

Fullerton, Howard N., Jr., 1997. "Labor Force 2006: Slowing Down and Changing Composition." *Monthly Labor Review* (November):23–38.

———. 1999. "Labor Force Projections to 2008: Steady Growth and Changing Composition." *Monthly Labor Review* (November):19–32.

Furstenberg, Frank, and Andrew Cherlin. 1991. *Divided Families: What Happens to Children When Parents Part.* Cambridge, MA: Harvard University Press.

G

Gable, Donna. 1993a. "On TV, Lifestyles of the Slim and Entertaining." *USA Today,* July 27, p. 3D.

———. 1993b. "Series Shortchange Working-Class and Minority Americans." *USA Today,* August 30, p. 3D.

Gabor, Andrea. 1995. "Crashing the 'Old Boy' Party." *New York Times,* January 8, sec. 3, pp. 1, 6.

Galant, Debra. 2000. "Finding a Substitute for Office Chitchat." *New York Times,* February 16, sec. Retirement, p. 20.

Gale, Elaine. 1999. "A New Point of View." *Los Angeles Times,* January 11, pp. B1, B3.

Gamson, Josh. 1989. "Silence, Death, and the Invisible Enemy: AIDS Activism and Social Movement 'Newness.'" *Social Problems* 36(October): 351–367.

Gans, Herbert J. 1991. *People, Plans, and Policies: Essays on Poverty, Racism, and Other National Urban Problems.* New York: Columbia University Press and Russell Sage Foundation.

———. 1995. *The War against the Poor: The Underclass and Antipoverty Policy.* New York: Basic Books.

Gardner, Carol Brooks. 1989. "Analyzing Gender in Public Places: Rethinking Goffman's Vision of Everyday Life." *American Sociologist* 20(Spring):42–56.

———. 1990. "Safe Conduct: Women, Crime, and Self in Public Places." *Social Problems* 37(August):311–328.

———. 1995. *Passing By: Gender and Public Harassment.* Berkeley: University of California Press.

Garfinkel, Harold. 1956. "Conditions of Successful Degradation Ceremonies." *American Journal of Sociology* 61(March):420–424.

Garner, Roberta. 1996. *Contemporary Movements and Ideologies.* New York: McGraw-Hill.

———. 1999. "Virtual Social Movements." Presented at Zaldfest: A conference in honor of Mayer Zald. September 17, Ann Arbor, MI.

Garreau, Joel. 1991. *Edge City: Life on the New Frontier.* New York: Doubleday.

Garza, Melita Marie. 1993. "The Cordi-Marian Annual Cotillion." *Chicago Tribune,* May 7, sec. C, pp. 1, 5.

Gates, Henry Louis, Jr. 1991. "Delusions of Grandeur." *Sports Illustrated* 75(August 19):78.

———. 1999. "One Internet, Two Nations." *New York Times,* October 31, p. A15.

Gauette, Nicole. 1998. "Rules for Raising Japanese Kids." *Christian Science Monitor,* October 14, pp. B1, B6.

Gay Men's Health Crisis. 2000. "Facts and Statistics." Accessed February 1, 2000 (http://www.gmhc.org/basics/statmain.html).

Gearty, Robert. 1996. "Beware of Pickpockets." *Chicago Daily News,* November 19, p. 5.

Gecas, Viktor. 1982. "The Self-Concept." Pp. 1–33 in *Annual Review of Sociology, 1982,* edited by Ralph H. Turner and James F. Short, Jr. Palo Alto, CA: Annual Reviews.

———. 1992. "Socialization." Pp. 1863–1872 in *Encyclopedia of Sociology,* vol. 4, edited by Edgar F. Borgatta and Marie L. Borgatta. New York: Macmillan.

Geckler, Cheri. 1995. *Practice Perspectives and Medical Decision-Making in Medical Residents: Gender Differences—A Preliminary Report.* Wellesley, MA: Center for Research on Women.

Gelles, Richard J., and Claire Pedrick Cornell. 1990. *Intimate Violence in Families.* 2d ed. Newbury Park, CA: Sage.

General Accounting Office. 2000. *Women's Health: NIH Has Increased Its Efforts to Include Women in Research.* Washington, DC: U.S. Government Printing Office.

Gerth, H. H., and C. Wright Mills. 1958. *From Max Weber: Essays in Sociology.* New York: Galaxy.

Geyh, Paul. 1998. "Feminism Fatale?" *Chicago Tribune,* July 26, sec. 13, pp. 1, 6.

Gillespie, Mark. 1999. "Poll Releases, April 6, 1999: U.S. Gun Ownership Continues Broad Decline." Accessed July 2, 2000 (http://www.gallup.com/poll/releases/pr990406.asp).

Giordano, Peggy C., Stephen A. Cernkovich, and Alfred DeMaris. 1993. "The Family and Peer Relations of Black Adolescents." *Journal of Marriage and Family* 55(May):277–287.

Giroux, Henry A. 1988. *Schooling and the Struggle for Public Life: Critical Pedagogy in the Modern Age.* Minneapolis: University of Minnesota Press.

Glauber, Bill. 1998. "Youth Binge Drinking Varies Around World." *St. Louis Post-Dispatch,* February 9, p. E4.

Global Reach. 2000. *Global Internet Statistics* (by language). September 30, 2000. Accessed November 7, 2000 (http://www.glreach.com/globstats/index.php3).

Goffman, Erving. 1959. *The Presentation of Self in Everyday Life.* New York: Doubleday.

———. 1961. *Asylums: Essays on the Social Situation of Mental Patients and Other Inmates.* Garden City, NY: Doubleday.

———. 1963a. *Stigma: Notes on Management of Spoiled Identity.* Englewood Cliffs, NJ: Prentice-Hall.

———. 1963b. *Behavior in Public Places.* New York: Free Press.

———. 1971. *Relations in Public.* New York: Basic Books.

———. 1979. *Gender Advertisements.* New York: Harper and Row.

Goldberg, Carey. 1998. "Little Drop in College Binge Drinking." *New York Times,* August 11, p. A14.

Golden, Frederic. 1999. "Who's Afraid of Frankenfood?" *Time,* November 29, pp. 49–50.

Goldman, Benjamin A., and Laura Fitton. 1994. *Toxic Wastes and Race Revisited: An Update of the 1987 Report on the Racial and Social Economic Characteristics of Communities with Hazardous Waste.* Washington, DC: Center for Policy Alternatives, United Church of Christ Commission for Racial Justice, and NAACP.

Goldman, Robert, and Stephen Papson. 1998. *Nike Culture: The Sign of the Swoosh.* London: Sage Publications.

Goldstein, Greg. 1998. "World Health Organization and Housing." Pp. 636–637 in *The Encyclopedia of Housing,* edited by Willem van Vliet. Thousand Oaks, CA: Sage Publications.

Goldstein, Melvyn C., and Cynthia M. Beall. 1981. "Modernization and Aging in the Third and Fourth World: Views from the Rural Hinterland in Nepal." *Human Organization* 40(Spring): 48–55.

Goleman, Daniel, 1991. "New Ways to Battle Bias: Fight Acts, Not Feelings." *New York Times,* July 16, pp. C1, C8.

Goliber, Thomas J. 1997. "Population and Reproductive Health in Sub-Saharan Africa." *Population Bulletin* 52(December).

Goode, Erica. 1999. "For Good Health, It Helps to Be Rich and Important." *New York Times,* June 1, pp. 1, 9.

Goode, William J. 1959. "The Theoretical Importance of Love." *American Sociological Review* 24(February):38–47.

Goodgame, Dan. 1993. "Welfare for the Well-Off." *Time* 141(February 22): 36–38.

Gottdiener, Mark, and Joe R. Feagin. 1988. "The Paradigm Shift in Urban Sociology." *Urban Affairs Quarterly* 24(December):163–187.

———, and Ray Hutchison. 2000. *The New Urban Sociology.* 2d ed. New York: McGraw-Hill.

Gottfredson, Michael, and Travis Hirschi. 1990. *A General Theory of Crime.* Palo Alto, CA: Stanford University Press.

Gottschalk, Peter, Sara McLanahan, and Gary Sandefur. 1994. "The Dynamics and Intergenerational Transmission of Poverty and Welfare Participation." Pp. 85–108 in *Confronting Poverty: Prescriptions for Change,* edited by Sheldon H. Danziger, Gary D. Sandefur, and Daniel H. Weinburg. Cambridge, MA: Harvard University Press.

Gough, E. Kathleen. 1974. "Nayar: Central Kerala." Pp. 298–384 in *Matrilineal Kinship,* edited by David Schneider and E. Kathleen Gough. Berkeley: University of California Press.

Gouldner, Alvin. 1960. "The Norm of Reciprocity." *American Sociological Review* 25(April):161–177.

———. 1970. *The Coming Crisis of Western Sociology.* New York: Basic Books.

Gove, Walter R., ed. 1980. *The Labelling of Deviance.* 2d ed. Beverly Hills, CA: Sage.

———. 1987. "Sociobiology Misses the Mark: An Essay on Why Biology but Not Sociobiology Is Very Relevant to Sociology." *American Sociologist* 18(Fall):258–277.

Gramsci, Antonio. 1929. "Selections from the Prison Notebooks." In Quintin Hoare and Geoffrey Nowell Smith, eds. London: Lawrence and Wishort.

Greeley, Andrew M. 1989. "Protestant and Catholic: Is the Analogical Imagination Extinct?" *American Sociological Review* 54(August):485–502.

Green, Dan S., and Edwin D. Driver. 1978. "Introduction." Pp. 1–60 in *W. E. B. DuBois on Sociology and the Black Community,* edited by Dan S. Green and Edwin D. Driver. Chicago: University of Chicago Press.

Greenburg, Jan Crawford. 1999. "Sampling for Census Restricted." *Chicago Tribune,* January 26, pp. 1, 10.

Greene, Jay P. 1998. "A Meta-Analysis of the Effectiveness of Bilingual Education." Sponsored by the Toms River Policy Initiative. Accessed July 1, 1998 (http://data.Fas.harvard.edu/pepg/biling.htm).

Greenhouse, Linda. 1998a. "High Court Ruling Says Harassment Includes Same Sex." *New York Times,* March 5, pp. A1, A17.

———. 1998b. "Overturning of Late-Term Abortion Ban Is Let Stand." *New York Times,* March 24, p. A13.

Greenhouse, Steven. 1998. "Equal Work, Less-Equal Perks." *New York Times,* March 30, p. C1.

Grimsley, Kirstin Downey. 1997. "Big Boss May Be Watching—and Listening." *Washington Post National Weekly Edition,* June 2, p. 20.

Grossman, David C. et al. 1997. "Effectiveness of a Violence Prevention Curriculum among Children in Elementary School." *Journal of the American Medical Association* 277(May 28):1605–1617.

Groves, Martha. 1999. "New Adoptions Open Up the Family Circle." *Los Angeles Times,* August 8, p. A3.

Groza, Victor, Daniela F. Ileana, and Ivor Irwin. 1999. *A Peacock or a Crow: Stories, Interviews, and Commentaries on Romanian Adoptions.* Euclid, OH: Williams Custom Publishing.

Guralnik, Jack M. et al. [5 authors]. 1993. "Educational Status and Active Life Expectancy among Older Blacks and Whites." *New England Journal of Medicine* 329(July 8):110–116.

Guterman, Lila. 2000. "Why the 25-Year-Old Battle over Sociology Is More than Just 'An Academic Sideshow.'" *Chronicle of Higher Education,* July 7, pp. A17–A18.

Gutiérrez, Gustavo. 1990. "Theology and the Social Sciences," in Paul E. Sigmund, *Liberation Theology at the Crossroads: Democracy or Revolution?* New York: Oxford University Press, pp. 214–225.

Gwynne, S. C., and John F. Dickerson. 1997. "Lost in the E-Mail." *Time* 149(April 21):88–90.

H

Haas, Michael, ed. 1999. *The Singapore Puzzle.* Westport, CT: Praeger.

Hacker, Andrew. 1964. "Power to Do What?" Pp. 134–146 in *The New Sociology,* edited by Irving Louis Horowitz. New York: Oxford University Press.

Hacker, Helen Mayer. 1951. "Women as a Minority Group." *Social Forces* 30(October):60–69.

———. 1974. "Women as a Minority Group, Twenty Years Later." Pp. 124–134 in *Who Discriminates against Women?,* edited by Florence Denmark. Beverly Hills, CA: Sage.

Hafner, Katie. 2000. "For the Well Connected, All the World's an Office." *New York Times,* March 30, pp. D1, D7.

Hahn, Harlan. 1993. "The Political Implications of Disability Definitions and Data." *Journal of Disability Policy Studies* 4(2):41–52.

Haines, Valerie A. 1988. "Is Spencer's Theory an Evolutionary Theory?" *American Journal of Sociology* 93(March):1200–1223.

Halal, William E. 1992. "The Information Technology Revolution." *Futurist* 26(July–August):10–15.

Halbfinger, David M. 1998. "As Surveillance Cameras Peer, Some Wonder if They Also Pry." *New York Times,* February 22, p. A1.

Hall, Kay. 1999. "Work From Here." *Computer User* 18(November):32.

Hall, Mimi. 1993. "Genetic-Sex-Testing a Medical Mine Field." *USA Today,* December 20, p. 6A.

Hall, Peter. 1977. *The World Cities.* London: Weidenfeld and Nicolson.

Hall, Robert H. 1982. "The Truth about Brown Lung." *Business and Society Review* 40(Winter 1981–82):15–20.

Hallinan, Maureen T. 1997. "The Sociological Study of Social Change." *American Sociological Review* 62(February):1–11.

Hani, Yoko. 1998. "Hot Pots Wired to Help the Elderly." *Japan Times Weekly International Edition,* April 13, p. 16.

Hansell, Saul. 1999. "Amazon's Risky Christmas." *New York Times,* November 3, sec. 3, pp. 1, 15.

Hara, Hiroko. 2000. "Homeless Desperately Want Shelter, Jobs." *Japan Times International* 40(January 16), p. 14.

Harap, Louis. 1982. "Marxism and Religion: Social Functions of Religious Belief." *Jewish Currents* 36(January): 12–17, 32–35.

Harlow, Harry F. 1971. *Learning to Love.* New York: Ballantine.

Harmon, Amy. 1998. "The Law Where There Is No Land." *New York Times,* March 16, pp. C1, C9.

Harrah's Entertainment. 1996. *Harrah Survey of Casino Entertainment.* Memphis, TN: Harrah's Entertainment.

Harrington, Michael. 1980. "The New Class and the Left." Pp. 123–138 in *The New Class,* edited by B. Bruce-Briggs. Brunswick, NJ: Transaction.

Harris, Chauncy D., and Edward Ullman. 1945. "The Nature of Cities." *Annals of the American Academy of Political and Social Science* 242(November):7–17.

Harris, David. 1999. *Driving While Black: Racial Profiling on Our Nation's Highways.* New York: American Civil Liberties Union.

Harris, Judith Rich. 1998. *The Nurture Assumption: Why Children Turn Out the Way They Do.* New York: Free Press.

Harris, Marvin. 1997. *Culture, People, Nature: An Introduction to General Anthropology.* 7th ed. New York: Longman.

Hartjen, Clayton A. 1978. *Crime and Criminalization.* 2d ed. New York: Praeger.

Haub, Carl, and Deana Cornelius. 1999. *1999 World Population Data Sheet.* Washington, DC: Population Reference Bureau.

———, and ———. 2000. *2000 World Population Data Sheet.* Washington, DC: Population Reference Bureau.

Haviland, William A. 1999. *Cultural Anthropology (Case Studies in Cultural Anthropology).* 9th ed. Ft. Worth: Harcourt Brace.

Hayward, Mark D., William R. Grady, and Steven D. McLaughlin. 1987. "Changes in the Retirement Process." *Demography* 25(August):371–386.

Health Care Financing Administration. 2000. *National Health Expenditures Projections: 1998–2008.* Accessed October 1, 2000. (http://www.hcfa.gov/stats/NHE-Proj/proj1998/default.htm).

Heckert, Druann, and Amy Best. 1997. "Ugly Duckling to Swan: Labeling Theory and the Stigmatization of Red Hair." *Symbolic Interaction* 20(No. 4):365–384.

Hedley, R. Alan. 1992. "Industrialization in Less Developed Countries." Pp. 914–920 in *Encyclopedia of Sociology,* vol. 2, edited by Edgar F. Borgatta and Marie L. Borgatta. New York: Macmillan.

Heikes, E. Joel. 1991. "When Men Are the Minority: The Case of Men in Nursing." *Sociological Quarterly* 32(3): 389–401.

Heise, Lori, M. Ellsberg, and M. Gottemuelle. 1999. "Ending Violence Against Women." *Population Reports,* ser. L, no. 11. Baltimore: Johns Hopkins University School of Public Health.

Henley, Nancy, Mykol Hamilton, and Barrie Thorne. 1985. "Womanspeak and Manspeak: Sex Differences and Sexism in Communication, Verbal and Nonverbal." Pp. 168–185 in *Beyond Sex Roles,* 2d ed., edited by Alice G. Sargent. St. Paul, MN: West.

Henly, Julia R. 1999. "Challenges to Finding and Keeping Jobs in the Low-Skilled Labor Market." *Poverty Research News* 3(No. 1):3–5.

Henneberger, Melinda. 1995. "Muslims Continue to Feel Apprehensive." *New York Times,* April 14, p. B10.

Henry, Mary E. 1989. "The Function of Schooling: Perspectives from Rural Australia." *Discourse* 9(April):1–21.

Herrmann, Andrew. 1994. "Survey Shows Increase in Hispanic Catholics." *Chicago Sun-Times,* March 10, p. 4.

Hersch, Patricia. 1998. *A Tribe Apart: A Journey into the Heart of the American Adolescence.* New York: Fawcett Books.

Herskovits, Melville J. 1930. *The Anthropometry of the American Negro.* New York: Columbia University Press.

———. 1941. *The Myth of the Negro Past.* New York: Harper.

———. 1943. "The Negro in Bahia, Brazil: A Problem in Method." *American Sociological Review* 8(August): 394–402.

Hess, John L. 1990. "Confessions of a Greedy Geezer." *The Nation* 250(April 2):451–455.

Hewlett, Sylvia Ann, and Cornel West. 1998. *The War Against Parents.* Boston: Houghton Mifflin.

Hillery, George A. 1955. "Definitions of Community: Areas of Agreement." *Rural Sociology* (2):111–123.

Hirschi, Travis. 1969. *Causes of Delinquency.* Berkeley: University of California Press.

Hochschild, Arlie Russell. 1973. "A Review of Sex Role Research." *American Journal of Sociology* 78(January): 1011–1029.

———. 1990. "The Second Shift: Employed Women Are Putting in Another Day of Work at Home." *Utne Reader* 38(March–April):66–73.

———, with Anne Machung. 1989. *The Second Shift: Working Parents and the Revolution at Home.* New York: Viking Penguin.

Hodge, Robert W., and Peter H. Rossi. 1964. "Occupational Prestige in the United States, 1925–1963." *American Journal of Sociology* 70(November): 286–302.

Hoebel, E. Adamson. 1949. *Man in the Primitive World: An Introduction to Anthropology.* New York: McGraw-Hill.

Hoffman, Adonis. 1997. "Through an Accurate Prism." *Los Angeles Times,* August 8, p. M1.

Hoffman, Donald L., and Thomas P. Novak. 1998. "Bridging the Racial Divide on the Internet." *Science* 200(April 17):390–391.

Hoffman, Lois Wladis. 1985. "The Changing Genetics/Socialization Balance." *Journal of Social Issues* 41(Spring):127–148.

Hofstede, Geert. 1997. *Cultures and Organizations: Software of the Mind.* Rev. ed. New York: McGraw-Hill.

Holden, Constance. 1980. "Identical Twins Reared Apart." *Science* 207(March 21):1323–1328.

———. 1987. "The Genetics of Personality." *Science* 257(August 7):598–601.

Hollingshead, August B. 1975. *Elmtown's Youth and Elmtown Revisited.* New York: Wiley.

Holmes, Steven A. 1997. "Leaving the Suburbs for Rural Areas." *New York Times,* October 19, p. 34.

Homans, George C. 1979. "Nature versus Nurture: A False Dichotomy." *Contemporary Sociology* 8(May):345–348.

Hondagneu-Sotelo, Pierrette. 1994. "Regulating the Unregulated? Domestic Workers' Social Networks." *Social Problems* 41(February):50–64.

Horgan, John. 1993. "Eugenics Revisited." *Scientific American* 268(June): 122–128, 130–133.

Horn, Jack C., and Jeff Meer. 1987. "The Vintage Years." *Psychology Today* 21(May):76–77, 80–84, 88–90.

Horovitz, Bruce. 1995. "Marketers Tap Data We Once Called Our Own." *USA Today,* December 19, pp. A1, A2.

Horowitz, Helen Lefkowitz. 1987. *Campus Life.* Chicago: University of Chicago Press.

Horowitz, Irving Louis. 1983. *C. Wright Mills: An American Utopia.* New York: Free Press.

Horwitt, Sanford D. 1989. *Let Them Call Me Rebel: Saul Alinsky—His Life and Legacy.* New York: Knopf.

Hosokawa, William K. 1969. *Nisei: The Quiet Americans.* New York: Morrow.

Housing and Urban Development. 1999. *Stuart B. McKinney Homeless Programs.* Washington, DC: U.S. Government Printing Office.

Hout, Michael. 1988. "More Universalism, Less Structural Mobility: The American Occupational Structure in the 1980s." *American Journal of Sociology* 91(May):1358–1400.

Howard, Judith A. 1999. "Border Crossings between Women's Studies and Sociology." *Contemporary Sociology* 28(September):525–528.

Howard, Michael C. 1989. *Contemporary Cultural Anthropology.* 3d ed. Glenview, IL: Scott, Foresman.

Huang, Gary. 1988. "Daily Addressing Ritual: A Cross-Cultural Study." Presented at the annual meeting of the American Sociological Association, Atlanta.

Huber, Bettina J. 1985. *Employment Patterns in Sociology: Recent Trends and Future Prospects.* Washington, DC: American Sociological Association.

Huddy, Leonie, Joshua Billig, John Bracciodieta, Lois Hoeffler, Patrick J. Moynihan, and Patricia Pugliani. 1997. "The Effect of Interviewer Gender on the Survey Response." *Political Behavior* 19(September):197–220.

Huffstutter, P. J., Tini Tran, and David Reyes. 1999. "Pirates of the High-Tech Age." *Los Angeles Times,* July 25, pp. A1, A28–A29.

Hughes, Everett. 1945. "Dilemmas and Contradictions of Status." *American Journal of Sociology* 50 (March): 353–359.

Human Rights Campaign. 2000. "Hate Crime Laws that Include 'Sexual Orientation.'" Accessed August 6, 2000 (http://www.hrc.org/mindset_issues .asp).

Hunt, Geoffrey et al. 1993. "Changes in Prison Culture: Prison Gangs and the Case of the 'Pepsi Generation.'" *Social Problems* 40(August):398–409.

Hunter, Herbert, ed. 2000. *The Sociology of Oliver C. Cox: New Perspectives: Research in Race and Ethnic Relations,* vol. II. Stanford, CT: JAI Press.

Hunter, James Davison. 1991. *Culture Wars: The Struggle to Define America.* New York: Basic Books.

Hurh, Won Moo. 1994. *Korean Immigrants in America: A Structural Analysis of Ethnic Confinement and Adhesive Adaptation.* Rutherford, NJ: Fairleigh Dickinson University Press.

———. 1998. *The Korean Americans.* Westport, CT: Greenwood Press.

Hurn, Christopher J. 1985. *The Limits and Possibilities of Schooling.* 2d ed. Boston: Allyn and Bacon.

———, and Kwang Chung Kim. 1998. "The 'Success' Image of Asian Americans: Its Validity, and Its Practical and Theoretical Implications." *Ethnic and Racial Studies* 12(October):512–538.

Hurst, Erik, Ming Ching Luoh, and Frank P. Stafford. 1996. "Wealth Dynamics of American Families, 1984–1994." Institute for Social Research, University of Michigan, Ann Arbor, MI. Unpublished paper.

I

Ibarra, Herminia. 1995. "Race, Opportunity, and Diversity of Social Circles in Managerial Networks." *Academy of Management Journal* 38(3):673–703.

Illinois Coalition Against the Death Penalty. 2000. "Basic Facts on the Death Penalty in Illinois." Accessed February 17, 2000 (http://www. keynet/nicadp/).

Immigration and Naturalization Service. 1999a. *Legal Immigration, Fiscal Year 1998.* Washington, DC: U.S. Government Printing Office.

——— 1999b. *1997 Statistical Yearbook of the Immigration and Naturalization Service.* Washington, DC: U.S. Government Printing Office.

Inglehart, Ronald, and Wayne E. Baker. 2000. "Modernization, Cultural Change, and the Persistence of Traditional Values." *American Sociological Review* 65(February):19–51.

Institute of International Education. 1998. "Foreign Students in U.S. Institutions 1997–98." *Chronicle of Higher Education* 45(December 11):A67.

Instituto del Tercer Mundo. 1999. *The World Guide 1999/2000.* Oxford, England: New International Publications.

Inter-Parliamentary Union. 1999. "Women in National Parliaments. Situation as of 30 September 1999." Accessed October 3, 1999 (http://www. ipu.org/wmn-e/classif.htm). Geneva, Switzerland: Inter-Parliamentary Union.

———. 2000. "Women in Parliaments: Situations as of 15 September 2000."

Accessed August 27, 2000 (http://www.ipu.org/wmn-e/classif.htm).

International Monetary Fund. 2000. *World Economic Outlook: Asset Prices and the Business Cycle.* Washington, DC: International Monetary Fund.

Irwin, Katherine. 1998. "Getting a Tattoo: Self Transformation and Defining Deviance Down." Presented at the annual meeting of the American Sociological Association, San Francisco.

———. 1999a. "Getting a First Tattoo: Techniques of Legitimation and Social Change." University of Colorado, Boulder, CO. Unpublished paper.

———. 1999b. "Body Deviant's Subculture." University of Colorado, Boulder, CO. Unpublished paper.

———. 2000. "Becoming a Body Deviant: The Process of Collecting Tattoos." Presented at the annual meeting of the American Sociological Association, Washington.

J

Jackson, Elton F., Charles R. Tittle, and Mary Jean Burke. 1986. "Offense-Specific Models of the Differential Association Process." *Social Problems* 33(April):335–356.

Jackson, Philip W. 1968. *Life in Classrooms.* New York: Holt.

Jacobson, Jodi. 1993. "Closing the Gender Gap in Development." Pp. 61–79 in *State of the World,* edited by Lester R. Brown. New York: Norton.

Janofsky, Michael. 1999. "New Mexico Bans Creationism from State Curriculum." *New York Times,* October 9, p. A7.

Japan Times Staff. 1999. "80% Back Capital Punishment." *Japan Times International Edition* 14(December 7):8.

Jasper, James M. 1997. *The Art of Moral Protest: Culture, Biography, and Creativity in Social Movements.* Chicago: University of Chicago Press.

Jehl, Douglas. 1999. "The Internet's 'Open Sesame' Is Answered Warily." *New York Times,* March 18, p. A4.

Jencks, Christopher. 1994. *The Homeless.* Cambridge, MA: Harvard University Press.

Jenkins, Richard. 1991. "Disability and Social Stratification." *British Journal of Sociology* 42(December):557–580.

Jennings, M. Kent, and Richard G. Niemi. 1981. *Generations and Politics.* Princeton, NJ: Princeton University Press.

Jobtrak.com. 2000a. "Jobtrak.com's Poll Finds that Students and Recent Grads Only Plan to Stay with Their First Employer No Longer than Three Years." Press release January 6. Accessed June 29, 2000 (http://static.jobtrak.com/mediacenter/press_polls/poll_010600.html).

———. 2000b. "79% of College Students Find the Quality of an Employer's Website Important in Deciding Whether or Not to Apply for a Job." Accessed on June 29, 2000 (http://static.jobtrak.com/mediacenter/press_polls/polls_061200.html).

Johnson, Anne M., Jane Wadsworth, Kaye Wellings, and Julie Field. 1994. *Sexual Attitudes and Lifestyles.* Oxford: Blackwell Scientific.

Johnson, Benton. 1975. *Functionalism in Modern Sociology: Understanding Talcott Parsons.* Morristown, NJ: General Learning.

Johnson, Dirk. 1993. "More and More, the Single Parent Is Dad." *New York Times,* August 31, pp. A1, A15.

———. 1996b. "Rural Life Gains New Appeal, Turning Back a Long Decline." *New York Times,* September 23, pp. A1, B6.

Johnson, George. 1999. "It's a Fact: Faith and Theory Collide Over Evolution." *New York Times,* August 15, sec. 4, pp. 1, 12.

Johnston, David Cay. 1996. "The Divine Write-Off." *New York Times,* January 12, pp. D1, D6.

Jolin, Annette. 1994. "On the Backs of Working Prostitutes: Feminist Theory and Prostitution Policy." *Crime and Delinquency* 40(No. 2):69–83.

Jones, Arthur F., Jr., and Daniel H. Weinberg. 2000. "The Changing Shape of the Nation's Income Distribution." *Current Population Reports,* ser. P60, no. 204. Washington, DC: US Government Printing Office.

Jones, Charisse. 1999. "Minority Farmers Say They've Been Cheated." *USA Today,* January 5, p. 9A.

Jones, James T., IV. 1988. "Harassment Is Too Often Part of the Job." *USA Today,* August 8, p. 5D.

Jones, Stephen R. G. 1992. "Was There a Hawthorne Effect?" *American Journal of Sociology* 98(November):451–568.

Jordan, Mary. 1996. "Out of the Kitchen, Onto the Ballot." *Washington Post National Weekly Edition,* October 21, P. 16.

Juhasz, Anne McCreary. 1989. "Black Adolescents' Significant Others." *Social Behavior and Personality* 17(2):211–214.

K

Kaiser Family Foundation. 2000. *The State of the HIV/AIDS Epidemic in America.* Menlo Park, CA: Kaiser Family Foundation.

Kalb, Claudia. 1999. "Our Quest to Be Perfect." *Newsweek* 134(August 9):52–59.

Kanagae, Haruhiko. 1993. "Sexual Harassment in Japan: Findings from Survey Research." Presented at the annual meeting of the Pacific Sociological Association, Portland, OR.

Kanellos, Nicholás. 1994. *The Hispanic Almanac: From Columbus to Corporate America.* Detroit: Visible Ink Press.

Kang, Mee-Eun. 1997. "The Portrayal of Women's Images in Magazine Advertisements: Goffman's Gender Analysis Revisited." In *Sex Roles* 37(December):979–996.

Kantrowitz, Barbara, and Pat Wingert. 1999. "Beyond Littleton: How Well Do You Know Your Kids?" *Newsweek,* May 10, pp. 36–40.

Katovich, Michael A. 1987. Correspondence. June 1.

Katz, Michael. 1971. *Class, Bureaucracy, and the Schools: The Illusion of Educational Change in America.* New York: Praeger.

Keating, Noah and Brenda Munro. 1988. "Farm Women/Farm Work." *Sex Roles* 19(August):155–168.

Kelley, Robin D. G. 1996. "Freedom Riders (the Sequel)." *The Nation* 262(February 5):18–21.

Kelly, Katy, and Doug Levy. 1995. "HMOs Dogged by Issue of Cost vs. Care." *USA Today,* October 17, pp. D1, D2.

Kelsoe, John R. et al. [12 authors]. 1989. "Re-evaluation of the Linkage Relationship between Chromosome LTP Loci and the Gene for Bipolar Affective Disorder in the Old Order Amish." *Nature* 342(November 16): 238–243.

Kemper, Vicki, and Viveca Novak. 1991. "Health Care Reform: Don't Hold Your Breath." *Washington Post National Weekly Edition* 8(October 28):28.

Kennedy, Bruce P., Ichiro Kawachi, and Deborah Prothrow-Stith. 1996. "Income Distribution and Mortality: Cross Sectional Ecological Study of the Robin Hood Index in the United States." *British Medical Journal* 312(April 20):1004–1007.

Kennickell, Arthur B., Martha Starr-McCluer, and Brian J. Surette. 2000. "Recent Changes in U.S. Family Finances: Results from the 1998 Survey of Consumer Finances." *Federal Reserve Bulletin* (January):1–29.

Kent, Mary Mederios. 1999. "Shrinking Societies Favor Procreation." *Population Today* 27(December):4–5.

Kephart, William M., and William M. Zellner. 1998. *Extraordinary Groups: An Examination of Unconventional Life-Styles.* 6th ed. New York: St. Martin's.

Kerbo, Harold R. 1996. *Social Stratification and Inequality: Class Conflict in Historical and Comparative Perspective.* 3d ed. New York: McGraw-Hill.

———. 2000. *Social Stratification and Inequality: Class Conflict in Historical, Comparative, and Global Perspective.* New York: McGraw-Hill.

Kerr, Clark. 1960. *Industrialization and Industrial Man: The Problems of Labor and Management in Economic Growth.* Cambridge, MA: Harvard University Press.

Kilborn, Peter T. 1999. "Gimme Shelter: Same Song, New Time." *New York Times,* December 5, p. 5.

———. 2000. "Learning at Home, Students Take the Lead." *New York Times,* May 24, pp. A1, A17.

Kim, Kwang Chung. 1999. *Koreans in the Hood: Conflict with African Americans.* Baltimore: Johns Hopkins University Press.

King, Anthony. 1998. "London Mayor Is Casualty of Voters' Apathy." *The Daily Telegraph* (London), May 19, p. 12.

King, Leslie. 1998. "'France Needs Children': Pronatalism, Nationalism, and Women's Equity." *Sociological Quarterly* 39(Winter):33–52.

———, and Madonna Harrington Meyer. 1997. "The Politics of Reproductive Benefits: U.S. Insurance Coverage of Contraceptive and Infertility Treatments." *Gender and Society* 11(February):8–30.

Kinsey, Alfred C., Wardell B. Pomeroy, and Clyde E. Martin. 1948. *Sexual Behavior in the Human Male.* Philadelphia: Saunders.

———, ———, and Paul H. Gebhard. 1953. *Sexual Behavior in the Human Female.* Philadelphia: Saunders.

Kinzer, Stephen. 1993. "German Court Restricts Abortion, Angering Feminists and the East." *New York Times,* May 29, pp. 1, 3.

Kirk, Margaret O. 1995. "The Temps in the Gray Flannel Suits." *New York Times,* December 17, p. F13.

Kitchener, Richard F. 1991. "Jean Piaget: The Unknown Sociologist." *British Journal of Sociology* 42(September): 421–442.

Kleinknecht, William. 1996. *The New Ethnic Mobs: The Changing Face of Organized Crime in America.* New York: Free Press.

Kohn, Alfie. 1988. "Girltalk, Guytalk." *Psychology Today* 22(February): 65–66.

Kohn, Melvin L. 1970. "The Effects of Social Class on Parental Values and Practices." Pp. 45–68 in *The American Family: Dying or Developing,* edited by David Reiss and H. A. Hoffman. New York: Plenum.

Kolata, Gina. 1998. "Infertile Foreigners See Opportunity in U.S." *New York Times,* January 4, pp. 1, 12.

———. 2000. *Clone. The Road to Dolly, and the Path Ahead.* New York: William Morrow.

———. 2000b. "Web Research Transforms Visit to the Doctor." *New York Times.* (March 6): A1, A18.

Komarovsky, Mirra. 1991. "Some Reflections on the Feminist Scholarship in Sociology." Pp. 1–25 in *Annual Review of Sociology, 1991,* edited by W. Richard Scott and Judith Blake. Palo Alto, CA: Annual Reviews.

Kortenhaus, Carole M., and Jack Demarest. 1993. "Gender Role Stereotyping in Children's Literature: An Update." *Sex Roles* 28(3–4):219–232.

Kourvetaris, George. 1999. "The Greek-American Family: A Generational Approach." Pp. 68–101 in *Ethnic Families in America: Patterns and Variations,* 4th ed., edited by Charles H. Mindel, Robert W. Habenstein, and Roosevelt Wright, Jr. Upper Saddle River, NJ: Prentice-Hall.

Kovaleski, Serge F. 1999. "Choosing Alternative Medicine by Necessity." *Washington Post National Weekly Edition* 16(April 5):16.

Krach, Constance A., and Victoria A. Velkoff. 1999. "Centenarians in the United States 1990." *Current Population Reports,* ser. P-23, no. 199RV. Washington, DC: U.S. Government Printing Office.

Kraut, Robert et al. 1998. "Internet Paradox: A Social Technology That Reduces Social Involvement and Psychological Well-Being." *American Psychologist* 55(September):1017–1031.

Kristof, Nicholas D. 1995. "Japan's Invisible Minority: Better Off Than in Past, but Still Outcasts," *New York Times,* November 30, p. A18.

———. 1998. "As Asian Economies Shrink, Women Are Squeezed Out." *New York Times,* June 11, pp. A1, A12.

Kunkel, Dale et al. 1999. *Sex on TV: A Biennial Report to Kaiser Family Foundation.* Santa Barbara, CA: University of California, Santa Barbara.

Kuptsch, Christine, and David M. Mazie. 1999. "Social Protection." Pp. 316–318 in *Enyclopedia Britannica Yearbook 1999.* Chicago: Encyclopedia Britannica.

Kwong, Peter, and JoAnn Lum. 1988. "Chinese-American Politics: A Silent Minority Tests Its Clout." *The Nation* 246(January 16):49–50, 52.

Kyodo News International. 1998a. "More Japanese Believe Divorce Is Acceptable." *Japan Times* 38(January 12), p. B4.

L

Labaree, David F. 1986. "Curriculum, Credentials, and the Middle Class: A Case Study of a Nineteenth Century High School." *Sociology of Education* 59(January):42–57.

Ladner, Joyce. 1973. *The Death of White Sociology.* New York: Random Books.

La Ganga, Maria L. 2000. "The Age of the Aging Electorate." *Los Angeles Times,* January 13, pp. A1, A17.

Lakoff, Robin Tolmach. 2000. *The Language War*. Berkeley: University of California Press.

Landers, Robert K. 1988. "Why America Doesn't Vote." *Editorial Research Reports* (*Congressional Quarterly*) *8* pt. 1, pp. 82–95.

Landtman, Gunnar. 1968. *The Origin of Inequality of the Social Class*. New York: Greenwood (original edition 1938, Chicago: University of Chicago Press).

Lang, Eric. 1992. "Hawthorne Effect." Pp. 793–794 in *Encyclopedia of Sociology*, vol. 2, edited by Edgar F. Borgatta and Marie L. Borgatta. New York: Macmillan.

Lappé, Anthony. 1999 "There Is No Average Day When You Live in a Tree." *New York Times Magazine*, December 12, p. 29.

Lappin, Todd. 1996. "Aux Armes, Netizens!" *The Nation* 262(February 26): 6–7.

Larson, Jan. 1996. "Temps Are Here to Stay." *American Demographics* 18(February):26–31.

Lassey, Marie L., William R. Lassey, and Martin J. Jinks. 1997. *Health Care Systems around the World: Characteristics, Issues, Reforms*. Upper Saddle River, NJ: Prentice-Hall.

Lasswell, Harold D. 1936. *Politics: Who Gets What, When, How*. New York: McGraw-Hill.

L.A. Times Poll. 2000. "Abortion Poll." *Los Angeles Times*, June 18, p. A14.

Lauer, Robert H. 1982. *Perspectives on Social Change*. 3d ed. Boston: Allyn and Bacon.

Laumann, Edward O., John H. Gagnon, and Robert T. Michael. 1994a. "A Political History of the National Sex Survey of Adults." *Family Planning Perspectives* 26(February):34–38.

———, ———, ———, and Stuart Michaels. 1994b. *The Social Organization of Sexuality: Sexual Practices in the United States*. Chicago: University of Chicago Press.

Leacock, Eleanor Burke. 1969. *Teaching and Learning in City Schools*. New York: Basic Books.

Leavell, Hugh R., and E. Gurney Clark. 1965. *Preventive Medicine for the Doctor in His Community: An Epidemiologic Approach*. 3d ed. New York: McGraw-Hill.

Lee, Barrett A. 1992. "Homelessness." Pp. 843–847 in *Encyclopedia of Sociology*, vol. 2, edited by Edgar F. Borgatta and Marie L. Borgatta. New York: Macmillan.

Lee, Heon Cheol. 1999. "Conflict Between Korean Merchants and Black Customers: A Structural Analysis." Pp. 113–130 in *Koreans in the Hood: Conflict with African Americans*, edited by Kwang Chung Kim. Baltimore: Johns Hopkins University Press.

Lehne, Gregory K. 1995. "Homophobia among Men: Supporting and Defining the Male Role." Pp. 325–336 in *Men's Lives*, edited by Michael S. Kimmel and Michael S. Messner. Boston: Allyn and Bacon.

Leinward, Donna. 2000. "20% Say They Used Drugs with Their Mom and Dad." *USA Today*, August 24, pp. 1A, 2A.

Lemann, Nicholas. 1991. "The Other Underclass." *Atlantic Monthly* 268(December):96–102, 104, 107–108, 110.

Lengermann, Patricia Madoo, and Jill Niebrugge-Brantley. 1998. *The Women Founders: Sociology and Social Theory, 1830–1930*. Boston: McGraw-Hill.

Lenski, Gerhard. 1966. *Power and Privilege: A Theory of Social Stratification*. New York: McGraw-Hill.

———, Jean Lenski, and Patrick Nolan. 1995. *Human Societies: An Introduction to Macrosociology*. 7th ed. New York: McGraw-Hill.

Leo, John. 1987. "Exploring the Traits of Twins." *Time* 129(January 12):63.

Leon, Sy. 1996. *None of the Above: Why Non-Voters Are America's Political Majority*. San Francisco: Fox and Wilkes.

Levin, Jack, and William C. Levin. 1980. *Ageism*. Belmont, CA: Wadsworth.

Levinson, Arlene. 1984. "Laws for Live-In Lovers." *Ms.* 12(June):101.

Lewin, Tamar. 1992. "Hurdles Increase for Many Women Seeking Abortions." *New York Times*, March 15, pp. 1, 18.

———. 1997. "Abortion Rate Declined Again in '95, U.S. Says, but Began Rising Last Year." *New York Times*, December 5, p. A10.

———. 1998. "Report Finds Girls Lagging Behind Boys in Technology." *New York Times*, October 14, p. B8.

———. 1998a. "Debate Centers on Definition of Harassment." *New York Times*, March 22, pp. A1, A20.

———. 2000. "Differences Found in Care with Stepmothers." *New York Times*, August 17, p. A16.

Lewis, Anthony. 1999. "Abroad at Home: Something Rich and Strange," *New York Times* (October 12): accessed at *The New York Times on the Web*.

Liao, Youlian, Daniel L. McGee, Guichan Cao, and Richard S. Cooper. 2000. "Quality of the Last Year of Life of Older Adults: 1986–1993." *Journal of American Medical Association* 283(January 26):512–518.

Lieberman, David. 1999. "On the Wrong Side of the Wires." *USA Today*, October 11, pp. B1, B2.

Liebow, Elliot. 1993. *Tell Them Who I Am: The Lives of Homeless Women*. New York: Free Press.

Light, Ivan. 1999. "Comparing Incomes of Immigrants." *Contemporary Sociology* 28(July):382–384.

Liker, Jeffrey K., Carol J. Hoddard, and Jennifer Karlin. 1999. "Perspectives on Technology and Work Organization." Pp. 575–596 in *Annual Review of Sociology 1999*, edited by Karen S. Cook and John Hagen. Palo Alto, CA: Annual Reviews.

Lillard, Margaret. 1998. "Olympics Put Spotlight on Women's Hockey." *Rocky Mountain News*, February 1, p. 8C.

Lilliston, Ben. 1994. "Corporate Welfare Costs More Than Welfare to the Poor, Group Reports." *The Daily Citizen*, January 18, p. 8.

Lin, Na, and Wen Xie. 1988. "Occupational Prestige in Urban China." *American Journal of Sociology* 93(January):793–832.

Lin, Nan. 1999. "Social Networks and Status Attainment." Pp. 467–487 in *Annual Review of Sociology 1999*, edited by Karen S. Cook and John Hagen. Palo Alto, CA: Annual Reviews.

Lindholm, Charles. 1999. "Isn't it Romantic?" *Culture Front Online* Spring:1–5.

Lindner, Eileen, ed. 1998. *Yearbook of American and Canadian Churches, 1998*. Nashville: Abingdon Press.

———, ed. 2000. *Yearbook of American and Canadian Churches*. Nashville: Abingdon Press.

Linn, Susan, and Alvin F. Poussaint. 1999. "Watching Television: What Are Children Learning About Race and

Ethnicity?" *Child Care Information Exchange* 128(July):50–52.

Linton, Ralph. 1936. *The Study of Man: An Introduction.* New York: Appleton-Century.

Lipset, Seymour Martin.1996. *American Exceptionalism: A Double-Edged Sword.* New York: Norton.

Lipson, Karen. 1994. "'Nell' Not Alone in the Wilds." *Los Angeles Times*, December 19, pp. F1, F6.

Liska, Allen E., and Steven F. Messner. 1999. *Perspectives on Crime and Deviance.* 3d ed. Upper Saddle River, NJ: Prentice-Hall.

Livernash, Robert, and Eric Rodenburg. 1998. "Population Change, Resources, and the Environment." *Population Bulletin* 53(March).

Llanes, José. 1982. *Cuban Americans: Masters of Survival.* Cambridge, MA: Abt Books.

Lofflin, John. 1988. "A Burst of Rural Enterprise." *New York Times*, January 3, sec. 3, pp. 1, 23.

Lofland, Lyn H. 1975. "The 'Thereness' of Women: A Selective Review of Urban Sociology." Pp. 144–170 in *Another Voice,* edited by M. Millman and R. M. Kanter. New York: Anchor/Doubleday.

Logan, John R., and Richard D. Alba. 1995. "Who Lives in Affluent Suburbs? Racial Differences in Eleven Metropolitan Regions." *Sociological Focus* 28(October):353–364.

Lohr, Steve. 1994. "Data Highway Ignoring Poor, Study Charges." *New York Times*, May 24, pp. A1, D3.

Longman, Phillip. 1999. "The World Turns Gray." *U.S. News & World Report* 126(March 1):30–35.

Longworth, R. C. 1993. "UN's Relief Agendas Put Paperwork before People." *Chicago Tribune*, September 14, pp. 1, 9.

———. 1996. "Future Shock: The Graying of the Industrial World." *Chicago Tribune*, September 4, pp. 1, 20.

Lorber, Judith. 1994. *Paradoxes of Gender.* New Haven, CT: Yale University Press.

Los Angeles Times. 1995. "Multicultural Medicine." October 21, p. B7.

Lott, John R., Jr. 1998. *More Guns, Less Crime: Understanding Crime and Gun Control Laws.* Chicago: University of Chicago Press.

Lowry, Brian, Elizabeth Jensen, and Greg Braxton. 1999. "Networks Decide Diversity Doesn't Pay." *Los Angeles Times*, July 20, p. A1.

Lukacs, Georg. 1923. *History and Class Consciousness.* London: Merlin.

Luker, Kristin. 1984. *Abortion and the Politics of Motherhood.* Berkeley: University of California Press.

———. 1996. *Dubious Conceptions: The Politics of Teenage Pregnancy.* Cambridge, MA: Harvard University Press.

———. 1999. "Is Academic Sociology Politically Obsolete?" *Contemporary Sociology* 28(January):5–10.

Lum, Joann, and Peter Kwong. 1989. "Surviving in America: The Trials of a Chinese Immigrant Woman." *Village Voice* 34(October 31):39–41.

Luo, Michael. 1999. "Megachurches Search for Ideas to Grow Again." *Los Angeles Times*, June 7, pp. B1, B3.

Luster, Tom, Kelly Rhoades, and Bruce Haas. 1989. "The Relation between Parental Values and Parenting Behavior: A Test of the Kohn Hypothesis." *Journal of Marriage and the Family* 51(February):139–147.

Lustig, Myron W., and Jolene Koester. 1999. *Intercultural Competence.* 3d ed. New York: Longman.

Lyotard, Jean François. 1993. *The Postmodern Explained: Correspondence, 1982–1985.* Minneapolis: University of Minnesota Press.

M

MacFarquhar, Neil. 1999. "For First Time in War, E-Mail Plays a Vital Role." *New York Times*, March 29, p. A12.

Mack, Raymond W., and Calvin P. Bradford. 1979. *Transforming America: Patterns of Social Change.* 2d ed. New York: Random House.

MacLeod, Alexander. 2000. "UK Moving to Open All (E-) Mail." *The Christian Science Monitor,* May 5, pp. 1, 9.

Magnier, Mark. 1999. "Equality Evolving in Japan." *Los Angeles Times*, August 30, pp. A1, A12.

Maguire, Brendan. 1988. "The Applied Dimension of Radical Criminology: A Survey of Prominent Radical Criminologists." *Sociological Spectrum* 8(2):133–151.

Maines, David R. 1977. "Social Organization and Social Structure in Symbolic Interactionist Thought." Pp. 235–259 in *Annual Review of Sociology, 1977,* edited by Alex Inkles. Palo Alto, CA: Annual Reviews.

———. 1982. "In Search of Mesostructure: Studies in the Negotiated Order." *Urban Life* 11(July):267–279.

Malcolm X, with Alex Haley. 1964. *The Autobiography of Malcolm X.* New York: Grove.

Malthus, Thomas Robert. 1798. *Essays on the Principle of Population.* New York: Augustus Kelly, Bookseller; reprinted in 1965.

———, Julian Huxley, and Frederick Osborn. [1824] 1960. *Three Essays on Population.* Reprint, New York: New American Library.

Mann, Jim. 2000. "India: Growing Implications for U.S." *Los Angeles Times,* May 17, p. A5.

Manson, Donald A. 1986. *Tracking Offenders: White-Collar Crime.* Bureau of Justice Statistics Special Report. Washington, DC: U.S. Government Printing Office.

Marklein, Mary Beth. 1996. "Telecommuters Gain Momentum." *USA Today,* June 18, p. 6E.

Marks, Alexandra. 1998. "Key Swing Vote in 1998: Women," *Christian Science Monitor,* July 14, p. 3.

Martin, Philip, and Elizabeth Midgley. 1999. "Immigrants to the United States." *Population Bulletin* 54(June):1–42.

Martin, Philip, and Jonas Widgren. 1996. "International Migration: A Global Challenge." *Population Bulletin* 51(April).

Martin, Susan E. 1994. "Outsider Within the Station House: The Impact of Race and Gender on Black Women Politics." *Social Problems* 41(August):383–400.

Martineau, Harriet. 1896. "Introduction" to the translation of *Positive Philosophy* by Auguste Comte. London: Bell.

———. [1837] 1962. *Society in America.* Edited, abridged, with an introductory essay by Seymour Martin Lipset. Reprint, Garden City, NY: Doubleday.

Martyna, Wendy. 1983. "Beyond the He/Man Approach: The Case for Nonsexist Language." Pp. 25–37 in *Language, Gender and Society,* edited by Barrie Thorne, Cheris Kramorae, and Nancy Henley. Rowley, MA: Newly House.

Marx, Karl, and Friedrich Engels. [1847] 1955. *Selected Work in Two Volumes.* Reprint, Moscow: Foreign Languages Publishing House.

Masaki, Hisane. 1998. "Hashimoto Steps Down." *The Japan Times* 38 (July 20):1–5.

Mascia-Lees, Frances E., and Patricia Sharp, eds. 1992. *Tattoo, Torture, Mutilation, and Adornment: The Denaturalization of the Body in Culture and Text.* Albany: State University of New York Press.

Mason, J. W. 1998. "The Buses Don't Stop Here Anymore." *American Prospect* 37(March):56–62.

Massey, Douglas S., and Nancy A. Denton. 1993. *American Apartheid: Segregation and the Making of the Underclass.* Cambridge, MA: Harvard University Press.

Matloff, Norman. 1998. "Now Hiring! If You're Young." *New York Times,* January 26, p. A21.

Matrix Information and Directory Services. 1999. "Current World Map of the Internet." Austin, TX: MIDS. Also accessible online (http://www.mids.org/mapsale/world/index.html).

Matsushita, Yoshiko. 1999. "Japanese Kids Call for a Sympathetic Ear." *Christian Science Monitor,* January 20, p. 15.

Matthews, Jay. 1999. "A Home Run for Home Schooling." *Washington Post National Weekly Edition* 16(March 29):34.

Mauro, Tony. 1999. "Will Every Childish Taunt Turn Into a Federal Case?" *USA Today,* May 25, pp. A1, A2.

Maxwell, Joe. 1992. "African Megachurch Challenged over Teaching." *Christianity Today* 36(October 5):58.

Mayer, Karl Ulrich, and Urs Schoepflin. 1989. "The State and the Life Course." Pp. 187–209 in *Annual Review of Sociology, 1989,* edited by W. Richard Scott and Judith Blake. Palo Alto, CA: Annual Reviews.

Mayor's Task Force on Homelessness. 1997. *Report to Wheaton City Council on the Mayor's Task Force on Homelessness.* Wheaton, IL: Mayor's Task Force on Homelessness.

McClung, H. Juhling, Robert D. Murray, and Leo A. Heitlinger. 1998. "The Internet as a Source for Current Patient Information." *Pediatrics* 10(June 6): electronic edition.

McCormick, John, and Claudia Kalb. 1998. "Dying for a Drink." *Newsweek,* June 15, pp. 30–31, 33–34.

McCreary, D. 1994. "The Male Role and Avoiding Femininity." *Sex Roles* 31: 517–531.

McDonald, Kim A. 1999. "Studies of Women's Health Produce a Wealth of Knowledge on the Biology of Gender Differences." *Chronicle of Higher Education* 45(June 25):A19, A22.

McFalls, Joseph A., Jr. 1998. "Population: A Lively Introduction." *Population Bulletin* 53(September).

———, Brian Jones, and Bernard J. Gallegher III. 1984. "U.S. Population Growth: Prospects and Policy." *USA Today,* January, pp. 30–34.

McGue, Matt, and Thomas J. Bouchard Jr. 1998. "Genetic and Environmental Influence on Human Behavioral Differences." Pp. 1–24 in *Annual Review of Neurosciences.* Palo Alto, CA: Annual Reviews.

McGuire, Meredith B. 1981. *Religion: The Social Context.* Belmont, CA: Wadsworth.

———. 1992. *Religion: The Social Context.* 3d ed. Belmont, CA: Wadsworth.

McIntosh, Peggy. 1988. "White Privilege and Male Privilege: A Personal Account of Coming to See Correspondence Through Work and Women's Studies." Working Paper No. 189, Wellesley College Center for Research on Women, Wellesley, MA.

McKenzie, Evan. 1994. *Privatopia: Homeowner Associations and the Rise of Residential Private Government.* New Haven, CT: Yale University Press.

McKinlay, John B., and Sonja M. McKinlay. 1977. "The Questionable Contribution of Medical Measures to the Decline of Mortality in the United States in the Twentieth Century." *Milbank Memorial Fund Quarterly* 55(Summer):405–428.

McKinley, James C., Jr. 1999. "In Cuba's New Dual Economy, Have-Nots Far Exceed Haves." *New York Times,* February 11, pp. A1, A6.

McKinnon, Jesse and Karen Humes. 2000. "The Black Population in the United States." *Current Population Reports.* Ser. P20 No. 530. Washington, DC: US Government Printing Office.

McLane, Daisann. 1995. "The Cuban-American Princess." *New York Times Magazine,* February 26, pp. 42–43.

McLaughlin, Abraham. 1998. "Tales of Journey from Death Row to Freedom." *Christian Science Monitor,* November 16, p. 2.

McNamara, Robert S. 1992. "The Population Explosion." *The Futurist* 26 (November–December):9–13.

Mead, George H. 1934. In *Mind, Self and Society,* edited by Charles W. Morris. Chicago: University of Chicago Press.

———. 1964a. In *On Social Psychology,* edited by Anselm Strauss. Chicago: University of Chicago Press.

———. 1964b. "The Genesis of the Self and Social Control." Pp. 267–293 in *Selected Writings: George Herbert Mead,* edited by Andrew J. Reck. Indianapolis: Bobbs-Merrill.

Mead, Margaret. [1935] 1963. *Sex and Temperament in Three Primitive Societies.* Reprint, New York: Morrow.

———. 1973. "Does the World Belong to Men—Or to Women?" *Redbook* 141(October):46–52.

Mechanic, David, and David Rochefort. 1996. "Comparative Medical Systems." Pp. 475–494 in *Annual Review of Sociology, 1996,* edited by John Hagan. Palo Alto, CA: Annual Reviews.

Mehren, Elizabeth. 1999. "Working 9 to 5 at Age 95." *USA Today,* May 5, pp. A1, A21–A22.

Melia, Marilyn Kennedy. 2000. "Changing Times." *Chicago Tribune,* January 2, sec. 17, pp. 12–15.

Melson, Robert. 1986. "Provocation or Nationalism: A Critical Inquiry into the Armenian Genocide of 1915." Pp. 61–84 in *The Armenian Genocide in Perspective,* edited by Richard G. Hovannisian. Brunswick, NJ: Transaction.

Mendez, Jennifer Brikham. 1998. "Of Mops and Maids: Contradictions and Continuities in Bureaucratized Domestic Work." *Social Problems* 45(February):114–135.

Merton, Robert K. 1968. *Social Theory and Social Structure.* New York: Free Press.

———, and Alice S. Kitt. 1950. "Contributions to the Theory of Reference Group Behavior." Pp. 40–105 in *Continuities in Social Research: Studies in the Scope and Method of the American Soldier,* edited by Robert K. Merton and Paul L. Lazarsfeld. New York: Free Press.

———, G. C. Reader, and P. L. Kendall. 1957. *The Student Physician.* Cambridge, MA: Harvard University Press.

Messner, Michael A. 1997. *Politics of Masculinities: Men in Movements.* Thousand Oaks, CA: Sage.

Meyers, Thomas J. 1992. "Factors Affecting the Decision to Leave the Old Order Amish." Presented at the annual meeting of the American Sociological Association, Pittsburgh.

Michels, Robert. 1915. *Political Parties.* Glencoe, IL: Free Press (reprinted 1949).

Mifflin, Lawrie. 1999. "Many Researchers Say Link Is Already Clear on Media and Youth Violence." *New York Times,* May 9, p. 23.

Migration News. 1998a. "Canada: Immigration, Diversity Up." 5(January). Accessed May 22, 1998 (http://migration.ucdavis.edu).

———. 1998b. "Immigration in EU, France: New Law, Australia: Immigration Unchanged." 5(May). Accessed May 6, 1998 (http://migration.ucdavis.edu).

Milgram, Stanley. 1963. "Behavioral Study of Obedience." *Journal of Abnormal and Social Psychology* 67(October):371–378.

———. 1975. *Obedience to Authority: An Experimental View.* New York: Harper and Row.

Miller, David L., and Richard T. Schaefer. 1993. "Feeding the Hungry: The National Food Bank System as a Non-Insurgent Social Movement." Presented at the annual meeting of the Midwest Sociological Society, Chicago.

Miller, D. W. 2000. "Sociology, Not Engineering May Explain Our Vulnerability to Technological Disaster." *Chronicle of Higher Education* (October 15):A19–A20.

Miller, Greg. 1999. "Internet Fueled Global Interest in Disruptions." *Chicago Tribune,* December 2, p. A24.

Miller, G. Tyler, Jr. 1972. *Replenish the Earth: A Primer in Human Ecology.* Belmont, CA: Wadsworth.

Miller, Michael. 1998. "Abortion by the Numbers." *The Village Voice* 43, January 27, p. 58.

Mills, C. Wright. 1956. *The Power Elite.* New York: Oxford University Press.

———. 1959. *The Sociological Imagination.* London: Oxford University Press.

Mills, Robert J. 2000. "Health Insurance Coverage." *Current Population Reports,* ser. P60, no. 211. Washington, DC: U.S. Government Printing Office.

Milton S. Eisenhower Foundation. 1999. *To Establish Justice, To Insure Domestic Tranquility: A Thirty Year Update of the National Commission on the Causes and Prevention of Violence.* Washington, DC: Milton S. Eisenhower Foundation.

Miner, Horace. 1956. "Body Ritual Among the Nacirema." *American Anthropologist* 58(June):503–507.

Mingle, James R. 1987. *Focus on Minorities.* Denver: Education Commission of the States and the State Higher Education Executive Officers.

Mizrahi, Terry. 1986. *Getting Rid of Patients.* New Brunswick, NJ: Rutgers University Press.

Moffatt, Susan. 1995. "Minorities Found More Likely to Live Near Toxic Sites." *Los Angeles Times,* August 30, pp. B1, B3.

Mogelonsky, Marcia. 1996. "The Rocky Road to Adulthood." *American Demographics* 18(May):26–29, 32–35, 56.

Monaghan, Peter. 1993. "Sociologist Jailed Because He 'Wouldn't Snitch' Ponders the Way Research Ought to Be Done." *Chronicle of Higher Education* 40(September 1):A8, A9.

Monteiro, Lois A. 1998. "Ill-Defined Illnesses and Medically Unexplained Symptoms Syndrome." *Footnotes* 26(February):3, 6.

Moore, Wilbert E. 1968. "Occupational Socialization." Pp. 861–883 in *Handbook of Socialization Theory and Research,* edited by David A. Goslin. Chicago: Rand McNally.

Morehouse Medical Treatment and Effectiveness Center. 1999. *A Synthesis of the Literature: Racial and Ethnic Differences in Acccess to Medical Care.* Menlo Park, CA: Henry J. Kaiser Family Foundation.

Morehouse Research Institute and Institute for American Values. 1999. *Turning the Corner on Father Absence in Black America.* Atlanta: Morehouse Research Institute and Institute for American Values.

Morin, Richard. 1999. "Not a Clue." *Washington Post National Weekly Edition* 16(June 14):34.

———. 2000. "Will Traditional Polls Go the Way of the Dinosaur?" *Washington Post National Weekly Edition* 17(May 15):34.

Morland, John, Jr. 1996. "The Individual, the Society, or Both? A Comparison of Black, Latino, and White Beliefs about the Causes of Poverty." *Social Forces* 75(December):403–422.

Morris, Aldon. 2000. "Reflections on Social Movement Theory: Criticisms and Proposals." *Contemporary Sociology* 29(May):445–454.

Morris, Bonnie Rothman. 1999. "You've Got Romance! Seeking Love on Line." *New York Times,* August 26, p. D1.

Morrison, Denton E. 1971. "Some Notes toward Theory on Relative Deprivation, Social Movements, and Social Change." *American Behavioral Scientist* 14(May–June):675–690.

Morrow, John K. 1997. "Of Sheep Cloning and Cold Fusion." *Chicago Tribune,* March 7, p. 23.

Morse, Arthur D. 1967. *While Six Million Died: A Chronicle of American Apathy.* New York: Ace.

Morse, Jodie. 1999. "Cracking Down on the Homeless." *Time,* December 2000, pp. 69–70.

Moseley, Ray. 2000. "Britons Watch Health Service Fall to Its Knees." *Chicago Tribune,* January 22, pp. 1, 2.

Moskos, Charles C., Jr. 1991. "How Do They Do It?" *New Republic* 205(August 5):20.

Mosley, J., and E. Thomson. 1995. Pp. 148–165 in *Fatherhood: Contemporary Theory, Research and Social Policy,* edited by W. Marsiglo. Thousand Oaks, CA: Sage.

MOST. 1999. MOST Quarterly. Internet vol. 1. Accessed July 19, 1999 (http://www.mostonline.org/qtrly/qtrly-index.htm).

Murdock, George P. 1945. "The Common Denominator of Cultures." Pp. 123–142 in *The Science of Man in the World Crisis,* edited by Ralph Linton. New York: Columbia University Press.

———. 1949. *Social Structure.* New York: Macmillan.

———. 1957. "World Ethnographic Sample." *American Anthropologist* 59(August): 664–687.

Murphy, Caryle. 1993. "Putting Aside the Veil." *Washington Post National Weekly Edition* 10 (April 12–18): pp. 10–11.

Murphy, Dean E. 1997. "A Victim of Sweden's Pursuit of Perfection." *Los Angeles Times*, September 2, pp. A1, A8.

N

Nader, Laura. 1986. "The Subordination of Women in Comparative Perspective." *Urban Anthropology* 15(Fall–Winter):377–397.

Naifeh, Mary. 1998. "Trap Door? Revolving Door? Or Both? Dynamics of Economic Well-Being, Poverty 1993–94." *Current Population Reports*, ser. P-70, no. 63. Washington, DC: U.S. Government Printing Office.

Nakane, Chie. 1970. *Japanese Society*. Berkeley: University of California Press.

Nakao, Keiko, and Judith Treas. 1990. *Computing 1989 Occupational Prestige Scores*. Chicago: NORC.

———, and ———. 1994. "Updating Occupational Prestige and Socioeconomic Scores: How the New Measures Measure Up." Pp. 1–72 in *Sociological Methodology, 1994,* edited by Peter V. Marsden. Oxford: Basil Blackwell.

Nash, Manning. 1962. "Race and the Ideology of Race." *Current Anthropology* 3(June):285–288.

National Abortion and Reproductive Rights Action League. 1999b. "NARAL Factsheets: Public Funding for Abortion." Accessed October 9, 1999 (http://www.naral.org/ publications/facts/1999/public_ funding.html).

National Advisory Commission on Criminal Justice. 1976. *Organized Crime*. Washington, DC: U.S. Government Printing Office.

National Center for Educational Statistics. 1997. "Digest of Education Statistics 1997." Washington, DC: U.S. Government Printing Office. Accessed September 29, 1999 (http://nces.ed. gov/pubs).

———. 1998. *Students' Report of School Crime: 1989 and 1995*. Washington, DC: U.S. Government Printing Office.

———. 1999. *Digest of Education Statistics, 1998*. Washington, DC: U.S. Government Printing Office.

National Center for Health Statistics. 1974. *Summary Report: Final Divorce Statistics, 1974*. Washington, DC: U.S. Government Printing Office.

———. 1990. *Annual Survey of Births, Marriages, Divorces, and Deaths: United States, 1989*. Washington, DC: U.S. Government Printing Office.

———. 1997a. *U.S. Deceased Life Tables for 1989–91*. Washington, DC: U.S. Government Printing Office.

———. 1997b. "Births and Deaths: United States, 1996." *Monthly Vital Statistics Report* 46(September 11).

———. 1999. "Infant, Neonatal, and Postnatal Mortality Rates by Race and Sex." *National Vital Statistics Report* 47(June 30):86–87.

———. 2000. "Births, Marriages, Divorces, and Deaths: Provisional Data for January 1999." *Monthly Vital Statistics Reports* 48(January 25):1–2.

National Center on Elder Abuse. 1998. *The National Elder Abuse Incidence Study*. Washington, DC: American Public Human Services Association.

National Center on Women and Family Law. 1996. *Status of Marital Rape Exemption Statutes in the United States*. New York: National Center on Women and Family Law.

National Homeschool Association. 1999. *Homeschooling Families: Ready for the Next Decade*. Accessed November 19, 2000 (http://www.n-h-a.org/decade. htm).

National Institute on Aging. 1999a. *Early Retirement in the United States*. Washington, DC: U.S. Government Printing Office.

———. 1999b. *The Declining Disability of Older Americans*. Washington, DC: U.S. Government Printing Office.

National Law Center on Homelessness and Poverty. 1996. *Mean Sweeps: A Report on Anti-Homeless Laws, Litigation, and Alternatives in 50 United States Cities*. Washington, DC: National Law Center on Homelessness and Poverty.

National Marriage Project. 2000. *The State of Our Unions*. New Brunswick, NJ: The National Marriage Project.

National Organization of Men Against Sexism (NOMAS). 1999. "Statement of Principles." Accessed October 11, 1999 (http://www.nomas.org/ statemt_of_principles.htm).

National Partnership for Women and Families. 1998. *Balancing Acts: Work/Family Issues on Prime-Time TV. Executive Summary*. Washington, DC: The National Partnership for Women and Families.

National Telecommunications and Information Administration. 2000. *Falling Through the Net: Toward Digital Inclusion*. Washington, DC: U.S. Government Printing Office.

National Vital Statistics Reports. 2000. "Births, Marriages, Divorces and Deaths: Provisional Data for October 1999." *National Vital Statistics Reports* 48(September 6).

Navarro, Vicente. 1984. "Medical History as Justification Rather Than Explanation: A Critique of Starr's *The Social Transformation of American Medicine*." *International Journal of Health Services* 14(4):511–528.

Nelson, Jack. 1995. "The Internet, the Virtual Community, and Those with Disabilities." *Disability Studies Quarterly* 15(Spring):15–20.

NetCoalition.com. 2000. "NetCoalition Joins Friend of the Court Brief in Napster Case." Press release, August 30. Washington, DC: NetCoalition.com.

Neuborne, Ellen. 1996. "Vigilantes Stir Firms' Ire with Cyber-antics." *USA Today,* February 28, pp. A1, A2.

Newman, William M. 1973. *American Pluralism: A Study of Minority Groups and Social Theory*. New York: Harper and Row.

Newsday. 1997. "Japan Sterilized 16,000 Women." September 18, p. A19.

New York Times. 1993a. "Child Care in Europe: Admirable but Not Perfect, Experts Say." February 15, p. A13.

———. 1995. "Reverse Discrimination of Whites Is Rare, Labor Study Reports." March 31, p. A23.

———. 1998. "2 Gay Men Fight Town Hall for a Family Pool Pass Discount." July 14, p. B2.

———. 1999a. "Woman Strikes Deal to Quit Redwood Home." December 19, p. 33.

———. 2000. "Technology's Gender Gap." September 5, p. A26.

Nibert, David. 2000. *Hitting the Lottery Jackpot: Government and the Taxing of Dreams*. New York: Monthly Review Press.

NICHD. 1999a. "Higher Quality Care Related to Less Problem Behavior." Accessed July 28, 1999 (http://www.nih.gov/nichd/docs/news/DAYCAR99.htm).
———. 1999b. "Child Outcomes When Child Care Center Classes Meet Recommended Standards for Quality." *American Journal of Public Health* 89(July):1072–1077.

Nie, Norman H. 1999. "Tracking Our Techno-Future." *American Demographics* (July):50–52.
———, and Lutz Erbring. 2000. "Study of the Social Consequences of the Internet." Accessible online (http://www.stanford.edu/group/sigss/). Palo Alto, CA: Stanford Institute for the Quantitative Study of Society.

Nielsen, Joyce McCarl, Glenda Walden, and Charlotte A. Kunkel. 2000. "Gendered Heteronormativity: Empirical Illustrations in Everyday Life." *Sociological Quarterly* 41(No. 2):283–296.

Nixon, Howard L., II. 1979. *The Small Group.* Englewood Cliffs, NJ: Prentice-Hall.

Nock, Steven L., James D. Wright, and Laura Sanchez. 1999. "America's Divorce Problem." *Society* 36(May/June): 43–52.

Nolan, Patrick, and Gerhad Lenski. 1999. *Human Societies: An Introduction to Macrosociology.* New York: McGraw-Hill.

Noll, Roger G., and Andrew Zimbalist. 1997. *Sports, Jobs and Taxes: The Economic Impact of Sports Teams and Stadiums.* Washington, DC: The Brookings Institution.

Noonan, Rita K. 1995. "Women against the State: Political Opportunities and Collective Action Frames in Chile's Transition to Democracy." *Sociological Forum* 10:81–111.

NORC (National Opinion Research Center). 1994. *General Social Surveys 1972–1994.* Chicago: National Opinion Research Center.

North Carolina Abecedarian Project. 2000. *Early Learning, Later Success: The Abecedarian Study.* Chapel Hill, NC: Frank Porter Graham Child Development Center.

Novak, Tim, and Jon Schmid. 1999. "Lottery Picks Split by Race, Income." *Chicago Sun-Times,* June 22, pp. 1, 24, 25.

Nussbaum, Daniel. 1998. "Bad Air Days." *Los Angeles Times Magazine,* July 19, pp. 20–21.

O

Oberschall, Anthony. 1973. *Social Conflict and Social Movements.* Englewood Cliffs, NJ: Prentice-Hall.

O'Donnell, Mike. 1992. *A New Introduction to Sociology.* Walton-on-Thames, United Kingdom: Thomas Nelson and Sons.

O'Donnell, Rosie. 1998. Statement at the National Partnership for Women and Families Annual Luncheon, June 10.

Office of Justice Programs. 1999. "Transnational Organized Crime." *NCJRS Catalog* 49(November/December):21.

Ogburn, William F. 1922. *Social Change with Respect to Culture and Original Nature.* New York: Huebsch (reprinted 1966, New York: Dell).
———, and Clark Tibbits. 1934. "The Family and Its Functions." Pp. 661–708 in *Recent Social Trends in the United States,* edited by Research Committee on Social Trends. New York: McGraw-Hill.

O'Hare, William P., and Brenda Curry-White. 1992. "Is There a Rural Underclass?" *Population Today* 20(March): 6–8.

Okano, Kaori, and Motonori Tsuchiya. 1999. *Education in Contemporary Japan: Inequality and Diversity.* Cambridge: Cambridge University Press.

Oliver, Melvin L., and Thomas M. Shapiro. 1995. *Black Wealth/White Wealth: New Perspectives on Racial Inequality.* New York: Routledge.

Orum, Anthony M. 1989. *Introduction to Political Sociology: The Social Anatomy of the Body Politic.* 3d ed. Englewood Cliffs, NJ: Prentice-Hall.
———. 2001. *Introduction to Political Sociology.* 4th ed. Upper Saddle River, NJ: Prentice-Hall.

Orwell, George. 1949. *1984.* New York: Harcourt Brace Jovanovich.

Ostling, Richard N. 1993. "Religion." *Time International,* July 12, p. 38.

Ouellette, Laurie. 1993. "The Information Lockout." *Utne Reader,* September–October, pp. 25–26.

Owens, Lynn, and L. Kendall Palmer. 2000. *Public Betrayals and Private Portrayals: Activist Intention in Tension on the WWW.* Presented at the annual meeting of the American Sociological Association, Washington, DC.

P

Pagani, Steve. 1999. "End the 'Culture of Death,' Pope Tells America." Reuters Wire Service, January 23.

Page, Charles H. 1946. "Bureaucracy's Other Face." *Social Forces* 25 (October):89–94.

Palen, J. John. 1995. "The Suburban Revolution: An Introduction." *Sociological Focus* 28(October):347–351.

Pappas, Gregory et al. [4 authors]. 1993. "The Increasing Disparity in Mortality between Socioeconomic Groups in the United States, 1960 and 1986." *New England Journal of Medicine* 329(July 8):103–109.

Park, Robert E. 1916. "The City: Suggestions for the Investigation of Human Behavior in the Urban Environment." *American Journal of Sociology* 20(March):577–612.
———. 1936. "Succession, an Ecological Concept." *American Sociological Review* 1(April):171–179.

Parker, Suzi. 1998. "Wedding Boom: More Rings, Tuxes, Bells, and Brides." *Christian Science Monitor,* July 20, pp. 1, 14.

Parsons, Talcott. 1951. *The Social System.* New York: Free Press.
———. 1966. *Societies: Evolutionary and Comparative Perspectives.* Englewood Cliffs, NJ: Prentice-Hall.
———. 1972. "Definitions of Health and Illness in the Light of American Values and Social Structure." Pp. 166–187 in *Patients, Physicians and Illness,* edited by Gartley Jaco. New York: Free Press.
———. 1975. "The Sick Role and the Role of the Physician Reconsidered." *Milbank Medical Fund Quarterly, Health and Society* 53(Summer): 257–278.
———, and Robert Bales. 1955. *Family, Socialization, and Interaction Process.* Glencoe, IL: Free Press.

Pasternak, Judy. 1998. "'Edge City' Is Attempting to Build a Center." *Los Angeles Times,* January 1, p. A5.

Pate, Antony M., and Edwin E. Hamilton. 1992. "Formal and Informal Deterrents to Domestic Violence: The Dade County Spouse Assault Experiment." *American Sociological Reviews* 57(October):691–697.

Patterson, Orlando. 1998. "Affirmative Action." *Brookings Review* 16(Spring):17–23.

Patton, Carl V., ed. 1988. *Spontaneous Shelter: International Perspectives and Prospects*. Philadelphia: Temple University Press.

Paulson, Amanda. 2000. "Where the School Is Home." *Christian Science Monitor*, October 10, pp. 18–21.

Pear, Robert. 1983. "$1.5 Billion Urged for U.S. Japanese Held in War." *New York Times*, June 17, pp. A1, D16.

———. 1996. "Clinton Endorses the Most Radical of Welfare Trials." *New York Times*, May 19, pp. 1, 20.

———. 1997a. "New Estimate Doubles Rate of H.I.V. Spread." *New York Times*, November 26, p. A6.

———. 1997b. "Now, the Archenemies Need Each Other." *New York Times*, June 22, sec. 4, pp. 1, 4.

Pelton, Tom. 1994. "Hawthorne Works' Glory Now Just So Much Rubble." *Chicago Tribune*, April 18, pp. 1, 6.

Perkins, Craig, and Patsy Klaus. 1996. *Criminal Victimization 1994*. Washington, DC: U.S. Government Printing Office.

Perlez, Jane. 1996. "Central Europe Learns about Sex Harassment." *New York Times*, October 3, p. A3.

Perrow, Charles. 1999. *Normal Accidents: Living with High Risk Technologies*. Updated edition. New Brunswick, NJ: Rutgers University Press.

———. 1986. *Complex Organizations*. 3d ed. New York: Random House.

Perry, Suzanne. 1998a. "Human Rights Abuses Get Internet Spotlight." Reuters, February 4.

———. 1998b. "U.S. Data Companies Oppose Primary Laws." Reuters, March 19.

Pescovitz, David. 1999. "Sons and Daughters of HAL Go on Line." *New York Times*, March 18, pp. D1, D8.

Peter, Laurence J., and Raymond Hull. 1969. *The Peter Principle*. New York: Morrow.

Petersen, William. 1979. *Malthus*. Cambridge, MA: Harvard University Press.

Phelan, Michael P., and Scott A. Hunt. 1998. "Prison Gang Members' Tattoos as Identity Work: The Visual Comments of Moral Careers." *Symbolic Interaction* 21(No. 3):277–298.

Phillips, E. Barbara. 1996. *City Lights: Urban–Suburban Life in the Global Society*. New York: Oxford University Press.

Piaget, Jean. 1954. *The Construction of Reality in the Child*. Translated by Margaret Cook. New York: Basic Books.

Piller, Charles. 2000. "Cyber-Crime Loss at Firms Doubles to $10 Billion." *Los Angeles Times*, May 22, pp. C1, C4.

Pinderhughes, Dianne. 1987. *Race and Ethnicity in Chicago Politics: A Reexamination of Pluralist Theory*. Urbana: University of Illinois Press.

Platt, Steve. 1993. "Without Walls." *Statesman and Society* 6(April 2):5–7.

Plomin, Robert. 1989. "Determinants of Behavior." *American Psychologist* 44(February):105–111.

Pollack, Andrew. 1996. "It's See No Evil, Have No Harassment in Japan." *New York Times*, May 7, pp. D1, D6.

Pollard, Kelvin M. 1994. "Population Stabilization No Longer in Sight for U.S." *Population Today* 22(May):1–2.

Pomfret, John. 2000. "A New Chinese Revolution." *Washington Post National Weekly Edition*, February 21, pp. 17–19.

Ponczek, Ed. 1998. "Are Hiring Practices Sensitive to Persons with Disabilities?" *Footnotes* 26(No. 3):5.

Popenoe, David, and Barbara Dafoe Whitehead. 1999. *Should We Live Together? What Young Adults Need to Know About Cohabitation Before Marriage*. Rutgers, NJ: The National Marriage Project.

Population Reference Bureau. 1978. "World Population: Growth on the Decline." *Interchange* 7(May):1–3.

———. 1996. "Speaking Graphically." *Population Today* 24(June/July):b.

———. 2000. "More Youths Take Alternative Route to Finish High School." *Population Today* 28(January):7.

Porter, Rosalie Pedalino. 1997. "The Politics of Bilingual Education." *Society* 34(No. 6):31–40.

Power, Carla. 1998. "The New Islam." *Newsweek* 131(March 16):34–37.

Powers, Mary G., and Joan J. Holmberg. 1978. "Occupational Status Scores: Changes Introduced by the Inclusion of Women." *Demography* 15(May):183–204.

Princeton Religion Research Center. 2000a. "Nearly Half of Americans Describe Themselves as Evangelicals." *Emerging Trends* 22(April):5.

———. 2000b. "Latest Religious Preferences for U.S." *Emerging Trends* 22(March):2.

Pula, James S. 1995. *Polish Americans: An Ethnic Community*. New York: Twayne.

Purnick, Joyce. 1996. "G.O.P. Quest to Narrow Gender Gap." *New York Times*, November 14, p. B1.

Putnam, Robert D. 2000. *Bowling Alone: The Collapse and Revival of American Community*. New York: Simon and Schuster.

Pyle, Amy. 1998. "Opinions Vary on Studies That Back Bilingual Classes." *Los Angeles Times*, March 2, pp. B1, B3.

Q

Quadagno, Jill. 1999. *Aging and the Life Course: An Introduction to Social Gerontology*. New York: McGraw-Hill.

Quinney, Richard. 1970. *The Social Reality of Crime*. Boston: Little, Brown.

———. 1974. *Criminal Justice in America*. Boston: Little, Brown.

———. 1979. *Criminology*. 2d ed. Boston: Little, Brown.

———. 1980. *Class, State and Crime*. 2d ed. New York: Longman.

R

Ramet, Sabrina. 1991. *Social Currents in Eastern Europe: The Source and Meaning of the Great Transformation*. Durham, NC: Duke University Press.

Ravitch, Diane. 2000. *Left Back: A Century of Failed School Reforms*. New York: Simon and Schuster.

Reddick, Randy, and Elliot King. 2000. *The Online Student: Making the Grade on the Internet*. Fort Worth: Harcourt Brace.

Reese, William A., II, and Michael A. Katovich. 1989. "Untimely Acts: Extending the Interactionist Conception of Deviance." *Sociological Quarterly* 30(2):159–184.

Reinharz, Shulamit. 1992. *Feminist Methods in Social Research*. New York: Oxford University Press.

Stearn, J. 1993. "What Crisis?" *Statesmen and Society* 6(April 2):7–9.

Stedman, Nancy. 1998. "Learning to Put the Best Shoe Forward." *New York Times,* October 27.

Stein, Leonard. 1967. "The Doctor–Nurse Game." *Archives of General Psychiatry* 16:699–703.

Steinfeld, Edward S. 1999. "Beyond the Transition: China's Economy at Century's End." *Current History* 98(September):271–275.

Stenning, Derrick J. 1958. "Household Viability among the Pastoral Fulani." Pp. 92–119 in *The Developmental Cycle in Domestic Groups,* edited by John R. Goody. Cambridge, Eng.: Cambridge University Press.

Stephen, Elizabeth Hervey. 1999. "Assisted Reproductive Technologies: Is the Price Too High?" *Population Today* (May):1–2.

Sternberg, Steve. 1999. "Virus Makes Families Pay Twice." *USA Today,* May 24, p. 6D.

Sterngold, James. 1992. "Japan Ends Fingerprinting of Many Non-Japanese," *New York Times* May 21, p. A11.

Stevens, Ann Huff. 1994. "The Dynamics of Poverty Spells: Updating Bane and Ellwood." *American Economic Review* 84 (May):34–37.

Stevenson, David, and Barbara L. Schneider. 1999. *The Ambitious Generation: America's Teenagers, Motivated but Directionless.* New Haven: Yale University Press.

Stevenson, Robert J. 1998. *The Boiler Room and Other Telephone Sales Scams.* Urbana, IL: University of Illinois Press.

Stolberg, Sheryl. 1995. "Affirmative Action Gains Often Come at a High Cost." *Los Angeles Times,* March 29, pp. A1, A13–A16.

Stolberg, Sheryl Gay. 2000. "Alternative Care Gains a Foothold." *New York Times,* January 31, pp. A1, A16.

Stoll, Clifford. 1995. *Silicon Snake Oil: Second Thoughts on the Information Superhighway.* New York: Anchor/Doubleday.

Stoughton, Stephanie, and Leslie Walker. 1999. "The Merchants of Cyberspace." *Washington Post National Weekly Edition* 16(February 15):18.

Strassman, W. Paul. 1998. "Third World Housing." Pp. 589–592 in *The Encyclopedia of Housing,* edited by Willem van Vliet. Thousand Oaks, CA: Sage.

Straus, Murray A. 1994. "State-to-State Differences in Social Inequality and Social Bonds in Relation to Assaults on Wives in the United States." *Journal of Comparative Family Studies* 25(Spring):7–24.

Strauss, Anselm. 1977. *Negotiations: Varieties, Contexts, Processes, and Social Order.* San Francisco: Jossey Bass.

Strom, Stephanie. 2000a. "In Japan, the Golden Years Have Lost Their Glow." *New York Times,* February 16, 7.

———. 2000b. "Tradition of Equality Fading in New Japan." *New York Times,* January 4, pp. A1, A6.

Strum, Charles. 1993. "Schools' Tracks and Democracy." *New York Times,* April 1, pp. B1, B7.

Sugimoto, Yoshio. 1997. *An Introduction to Japanese Society.* Cambridge, Eng.: Cambridge University Press.

Sumner, William G. 1906. *Folkways.* New York: Ginn.

Sutherland, Edwin H. 1937. *The Professional Thief.* Chicago: University of Chicago Press.

———. 1940. "White-Collar Criminality." *American Sociological Review* 5(February):1–11.

———. 1949. *White Collar Crime.* New York: Dryden.

———. 1983. *White Collar Crime: The Uncut Version.* New Haven, CT: Yale University Press.

———, and Donald R. Cressey. 1978. *Principles of Criminology.* 10th ed. Philadelphia: Lippincott.

Suttles, Gerald D. 1972. *The Social Construction of Communities.* Chicago: University of Chicago Press.

Swanson, Stevenson. 1999. "Shaker Ranks Down to the Faithful Few." *Chicago Tribune,* April 4, p. 6.

——— and Jim Kirk. 1998. "Satellite Outage Felt by Millions." *Chicago Tribune,* May 21, pp. 1, 26.

Szasz, Thomas S. 1971. "The Same Slave: An Historical Note on the Use of Medical Diagnosis as Justificatory Rhetoric." *American Journal of Psychotherapy* 25(April):228–239.

T

Taeuber, Cynthia M. 1992. "Sixty-Five Plus in America." *Current Population Reports,* ser. P-23, no. 178. Washington, DC: U.S. Government Printing Office.

Tagliabue, John. 1996. "In Europe, a Wave of Layoffs Stuns White-Collar Workers." *New York Times,* June 20, pp. A1, D8.

Takezawa, Yasuko I. 1995. *Breaking the Silence: Redress and Japanese American Ethnicity.* Ithaca, NY: Cornell University Press.

Talbot, Margaret. 1998. "Attachment Theory: The Ultimate Experiment." *New York Times Magazine,* May 24, pp. 4–30, 38, 46, 50, 54.

Tannen, Deborah. 1990. *You Just Don't Understand: Women and Men in Conversation.* New York: Ballantine.

———. 1994a. *Talking from 9 to 5.* New York: William Morris.

———. 1994b. *Gender and Discourse.* New York: Oxford University Press.

Taylor, Verta. 1995. "Watching for Vibes: Bringing Emotions into the Study of Feminist Organizations." Pp. 223–233 in *Feminist Organizations: Harvest of the New Women's Movement,* edited by Myra Marx Ferree and Patricia Yancy Martin. Philadelphia: Temple University Press.

Telsch, Kathleen. 1991. "New Study of Older Workers Finds They Can Become Good Investments." *New York Times,* May 21, p. A16.

Terry, Sara. 2000. "Whose Family? The Revolt of the Child-Free." *Christian Science Monitor,* August 29, pp. 1, 4.

Theberge, Nancy. 1997. "'It's Part of the Game'—Physicality and the Production of Gender in Women's Hockey." *Gender and Society* 11(February): 69–87.

Third International Mathematics and Science Study. 1998. *Mathematics and Science Achievement in the Final Year of Secondary School.* Boston, MA: TIMSS International Study Center.

Thomas, Gordon, and Max Morgan Witts. 1974. *Voyage of the Damned.* Greenwich, CT: Fawcett Crest.

Thomas, Jim. 1984. "Some Aspects of Negotiating Order: Loose Coupling and Mesostructure in Maximum Security Prisons." *Symbolic Interaction* 7(Fall): 213–231.

Thomas, Pattie and Erica A. Ownes. 2000 "Age Cure!: The Business of Passing." Present at the annual meeting of the American Sociological Association, Washington, DC.

Thomas, Robert McG., Jr. 1995. "Maggie Kuhn, 89, the Founder of the Gray Panthers, Is Dead." *New York Times,* April 23, p. 47.

Thomas, William I. 1923. *The Unadjusted Girl.* Boston: Little, Brown.

Thomson, Elizabeth, and Ugo Colella. 1992. "Cohabitation and Marital Stability: Quality or Commitment?" *Journal of Marriage and the Family* 54(May):259–267.

Thornton, Russell. 1987. *American Indians Holocaust and Survival: A Population History Since 1492.* Norman: University of Oklahoma Press.

Tierney, John. 1990. "Betting the Planet." *New York Times Magazine,* December 2, pp. 52–53, 71, 74, 76, 78, 80–81.

Tilly, Charles. 1993. *Popular Contention in Great Britain 1758–1834.* Cambridge, MA: Harvard University Press.

Tolbert, Kathryn. 2000. "In Japan, Traveling Alone Begins at Age 6." *Washington Post National Weekly Edition* 17(May 15):17.

Tonkinson, Robert. 1978. *The Mardudjara Aborigines.* New York: Holt.

Tönnies, Ferdinand. [1887] 1988. *Community and Society.* Rutgers, NJ: Transaction.

Topolnicki, Denise M. 1993. "The World's 5 Best Ideas." *Money* 22(June):74–83, 87, 89, 91.

Touraine, Alain. 1974. *The Academic System in American Society.* New York: McGraw-Hill.

Treas, Judith. 1995. "Older Americans in the 1990s and Beyond." *Population Bulletin* 50(May).

Treiman, Donald J. 1977. *Occupational Prestige in Comparative Perspective.* New York: Academic.

Tuchman, Gaye. 1992. "Feminist Theory." Pp. 695–704 in *Encyclopedia of Sociology,* vol. 2, edited by Edgar F. Borgatta and Marie L. Borgatta. New York: Macmillan.

Tucker, James. 1993. "Everyday Forms of Employee Resistance." *Sociological Forum* 8(March):25–45.

Tumin, Melvin M. 1953. "Some Principles of Stratification: A Critical Analysis." *American Sociological Review* 18(August):387–394.

———. 1985. *Social Stratification.* 2d ed. Englewood Cliffs, NJ: Prentice-Hall.

Ture, Kwame, and Charles Hamilton. 1992. *Black Power: The Politics of Liberation.* Rev. ed. New York: Vintage Books.

Turkle, Sherry. 1995. *Life on the Screen: Identity in the Age of the Internet.* New York: Simon and Schuster.

———. 1999. "Looking Toward Cyberspace: Beyond Grounded Sociology," *Contemporary Sociology* 28(November):643–654.

Turner, Bryan S., ed. 1990. *Theories of Modernity and Postmodernity.* Newbury Park, CA: Sage.

Turner, Craig. 1998. "U.N. Study Assails U.S. Executions as Biased." *Los Angeles Times,* March 4, p. A1.

Turner, J. H. 1985. *Herbert Spencer: A Renewed Application.* Beverly Hills, CA: Sage.

Turner, Margery Austin, and Felicity Skidmore, eds. 1999. *Mortgage Lending Discrimination: A Review of Existing Evidence.* Washington, DC: Urban Institute.

Twaddle, Andrew. 1974. "The Concept of Health Status." *Social Science and Medicine* 8(January):29–38.

Tyler, William B. 1985. "The Organizational Structure of the School." Pp. 49–73 in *Annual Review of Sociology, 1985,* edited by Ralph H. Turner. Palo Alto, CA: Annual Reviews.

U

Uchitelle, Louis. 1996. "More Downsized Workers Are Returning as Rentals." *New York Times,* December 8, pp. 1, 34.

———. 1999. "Divising New Math to Define Poverty." *New York Times,* October 18, pp. A1, A14.

UNAIDS. 2000. *Report on the Global HIV/AIDS Epidemic, June 2000.* Geneva, Switzerland: Joint United Nations' Programme on HIV/AIDS (UNAIDS).

United Nations. 1995. *The World's Women, 1995: Trends and Statistics.* New York: United Nations.

United Nations Development Programme. 1995. *Human Development Report 1995.* New York: Oxford University Press.

United Nations Human Rights Commission. 1997. "U.N. Human Rights Commission Acts on Texts." M2 PressWire. 4/9.

United Nations Population Division. 1998a. "Demographic Input of HIV/AIDS." Accessed (http://www.undp.org/popin/wdtrends/demoimp.htm).

———. 1998b. *World Abortion Policies.* New York: Department of Economic and Social Affairs, UNPD.

———. 1999. *The World at Six Billion.* New York: UNPD.

U.S. Conference of Mayors. 1999. *A Status Report on Hunger and Homelessness in America's Cities.* Washington: U.S. Conference of Mayors.

U.S. English. 1999. "States with Official English Laws." Accessed July 27, 1999 (http://www.us-english.org/states.htm).

Uttley, Alison. 1993. "Who's Looking at You, Kid?" *Times Higher Education Supplement* 30(April 30):48.

V

Vallas, Steven P. 1999. "Rethinking Post-Fordism: The Meaning of Workplace Flexibility." *Sociological Theory* 17(March):68–101.

van den Berghe, Pierre. 1978. *Race and Racism: A Comparative Perspective.* 2d ed. New York: Wiley.

Vanderpool, Tim. 1995. "Secession of the Successful." *Utne Reader* (November–December):32, 34.

Vanneman, Reeve, and Lynn Weber Cannon. 1987. *The American Perception of Class.* Philadelphia: Temple University Press.

Van Slambrouck, Paul. 1998. "In California, Taking the Initiative—Online." *Christian Science Monitor,* November 13, pp. 1, 11.

———. 1999a. "Netting a New Sense of Connection." *Christian Science Monitor,* May 4, pp. 1, 4.

———. 1999b. "Newest Tool for Social Protest: The Internet." *Christian Science Monitor,* June 18, p. 3.

van Vucht Tijssen, Lieteke. 1990. "Women between Modernity and Postmodernity." Pp. 147–163 in *Theories of Modernity and Postmodernity,* edited by Bryan S. Turner. London: Sage.

Vaughan, Diane. 1996. *The Challenger Launch Decision: Risky Technology, Culture, and Deviance at NASA.* Chicago: University of Chicago Press.

———. 1999. "The Dark Side of Organizations: Mistake, Misconduct, and Disaster." Pp. 271–305 in *Annual Review of Sociology*, edited by Karen J. Cook and John Hagan. Palo Alto: Annual Reviews.

Veblen, Thorstein. 1919. *The Vested Interests and the State of the Industrial Arts.* New York: Huebsch.

Vega, William A. 1995. "The Study of Latino Families: A Point of Departure." Pp. 3–17 in *Understanding Latino Families: Scholarship, Policy, and Practice*, edited by Ruth E. Zambrana. Thousand Oaks, CA: Sage.

Venkatesh, Sudhir Alladi. 1997. "The Social Organization of Street Gang Activity in an Urban Ghetto." *American Journal of Sociology* 103(July): 82–111.

Ventura, Stephanie J., and Christine A. Bachrach. 2000. "Nonmarital Childbearing in the United States, 1990–91." *National Vital Statistics Reports* 48 (October 18).

———, Joyce A. Martin, Sally C. Curtin, T. J. Mathews, and Melissa M. Park. 2000a. "Births: Final Data for 1998." *National Vital Statistics Reports* 48(March 28).

Verhovek, Sam Howe. 1997. "Racial Tensions in Suit Slowing Drive for 'Environmental Justice,'" *New York Times*, September 7, pp. 1, 16.

Vernon, Glenn. 1962. *Sociology and Religion.* New York: McGraw-Hill.

Vernon, Jo Etta A. et al. [4 authors]. 1990. "Media Stereotyping: A Comparison of the Way Elderly Women and Men Are Portrayed on Prime-Time Television." *Journal of Women and Aging* 2(4):55–68.

Vidaver, R. M. et al. 2000. "Women Subjects in NIH-funded Clinical Research Literature: Lack of Progress in Both Representation and Analysis by Sex. *Journal of Women's Health Gender Based Medicine* 9(June):495–504.

Vladimiroff, Christine. 1998. "Food for Thought." *Second Harvest Update* (Summer):2.

Vobejda, Barbara, and Judith Havenmann. 1997. "Experts Say Side Income Could Hamper Reforms." *Washington Post*, November 3, p. A1.

W

Wacquant, Loïc J. D. 1993. "When Cities Run Riot." *UNESCO Courier* (February), pp. 8–15.

Wages for Housework Campaign. 1999. *Wages for Housework Campaign.* Circular. Los Angeles.

Wagley, Charles and Marvin Harris. 1958. *Minorities in the New World: Six Case Studies.* New York: Columbia University Press.

Wallace, Ruth A., and Alison Wolf. 1980. *Contemporary Sociological Theory.* Englewood Cliffs, NJ: Prentice-Hall.

Wallerstein, Immanuel. 1974. *The Modern World System.* New York: Academic Press.

———. 1979. *Capitalist World Economy.* Cambridge, Eng.: Cambridge University Press.

———. 2000. *The Essential Wallerstein.* New York: The New Press.

Wallerstein, Judith S., Judith M. Lewis, and Sandra Blakeslee. 2000. *The Unexpected Legacy of Deviance.* New York: Hyperion.

Wallis, Claudia. 1987. "Is Mental Illness Inherited?" *Time* 129(March 9):67.

Walzer, Susan. 1996. "Thinking about the Baby: Gender and Divisions of Infant Care." *Social Problems* 43(May):219–234.

Waring, Marilyn. 1988. *If Women Counted: A New Feminist Economics.* San Francisco: Harper and Row.

Warner, Judith. 1996. "France's Anti-abortion Movement Gains Momentum." *Ms.* 7(September–October): 20–21.

Watts, Jerry G. 1990. "Pluralism Reconsidered." *Urban Affairs Quarterly* 25(June):697–704.

Weber, Bruce, Greg Duncan, and Leslie Whitener. 2000. "Rural Dimensions of Welfare Reform." *Poverty Research News* 4(September–October):3–4.

Weber, Max. [1913–1922] 1947. *The Theory of Social and Economic Organization.* Translated by A. Henderson and T. Parsons. New York: Free Press.

———. [1904] 1949. *Methodology of the Social Sciences.* Translated by Edward A. Shils and Henry A. Finch. Glencoe, IL: Free Press.

———. [1904] 1958a. *The Protestant Ethic and the Spirit of Capitalism.* Translated by Talcott Parsons. New York: Scribner.

———. [1916] 1958b. *The Religion of India: The Sociology of Hinduism and Buddhism.* New York: Free Press.

Wechsler, Henry. 2000. "Binge Drinking: Should We Attack the Name or the Problem?" *Chronicle of Higher Education* 47(October 20):B12–13.

Wechsler, Henry et al. 2000. "College Binge Drinking in the 1990s: A Continuing Program." *Journal of American College Health* 48(March):199–210.

Weeks, John R. 1999. *Population: An Introduction to Concepts and Issues.* 7th ed. Belmont, CA: Wadsworth.

Weinstein, Deena. 1999. *Knockin' The Rock: Defining Rock Music as a Social Problem.* New York: McGraw-Hill/Primis.

———. 2000. *Heavy Metal: The Music and Its Culture.* Cambridge, MA: Da Capo.

———, and Michael A. Weinstein. 1999. "McDonaldization Enframed." Pp. 57–69 in *Resisting McDonaldization*, edited by Barry Smart. London: Sage.

Weisman, Steven R. 1992. "Landmark Harassment Case in Japan." *New York Times*, April 17, p. A3.

Weiss, Rick. 1998. "Beyond Test-Tube Babies." *Washington Post National Weekly Edition* 15(February 16):6–7.

Welfare to Work Partnership. 2000. "Business Partners Find Success but Call for Renewed Community Action." *Trends in Executive Opinions* (2000 Series No. 1), p.1.

Wellman, Barry et al. [6 authors]. 1996. "Computer Networks as Social Networks: Collaborative Work, Telework, and Virtual Community." Pp. 213–238 in *Annual Review of Sociology, 1996*, edited by John Hagan. Palo Alto, CA: Annual Reviews.

Welsh, Sandy. 1999. "Gender and Sexual Harassment." Pp. 169–190 in *Annual Review of Sociology, 1999*, edited by Karen S. Cook and John Hagan. Palo Alto, CA: Annual Reviews.

West, Candace, and Don H. Zimmerman. 1983. "Small Insults: A Study of Interruptions in Cross Sex Conversations between Unacquainted Persons."

Pp. 86–111 in *Language, Gender, and Society,* edited by Barrie Thorne, Cheris Kramarae, and Nancy Henley. Rowley, MA: Newbury House.

———, and ———. 1987. "Doing Gender." *Gender and Society* 1(June): 125–151.

Whyte, William Foote. 1981. *Street Corner Society: Social Structure of an Italian Slum.* 3d ed. Chicago: University of Chicago Press.

———. 1989. "Advancing Scientific Knowledge through Participatory Action Research." *Sociological Forum* 4(September):367–385.

Wickham, DeWayne. 1998. "Affirmative Action not in Real Jeopardy." *USA Today,* April 7, p. 13A.

Wickman, Peter M. 1991. "Deviance." Pp. 85–87 in *Encyclopedic Dictionary of Sociology,* 4th ed., by Dushkin Publishing Group. Guilford, CT: Dushkin.

Wiener, Jon. 1994. "Free Speech on the Internet." *The Nation* 258(June 13): 825–828.

Wilford, John Noble. 1997. "New Clues Show Where People Made the Great Leap to Agriculture." *New York Times,* November 18, pp. B9, B12.

Wilhelm, Anthony. 1998. *Buying into the Computer Age: A Look at Hispanic Families.* Claremont, CA: The Thom Rivera Policy Institute.

Wilkinson, Tracy. 1999 "Refugees Forming Bonds on Web." *Los Angeles Times,* July 31, p. A2.

Willet, Jeffrey G., and Mary Jo Deegan. 2000. "Liminality? and Disability: The Symbolic Rite of Passage of Individuals with Disabilities." Presented at the annual meeting of the American Sociological Association, Washington, DC.

Williams, Carol J. 1995. "Taking an Eager Step Back." *Los Angeles Times,* June 3, pp. A1, A14.

Williams, David R., and Chiquita Collins. 1995. "U.S. Socioeconomic and Racial Differences in Health: Patterns and Explanations." Pp. 349–386 in *Annual Review of Sociology, 1995,* edited by John Hagan. Palo Alto, CA: Annual Reviews.

Williams, Lena. 1995. "Not Just a White Man's Game: Blacks in Business Master the Art of Networking." *New York Times,* November 9, pp. D1, D10.

Williams, Patricia J. 1997. "Of Race and Risk." *The Nation.* Digital Edition. Accessed December 12, 1999 (http://www.thenation.com).

Williams, Robin M., Jr. 1970. *American Society.* 3d ed. New York: Knopf.

———, in collaboration with John P. Dean and Edward A. Suchman. 1964. *Strangers Next Door: Ethnic Relations in American Communities.* Englewood Cliffs, NJ: Prentice-Hall.

Williams, Simon Johnson. 1986. "Appraising Goffman." *British Journal of Sociology* 37(September):348–369.

Williams, Wendy M. 1998. "Do Parents Matter? Scholars Need to Explain What Research Really Shows." *Chronicle of Higher Education* 45(December 11): B6–B7.

Wilmut, Ian et al. [5 authors]. 1997. "Viable Offering Derived from Fetal and Adult Mammalian Cells." *Nature* 385(February 27):810–813.

Wilson, Edward O. 1975. *Sociobiology: The New Synthesis.* Cambridge, MA: Harvard University Press.

———. 1978. *On Human Nature.* Cambridge, MA: Harvard University Press.

Wilson, John. 1973. *Introduction to Social Movements.* New York: Basic Books.

Wilson, Warner, Larry Dennis, and Allen P. Wadsworth, Jr. 1976. "Authoritarianism Left and Right." *Bulletin of the Psychonomic Society* 7(March):271–274.

Wilson, William Julius. 1980. *The Declining Significance of Race: Blacks and Changing American Institutions.* 2d ed. Chicago: University of Chicago Press.

———. 1987. *The Truly Disadvantaged: The Inner City, the Underclass and Public Policy.* Chicago: University of Chicago Press.

———, ed. 1989. *The Ghetto Underclass: Social Science Perspectives.* Newbury Park, CA: Sage.

———. 1996. *When Work Disappears: The World of the New Urban Poor.* New York: Knopf.

———. 1999a. "Towards a Just and Livable City: The Issues of Race and Class." Address at the Social Science Centennial Conference, April 23, 1999. Chicago, IL: DePaul University.

———. 1999b. *The Bridge Over the Racial Divide: Rising Inequality and Coali-*

tion Politics. Berkeley: University of California Press.

Winsberg, Morton. 1994. "Specific Hispanics." *American Demographics* 16(February):44–53.

Winter, J. Alan. 1977. *Continuities in the Sociology of Religion.* New York: Harper and Row.

Wirth, Louis. 1928. *The Ghetto.* Chicago: University of Chicago Press.

———. 1938. "Urbanism as a Way of Life." *American Journal of Sociology* 44(July):1–24.

Wiseman, Paul. 2000. "China's Little Emperors: The Offspring of Policy." *USA Today,* February 23, p. 10D.

Wolf, Naomi. 1991. *The Beauty Myth.* New York: Anchor Books.

———. 1992. *The Beauty Myth: How Images of Beauty Are Used against Women.* New York: Anchor.

Wolf, Richard. 1996. "States Can Expect Challenges after Taking over Welfare." *USA Today,* October 1, p. 8A.

Wolff, Edward N. 1999. "Recent Trends the Distribution of Household Wealth Ownership." In *Back to Shared Prosperity: The Growing Inequality of Wealth and Income in America,* edited by Ray Marshall. New York: M.E. Sharpe.

Wolinsky, Fredric P. 1980. *The Sociology of Health.* Boston: Little, Brown.

Wolraich et al. 1998. "Guidance for Effective Discipline." *Pediatrics* 101(April):723–728.

Women's International Network. 1995. "Working Women: 4 Country Comparison." *WIN News* 21(September 9): 82.

Wood, Daniel B. 2000. "Minorities Hope TV Deals Don't Just Lead to 'Tokenism.'" *Christian Science Monitor,* January 19.

Woodard, Colin. 1998. "When Rate Learning Fails against the Test of Global Economy." *Christian Science Monitor,* April 15, p. 7.

Wooden, Wayne. 1995. *Renegade Kids, Suburban Outlaws: From Youth Culture to Delinquency.* Belmont, CA: Wadsworth.

World Bank. 1995. *World Development Report 1994: Workers in an Integrating World.* New York: Oxford University Press.

———. 1996. *World Development Report 1996: From Plan to Market.* New York: Oxford University Press.

p. 299. Bill Truslow/Liaison
p. 302. Blair Seitz/Photo Researchers
p. 303. Cliff Moore/Princeton Stock Photo
p. 305. Richard Hutchings/Photo Researchers
p. 308. Jon Bradley/Tony Stone
p. 310. James D. Wilson/Woodfin Camp
p. 312. © Andy Warhol Foundation, Inc./Art Resource

Chapter 12

Chapter opener: Thomas Coex/Agence France Press
p. 323. Richard Vogel/Liaison
p. 324. Tom Pidgeon/AP Photo
p. 326. Lara Jo Regan/Liaison
p. 328. Steve McCurry/Magnum
p. 335. Mary Kate Denny/Photo Edit
p. 336. Joe McNally/Sygma
p. 338. Beringer-Dratch/Picture Cube
p. 341. Bob Daemmrich/Stock Boston
p. 343. James Marshall/Image Works
p. 344. Rob Crandall/Image Works

Chapter 13

Chapter opener: Milton Glaser
p. 355. Reuters/Claro Cortes/Archive Photos
p. 356. AP Photo
p. 358. Bob Daemmrich/Stock Boston
p. 361. Robert Matheu/Courtesy Rock the Vote
p. 367. AP Photo
p. 368. Bob Daemmrich/Stock Boston
p. 370. Stacy Pick/Stock Boston

Chapter 14

Chapter opener: Designed by Gran Fury/Reproduced by permission of the New York Public Library, Astor, Lenox, and Tilden Foundations.
p. 382. Remy De LaMauviniere/AP Photo
p. 382. Corbis Bettmann
p. 386. A. Ramey/Woodfin Camp
p. 389. Wally McNamee/Woodfin Camp
p. 391. Jonathan Nouro/Photo Edit
p. 392. Stephanie Maze/Woodfin Camp
p. 392. David Austen/Stock Boston
p. 393. Stephen Agricola/Stock Boston
p. 395. Chris Brown/Saba
p. 396. Eric Bouvet/Gamma Liaison
p. 398. Michael Keller/Picture Cube
p. 399. Bill Aron/Photo Edit
p. 403. A. Ramey/WoodfinCamp
p. 407. Charles Gupton/Tony Stone

Chapter 15

Chapter opener: Barry Dawson, *Street Graphics India* (New York: Thames & Hudson, 1999), p. 110.
p. 416. Image Works Archives
p. 422. M.J. Griffith/Photo Researchers
p. 424. Jean Marc Gibous/Gamma Liaison
p. 426. Jim Pickerall/Stock Boston
p. 427. David Young-Wolff/PhotoEdit
p. 429. Joe Sohm/Image Works
p. 431. Gerard J. Burkhart/Liaison
p. 433. AP Photo
p. 436. AP Photo

Chapter 16

Chapter opener: Image courtesy of Warp Records
p. 448. Frederique Jouval/Sygma
p. 448. Frederique Jouval/Sygma
p. 450. Lisa Terry/Gamma Liaison
p. 451. Chris O'Meara/AP Photo
p. 455. Jim West/Impact Visuals
p. 456. Reuters/Shaun Best/Archive Photos
p. 457. Joe Sohm/Image Works
p. 461. AP Photo
p. 463. Stan Godlewski
p. 468. AP Photo

Table of Contents

Name Index

Subject Index

APPLICATIONS OF SOCIOLOGY'S MAJOR THEORETICAL APPROACHES

Sociology provides comprehensive coverage of the major sociological perspectives. The summary table below includes a sample of the topics in this text that have been explored using these approaches. The numbers in parentheses indicate chapters of text coverage.

FUNCTIONALIST PERSPECTIVE

Defined and Explained (1)
Adoption (11)
Aging and Disengagement Theory (10)
AIDS and Social Networks (5)
Anomie Theory of Deviance (7)
Bilingualism (3)
Culture (3)
Davis and Moore's View of Stratification (8)
Dominant Ideology (3)
Durkheim's View of Deviance (7)
Dysfunctions of Racism (9)
Education Transmitting Culture (12)
Education Promoting Social and Political Integration (12)
Equilibrium Model of Social Change (16)
Family (11)
Formal Organizations (6)
Gan's Functions of Poverty (8)
Gender Stratification (10)
Health and Illness (18)
Immigration (9)
In-Groups and Out-Groups (6)
Integrative Function of Religion (12)
Internet (16)
Knockin' the Rock (3)
Language (3)
Modernization Theory (8)
Racism and the Dominant Group (9)
Sex Selection (16)
Sick Role (14)
Social Change (16)
Social Control (7)
Social Control and Education (12)
Social Institutions (5)
Social Networks (5)
Socialization in Schools (4)
Television (1)
Urban Ecology (15)

CONFLICT PERSPECTIVE

Defined and Explained (1)
Abortion (10)
Adoption (11)
Affirmative Action (12)
Aging and Age Stratification (10)
AIDS Crisis (5)
Bilingualism (3)
Chaos Theory (16)
Corporate Welfare (8)
Correspondence Principle (12)
Culture (3)
Day Care Funding (4)
Deviance (7)
Disability as a Master Status (5)
Domestic Violence (11)
Dominant Ideology (3,8)
Education and Bestowal of Status (12)
Electronic Redlining (16)
Elite Model of the U.S. Power Structure (12)
Environmental Issues (15)
Exploitation Theory of Racial Subordination (9)
Gender Stratification (10)
Health and Illness (14)
Hidden Curriculum (12)
Immigration (9)
Inequality and Technology (8,16)
In-Groups and Out-Groups (6)
Iron Law of Oligarchy (6)
Language (3)
Liberation Theology (12)
Marx's View of Capitalism (8)
Medicalization of Society (14)
Model Minority (9)
New Urban Sociology (15)
Physician-patient Interaction (14)
Political Socialization (12)
Privacy and Technology (16)
Racism and Health (14)
Religion and Social Control (12)
Reproductive Technology (11)
Resistance to Social Change (16)
School Prayer (12)
Sexism in Education (12)
Sexual Harassment (6)
Social Change (16)
Social Control (7)
Social Institutions (5)
Subordination of Racial Groups through Stereotyping (9)
Television (1)
Television and Social Reality (4)
Titanic (8)
Tracking (12)
Victimless Crimes (7)
White-Collar Crime (7)
Women and Education (12)
Women and Social Class (8)
World Systems Analysis (8)
World Technology Gap (16)

INTERACTIONIST PERSPECTIVE

Defined and Explained (1)
Aging and Activity Theory (10)
Contact Hypothesis and Interracial Contact (9)
Differential Association (7)
Dramaturgical Approach (4)
Education (12)
Electronic Forms of Communication (16)
Gender Stratification (10)
Health and Illness (14)
Human Relations Approach to Bureaucracies (6)
Impact of AIDS (5)
Knockin' the Rock (7)
Language (3)
Negotiated Order (5)
Physician-patient Interactions (14)
Political Socialization (12)
Pressure to Pray in Schools (12)
Privacy and Technology (16)
Reproductive Technology (11)
Small Groups (6)
Social Institutions (5)
Survivor Coalition-Building (6)
Teacher-Expectancy Effect (12)
Teenage Pregnancy (4)
Television (1)
Unwed Mother Stigma (11)

LABELING THEORY

Defined and Explained (7)
Being Old (10)
Health and Illness (14)
Knockin' the Rock (3)
People with AIDS (5,14)
People with Disabilities (5)
Presentation of Self (4)
Self-fulfilling Prophecy (9)
Societal Reaction Theory (7)
Teacher-Expectancy Effect (12)
Victimless Crimes (7)